Space, Time, and Archaeological Landscapes

INTERDISCIPLINARY CONTRIBUTIONS
TO ARCHAEOLOGY

Space, Time, and Archaeological Landscapes

Edited by

JACQUELINE ROSSIGNOL

University of New Mexico
Albuquerque, New Mexico

and

LuANN WANDSNIDER

University of Nebraska–Lincoln
Lincoln, Nebraska

Plenum Press • *New York and London*

Library of Congress Cataloging-in-Publication Data

Space, time, and archaeological landscapes / edited by Jacqueline
Rossignol and LuAnn Wandsnider.
        p.   cm. -- (Interdisciplinary contributions to archaeology)
    Outgrowth of a symposium held at the 53rd Annual Meeting of the
Society for American Archaeology in Phoenix, Ariz. in 1988.
    Includes bibliographical references and index.
    ISBN 0-306-44161-6
    1. Ethnoarchaeology--Congresses. 2. Distributional archaeology-
-Congresses. 3. Land settlement patterns--Congresses.
I. Rossignol, Jacqueline. II. Wandsnider, LuAnn. III. Series.
CC79.E85S63 1992
930.1--dc20
                                                      92-17145
                                                           CIP

ISBN 0-306-44161-6

© 1992 Plenum Press, New York
A Division of Plenum Publishing Corporation
233 Spring Street, New York, N.Y. 10013

Printed in the United States of America

Contributors

Charlotte Beck • Department of Anthropology, Hamilton College, Clinton, New York 13323

Lewis R. Binford • Department of Anthropology, Southern Methodist University, Dallas, Texas 75275

Eileen L. Camilli • Department of Anthropology, University of New Mexico, Albuquerque, New Mexico 87131

Claudia Chang • Department of Anthropology and Sociology, Sweet Briar College, Sweet Briar, Virginia 24595

Robert E. Dewar • Department of Anthropology, University of Connecticut, Storrs, Connecticut 06269

Robert C. Dunnell • Department of Anthropology DH-05, University of Washington, Seattle, Washington 98195

James I. Ebert • Ebert and Associates, 3700 Rio Grande Boulevard N.W., Suite 3, Albuquerque, New Mexico 87109

Stanton W. Green • Department of Anthropology, University of South Carolina, Columbia, South Carolina 29208

George T. Jones • Department of Anthropology, Hamilton College, Clinton, New York 13323

Edwin R. Hajic • Quaternary Studies Program, Illinois State Museum, Springfield, Illinois 62706

Kevin A. McBride • Department of Anthropology, University of Connecticut, Storrs, Connecticut 06269

Mark G. Macklin • Department of Geography, University of Newcastle-Upon-Tyne, Newcastle-Upon-Tyne NE1 7RU, England

Jacqueline Rossignol • Department of Anthropology, University of New Mexico, Albuquerque, New Mexico 87131

Sarah H. Schlanger • Museum of New Mexico, Office of Archaeological Studies, P.O. Box 2087, Santa Fe, New Mexico 87504

C. Russell Stafford • Department of Anthropology, Indiana State University, Terre Haute, Indiana 47809

LuAnn Wandsnider • Department of Anthropology, University of Nebraska–Lincoln, Lincoln, Nebraska 68588-0368

Marek Zvelebil • Department of Archaeology and Prehistory, University of Sheffield, Sheffield S10 2TN, England

Preface

The last 20 years have witnessed a proliferation of new approaches in archaeological data recovery, analysis, and theory building that incorporate both new forms of information and new methods for investigating them. The growing importance of survey has meant an expansion of the spatial realm of traditional archaeological data recovery and analysis from its traditional focus on specific locations on the landscape—archaeological sites—to the incorporation of data both on-site and off-site from across extensive regions. Evolving survey methods have led to experiments with nonsite and distributional data recovery as well as the critical evaluation of the definition and role of archaeological sites in data recovery and analysis. In both survey and excavation, the geomorphological analysis of landscapes has become increasingly important in the analysis of archaeological materials. Ethnoarchaeology—the use of ethnography to sharpen archaeological understanding of cultural and natural formation processes—has concentrated study on the formation processes underlying the content and structure of archaeological deposits. These actualistic studies consider patterns of deposition at the site level and the material results of human organization at the regional scale. Ethnoarchaeological approaches have also affected research in theoretical ways by expanding investigation into the nature and organization of systems of land use per se, thus providing direction for further study of the material results of those systems.

Although new and stimulating ways to investigate the archaeological record continue to enliven the discipline, much work remains to be done on the appropriate use of these methods in pursuing processual goals of archaeology, as well as their integration to form an overall strategy of archaeological inquiry.

In 1987 the editors sought participants for an edited volume that would evaluate traditional concepts of data recovery, analysis, and theory building, with a regional emphasis, and explore productive ways to integrate distributional survey, geomorphology, formation processes, and ethnoarchaeological studies. American and European participants were brought together for a symposium at the 53rd Annual Meeting of the Society for American Archaeology in Phoenix, Arizona, titled "Beyond Boundaries in Time and Space: The Utility of the Site Concept."

The symposium took as its central theme the specific goal of evaluating the traditional definition, identification, and analysis of the archaeological site, with an emphasis on alternate ways to organize regional data recovery and analysis. The success of the symposium generated much enthusiasm among the participants, and 13 of the 19 participants expressed an interest in further developing the theme of the integration of concepts, techniques, and methods for developing an effective regional approach to archaeology, as well as the exploration of alternate ways to conceptualize archaeological problems.

After intensive review of the symposium papers, the editors narrowed the focus to the investigation of past systems of land use by prehistoric hunter–gatherers and agropastoralists. Authors worked within the framework of a carefully considered landscape perspective. Partially derived from American and European geography and archaeology, our notion of archaeological landscape embodies the view that the distribution of archaeological artifacts and features relative to elements of the landscape (and not merely the spatial relationships among artifacts and features) provide insight into social and economic organizations in the past. One important difference, however, distinguished our notion of the landscape from others: Our notion of archaeological landscape includes the explicit incorporation of natural and cultural formation processes, not just within sites but across entire regions. By structuring our notion of archaeological landscapes in this way, we hoped to integrate the archaeological and ethnoarchaeological study of systems of land use as they are organized across space with new techniques for recognizing, and utilizing, insight from the study of natural and cultural formation processes. We hoped that the conscious incorporation of normally distinct archaeological studies would result in a synergy that would promote effective methods of archaeological inference and theory building for understanding past use of the landscape.

Within this context, the authors were asked to selectively evaluate, and/or provide analytical justification for a series of related topics within the volume landscape approach based on research projects in which they were currently involved: The topics included site versus nonsite approaches to archaeological and ethnoarchaeological data recovery and the subsequent impact on data analysis and theory building; problems and advantages in incorporating elements derived from studies of landscape geomorphology and natural and cultural formation processes; and problems and advantages in incorporating landscape elements into analysis and theory building. Authors were encouraged to discuss the disjunction between the new methods of data collection and analysis and traditional frameworks of archaeological interpretation and propose new ways to structure how we think about systems in the past and how we analyze the material results of these systems.

The archaeological and ethnoarchaeological examples provided in this volume are from Europe and America and span both arid and temperate environments. We believe the landscape approach proposed in this volume, by scrutinizing the use of site and acknowledging natural and cultural formation processes, incorporates a greater proportion of the potential archaeological variability in the making of inferences about the past use of landscapes. The approaches and views presented by the authors are wide ranging and diverse and sometimes at odds with one another—a potentially productive development. The variety and contrast of approaches generate a synergy that promotes archaeological theory building. We think that the strategies presented by the authors provide new, productive directions for the use of the many exciting techniques and methods now at our disposal.

We wish to thank the authors for their contributions, their encouragement, and their patience. We also thank the symposium coorganizers, Eileen Camilli and Jim Ebert, and other symposia participants—especially John Cherry, Jack Davis, and Rob Foley—for their contributions. For comments on early drafts of the volume, we thank the various anonymous reviewers. For assistance and insight on the structure of the volume, we thank Roger Anyon, Bob Dewar, Steve Kuhn, Bob Leonard, Mary Stiner, and Patrice Teltser. We would also like to thank Peter Ainsworth, Jack Davis, Robert Dunnell, T. J. Ferguson, Keith Kintigh, and Mark Varien for comments on early drafts of parts of the volume, and June-el Piper for editorial and technical advice. Over the years we have benefited from innumerable conversations on this topic with many researchers. These individuals are responsible (but in no way accountable) in part for the eventual content of this volume. For this assistance we acknowledge Roger Anyon, Lew Binford, Bob Dewar, Tom Jones, Signa Larralde, Bob Leonard, K. Paddayya, Michael Shott, and Alan Sullivan. For invaluable insight into the nature of the creative process, the senior editor would like to thank Holly Roberts. Finally, we would like to thank Michael Jochim and Eliot Werner for their encouragement and support.

Contents

**Chapter 3 • Seeing the Present and Interpreting the Past—and
Keeping Things Straight**......................... 43

Lewis R. Binford

**PART III. THE SPATIAL DIMENSION OF
ARCHAEOLOGICAL LANDSCAPES**

**Chapter 4 • Archaeological Landscapes: The Ethnoarchaeology
of Pastoral Land Use in the Grevena Province of
Northern Greece**................................ 65

Claudia Chang

Chapter 7 • Landscape Scale: Geoenvironmental Approaches to Prehistoric Settlement Strategies 137

C. Russell Stafford and Edwin R. Hajic

PART IV. THE TEMPORAL DIMENSION OF ARCHAEOLOGICAL LANDSCAPES

Chapter 8 • Chronological Resolution in Distributional Archaeology..................................... 167

George T. Jones and Charlotte Beck

PART V.   POSTSCRIPT AND PROSPECTUS

Part I

Introduction

Chapter **1**

Concepts, Methods, and Theory Building
A Landscape Approach

JACQUELINE ROSSIGNOL

INTRODUCTION

Space, Time, and Archaeological Landscapes investigates the relationship between the methods and goals of processual archaeology in the 1990s. Processual archaeologists attempt to bring a scientific structure to understanding change in social and economic systems, in the context of theories of adaptation and evolution. The contributors to this volume explore ways to profitably formulate archaeological problems and to link methods with theories in the scientific way associated with the aspirations of processual archaeology. Authors present their research in light of three questions:

1. How can "scientifically compatible" approaches, that is, ones that allow archaeologists to give observations consistent and explicit meanings, be integrated to address the processual questions we bring to the record?
2. Are concepts considered fundamental to archaeology, such as the site, inadequate for a scientific archaeology? If so, what concepts are more compatible with a scientific archaeology?

JACQUELINE ROSSIGNOL • Department of Anthropology, University of New Mexico, Albuquerque, New Mexico 87131.

Space, Time, and Archaeological Landscapes, edited by Jacqueline Rossignol and LuAnn Wandsnider. Plenum Press, New York, 1992.

3. How can scientifically compatible approaches be combined so as to enhance theory building?

Specifically, contributors focus on whether the site concept is compatible with scientific inquiry—the aim of processual archaeology—and evaluate techniques, methods, and approaches that may have more promise for encouraging scientific methods. Concentration is on approaches that include the study of cultural and natural formation processes, taphonomy, ethnoarchaeology, and distributional forms of data recovery. With the exception of the latter survey technique, focus is on approaches emphasizing actualistic studies and the role that these studies play in a scientific archaeology.

A common goal, the explication of stability and change in hunter–gatherer and agropastoral subsistence strategies as they are deployed over landscapes, unites the authors. This goal provides the context for the evaluation of concepts and the incorporation of scientifically compatible approaches. The scope of the volume is limited to noncomplex societies in order to take advantage of the close ecological links that hunter–gatherer and village-level agropastoralists have with the landscape. This interaction can be exploited in studies specifically designed to investigate land use, through a landscape perspective. Partially derived from American and European geography and archaeology, our landscape perspective embodies the view that the distribution of archaeological artifacts and features relative to elements of the landscape (and not merely the spatial relationships among artifacts and features) provide insight into social and economic organization in the past. By concentrating on land use, potentially synergistic relationships among environmental systems, landscape physiography and the spatial aspects of human land use strategies can be explored and exploited.

We define *landscape approach* as the archaeological investigation of past land use by means of a landscape perspective, combined with the conscious incorporation of regional geomorphology, actualistic studies (taphonomy, formation processes, ethnoarchaeology), and marked by ongoing reevaluation and innovation of concepts, methods, and theory. This landscape approach not only provides a common theater for a variety of archaeologists to interact, but, more importantly, it provides a directed, but flexible, orientation for theory building.

In other words, our landscape approach addresses regional-level problems in archaeology by capitalizing on the interaction among regional-level geological, ecological, and actualistic studies. This framework takes inspiration from Butzer's contextual approach (Butzer 1982; see also Hassan 1979) and Foley's regional taphonomic and off-site approach (Foley 1981a,b).

Our landscape approach differs substantially from landscape archaeology. Because of their explicitly historical emphasis, method and interpretation of landscape archaeologists do not incorporate ecological and geological system variables. Both British and American practitioners of landscape archaeology assert an historical and (Hodderian) contextual focus for the discipline (Roberts 1987; Deetz 1990; Crumley and Marquardt 1990).

THE SYSTEMIC PARADIGM

Concurrent with the reemergence of evolutionary problems in archaeology that took place in the 1960s was a concern to address those problems in an explicitly scientific way (Willey and Sabloff 1980:195; Dunnell 1986:39–40). More precisely, archaeologists wanted to investigate methods of inference that ultimately lead to knowing the past, rather than to speculating about it. The predominant paradigm that has emerged from the self-conscious evaluation of archaeological methods stresses the investigation of behavioral and formational *systems* underlying the organization of the archaeological record (Willey and Sabloff 1980:186; Dunnell 1986:38).

The underlying premises of the systemic paradigm emphasize the interaction of several levels of system. For example, hunter–gatherer and agropastoral subsistence systems are made up of adaptive[1] strategies organized over space and through time. These strategies incorporate plant and animal species utilized by people, and by extension, the physical and biological environmental factors that constrain or encourage those species. Both the environmental systems of the resource species, and the human subsistence strategies with which they interact, are organized according to ecological principles.

Ultimately, adaptive strategies are of interest to the processual archaeologist because adaptations have systemic properties, and these systemic properties are responsible for the organization underlying the archaeological record (Binford 1978a:3). Furthermore, understanding change in systems of adaptation—culture[2] change—and the implications of those changes for cultural evolution, is the ultimate aim of processual studies. The challenge to the processual archaeologist is to discover how the interaction of human subsistence systems and environmental systems is reflected in the organization of archaeological remains. For the archaeologists in this volume, the interaction of human subsistence systems and environmental systems is a primary concern of processual study.

[1] Adaptation can be defined as *conformity* between the organism and its environment. Organisms may be thought of as "tracking" their environments in both ecological and evolutionary time, changing as their environments change. Such environmental tracking may be physiological (as in acclimation), behavioral (including learning), and/or genetic (evolutionary [biological]), depending on the time scale of environmental change (Pianka 1983:85–87, emphasis added). We add cultural or extrasomatic mechanisms of inheritance to Pianka's discussion of environmental tracking (Binford 1989b:471–472).

[2] Culture is assumed to be the extrasomatic means of adaptation and not dependent upon genetic mechanisms for its form or biological reproduction for its transmission (White 1959).

NEW METHODS AND CONCEPTS IN ARCHAEOLOGY

The past 20 years have witnessed the development of new and potentially powerful methods for investigating the various systems underlying the organization of the archaeological record. By far, the most influential methods implement actualistic studies (e.g., Schiffer 1976; Binford 1978a; Yellen 1977). Actualistic studies examine present-day, ongoing systems of dynamics that can be related to the deposition of archaeological remains. Actualistic studies come in three forms: inquiry into formation of the fossil assemblages (taphonomy), investigation of the effects of interactive human and natural processes on archaeological assemblages, and examination of the impact of hunter–gatherer and agropastoral mobility strategies on locations of the landscape. Geomorphology, the study of land form history, or morphogenesis, supports taphonomic and formation process studies by investigating formation processes at a regional scale.

Taphonomy developed in association with paleontology and concerns the processes and resultant biases whereby the fossil record is formed (Foley 1981b:157). Behrensmeyer and Kidwell (1985) define the fossil record as "the result of a dynamic, evolving, integrated system of biological and sedimentological processes." Investigation of this biological–sedimentological matrix expanded into the archaeological field, and research is conducted actualistically in an effort to gain an understanding of the numerous, complex processes that produce both early man paleontological deposits as well as archaeological deposits. Although most work has been conducted at the site level, regional-level concern with taphonomic processes is increasing (Foley 1981a,b; Dunnell and Dancy 1983).

Formation process studies, a closely related approach, targets explicitly the interaction between anthropogenic and natural processes especially within archaeological sites. Formally introduced and developed by Schiffer in the late 1970s, formation process studies capitalized on the observation that both natural and cultural formation processes that contribute to the material record of past systems are *regular*. These regular processes serve as a systematic link between archaeological remains and past cultural systems (Schiffer 1976:12). Schiffer attempts to use this relationship to parse out these intervening processes, hopefully revealing the original "undisturbed" record (1976:13; cf. Binford 1981), a goal shared by many taphonomists working on paleontological deposits.

These regular processes can also be used, however, to attain a more complete understanding of the systematic dynamics underlying the record. Cultural formation processes influence the structure of the archaeological record in myriad ways, ranging from the initial episodes of anthropogenic modification of locations on the landscape, to repeated discard of artifacts as use of the location continues, abandonment, reuse of locations, and finally, excavation. Natural formation processes, such as erosion, alluviation and aeolian deposition, interact with cultural processes and further modify locations. Actualistic study of formation processes, by isolating and explicitly defining this series of processes, examines the fundamental nature of the interface between the archaeological record and the environmental and physiographic matrix within which it is embedded (e.g., Foley 1981b; Wandsnider 1989).

Ethnoarchaeology is another actualistic approach that explores anthropogenic impact on archaeological matrices in light of the systemic *regional* patterns of human behavior over space and through time. These latter studies focus on the cross-cultural study of hunter–gatherer and agropastoralist systems and try to isolate systemic elements, especially as they are correlated with different environments (Binford 1980; Kelly 1983). Ethnoarchaeology is performed on mainly two scales; at the site level and at the landscape scale. Site-level research emphasizes spatial patterns of deposition resulting from specific activities, usually of short temporal duration, and is often closely allied with the formal study of formation processes as advocated by Schiffer (however, cf. Binford 1978b).

Landscape-scale ethnoarchaeological research investigates the organization of subsistence strategies at the regional level, how these strategies shift through time, and how organization impacts the structure of the archaeological record. Research has focused on isolating behavioral elements of subsistence strategies and establishing their range and variety cross-culturally. One such element is mobility. Actualistic research reveals that environmental parameters, for example, the variety, placement on the landscape, and seasonal availability of resources, influence mobility strategies among hunter–gatherers. In turn, mobility strategies of hunter–gatherer and agropastoral groups have direct impact on the structure of artifactual remains at locations (Binford 1980,1982). Other elements of subsistence strategies whose roles in subsistence behavior have been illuminated include storage, curation, and tethering of mobility systems to certain resources.

Although actualistic studies of the systemic organization of behavior can operate simultaneously at the site and landscape scale and research at the landscape scale has made a significant contributions to theory building (e.g. Binford 1980,1982), site-based formation processes and ethnoarchaeology have been emphasized at the expense of the incorporation of landscape morphogenesis and the development of landscape-scale ethnoarchaeology.

Finally, nonsite, or distributional forms of data recovery (Thomas 1975; Dunnell and Dancy 1983; Ebert 1986) as well as off-site conceptualization of archaeological region (Foley 1981a,b) are proposed as systems of data recovery more compatible with systemic aspects of the archaeological record. Nonsite or distributional approaches define the artifact as the primary unit of observation and analysis and forego the site concept altogether. The off-site approach, as presented by Foley, subsumes sites under a regional data recovery program that stresses the distributions of materials between traditionally defined sites and the regionwide taphonomic influences on the archaeological record.

In order for archaeological research to be scientific, the questions about the record must be formulated so that archaeological elements or groups of elements are given meanings that are consistent and explicit and do not change and shift between applications. Explicit and reliable meanings are important because without them we cannot reliably observe diversity in the record. Diversity and change in diversity is the subject of an evolutionary study (Dunnell 1980).

Actualistic studies of taphonomy, formation processes, and human subsistence strategies, as well as the incorporation of morphogenic studies at the landscape scale, seek to identify the impact of one set of well-defined variables on another. The actualistic study of formation processes at the site level and the incorporation of geomorphological principles at the landscape scale, have generated detailed accounts of the interaction between natural and anthropogenic deposition patterns. These accounts more than anything successfully discourage archaeologists from attempting to directly infer meaning from the archaeological record (Kroll and Price 1991:7). Likewise, actualistic studies of subsistence strategies has introduced a sizable array of organized variables that archaeologists and other anthropologists could have scarcely guessed at before the advent of ethnoarchaeology. The result has been a more thorough, methodological consideration of the entire range of dynamics underlying the archaeological record.

LINKING METHOD AND THEORY

Although methods incorporating actualistic studies of taphonomy, formation processes, and human subsistence strategies have greatly expanded our knowledge of the record, and our understanding of the problem of past systems, the impact of actualistic studies on the way we think about the past has been less successful. Archaeologists have difficulty linking the results of actualistic studies with the questions concerning culture change. The results of actualistic studies are not used to inform on the nature of the world; more often they are used as "cautionary tales" to criticize studies that have utilized flawed definitions or to question traditional conceptualizations of the record. We identify several reasons why useful methods have not had the impact that they should have had.

1. *Failure to link actualistic studies with general theory.* Binford (1977:6–7) has suggested that theory building proceeds at two stages. Actualistic studies are crucial to the first stage—the development of middle-range theory—defined by Binford as those studies that link the archaeological static record with knowledge of formational and behavioral dynamics. The second stage of theory building is to link middle-range research with general theory questions about the nature of human culture and culture change—questions that reflect the goals of processual archaeology. Although considerable headway has been made at the actualistic

level, the second stage of theory building, linking the results of actualistic studies with general theory, is poorly developed (see also Renfrew 1982).

2. *Attempting to integrate scientific with nonscientific conventions.* Attempts by archaeologists to combine methods designed to explore systemic phenomena with traditional concepts in archaeology poorly suited for systemic exploration have marked much of archaeological research over the past 20 years. The site concept and standard or traditional settlement pattern approaches are specifically implicated in this problem and are dealt with extensively in this volume (e.g., Dunnell, Binford, Chang, Dewar, and McBride). Briefly, overdependence on a site approach is implicated in (a) the neglect of dispersed "off-site" materials that are important for investigating land use at the regional scale, (b) inexact or vague definitions at the observational level, making data collection and statistical analysis difficult, and (c) a tendency to treat sites as monolithic entities, underestimating the complexity of occupation-component interaction.

3. *Poor integration of the structure of the archaeological record with concepts derived from actualistic studies of land use strategies.* For example, as Kroll and Price (1991:2–3) note, archaeologists often invest considerable energy into spatial analysis designed to isolate activity areas in archaeological deposits, without considering the organization of the behaviors responsible for activity areas. Factors influencing the structure of activity areas within sites are often dependent on the character of strategies at the regional scale, not to mention intervening formation processes.

4. *Poor integration of methods directed at either analysis of the record or analysis of human systems.* Although new approaches are employed with enthusiasm, they are poorly integrated. Archaeologists tend to specialize, often focusing on a specific technique such as lithic analysis or a method such as ethnoarchaeology. Archaeologists rarely have the opportunity or resources to simultaneously apply the range of methods required for a complete understanding of the archaeological problem.

Overall, the failure of the processual method has been a failure to link between scales and across scales with general theory and a tendency to integrate scientific with nonscientific goals. Although new methods are structurally compatible with scientific approaches, in a fundamental way they often are not linked to any theoretical goal. The links between archaeological method and the scientific goal of knowing the empirical world has only been partially forged.

For archaeology there are two major theory-building problems: The first is reliably linking our understanding of universal dynamics with the static record in order to correctly infer dynamics. This problem is akin to the geologist's problem of linking present-day erosional and depositional processes with the static record of accretional events in the past as revealed by the geological record, so that he or she can correctly infer the causes of the present-day geological landscape.

Actualistic studies seek to make similar links between statics and dynamics. Fortunately, the implementation of actualistic studies in archaeology is well on its way to improving our knowledge of the natural and behavioral processes that determine the structure of the archaeological record (Thomas 1986:237–240).

The other problem of archaeology is making sure that the methods we apply to the record are relevant to general theory—that the methods interact with theories about past cultural organization and culture change. In other words, research in formational and ethnoarchaeological actualistic studies must be kept on course, so it does not veer off into trivial applications. Binford has suggested a "linking" set of questions between theory and methodology that can serve to keep methodological studies on track (and not reduce them to interesting facts about the data, or "cautionary tales"). These are (1) What uniformitarian assumptions can we make about natural and cultural dynamics in the present day that we can reliably project back into the past? (2) Why do humans behave the way they do at different times and places? (3) How can we make sense of recognized patterns of change and diversity in organized human behavior? (Binford 1977:6).

Most of the chapters in this volume are organized around one or more of these linking questions. In terms of the first question—what assumptions can be projected back into the past?—many of the chapters in this volume focus on the fact that the record is organized based on regular (and predictable) patterns of formation and that the interaction of human strategies with the environment is based on general, or uniformitarian, ecological rules. The challenge is working out what aspects of those systems are relevant to understanding the formation of the record, the organization of subsistence strategies, the structure of the environment, and the interaction among all three.

In terms of understanding why humans behave the way they do at different times and places, the volume contributors incorporate ethnoarchaeological and cross-cultural studies of hunter–gatherer and agropastoral forms of land use into their archaeological investigations of land use. Making sense of the highly variable catalog of particular situations presented by cross-cultural study requires archaeologists to broaden inquiry to consideration of organizational characteristics, the underlying structure of societies based on environmental and demographic variables (Yellen 1989:106–116). By examining and referencing the ethnographic and ethnoarchaeological catalog of land use strategies, the authors in this volume begin to discern the elements underlying the environmental and demographic organization responsible for the structure of the archaeological record.

In terms of the third problem—making sense of patterns of change and diversity—it is difficult to conceptualize this problem in a study of land use without simultaneously considering the interacting taphonomical, formational, geomorphological, and ecological systems. In the first step toward addressing this problem, the relevant aspects of these concurring systems must be recognized and incorporated. The next step, pattern recognition, is dependent on how well we link our knowledge of the variables responsible for the character of the human–environmental interaction (the elements of subsistence system organization) with formation processes. Authors examine these patterns, in light of the complex structure of the record and the complexity of human organization, in order to gain increased knowledge of the past. In many ways this third problem, making sense of patterns of change and diversity in past systems of land use, is the goal of the volume.

STRUCTURE OF THE VOLUME

The volume consists of four sections: Part I is a general introduction to the entire volume. In the second part, Concepts and a Scientific Archaeology, authors evaluate concepts, and propose theoretical frameworks for research. In the next two parts, The Spatial Dimension of Archaeological Landscapes and The Temporal Dimension of Archaeological Landscapes, authors seek to incorporate and creatively combine various systemic approaches to archaeological questions: actualistic studies of human land use, actualistic studies of the systemic aspects of formation processes, and systemic study of the physiographic aspects of the landscape. In addressing these questions, the authors in the "space" section apply a landscape perspective to problems peculiar to the spatial dimension; in the "time" section, authors focus on the spatial–temporal interaction between behavioral occupation and archaeological components. In the closing chapter, Archaeological Landscape Studies: Postscript and Prospectus, Wandsnider provides an overview, discussion, and directions for future research.

The two contributions that make up the concepts section investigate the scientific utility of a concept central to today's practice of archaeology: the archaeological site. In the process of assessing the definition and use of *site* in archaeology, Dunnell rejects the site concept because of its fundamental analytical intractability. Binford, in an extended discussion on the appropriate structure for scientific research, and the role of evolutionary concepts in theory building, disagrees emphatically with Dunnell and defends the site concept as representing the nexus of interaction of various scales relevant to understanding organization. Both use their evaluation of site to expand into a discussion of the appropriate structure of archaeological inquiry. In spite of fundamental disagreements over the structure of archaeological research, and the role of evolutionary theory, both authors stress the importance of explicit and reliable concepts, and approve of the use of flexible, interactive spatial scales promoted by a landscape approach.

Hodges (1987:131) notes succinctly that "the use of space through time is the key asset in the archaeologist's armoury." The "space" and "time" sections present approaches designed to address, at least in part, the conceptual and methodological problems discussed in the first section. Authors in both these sections apply innovative concepts and methods in an attempt to identify behavioral-related organization underlying the structure of the record. Areas of research range from the humid Northeast and Midwest to the arid West of the United States, across the Atlantic to (humid) Ireland and (arid) Greece. Approaches include survey, survey and excavation, and one ethnoarchaeological study. The temporal scales covered and the landscape strategies examined are likewise wide ranging, from systems in operation over months, decades, and centuries to economic transformations taking place over thousands of years.

Authors carefully consider the utility of the site for conceptualizing problems at the regional level, and many (Chang, Stafford and Hajic, Camilli and Ebert, Zvelebil, Green and Macklin, Jones and Beck, and Wandsnider) take Dunnell's position that *site* is an inadequate conceptual and analytical unit. Dewar and McBride, in agreement with Binford, "rehabilitate" the site concept and argue convincingly for its relevance in understanding systems of land use. The conceptual investigation expands to the advantages and disadvantages of nonsite approaches, specifically, distributional approaches to data recovery. Alternative spatial concepts, such as the notion of "place" (Chang, Schlanger) and "landscape element" (Stafford and Hajic), and new temporal concepts, "episode" (Zvelebil, Green, and Macklin) and "medium-term processes" (Dewar and McBride), are investigated. Methodologically, all of the authors incorporate actualistic studies in either the data recovery stages by implementation of formation processes and geomorphology or in the interpretive phases by means of ethnoarchaeological studies of mobility, foraging strategies, and ethnographic studies of abandonment. Actualistic studies are sometimes incorporated at both the data recovery and interpretive stages.

The four chapters in the space section select and apply methods geared to the theoretical problem of where and why people in the past located themselves in relation to the environmental and physiographic landscapes. Problems of temporal resolution are set aside in order to concentrate on the spatial dimension of the archaeological record.

Two of the chapters concern relatively short-term agropastoral adaptations with a strong emphasis on the role of places on the landscape. Chang implements an actualistic method, ethnoarchaeology, in a study of organization of animal husbandry systems over space among Greek agropastoralists. Chang shows how a nonsite orientation can be used to revisualize a previously archaeologically invisible pastoral record and thus reveal architectural variability useful for examining agropastoral systems. Placement of these architectural facilities is interactive with several scales of landscape. This interaction in turn reveals the organization underlying the system of land use. Schlanger investigates the reuse of locations after residential abandonment in an approach that emphasizes the role of places on the landscape and dependable chronological markers in understanding systems of land use for prehistoric agriculturalists in the arid Southwest United States.

The latter two chapters of the space section investigate longer term, hunter–gatherer adaptations, with an emphasis on formation processes, variety of land form, and distributional data recovery. Camilli, in a study of prehistoric hunter–gatherers in the Southwest United States, incorporates a distributional approach, landscape physiography, and formation processes to present a new notion of archaeological visibility: The relative visibility of the archaeological remains on an abandoned location at least partly determine the chances of that location's reuse. Stafford and Hajic use a distributional approach and regional morphogenesis to identify and categorize assemblages and then relate them to several scales of land form present in the Illinois river valley. Use of independently derived measures of landscape scale and consideration of individual land form provide a method for measuring interaction between the landscape and lithic assemblages.

The four chapters in the time section address the perennial archaeological problem of determining not only the relative order of archaeological elements but at what temporal *resolution* these elements represent and what temporal resolutions we should be conceptualizing human behavior. These chapters fuse consideration of space and time by investigating the relationship between behavioral occupations and archaeological components.

Jones and Beck provide an overview of traditional approaches to chronological resolution. Archaic hunter–gatherers in Nevada are investigated using distributionally derived obsidian data that demonstrate a different method for conceptualizing and deriving chronological resolution for regions lacking temporal markers. The method also has potential for the investigation of occupation–component interaction. Zvelebil, Green, and Macklin use lithic assemblages and regional geomorphology to discuss, on the one hand, temporal resolution, and on the other, how the Mesolithic to Neolithic transition in Ireland is temporally structured in behavioral terms. The authors explicitly espouse a landscape approach and evaluate its utility. Dewar and McBride promote a scale of temporal resolution (medium-term processes) intermediate between ethnographic annual rounds and evolutionary change in a discussion of Terminal Archaic–Woodland phase hunter–gatherers in the Northeast United States. Wandsnider uses a simulation analysis to explore the development of archaeological landscapes subject to different frequencies and periodicities of use.

In the final chapter, Wandsnider provides an overview and discussion of the operational and conceptual issues raised in this volume and suggests directions for further research.

SUMMARY

Space, Time, and Archaeological Landscapes investigates the conceptual bases underlying a processual, scientific archaeology and explores the utility of a proposed landscape approach. This landscape approach is derived from the notion that the synergistic employment of studies of formation processes, taphonomy, ethnoarchaeology, and distributional approaches to data recovery can result in increased understanding of formational, ecological, and behavioral systems that influence the structure of the archaeological record.

The application of the landscape approach is in keeping with the goal of understanding change in social and economic systems, in the context of theories of evolution. Applying actualistic studies of taphonomy, formation processes and human subsistence strategies, and incorporation of landscape-scale morphogenic studies in an interactive approach, however, is not sufficient. Methods that make up the landscape approach are linked to general theory questions, or processual goals, through a series of three questions: (1) What uniformitarian assumptions can we make about natural and cultural dynamics in the present day that we can reliably project back into the past? (2) Why do humans behave the way they do at different times and places? (3) How does one make sense of recognized patterns of change and diversity in organized human behavior? This general agenda is applied to specific questions of organization, and change in organization, in studies of hunter–gatherer and agropastoral land use.

The editors present these chapters not only as examples of a potentially useful approach, but as useful exercises in theory building. These chapters present procedures that increase our understanding of the intellectual problems we are faced with and a clarification of things we need to learn more about in order to truly know, and understand, the archaeological record.

REFERENCES

Behrensmeyer, A. K., and Kidwell, S. M., 1985, Taphonomy's Contribution to Paleobiology, *Paleobiology* 11(1):105–109.

Binford, L. R., 1977, General Introduction, in: *For Theory Building in Archaeology* (L. R. Binford, ed.), Academic Press, New York, pp. 1–10.

Binford, L. R., 1978a, *Nunamiut Ethnoarchaeology*, Academic Press, New York.

Binford, L. R., 1978b, Dimensional Analysis of Behavior and Site Structure: Learning from an Eskimo Hunting Stand, *American Antiquity* 43(3):330–361.

Binford, L. R., 1980, Willow Smoke and Dogs' Tails: Hunter–Gatherer Settlement Systems and Archaeological Site Formation. *American Antiquity* 45(1):4–20.

Binford, L. R., 1981, Behavioral Archaeology and the "Pompeii Premise," *Journal of Anthropological Research* 37(3):195–208.

Binford, L. R., 1982, The Archaeology of Place, *Journal of Anthropological Archaeology* 1(1):5–31.

Binford, L. R., 1987, Researching Ambiguity: Frames of Reference and Site Structure, in: *Method and*

Theory in Activity Area Research (S. Kent, ed.), Columbia University Press, New York, pp. 449–512.

Binford, L. R., 1989a, Styles of Style, *Journal of Anthropological Archaeology* 8.

Binford, L. R., 1989b, Isolating the Transition to Cultural Adaptations: An Organizational Approach, in: *Debating Archaeology* (L. R. Binford, ed.), Academic Press, New York, pp. 464–481.

Butzer, K. W., 1982, *Archaeology as Human Ecology: Method and Theory for a Contextual Approach*, Cambridge University Press, Cambridge.

Crumley, C. L., and W. H. Marquardt, 1990, Landscape: A Unifying Concept in Regional Analysis, in: *Interpreting Space: GIS and Archaeology* (K. M. S. Allen, S. W. Green, and E. B. W. Zubrow, eds.), Taylor and Francis, London, pp. 73–79.

Deetz, J., 1990, Prologue: Landscapes as Cultural Statements, in: *Earth Patterns—Essays in Landscape Archaeology* (W. M. Kelso and R. Most, eds.), University Press of Virginia, Charlottesville, pp. 1–4.

Dunnell, R. C., 1980, Evolutionary Theory and Archaeology, in: *Advances in Archaeological Method and Theory* 3 (M. B. Schiffer, ed.), Academic Press, New York, pp. 35–99).

Dunnell, R. C., 1986, Five Decades of American Archaeology, in: *American Archaeology Past and Future* (D. J. Meltzer, Don D. Fowler, and J. A. Sabloff, eds.), Smithsonian Institution Press, Washington, pp. 23–49.

Dunnell, R. C., and Dancy, W. S., 1983, The Siteless Survey: A Regional Scale Data Collection Strategy, in: *Advances in Archaeological Method and Theory*, Volume 6 (M. B. Schiffer, ed.), Academic Press, New York, pp. 267–88.

Ebert, J. I. (1986), *Distributional Archaeology: Nonsite Discovery, Recording and Analytical Methods for Application to the Surface Archaeological Record*, Ph.D. dissertation, Department of Anthropology, University of New Mexico.

Foley, R., 1981a, *Off-site Archaeology and Human Adaptation in Eastern Africa: Analysis of Regional Artifact Density in the Amboseli, Southern Kenya*. Cambridge Monographs in African Archaeology 3. British Archaeological Reports, International Series 97.

Foley, R., 1981b, Off-site Archaeology: An Alternative Approach for the Short-sited, in: *Pattern of the Past—Studies in Honour of David Clarke* (I. Hodder, G. Issac, and N. Hammond, eds.), Cambridge University Press, Cambridge, pp. 157–183.

Hassan, F. A., 1979, Geoarchaeology: The Geologist and Archaeology, *American Antiquity* 44:267–270.

Hodges, R., 1987, Spatial Models, Anthropology and Archaeology, in: *Landscape and Culture—Geographical and Archaeological Perspectives* (J. M. Wagstaff, ed.), Basil Blackwell, Oxford, pp. 118–133.

Kelly, R. L., 1983, Hunter–Gatherer Mobility Strategies, *Journal of Anthropological Research* 39:277–306.

Kroll, E. M., and Price, T. D., eds., 1991, *The Interpretation of Archaeological Spatial Patterning*, Plenum Press, New York.

Kroll, E. M., and Price, T. D., 1991, Spatial Analysis of Ethnoarchaeological Sites, in: *The Interpretation of Archaeological Spatial Patterning*, (E. M. Kroll and T. D. Price, eds.), Plenum Press, New York, pp. 7–9.

Renfrew, C., 1982, Explanation Revisited, in: *Theory and Explanation in Archaeology* (C. Renfrew, M. J. Rowlands, and B. A. Segraves eds.), Academic Press, New York, pp. 5–23.

Roberts, B. K., 1987, Landscape Archaeology, in: *Landscape and Culture—Geographical and Archaeological Perspectives* (J. M. Wagstaff, ed.), Basil Blackwell, Oxford, pp. 77–95.

Schiffer, M. B., 1976, *Behavioral Archaeology*, Academic Press, New York.

Thomas, D. H., 1975, Nonsite Sampling in Archaeology: Up the Creek Without a Site?, in: *Sampling in Archaeology* (J. W. Mueller, ed.), University of Arizona Press, Tucson, pp. 61–81.

Thomas, D. H., 1986, Contemporary Hunter–Gatherer Archaeology in America, in: *American Archae-*

ology Past and Future (D. J. Meltzer, Don D. Fowler, and J. A. Sabloff, eds.), Smithsonian Institution Press, Washington, pp. 237–276.

Wandsnider, L., 1989, *Long-Term Land Use, Formation Processes, and the Structure of the Archaeological Landscape: A Case Study from Southwestern Wyoming*, Ph.D. dissertation, Department of Anthropology, University of New Mexico.

White, L. A., 1959, *The Evolution of Culture*, McGraw-Hill, New York.

Willey, G. R., and Sabloff, J. A., 1980, *A History of American Archaeology*, Second Edition, W. H. Freeman and Co., San Francisco.

Yellen, J. E., 1977, *Archaeological Approaches to the Present: Models for Reconstructing the Past*, Academic Press, New York.

Yellen, J. E., 1989, The Present and the Future of Hunter–Gatherer Studies, in: *Archaeological Thought in America* (C. C. Lamberg-Karlovsky, ed.), Cambridge University Press, Cambridge, pp. 89–116.

Part II

Concepts and a Scientific Archaeology

The two chapters in this section illustrate the important role of evaluation in a scientific approach to archaeology. In their respective chapters, Robert Dunnell and Lewis Binford evaluate the utility of the site concept, first by providing an historic overview, and then by elaborating the site concept's role in method and theory. Both authors use this initial discussion of *site* as an opportunity to develop their respective arguments on the structure of archaeological inquiry. Although both Dunnell and Binford stress the importance of explicit definition and reliable methods of observation, and the advantages of a multiscaler landscape approach, they part company over appropriate methodological goals. The divergence of these two explicitly scientific approaches emphasizes the importance of relationships among concepts in structuring research.

Dunnell advocates a siteless approach for archaeology—not because it is a useful method for exploring land use (as advocated by the editors of this volume) but because the site concept is fundamentally defective. Dunnell argues that sites are ambiguously defined, multifaceted entities that are stipulated rather than constructed from more basic elements (e.g., artifacts and features). Furthermore, the site—although often defined as a discrete entity—is operationally identified in the field by relative differences in artifact density. Because site definitions are mutable and multifarious, and the relationship between definition and identity in the field less than isomorphic, the site concept is deleterious to an explicitly empirical understanding of the surface archaeological record. Dewar and McBride's "component" (Chapter 10 in this volume), plagued by the same limitations, is included in his criticism.

Dunnell stresses the importance of developing methods for constructing units of historical association from smaller-scale observational units (e.g., artifacts). Rather than deriving these units by breaking down sites or assemblages into constituent elements, he forcefully advocates building up from smaller units to spatial aggregates of interpretive significance. In other words, distributional approaches are most properly used to support a completely different theoretical orientation to the record. Dunnell has elaborated this theoretical orientation in several publications (e.g., Dunnell 1971, 1986).

Dunnell observes (perhaps ruefully) that siteless approaches advocated by him in the past (Dunnell and Dancy 1983), although gaining currency in the practice of archaeological data recovery, are not applied with his corresponding methodological and theoretical goals. By and large, siteless or distributional approaches, and related off-site approaches as advocated by Thomas (1975) and Foley (1981a,b), are used to aid research specifically concerned with land use in a context of landscape or regional archaeology.

Dunnell's observation reflects almost exactly the composition of this volume: Of the five chapters espousing distributional data recovery, only Jones and Beck argue the importance of building interpretive structures from individual artifacts. The balance of the chapters use distributional approaches as a way to explicate land use.

Binford views the observational, methodological, and theoretical role of *site* and the goals and structure of scientific inquiry quite differently. Whereas Dunnell views the site concept as an insubstantial entity and a major impediment to the development of methods for the construction of spatial aggregates, Binford perceives sites as real archaeological and behavioral phenomena. Furthermore, *site* has a role to play in explicating an archaeological concept central to Binford's theoretical goals—organization.

For Binford, sites are the structural consequences of short-term organizations and events of the past. In Binford's view, the ambiguity that results when archaeologists attempt to acknowledge the behavioral and structural complexity of sites detracts from neither the site concept's importance nor its existence. The major difference between these authors' view of *site* is that Binford embeds a scale of behavioral meaning into the use of the site concept (as do most archaeologists) in a way Dunnell does not clearly acknowledge or consider as either relevant, or not relevant, to a conceptualization of site.

Dunnell stresses the importance of building up or constructing, from small-scale observational units to interpretive structure. Binford, in contrast, stresses identifying the structural results of dynamics. The focus of Binford's research is on the regular juxtapositioning of things in the past within sites, on places, and over landscapes, and understanding the organization of dynamics or systems responsible for them. Another fundamental difference between this view and Dunnell's is the character of instruments for measure. Although Dunnell implies in his chapter that instruments for measure are theory dependent. Binford explicitly states that instruments of measure be theory *in*dependent.

Binford develops his own argument for the structure of the record by taking Dunnell to task over his evolutionary views. Although Dunnell makes no reference to evolution in his chapter, he does elaborate on its role in archaeology in recent articles (Dunnell 1986, 1990).

In light of their basic agreement over the importance of explicit and reliable definitions, the divergence of Dunnell and Binford's views highlights the importance of evaluating the concepts themselves, the roles concepts play in methodology, and the role theoretical goals play in scientific archaeological inquiry. This section outlines issues basic to archaeological inquiry, the specifics of which are pursued in the "space" and "time" sections that follow.

REFERENCES

Dunnell, R. C., 1971, *Systematics in Prehistory*, The Free Press, New York.

Dunnell, R. C., 1986, Methodological Issues in Americanist Artifact Classification, in: *Advances in Archaeological method and Theory*, 9 (M. Schiffer, ed.), Academic Press, New York, pp. 149–207.

Dunnell, R. C., 1990, Aspects of the Application of Evolutionary Theory in Archaeology, in: *Archaeological Thought in America*, (C. C. Lamberg-Karlovsky, ed.), Cambridge University Press, Cambridge, pp. 35–49.

Dunnell, R. C., and Dancy, W. S., 1983, The Siteless Survey: A Regional Scale Data Collection Strategy, in: *Advances in Archaeological Method and Theory*, Volume 6 (M. B. Schiffer, ed.), Academic Press, New York, pp. 267–288.

Foley, R., 1981a, *Off-site Archaeology and Human Adaptation in Eastern Africa: Analysis of Regional Artifact Density in the Amboseli, Southern Kenya.* Cambridge Monographs in African Archaeology 3. British Archaeological Reports, International Series 97.

Foley, R., 1981b, Off-site Archaeology: An Alternative Approach for the Short-sited, in: *Pattern of the Past—Studies in Honour of David Clarke*, (I. Hodder, G. Issac, and N. Hammond, eds.), Cambridge University Press, Cambridge, pp. 157–183.

Thomas, D. H., 1975, Nonsite Sampling in Archaeology: Up the Creek without a Site?, in: *Sampling in Archaeology* (J. W. Mueller, ed.), University of Arizona Press, Tucson, pp. 61–81.

Chapter **2**

The Notion Site

ROBERT C. DUNNELL

INTRODUCTION

In spite of critiques that date to the early 1970s (Dancey 1971; Thomas 1975) the notion *site* is as ubiquitous as any archaeological concept in the current literature. Archaeologists look for, and find sites (e.g., site surveys); they record sites (e.g., state surveys, the National Register of Historic Places); they collect and/or excavate sites, they interpret sites; and incredibly, they even date sites. *Site* usually provides the framework for recording artifact provenience; it usually serves as a sampling frame at some level in most fieldwork (e.g., Binford 1964; McManomon 1981; Redman 1973); and, largely by default, it, or some partitioning of it (e.g., Dewar 1986), serves as the unit of artifact association. Site is, as usually depicted in introductory texts, a basic, if not the basic, unit of archaeology.

In English, site means place or location of:

> site (sit), n., 1. the position of a town, building, etc., esp. as to its environ-
> ment. 2. the area on which anything is, has been, or is to be located.
> (Barnhart and Stein 1958:1130)

Initially archaeologists simply borrowed *site* from English, along with its commonsense context. Subsequently it has acquired archaeological significance and is now used as a tool for conceptualizing the archaeological record. This chapter argues that the notion of site as an archaeological concept is defective, even

ROBERT C. DUNNELL • Department of Anthropology, DH-05, University of Washington, Seattle, Washington 98195.

Space, Time, and Archaeological Landscapes, edited by Jacqueline Rossignol and LuAnn Wandsnider. Plenum Press, New York, 1992.

deleterious to archaeology. Its use is warranted neither as a unit of observation nor as a unit of analysis.

SITE

Development of the Concept

Site has not always figured as prominently in archaeology as it does today. In the nineteenth century, archaeological attention focused on large scale, aboveground "monuments." Portable objects played a largely supplemental role, answering questions conjured by and phrased in terms of monuments (e.g., Atwater 1833; Squier and Davis 1848; C. Thomas 1894). Aboriginal artifacts unaccompanied by monumental works were often dismissed as "Indian" (Atwater 1833). Descriptive English terms, often with embedded functional connotation (e.g., fortification, cemetery, quarry, mound) took the place of generic terms like *site* (cf. C. Thomas 1894:28–33). In the eastern United States, largely sequent to the resolution of the Moundbuilder/Indian dichotomy (Silverberg 1968), more interest was directed to the places where artifacts occurred without associated aboveground works or fixed antiquities (Peabody and Moorehead 1904; Skinner and Schrabisch 1913). Functional English terms like *village* and *camp* were frequently used to designate such localities, but it is in this context that *site* seems to emerge as a generic archaeological term. Systematic efforts to catalog places of archaeological interest began in earnest in the 1920s (National Research Council 1930:3; e.g., Skinner and Schrabisch 1913; Funkhouser and Webb 1932;) and site became the basic unit of tabulation. By the WPA-CCC era (Quimby 1979), *site* was an ubiquitous term in the discipline.

Site was initially adopted from English, without formal justification or discussion, simply as a generic term to accommodate an increasingly sophisticated appreciation of the variety of forms that the archaeological record could take. Use of the term was confined to the ordinary meaning of the English word. Site was a place where something else, be it artifacts or monuments or a combination of the two, occurred.

In addition to site as a place, the town or settlement connotation of English site was carried over *sub rosa* as well. In only a few cases were direct equations to ethnographic settlements drawn explicitly (Dawson 1880; Smith 1910a). Certainly, in the absence of monuments, site was not applied routinely to the loci of isolated portable artifacts; more or less dense clusters of artifacts that could be supposed reasonably to represent former settlements are plainly implied. Given that site was unchanged from the natural language, it is not surprising that no one apparently saw any necessity to consider its use explicitly.

Not all early workers saw sites as empirical units. Holmes, for example, saw sites as concentrations of "implements" (1897). That Holmes should have taken this view is not surprising in light of his career-long focus on portable objects in contrast to the fixed antiquities focus of most of his contemporaries. Even so, his "concentration-of-artifacts" view is largely implicit and occasioned by the necessity of distinguishing quarry debris from parent material. Nonetheless, his conception is plainly quantitative rather than qualitative and presages both more modern notions of site as well as nonsite conceptions of the record. Holmes was not alone in taking the view, however implicit, that portable artifacts were the basic units of observation. Harland I. Smith, for example, used the notion of site much in the manner of his contemporaries (Smith 1910a). However, in his survey of the Yakima Valley in Washington, he sees regional abundance patterns of portable artifacts as recording prehistoric land use intensity in a virtually modern way (Smith 1910b).

Definitions[1] of *site* do not appear routinely until the midtwentieth century, and then typically in the context of explaining archaeology to neophytes. Apparently, all archaeologists knew what *sites* were, and the notion need only be explained to nonarchaeologists. This condition may not have changed. Champion's (1980) dictionary of archaeological terms has no entry under site. Recent and current texts present a plethora of definitions that differ only in minor detail; in fact, the bulk of the definitions of site seem to stem from two definitions, either employed singly or in combination, a phenomenon peculiar to textbooks that has recently been analyzed by Gould (1988).

Heizer formulated one influential notion of site:

> A site is any place, large or small, where there are to be found traces of ancient occupation or activity. The usual clue is the presence of artifacts . . . some [sites] . . . are as large as a city, others as small as the spot where an arrowhead lies. (Hole and Heizer 1973:86–87; see also Hole and Heizer 1965:33, 1969:59; Hole and Heizer 1973:86–87; Heizer and Graham 1967:14; Hester *et al.* 1975:13; cf. Fagan 1978:82, 1981:93)

This exposition treats site as a place, a place that is distinguished from other places by the presence of artifacts. Indeed, in the case of single-artifact sites, the notion is synonymous with provenience.

Another prominent account is presented by Phillips and Willey (1953) in their survey of archaeology that was to become *Method and Theory in American*

[1] The use of the word *definition*, especially in conjunction with *site*, is a particularly murky matter in archaeology. When archaeologists talk about defining sites, they are usually talking about identifying an empirical analog for a concept *site*, thus conflating epistemological and theoretical/ontological issues. Here I use *define* to mean stating the necessary and sufficient conditions for being a member of a class and *identify* to mean the process of ascertaining whether a particular thing meets the requirements of a definition and delineating its boundaries.

Archaeology (Willey and Phillips 1958). For them, site has a central role in archaeological theory:

> A site is the smallest *unit* of space dealt with by the archaeologist and the most difficult to define. Its physical limits, which may vary from a few square yards to as many square miles, are often impossible to fix. About the only requirement ordinarily demanded of the site is that it be fairly continuously covered by the remains of former occupation, and the general idea is that these pertain to a single unit of settlement, which may be anything from a small camp to a large city. . . . The site is the basic unit for stratigraphic studies. . . . It is in effect the minimum operational unit of geographic spaces. (Willey and Phillips 1958:18; cf. Hester 1976:83; J. W. Smith 1976:106; Fagan 1978:323; Sharer and Ashmore 1979:72–73) [emphasis added]

Willey and Phillips' site is a place distinguished by artifacts as in the Heizer definition. Their definition is, however, different in a number of significant respects. First, they plainly exclude the simple provenience notion of site. Single objects are not sites. Sites are groups of objects in spatial proximity. Far more important, however, is Willey and Phillips's frank discussion of the site as a *unit*, an archaeological unit. Their insistence on the site's basic or minimal nature and vertical and horizontal boundaries identify its function as a unit of association. Although clearly identified as an archaeological unit, implying archaeological construction, it is also clear that Willey and Phillips expect it to be congruent, in theory if somewhat more difficult in practice, with ethnographic settlement. This particular aspect of Willey and Phillips's concept was later elaborated by Chang (1967) in the context of settlement studies.

A third view of the notion of site is first expressed by Binford (1964) in his pathbreaking "A Consideration of Archaeological Research Designs":

> The site is a spatial cluster of cultural features or items, or both. The formal characteristics of a site are defined by *its* formal content and the spatial and associational structure of the population's cultural items and features present. (Binford 1964:431) [emphasis added]

Although foreshadowed in Vescelius's (1960) account of sampling, Binford's use of the notion is a clear departure from other definitions then current. First, site is no longer a place distinguished by artifacts; rather, site is comprised by the artifacts themselves and their spatial relations. It is more akin to the archaeological notion of assemblage than to the English meaning of site underlying the other definitions. Site has an entirely different complexion. Secondly, and in stark contrast to Willey and Phillips's notion, Binford makes it clear that sites are not justifiably regarded as homogeneous: "*areas within sites vary functionally*" (Binford 1964:432, emphasis in the original). In fact, combating the notion of homogeneity implied in the Willey and Phillips's concept became one of the major battle cries of the early new archaeology (e.g., Binford 1965; Flannery 1967;

Struever 1971). A third important contrast is apparent only from the context. Whereas both the Heizer and Willey and Phillips's notions formalized a preexisting idea, albeit from the perspective and bookkeeping needs of a field man on the one hand and the requirements of systematists on the other, Binford's definition was an effort to change a preexisting notion. The analytic consequences of such a change were outlined simultaneously (Binford 1964). There is one further feature of note. Although Binford's definition recognized that sites were not homogeneous spatial units, they were still treated as empirical units as witness the pronoun *its*. A site was a thing that could have contents and structure.

Given the popularity of the new archaeology in academic circles of the 1970s and 1980s, it is surprising that Binford's notion of site did not make a major impact in the literature. Of all the modern texts, only Sharer and Ashmore's account of the site notion makes any serious accommodation to Binford's conception of site (Sharer and Ashmore 1979:72–73, 95). Only in considerations of sampling (e.g., Ragir 1967:181) is Binford's notion common.

One might argue that textbook definitions bear little resemblance to the way in which archaeologists actually behave in relation to the archaeological record. Certainly important changes are evident. When Willey and Phillips wrote, sites were more or less homogeneous artifact mines. Their lack of interest in spatial patterning internal to sites is strong testimony on this point as Binford noted (1964:433). It is truly remarkable that while archaeologists began collecting artifacts using arbitrary horizontal grid systems sporadically in the late nineteenth century (Peabody and Moorehead 1904) and routinely so by the late 1930s, the first attempts to utilize these spatial data did not begin until the mid-1960s (e.g., Hanson, Dunnell, and Hardesty 1964).

Although not affecting the literature, the Binford notion has had a profound influence on practice precisely on this point. Treating sites as internally undifferentiated may persist in some contexts, but using individual artifacts or small aggregates of artifacts, that is, grid units, is now unremarkable. Today site is also sometimes used as a patently arbitrary convention that either signals a change in data recovery strategy in response to artifact density (e.g., Dunnell 1985) or resource management (e.g., Dewar 1986) or both (e.g., Warren 1982; Van Bueren 1990). The dominant contemporary view, however, regards sites as archaeologically relevant, empirical units that exist independently of the archaeologist. Thus they can be discovered, described, and interpreted in archaeologically meaningful ways.

LIABILITIES OF THE SITE NOTION

The problems posed by site can be divided into ontological (i.e., are sites "real," empirical archaeological entities), epistemological (i.e., how can we, how do we, delineate such units on the ground), and theoretical (i.e., what role should site play in the discipline's explanatory structure.

Ontological Status of Site

Programmatic statements aside, there seems little doubt in the minds of most archaeologists that sites exist. Any suggestion to the contrary is derided as a silly challenge to an obvious reality or a trivial quarrel over words, scale of observation, or interpretive interest. At one extreme, sites are thought to constitute the entirety of the archaeological record, that the record consists of a large number of discrete localities that are archaeologically relevant separated by vast spaces that have no significant archaeological content (e.g., MacCord 1988). This view seems to underlie most CRM law and regulation (e.g., U.S. Code, 1977, Executive Order 11593, especially in the original time frame) implicitly (cf. Wandsnider 1988). At the other extreme, sites are simply one form in which the archaeological record occurs, a high-density element that can be contrasted with a low density or "off-site" segment of the record (e.g., Doelle 1975, 1977; Plog *et al.* 1978; cf. Foley 1981:11). Neither position questions the reality of site. Culture historians regarded them as internally homogeneous artifact mines. New archaeologists view them as internally variable and patterned, but they remain entities nonetheless.

Both poles represent the same view of the nature of reality. Sites are regarded as things that can be observed rather than units that are constructed. If site were simply used as an English word to designate the location of one or more kinds of independently defined, archaeologically rationalized units, then the ontological status of site would be reduced to a trivial semantic issue. Their use, however, as units of observation, association, counting, and interpretation *necessarily* asserts their reality and archaeological relevance. Current understanding of the archaeological record does not supply any warrant for regarding sites as such elemental archaeological units. It is generally appreciated, even by those most strongly committed to the site notion (e.g., MacCord 1988), that the archaeological record is a contemporary phenomenon (Binford 1968:271). Consequently, the continuous distributions of artifacts that are taken to demark sites (e.g., Willey and Phillips 1958:18; P. Thomas 1986) are contemporary patterns and are not *a priori* archaeologically relevant units. Dewar recognizes this aspect of the notion and suggests that site might be useful in the management context (1986:77–78). However, as Dancey and I (Dunnell and Dancey 1983:271–272) observed earlier, even in the management context, the notion of site is deleterious because it leads to systematic exclusion of segments of the archaeological record (cf. Sullivan 1988; Wandsnider 1988) and limited utility of the included segment (e.g., May 1988).

Formation studies (e.g., Schiffer 1972, 1976, 1983, 1987) and taphonomic studies generally (see Foley 1981:10–14 for a discussion of taphonomy in relation to site) make it clear that sites, as they are observed by archaeologists, are created by the act of observation at a particular point in time. Materials are added, removed, and rearranged continuously in the archaeological record. No one would contest that settlements, camps, villages, activity loci, and the like can produce what we see today as more or less dense clusters of artifacts, but there is no necessary relation between such ethnographic concepts, many of which are themselves suspicious as units of ethnographic observation, and high-density clusters of artifacts. Not all such clusters are the product of behaviors implied by the ethnographic categories, nor do all such ethnographic units leave high-density artifact clusters. Settlement, occupation, and activities are not agents of deposition; at best they are highly interpretive summaries of relations among such agents. Sites are not units of deposition; they are accretionary phenomena. The historical relatedness of their pieces is highly variable and not directly correlated with spatial proximity.

My own Cold Water Farm study in Southeast Missouri (Dunnell 1985, 1988) illustrates this issue well. In order to examine the precision of surface collection techniques, I have recollected the same track in six successive years using the same protocol and under closely similar conditions. Sampling, imposed by plow-zone mechanics, interacting with artifact density makes single episodes of data recovery (Figure 1) unreliable; stable patterns emerge only when several seasons' data are combined (Figure 2) (Dunnell 1988). One of the products of this research is a series of density maps that relate artifact kind, frequency, and location to environmental, geographic, and technical parameters (Figures 1, 2). Among the patterns to emerge is the relatively heavy use of the land bordering the principal watercourse. Throughout the 11,000 years or so represented by the surface, isolated deposition events—events involving only a single object, most frequently bifaces or projectile points in functional condition but including a few other curated (Binford 1976) artifacts—happened with much greater frequency close to the slough than they did elsewhere. In at least two areas, this led to the formation of "clusters" (arbitrarily taken to be two or more artifacts separated by less than 10 meters) or sites in slightly higher or otherwise more "favorable" locations in this generally swampy terrain (Madsen and Dunnell 1989). During a brief period in the Middle Woodland (*ca.* A.D. 500), domestic settlement, a large series of historically related deposition events—events most frequently involving ceramics, debris from tool manufacture, and burned sediment—left additional dense clusters of artifacts in the same near-slough zone. Variation presumably in duration and formation process led to variable artifact densities among such areas, the lower end of which overlaps the "sites" built up from single events. In fact, such "sites" make an unknown contribution to the domestic clusters. Sometimes that contribution may be quite vexing. For example, domestic clusters generally lack functionally complete projectile points (manufacturing rejects and terminal biface

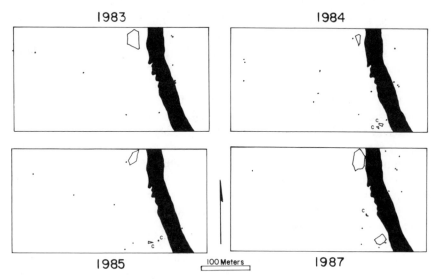

Figure 1. Distribution of artifacts and artifact clusters in the Cold Water Farm Tract plotted by season. Open polygons and localities marked "C" represent clusters; simple dots represent isolated objects. The dark vertical band marks the location of the former slough.

Figure 2. Distribution of artifacts and artifact clusters in the Cold Water Farm Tract as a composite of the four seasons' work shown in Figure 1. Open polygons and localities marked "C" represent clusters; crosses mark isolated lithic artifacts; circles mark isolated ceramic artifacts. The dark vertical band marks the location of the former slough.

reduction stages may be fairly common) presumably because relatively little hunting takes place inside the house or in the frontyard. In the Cold Water Farm case, this lack of points and lithics generally is exaggerated by the cost of rock, all of which has to be imported from a distance. Consequently, any projectile points "associated" with the domestic clusters, that is, found within their boundaries however drawn, are more likely to have arrived at their locations through deposition events unrelated to those comprising the bulk of the "site" than they are to be part of the domestic cluster events. Lest this example be dismissed as characterizing surface deposits alone, it should be remembered that virtually all buried, neatly stratified deposits started out as surface deposits.

If sites are not units of formation, then they have no legitimate role as units of observation. Concentrations of artifacts certainly do occur. They are the traditional focus of field archaeology. Objects found in spatial proximity, however, may have, and frequently do have, entirely unrelated histories that preclude a simple equation between spatial proximity and systemic relevance. Their composition and organization is strictly modern and archaeologic.

Epistemological Status of Site

The epistemological status of site is largely determined by its ontological status. Archaeologists have typically ignored the ontological questions; however, there is a general appreciation that site entails some noteworthy epistemological problems (Klinger 1976; Schiffer 1987:350). All of the modern textbook definitions of site are probably traceable to Hole and Heizer's definition: "Site is any place, large or small, where there are to be found traces of ancient occupation or activity. The usual clue is the presence of artifacts" (Hole and Heizer 1973:86–87; see also Hole and Heizer 1965:33; Heizer and Graham 1967:14; Hester et al. 1975:13; cf. Fagan 1978:82; 1981:93; 1987:102). Their guidelines for identification acknowledge the epistemological component of the concept. Most archaeologists, following the model of Hole and Heizer (e.g., Willey and Phillips 1958; Plog et al. 1978; Sharer and Ashmore 1979; Sharer 1987) seem to hold two contrary notions of site simultaneously. Goodyear et al. exemplify this dualism. With uncommon candor and insight they identify the site concept as "merely *a synthetic construct created by the archaeologist* to deal with varying spatial distributions of artifactual remains (1979:39, emphasis added). Yet on the very next page, "when a site was *encountered* . . . when a site was *discovered*" (Goodyear et al. 1979:40, emphasis added) plainly indicate that operationally even these otherwise critical scholars treat site as an empirical unit.

An even more common, but less introspective dualism occurs. On the one hand, sites are *real* things (and this is not regarded as problematic), but on the other, sites are difficult to "define" because they are not really things or qualities but rather concentrations or quantities. The impression these discussions leave is that the difficulties in implementing the notion of site arise because, although site boundaries do or did *exist,* they have been obscured by vegetation, sedimentation, or other unfavorable conditions of observation (e.g., Sharer and Ashmore 1979:72–73).

Some archaeologists employ site, or more frequently "cluster," simply to structure observation technique (e.g., Wilke and Thompson 1977; Warren 1982; Dunnell 1985), and thus the selection of a density threshold for site recognition is pragmatically determined and without archaeological significance. But for usages that accord *site* archaeological significance, determining the appropriate density thresholds is of paramount importance because that decision determines not only what is or is not a site (e.g., MacCord 1988), but also the size, shape, and location of sites and the artifacts that will be treated as a unit in subsequent analysis as well as its management status (DeBloois 1983; Sullivan 1988). Unfortunately, this decision is made typically in an *ad hoc* fashion when it is raised explicitly at all (cf. House and Schiffer 1975; Wilke and Thompson 1977:10–20; Plog *et al.* 1978:384–389; Nance 1980:173, 1983:300; Warren 1982:339–340; DeBloois 1983; Barber 1984; MacCord 1988:6–15). Plog *et al.*'s (1978:384–389) discussion in "Decision Making in Modern Surveys" is the most extended and analytic consideration of the concept in an epistemological context. They adopt a rather standard notion of site: "A *site* is a discrete and potentially interpretable locus of cultural materials" (Plog *et al.* 1978:389; emphasis in original). They go on to address the epistemological issues:

> By discrete, we mean *spatially bounded* with those boundaries marked by at least *relative changes in artifact densities.* By interpretable we mean that materials of sufficient quality and quantity are present for at least attempting and usually sustaining inferences about the behavior occurring at the locus. By cultural materials we mean artifacts, ecofacts, and features. (Plog *et al.* 1978:389; emphasis added)

Site is *defined* as a discrete entity that is interpretable as a unit in some sense. They are *identified,* however, by "relative" differences in artifact density. The meaning of *discrete* and *bounded* seems to lose something in transition from ontological to epistemological realms. Further, their notion of site has a strong operationalist component, that is, what is or is not a site depends on what one's methods of inference require, not on the ontological or even theoretical properties of the concept or, for that matter, empirical structure.

Plog *et al.* seem to recognize the weakness of their position for they go on:

> The notion of a density limit on site definitions [identifications] is problematic but not absurd. Such a definition [density threshold] should never be an absolute . . . it should be tied to some notion of interpretability in the specific context . . . [and] . . . it should be regarded by each member of every crew as a standard about which arguments are to occur and judgments are

to revolve. The occurrence of such argument and the focusing of such judgments are the most important effect of quantitative definitions [identifications] of sites. (Plog *et al.* 1978:389; bracketed words added)

In spite of their initial admonitions on the importance of uniform site recognition, they provide no means of achieving this objective, even glorying in the concept's practical ambiguity. Here we have a classic example of the all too common archaeological practice of regarding a problem as solved simply because it has been noticed and discussed.

Wilke and Thompson (1977:19–20) anticipate this kind of argument and actually constructed a context-specific, universally applicable algorithm for determining cluster boundaries. In a resource management context, they suggest that the threshold density for cluster boundaries be determined empirically by selecting the particular density level that maximizes the number of clusters. Such a threshold can be unambiguously determined because at threshold values higher than the optimal number, the number of clusters diminishes as an increasingly larger fraction of the artifacts no longer belong to sites, whereas at threshold values smaller than the optimal value, the number of sites diminishes because separate clusters are increasingly joined to form superclusters (Figure 3). This clever approach solves the problem of comparability in identification, but the units thus formed plainly have no archaeological meaning.

Most explicit concern over site identification arises in the survey context. Dewar (1986), however, identifies similar problems in the vertical dimension that is most often the focus in excavation, arguing that sites (concentrations of artifacts) should be distinguished from components (artifacts from the same period) and from occupations (artifacts from the same use) (cf. Dunnell 1971:182). Dewar, however, takes the horizontal integrity of site as a given. His approach amounts to subdividing sites, and it carries all of the ontological and epistemological baggage of site with it. He does note, however, that archaeologists want to and usually do interpret sites as if they were occupations but that occupations can actually be distinguished only rarely, if at all (cf. P. Thomas 1986). Binford (1981a) raises precisely the same issue, among others, in his discussion of the "Pompeii premise."

The Cold Water Farm projects illustrate still another facet of the epistemological difficulties posed by site. Although the distribution of artifacts in the tract is more or less constant from one collection to the next, the number, size, and shape of clusters differ dramatically from one examination to the next, presumably in consequence of changes in the record itself (i.e., ongoing formation processes) and sampling error (Figures 1, 2). Consequently, even if it were possible to devise a general algorithm to identify archaeologically relevant sites, it is still not reasonable to suppose that its application would yield a comparable set of sites.

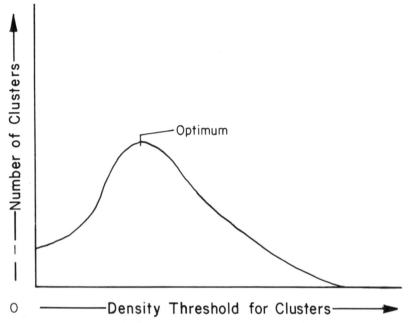

Figure 3. Relation between numbers of clusters and artifact density threshold for cluster recognition. As the density threshold for cluster recognition increases beyond the optimum, fewer areas meet the requirements for being a cluster; as the density threshold drops below the optimum, the number of clusters will also decrease as separate clusters coalesce toward a single global cluster.

Even though the epistemological problems with site have attracted archaeological attention, they have not been solved, nor is there any reason to suppose that they can be. If sites are concentrations rather than discrete things, then it *is* absurd, to use Plog *et al.*'s term, to suppose that they can be validly observed, discovered, or recorded.

Theoretical Status of the Site Concept

It is just as absurd, given that sites cannot be asserted to exist outside the present, to accord *site* any theoretical role in archaeology. But site is, of course, a major concept in the discipline's interpretive strategy. It *is* the *thing* that textbooks (and not a small amount of professional writing) talk about. It is the focus of most recovery programs (see Wildesen 1982:55–56, for a spirited defense of site in this role), many discussions of sampling, and many approaches to spatial analysis. Willey and Phillips (1958:18) cast site in explicit theoretical terms when they treat it as the minimal unit of association. Plog *et al.* (1978:389) regard it as a basic unit of interpretation, reflecting what is probably its most common theoretical role. Dewar's (1986) suggested modifications, although recognizing the issues involved, only shift the interpretive unit from site to part of site. Dewar's development of "remnant settlement pattern" research (Dewar and McBride, this volume; Dewar, 1991) is a thorough critique of the concept of site in settlement pattern studies. Increasingly, its role in structuring cultural resource management plans is being recognized as deleterious and producing a highly skewed managed record (e.g., Brooks 1979; Dunnell and Dancey 1983; May 1988; Barber 1984; Sullivan 1988; Wandsnider 1988; Van Sueren 1990.)

Site has no theoretical role because, to the extent that sites may be said to exist (concentrations of artifacts), sites are modern, contemporary phenomena, whereas archaeological interest lies in the systemic context. The theoretical functions for which the site concept has been expropriated uncritically are, however, real needs. We require a series of units, not just a single unit, of association within which counts and patterns are archaeologically meaningful. Such units must rest on historical connections between deposition events, not spatial proximity. In short, as I argued long ago (Dunnell 1971:181), we need units analogous to Dewar's occupation. The solution to the problem of identifying such units lies not in "refining" the notion of site or tinkering with density thresholds or other means of site delineation. Our methodological energies need to be redirected to developing methods of constructing units of historical association from smaller-scale observational units.

SITELESS CONCEPTION OF THE ARCHAEOLOGICAL RECORD

Introduction

Artifact can supply the smaller-scale observational unit. By artifact, I mean anything that displays any attribute, including location, as a consequence of human agency (cf. Spaulding 1960:438; Dunnell 1971:117). This is not the place to explore the full ramifications of the concept artifact. Although it shares some of the same features of its history with that of site, its central position in the discipline's theory and its ontological and epistemological status are far more secure (e.g., Spaulding 1960; Clarke 1968; Dunnell 1971, 1984; Binford, this volume). The idea of artifact and the ability to identify it securely were requisites to the establishment of archaeology (e.g., Grayson 1983), and they continue to be the subject of intense scrutiny (e.g., Binford 1981b). Plainly, artifact is not a minimal unit in archaeology; that distinction must rest with its defining artificial attributes. However, it is reasonably construed as the basic empirical unit of association, that is, a unit within which association is observational rather than inferential. Because artifacts as objects are time-transgressive, they acquire their attributes over potentially significant amounts of time; consequently simple spatial association within an object cannot be accepted uncritically as systemic. More importantly, whereas sites are never units of deposition, artifacts frequently are units of deposition or subdivisions of such units.

If artifact is taken to be the basic unit of observation, then the archaeological record becomes a more or less continuous distribution of artifacts on or near the surface of the planet (Dunnell and Dancey 1983:272), not a collection of sites waiting to be found. This conception of the nature of archaeological reality treats all variability in artifact density and kind as potentially explanatory. Consequently, the analytic task of archaeology is to explain the density and character of the more or less continuous distribution of artifacts. The high-density nodes that are the usual focal referent of site are, in this view, epiphenomena that arise in consequence of both natural and artificial agents of transport, weathering, and deposition and that can be wholly explained by processes operating on artifacts (cf. Schiffer 1987).

It is important to recognize that this is a fundamentally different conception of the nature of archaeological reality than that which spawned the site notion. It is not a view that can be reached by breaking down sites into smaller and smaller constituent elements. It proceeds in the other direction, building up to, rather than dividing, spatial aggregates of interpretive significance.

The siteless or nonsite view of the record is hardly new. At least three, apparently independent inventions of this kind of conception, have been made (Dancey 1971; D. Thomas 1975; Foley 1981; Dunnell and Dancey 1983), some dating back to the early 1970s. Although they were offered programmatically, the impact of these arguments has been limited largely to rationalizing research specifically concerned with land use, leading to yet another "kind of archaeology," distributional or landscape archaeology. The lack of a broader impact of the siteless view seems to lie in a failure to appreciate that the nonsite view is not a different interpretation of the discipline's subject matter but a different view of what the subject matter is. Further and pragmatically, the commonsense origin of site led to its early fixation in practice and law before we were equipped to appreciate the intellectual baggage or could anticipate the myriad of practical problems it entailed.

As Luedtke has recently surmised, this may simply express a general reluctance to abandon the essentialist ontology (Sober 1980; Dunnell 1982) of common sense: "most archaeologists are fundamentally attracted to categorical descriptive systems and view . . . [numerical expression of variability] . . . primarily as a means to the end of creating categories" (Luedtke 1986:90). Her analysis certainly describes the history of the site notion. Until the siteless conception of the archaeological record is recognized as an ontological as well as an epistemological departure from archaeological tradition, its impact will continue to be limited, and its theoretical and methodological potential, lodged primarily in the *construction* of interpretable artifact aggregates, will go unrealized.

Aggregate Construction

Because the siteless view has been linked to particular research questions rather than treated as an ontological change that affects all archaeological work, relatively little effort has been devoted to developing methodologies for the construction of archaeologically relevant spatial aggregates comparable to site. There are formidable problems in such method development to be sure, but there is no *a priori* reason to suppose they cannot be overcome. Key to such development is the growing appreciation that the formation of the archaeological record must be understood as a sedimentary process (e.g., Schiffer 1987; esp. Stein 1987). The attributes of objects indicative of weathering, transport, and depositional histories may well provide methods for ascertaining depositional contemporaneity. One such limited method has already been developed to distinguish the addition of recent glass in historic deposits (Hoover 1987). Abrasion and chemical weathering of other materials (e.g., Pinto *et al.* 1987) as well as analysis of artifact size (Dunnell 1986) offer similar potentials. In a more context-specific fashion, the routine examination of microartifacts makes it possible to distinguish incidental associations of macroartifacts from related deposition events by ascertaining whether certain classes of objects were manufactured at a particular location or simply deposited there (Dunnell 1986; Vance 1988; Madsen and Dunnell 1989).

A common complaint voiced against the siteless conception of the record is the supposed inability to date surface deposits (traditional critics almost always equate the siteless view with surface examination), a curious position because, as noted earlier, virtually all buried deposits were once surface deposits. The real basis for such complaints lies in the fact that C-14 dating cannot usually be employed. Radiocarbon dating cannot be used because, as a chemical method, it dates a chemical event (the isolation of a carbon reservoir from the atmospheric reservoir) and therefore requires a bridging argument to connect the dated event to some event of archaeological interest (Dean 1978; Dunnell and Readhead 1988). The notion of site as a unit of association has frequently served to link a piece of burned wood to a pattern or group of artifacts of particular composition. Without a means of association, the nonarchaeological events dated by C-14 can rarely be linked to archaeological events.

Yet there are other dating methods, obsidian hydration (Jones and Beck, this volume) and thermoluminescence dating (Aitken 1985), to name but two, that operate directly on a greater variety of artifacts and that typically date archaeologically relevant events. Certainly, the development of local relative and even absolute chronologies of objects is within the theoretical potential of these and other methods. The point is that the development of methods to effect a siteless approach to the archaeological record is possible. In fact, much of the preliminary research has already been done, but the development of methods for the construction of spatial aggregates has been frustrated by the notion of site and the assumptions it entails about the record.

SUMMARY AND CONCLUSIONS

Certainly, there is no reason to expunge the word *site* from the archaeological vocabulary if site is used simply to mean "location of." While the notion undoubtedly derives from this English sense of the word, it has grown to mean much more in archaeology. In contemporary usage, it is an unanalyzed concept denoting spatial aggregates of archaeological significance. Sites have become aggregates; location has become just a property of the site. Virtually all archaeological research and cultural resource management are structured at some level by the site notion.

Yet contemporary understanding of the formation of the archaeological record does not support the existence of sites as either observational or analytic units. The concentrations of artifacts that are taken to constitute sites are the products of numerous discrete events of deposition, the independence or relatedness of which must be empirically determined in order to obtain archaeologically meaningful units of association. There certainly is no harm in calling concentrations of artifacts sites, regardless of how one might define concentration, but it is difficult to see to what end when contemporary concentrations of artifacts are relevant neither to resource management nor archaeological research.

The siteless or nonsite view of the archaeological record is compatible with current understanding of formation processes. Because this conception of the archaeological record has been interpreted theoretically, its impact has been limited to studies focused on landscape use rather than affecting the way in which all archaeologists should approach understanding the archaeological record. Because the archaeological record is a nonrenewable resource, the notion *site* not only biases our understanding of the human past, but it is also rapidly leading to biased destruction of the record, forever impairing our understanding of the human past.

In the last analysis, site, *as an archaeological concept,* has no role to play in the discipline. Its uses are not warranted by its properties. It obscures crucial theoretical and methodological deficiencies, and it imparts a serious and unredeemable systematic error in recovery and management programs. In spite of the technical problems its abandonment will cause, the concept of archaeological site should be discarded.

ACKNOWLEDGMENTS

The writer appreciates the comments and assistance of the editors of this volume during the editorial process and for the opportunity to participate in the original symposium. M. D. Dunnell and F. C. Pierce read the manuscript in draft and made many helpful suggestions.

REFERENCES

Aitken, M. J., 1985, *Thermoluminescent Dating*, Academic Press, London.

Atwater, C., 1833, A Description of the Antiquities Discovered in the Western Country; Originally Communicated to the American Antiquarian Society, in: *The Writings of Caleb Atwater* (C. Atwater, ed.), Scott and Wright, Columbus, Ohio, pp. 9–165.

Barber, M. B., 1984, The Survey and Evaluation of Cultural Resources in Heavily Vegetated Areas: A U.S. Forest Service Approach, *Archaeological Society of Virginia Quarterly Bulletin* 39 (2).

Barnhart, C. L., and Stein, J. (eds.), 1958, *The American College Dictionary*, Random House, New York.

Binford, L. R., 1964, A Consideration of Archaeological Research Design, *American Antiquity* 29:425–441.

Binford, L. R., 1965, Archaeological Systematics and the Study of Culture Process, *American Antiquity* 31:203–210.

Binford, L. R., 1968, Some Comments on Historical Versus Processual Archaeology, *Southwestern Journal of Anthropology* 24:267–275.

Binford, L. R., 1976, Forty-Seven Trips: A Case Study in the Character of Some Formation Processes of the Archaeological Record, in: *The Interior Peoples of Northern Alaska* (E. S. Hall, Jr., ed.), National Museum of Man, Mercury Series, 49, Ottawa, pp. 299–381.

Binford, L. R., 1981a, Behavioral Archaeology and the Pompeii Premise, *Journal of Anthropological Research* 37:195–208.

Binford, L., 1981b, *Bones. Ancient Men and Modern Myths*, Academic Press, New York.

Brooks, R. L. 1979, Prehistoric Spot Finds, Localities, and Archaeological Context: A Cautionary Note from Kentucky, *Tennessee Anthropologist* 4:167–174.

Champion, S., 1980, *A Dictionary of Terms and Techniques in Archaeology*, Facts on File, New York.

Chang, K. C., 1967, *Rethinking Archaeology*, Random House, New York.

Clarke, D. L., 1968, *Analytical Archaeology*, Methuen, London.

Dancey, W. S., 1971, The Archaeological Survey: A Reorientation, Paper Presented at the 36th Annual Meeting of the Society for American Archaeology, Norman, Oklahoma.

Dawson, J. W., 1880, *Fossil Men and Their Modern Representatives*, Dawson Brothers, Montreal.

Dean, J. S., 1978, Independent Dating in Archaeological Analysis, *Advances in Archaeological Method and Theory* 1:223–255.

DeBloois, E. I., 1983, Managing Cultural Resources in the Highlands, in: *High Altitude Adaptations in the Southwest* (J. C. Winter, ed.), USDA Forest Service, Southwestern Region, Cultural Resources Management Report 2, Albuquerque, pp. 206–218.

Dewar, R. E., 1986, Discovering Settlement Systems of the Past in New England Site Distributions, *Man in the Northeast* 31:77–88.

Dewar, R. E., 1991, Dynamic Settlement Systems and Remnant Settlement Patterns, *American Antiquity* 56:604–620.

Doelle, W., 1975, *Prehistoric Resource Exploitation Within the Conoco Florence Project*, Archaeological Series No. 62, Arizona State Museum, Tempe.

Doelle, W., 1977, A Multiple Survey Strategy for Cultural Resource Management Studies, in: *Conservation Archaeology: A Guide for Cultural Resource Management Studies* (M. B. Schiffer and G. J. Gumerman, eds.), Academic Press, New York, pp. 201–209.

Dunnell, R. C., 1971, *Systematics in Prehistory*, Free Press, New York.

Dunnell, R. C., 1982, Science, Social Science and Common Sense: The Agonizing Dilemma of Modern Archaeology, *Journal of Anthropological Research* 38:1–25.

Dunnell, R. C., 1984, The Ethics of Significance Decisions, in: *Ethics and Values in Archaeology* (E. L. Green, ed.), Free Press, New York, pp. 62–74.

Dunnell, R. C., 1985, The Interpretation of Low Density Archaeological Records from Plowed Surfaces, Paper Presented at the 50th Annual Meeting of the Society for American Archaeology, Denver.

Dunnell, R. C., 1986, Theoretical Issues in the Interpretation of Microartifacts, Paper Presented at the 51st Annual Meeting of the Society for American Archaeology, New Orleans.

Dunnell, R. C., 1988, Low-Density Archaeological Records from Plowed Surfaces: Some Preliminary Considerations, *American Archaeology* 7:29–38.

Dunnell, R. C., and Dancey, W. S. 1983, The Siteless Survey: A Regional Scale Data Collection Strategy, *Advances in Archaeological Method and Theory* 6:267–287.

Dunnell, R. C., and Readhead, M. L., 1988, The Relation of Dating and Chronology: Comments on Chatters and Hoover (1986) and Butler and Stein (1988), *Quaternary Research*, 30:232–233.

Fagan, B. M., 1978, *In the Beginning. An Introduction to Archaeology*, 3rd ed., Little, Brown, and Co., Boston.

Fagan, B. M., 1981, *In the Beginning. An Introduction to Archaeology*, 4th ed., Little, Brown, and Co., Boston.

Fagan, B. M., 1987, *In the Beginning. An Introduction to Archaeology*, 6th ed., Little, Brown, and Co., Boston.

Flannery, K. V., 1967, Culture History Cultural Process: A Debate in American Archaeology, *Scientific American* 217:119–122.

Foley, R., 1981, *Off-Site Archaeology and Human Adaptation in Eastern Africa*, BAR International Series 97, Oxford.

Funkhouser, W. D., and Webb, W. S., 1932, *Archaeological Survey of Kentucky*, University of Kentucky Reports in Archaeology and Anthropology, 2, Lexington.

Goodyear, A. C., House, J. H., and Ackerly, N. W., 1979, *Laurens-Anderson. An Archaeological Study of the Inter-Riverine Piedmont*, Occasional Papers of the Institute of Archaeology and Anthropology, University of South Carolina, Columbia.

Gould, S. J., 1988, The Case of the Creeping Fox Terrier Clone, *Natural History* 1(1):16–24.

Grayson, D. K., 1983, *The Establishment of Human Antiquity*, Academic Press, New York.

Hanson, L. H., Dunnell, R. C., and Hardesty, D. L., 1964, *The Slone Site, Pike County, Kentucky*, National Park Service, Richmond.

Heizer, R. F., and Graham, J. A., 1967, *A Guide to Field Methods in Archaeology: Approaches to the Anthropology of the Dead*, rev. ed., National Press, Palo Alto.

Hester, J. J., 1976, *Introduction to Archaeology*, Holt, Rinehart & Winston, New York.

Hester, T. R., Heizer, R. F., and Graham, J. A., 1975, *Field Methods in Archaeology*, 6th ed., Mayfield, Palo Alto.

Hole, F., and Heizer, R. F., 1965, *An Introduction to Prehistoric Archaeology*, Holt, Rinehart & Winston, New York.

Hole, F., and Heizer, R. F., 1969, *An Introduction to Prehistoric Archaeology*, 2nd ed., Holt, Rinehart & Winston, New York.

Hole, F., and Heizer, R. F., 1973, *An Introduction to Prehistoric Archaeology*, 3rd ed., Holt, Rinehart & Winston, New York.

Holmes, W. H., 1897, Stone Implements of the Potomac-Chesapeake Tidewater Province, in: *Fifteenth Annual Report of the Bureau of Ethnology*, Government Printing Office, Washington, D.C. pp. 13–152.

Hoover, J., 1987, Postdepositional Alterations to Bottle Glass in a Plowed Field in Dunklin County, Missouri, Ms. in possession of author.

House, J. H., and Schiffer, M. B., 1975, Archaeological Survey in the Cache River Basin, in: *The Cache River Archaeological Project: An Experiment in Contract Archaeology* (assembled by M. B. Schiffer and J. H. House), Arkansas Archaeological Survey, Research Series, 8, Fayetteville, pp. 37–54.

Klinger, T. C., 1976, The Problem of Site Definition in Cultural Resource Management, *Arkansas Academy of Science Proceedings* 30:54–56.

Luedtke, B. E., 1986, Flexible Tools for Constructing the Past, *Man in the Northeast* 31:89–98.

MacCord, H., 1988, Where Do You Draw the Line?, *American Society for Conservation Archaeology, Report* 15(1):6–15.

Madsen, M. E., and Dunnell, R. C., 1989, Role of Microartifacts in Deducing Land Use from Low Density Records in Plowed Surfaces, Paper Presented at the 54th Annual Meeting of the Society for American Archaeology, Atlanta.

May, R. V., 1988, Broadside from the West: Response to Howard MacCord, *American Society for Conservation Archaeology Report* 15(2):10–14.

McManamon, P., 1981, Parameter Estimation and Site Discovery in the Northeast, *Contract Abstracts and CRM Archaeology* 1:43–48.

Nance, J. D., 1980, Non-Site Sampling in the Lower Cumberland River Valley, Kentucky, *Midcontinental Journal of Archaeology* 5:169–191.

Nance, J. D., 1983, Regional Sampling in Archaeological Survey: The Statistical Perspective, *Advances in Archaeological Method and Theory* 6:289–356.

National Research Council, 1930, *Guide Leaflet for Amateur Archaeologists*, Reprint and Circular Series of the National Research Council, No. 93, Washington, D.C.

Peabody, C., and Moorehead, W. K., 1904, *The Exploration of Jacobs Cavern, McDonald County, Missouri*, Department of Archaeology, Bulletin 1, Phillips Academy, Andover.

Phillips, P., and Willey, G. R., 1953, Method and Theory in American Archaeology: An Operational Basis for Culture-Historical Integration, *American Anthropologist* 55:615–633.

Pinto, I. V., Schiffer, M. B., Smith, S., and Skibo, J. M., 1987, Effects of Temper on Ceramic Abrasion Resistance: A Preliminary Investigation, *Archaeomaterials* 1:119–134.

Plog, S., Plog, F., and Wait, W., 1978, Decision Making in Modern Surveys, *Advances in Archaeological Method and Theory* 1:383–421.

Quimby, G. I., 1979, A Brief History of WPA Archaeology, in: *The Uses of Anthropology* (W. Goldschmidt, ed.), American Anthropological Association, Washington, D.C., pp. 110–123.

Ragir, S., 1967, A Review of Technologies for Archaeological Sampling, in: *A Guide to Field Methods in Archaeology. Approaches to the Anthropology of the Dead* (R. F. Heizer and J. A. Graham, eds.), National Press, Palo Alto, pp. 181–197.

Redman, C. L., 1973, Multistage Fieldwork and Analytic Techniques, *American Antiquity* 38:61–79.

Schiffer, M. B., 1972, Archaeological Context and Systemic Context, *American Antiquity* 37:156–165.

Schiffer, M. B., 1976, *Behavioral Archaeology*, Academic Press, New York.

Schiffer, M. B., 1983, Toward the Identification of Formation Processes, *American Antiquity* 48:675–706.

Schiffer, M. B., 1987, *Formation Processes of the Archaeological Record*, University of New Mexico Press, Albuquerque.

Sharer, R. J., 1987, *Archaeology: Discovering our Past*, Mayfield, Palo Alto, CA.

Sharer, R. J., and Ashmore, W., 1979, *Fundamentals of Archaeology*, Benjamin/Cummings, Menlo Park.

Silverberg, R., 1968, *Mound Builders of Ancient America: The Archaeology of a Myth*, New York Graphic Society, Greenwich.

Skinner, A., and Schrabisch, M., 1913, *A Preliminary Report of the Archaeological Survey of the State of New Jersey*, Geological Survey of New Jersey, Bulletin 9, Trenton.

Smith, H. I., 1910a, *The Prehistoric Ethnology of a Kentucky Site*, Anthropological Papers of the American Museum of Natural History, Vol. VI, Part II, New York.

Smith, H. I., 1910b, *The Archaeology of the Yakima Valley*, Anthropological Papers of the American Museum of Natural History, Vol. VI, Part I, New York.

Smith, J. W., 1976, *Foundations of Archaeology*, Glencoe Press, Beverly Hills.

Sober, E., 1980, Evolution, Population Thinking, and Essentialism, *Philosophy of Science* 47:350–383.

Spaulding, A. C., 1960, The Dimensions of Archaeology, in: *Essays in the Science of Culture. Essays in Honor of Leslie White* (G. E. Dole and R. L. Carneiro, eds.) T. Y. Crowell, New York, pp. 437–456.

Squire, E. G., and Davis, E. H., 1848, *Ancient Monuments of the Mississippi Valley*, Smithsonian Contributions to Knowledge, 1, Washington, D.C.

Stein, J. K., 1987, Deposits for Archaeologists, *Advances in Archaeological Method and Theory* 11:337–395.

Struever, S., 1971, Comments on Archaeological Data Requirements and Research Strategy, *American Antiquity* 36:9–19.

Sullivan, A. P., III, 1988, Current Issues in Regional Archaeology, in: *Tools to Manage the Past: Research Priorities for Cultural Resource Management in the Southwest*, (J. A. Tainter and R. H. Hamre, eds.), USDA Forest Service, General Technical Report RM-164, Fort Collins, pp. 81–89.

Thomas, C., 1894, Report on the Mound Explorations of the Bureau of Ethnology, *Twelfth Annual Report of the Bureau of Ethnology*, Washington, D.C., pp. 3–742.

Thomas, D. H., 1975, Nonsite Sampling in Archaeology: Up the Creek Without a Site? in: *Archaeological Sampling* (J. W. Mueller, ed.), University of Arizona Press, Tucson, pp. 61–81.

Thomas, P. A., 1986, Discerning Some Spatial Characteristics of Small, Short-Term, Single Occupation Sites: Implications for New England Archaeology, *Man in the Northeast* 31:99–121.

United States Code, 1977, Executive Order No. 11593, Protection and Enhancement of the Cultural Environment, 1971, Title 16, Section 470 (36FR9821).

Van Bueren, T. M., 1990, Where Do We Draw The Line? Some Thoughts on the Use of the 'Site' Concept, *Proceedings of the Society for California Archaeology* 4:213–219.

Vance, E. D., 1988, The Role of Microartifacts in Spatial Analysis, Ph.D. dissertation, Department of Anthropology, University of Washington, Seattle.

Vescelius, G. S., 1960, Archaeological Sampling: A Problem in Statistical Inference, in: *Essays in the Science of Culture. Essays in the Honor of Leslie A. White* (G. F. Dole and R. L. Carneiro, eds.), T. Y. Crowell, New York, pp. 457–470.

Wandsnider, L. A., 1988, Cultural Resources "Catch-22" and Empirical Justification for Discovering and Documenting Low-Density Archaeological Surfaces, in: *Tools to Manage the Past: Research for Cultural Resource Management in the Southwest* (J. A. Tainter and R. H. Hamre, eds.), USDA Forest Service, General Technical Report RM-164, Fort Collins, Colorado, pp. 90–97.

Warren, R. E., 1982, Prehistoric Settlement Patterns, in: *The Cannon Reservoir Human Ecology*

Project (M. J. O'Brien, R. E. Warren, and D. E. Lewarch, eds.), Academic Press, New York, pp. 337–368.

Wildesen, L. E., 1982, The Study of Impacts on Archaeological Sites, *Advances in Archaeological Method and Theory* 5:51–96.

Wilke, S., and Thompson, G., 1977, *Archaeological Survey of Western Kent County, Maryland*, Maryland Historical Trust, Department of Economic and Community Development, Annapolis.

Willey, G. R., and Phillips, P., 1958, *Method and Theory in American Archaeology*, University of Chicago Press, Chicago.

Chapter 3

Seeing the Present and Interpreting the Past—and Keeping Things Straight

LEWIS R. BINFORD

INTRODUCTION

In order to interpret what we see in the archaeological record, inferences must be made regarding (a) the formation processes of the material record and how they reflect the role that places played in the organization of the past and (b) how that role (and the organizations as well) changed through time. Two different strategies of "looking" are currently in vogue: site surveys and nonsite or distributional or landscape approaches. When interpretation is based on the paradoxical seriation/settlement pattern methodology, traditional site surveys are clearly not appropriate for addressing organizational questions. When interpretation is based on inferences (middle-range theory) as robust as those commonly used to identify features, however, the first question about the role that places played in the system can be addressed. On the other hand, nonsite approaches are more productively directed toward answering the second question.

It has been suggested that nonsite approaches necessitate a change in theoretical perspective—that the information gathered from the landscape

LEWIS R. BINFORD • Department of Anthropology, Southern Methodist University, Dallas, Texas 75275.

Space, Time, and Archaeological Landscapes, edited by Jacqueline Rossignol and LuAnn Wandsnider. Plenum Press, New York, 1992.

should be classified according to a predefined evolutionary framework (see Dunnell 1989; Leonard and Jones 1987). This stipulated framework is shown to be based on an incomplete understanding of Darwin's contributions to evolutionary theory. There is a failure to recognize the differences between what is needed to explain biological evolution and what is needed to explain cultural evolution, but more important, this framework ignores the problem of understanding archaeological variability that is organizational in reference. In addition, it represents an inaccurate understanding of the goals of science and the methods of independent testing of scientific propositions (for near total confusion on these issues, see Dunnell 1989). In this chapter I will discuss some of the theoretical and methodological implications of the use of data from site and nonsite investigations to address questions of organizational change and stability. This goal is different than that advocated by some proponents of "nonsite" approaches.

FEATURES, SITES, AND OTHER TYPES OF INFERENTIAL ARGUMENT: HOW WE "SEE" ORGANIZATION

More than 20 years ago K. C. Chang suggested to the field of archaeology that a shift was needed from the view that the artifact was the basic unit of observation to the view that the settlement should be seen as the "primary unit for conceptualization and operation" because we are "primarily interested in past peoples living in social groups having common cultural traditions" (1967a:39, 1967b). I objected to these suggestions then (Binford 1967, 1968) and continue to object to such approaches now. Let's explore these objections and expand them to a discussion of many interpretive themes common, if not dominant, in contemporary archaeology.

Perhaps we might begin with a few commonsense and long-standing ideas about archaeology. As Spaulding (1960) has so elegantly pointed out, archaeologists study artifacts. The artifact is the basic unit of observation for archaeologists. This seems to be a statement on which there can be little disagreement. If you ask archaeologists how they recognize sites, they will certainly reply that sites are places where there are concentrations of artifacts. Sites are conceptual generalizations about the spatial distribution of artifacts, and the artifacts are clearly the basic units of observation.

Let's ask our generic archaeologist another question. What is a feature? In answer to this question we can expect less-redundant answers and more disagreement among archaeologists. After some hesitation, I would expect the everyday archaeologist to tell us that features are the archaeological remains of ancient construction, or elements of the "built environment," or even "restructuring of nature" by human agents. I suggest that the difficulty in providing a clear operational definition of features (as opposed to sites) derives from a fundamental difference between the kinds of arguments required of archaeologists when they are called on to justify their claim for recognizing features as characteristics of the archaeological record as opposed to the kind of arguments required when they claim that they have recognized a "site."

Let's think for a moment about an experience most of us have shared. You are digging along in your "site," and you encounter some ashy lensing. This ashy deposit changes as you follow it with your Marshalltown into a matrix with flecks of burned clay and higher densities of charcoal. Digging deeper and in a slightly more bold manner you encounter vivid red staining on basement geological clays directly under the very heterogeneous lens of charcoal, ash, and scattered clumps of burned clay. Continuing your exploration laterally you may even encounter a little arc of stones judged to be geologically out of place. These rocks exhibit distinctive discoloration on one side—the side that is oriented toward the staining in the clay and the area where mixed contents of burned clay, charcoal, ash, and maybe even an increased frequency of long-bone splinters was noted. Continuing your explorations beyond the stones, you note a rather abrupt change, and the ashy lens disappears.

In this situation, most archaeologists would change their digging procedures, taking out feature forms and frequently changing their decisions about where to dig. Clearly now you need to dig in order to find the limits of this "feature" and therefore to be able to describe it differently than the "normal" way of describing "featureless" site deposits.

Why do we change our procedures? A more standard answer to this question can be expected than those that might be offered to the earlier one regarding what a feature is. Most of us would reply that features cannot be taken back to the lab for observation; they must be described in the field because the act of excavation destroys them. I suggest that in fact a different reason explains the change in procedures—a reason that is related to the fundamental difference in the character of argument between what is needed when one argues that one has seen a feature and what is common when one claims to have seen a "site."

I suggest that when archaeologists make the claim that they have seen a feature, this claim must be supported by the argument that a repetitive and complementary spatial arrangement among different things is demonstrable. In addition, it must be argued that this complementary structure made up of different things is recognizable by virtue of some understood or suspected organizational dynamics resulting in the regular juxtapositioning of different things in the past. Our ability to argue convincingly that we have encountered a feature depends upon (a) our ability to diagnose accurately the by-products of dynamic processes, such as the combustion of fuels, and (b) our ability to argue that these recognizable natural by-products are further organized by hominid/human agents—in this case, for example, the discrete localization of the by-products of combustion in conjunction with geologically out-of-place stones and the biased presence of long-bone splinters and other remains. In short, we must claim that we have recognized a structured and, importantly, complementary pattern among different things that has reference to past organizational dynamics. This claim is only as good as the arguments presented or alluded to in assertions that *structure* (a patterned arrangement of different things resulting from organized interaction among variables) is distributed in a complementary spatial pattern so as to implicate past dynamics of an understood form—in this case, the controlled burning of fuel in a single place.

Let's compare this understanding of feature recognition with our understanding of another commonly discussed archaeological unit—the site. As stated earlier, most archaeologists (operationally, at least) consider a site to be a spatial localization of artifacts, a concentration in space of recognizable by-products of human modification of natural materials: projectile points, lithic debris, fire-cracked rock, pottery sherds, food debris, and so forth. This aggregation criterion is regularly used for both horizontal "surface surveys" as well as vertical explorations within exposed stratified geological deposits. A site is a spatial concentration or high-density occurrence of artifacts. Archaeologists frequently argue about what constitutes an aggregation (e.g., how many artifacts per square meter), but these arguments are *operational*, not intellectual (*contra* Dunnell, this volume). Regardless of the operational conventions used, sites are recognized by the simple aggregation of material remains.

Here we note a major difference between the criteria for recognizing sites and the criteria for recognizing features. Many features may well be recognizable not by high densities of artifacts but instead by the particular structured relationships among different, otherwise naturally occurring phenomena—in our example, charcoal, unmodified stream cobbles, and heat-stained, geologically deposited clays. The strength of a claim for recognition of a feature does not depend on the presence of high densities of artifacts. Instead it is related to the claim that a particular, distinctive, structured arrangement of different things is unambiguously referable to a particular set of past dynamic conditions.

Are "sites" similar units? Certainly not. Clearly there are many different human patterns of organized land use that can result in aggregations of artifacts on a stable landscape. This would continue to be true regardless of the operational conventions adopted for recognition. Any argument regarding the character of potentially variable past organizations that could account for sites must be dependent on arguments analogous to those required to defend the claim for the recognition of a feature. We must be able to argue for a patterned regularity among different things that can be said to implicate the operation in the past of a common, organizing set of dynamics. When looking at spatial aggregates we must give equal weight to the consideration of many different natural processes, such as differential rates of erosion, burial, destruction, and so forth can reshape the spatial patterning of artifacts and their frequencies on the landscape available for us to observe. In short, a simple aggregation of artifacts does not directly implicate any unambiguous past processes, unlike the regular juxtaposition of the by-products of fuel combustion.

Archaeologists are impatient. They want to transform their observations of contemporary phenomena into descriptive or even explanatory statements about the past. Most traditional archaeologists, at least those who were my teachers, recognized this tendency and generally viewed surface collections and hence site recognition as the first steps to be taken in deciding where to dig. Excavation was considered to be the context of observation in which one had a chance to mount an argument for structure, for the patterned spatial juxtapositioning among different things within features or chronostratigraphic units. The recognition of those different things that went together enabled us to define ancient "cultures." Unfortunately, this approach depended on simple spatial association rather than the more sophisticated arguments required for defending the claims for features. It was this "envelope" strategy that I strongly criticized in *Bones* (Binford 1981a).

The serious exploration of surface-collected samples of artifacts from sites (which were defined as spatial aggregates of artifacts) gained in popularity among archaeologists under two separate trends in the archaeology of the 1940s and 1950s: first, the heated discussions of stylistic seriation as advocated by James Ford (1954, 1962), and second, the exploration of what came to be known as settlement-pattern studies resulting from the pioneering work of Gordon Willey (1953) and others. Both of these approaches relied heavily on surface surveys and "site" recognition to supply the data for arguments to the effect that the past was organized in distinctive ways. Seriation for temporal organization and settlement-pattern studies for dealing with the expectation that cultural systems had recognizable organizational properties (in that different things went together in complementary ways, as is generally characteristic of all systems) were welded together into an archaeological method.

Ironically, these two approaches, operating with very different assumptions about culture and the past, became methodologically linked in spite of their essential incompatibility (Binford 1989a). The classic seriational approach was strictly normative and assumed that cultures were internally homogeneous, representing consensus views as to the proper ways to conduct life. Settlement-pattern approaches assumed that cultural systems were internally differentiated and hence presented themselves as differentiated phenomena distributed in complementary ways. These phenomena could be used to infer properties of a past organization in the same way that features are recognizable as the complementary structured arrangement of different things. Here the archaeologist faced a dilemma. Many different things out there exist in the form of "sites." How do we know which demonstrably different sites go together to inform about past organizations?

In order to answer this question, the opposite assumptions, the assumptions of homogeneity common to seriational approaches, were adopted as a rescue methodology. Sites were recognized by simple aggregational criteria; they were then segregated by applying similarity criteria to their artifactual content (a seriational strategy). All sites with Folsom points became Paleoindian sites, all sites with high frequencies of certain types of ceramics became Pueblo II or perhaps Chacoan sites. Once the "sites" were categorized in terms of similarity criteria, this suite of "similar" sites was then examined for differences in site placement, size, or even frequencies of associated artifact classes not used in the original assignment of sites to phases or time periods. The differences were then cited as self-evident observations referable to differences in the settlement system. Little sites were microband camps, big sites were macroband camps (MacNeish 1958), or sites with higher than normal frequencies of projectile points were hunting camps, whereas sites with larger assemblage sizes and greater typological diversity of artifact classes were residential sites. Similarly, if all the sites with a similar projectile point "style" tended to cluster spatially along the margins of playas, to many it seemed clear that site placement in that system was biased in favor of playa-overlook locations, without taking postdepositional processes into consideration.

Despite all of our "advances," as Schiffer might say, this is still our dominant methodology. At the present time advances primarily consist of "cautionary tales" suggesting that the dominant methodology is flawed. For instance, long ago Joffre Coe was able to demonstrate that when stratigraphic criteria were used for temporal arrangement of projectile point styles one obtained a totally different view of the past than when seriational criteria were used. (See the contrasts in views of the past presented by Holland 1955 and Coe 1964, or the flap over the Carbon-14 dating of Snaketown features [Schiffer 1982].) Another example is the early distributional work in the Illinois Valley (Luchterhand 1970), which demonstrated that the clustered patterning of artifact forms on the contemporary land surface primarily reflected differential erosion and sedimentary burial and in no way was directly referable to preferential bias in the location of camps. Many examples to the effect that site size may respond to multiple use rather than simple differences among the sizes of groups that used the sites are common in our literature (Binford 1983a; Camilli 1983). Clearly the recycling of artifacts at sites by later occupants modifies the frequencies and associational patterning referable to the initial conditions of deposition. This growing body of "cautionary tales" explores the effects of various natural agents in restructuring the patterns of seeming aggregation and dispersion as well as the differential sorting of artifacts. These stories are challenges to the reliability of our dominant methodology for using site data to make direct inferences regarding past organizations.

Our methodology is flawed and riddled with ambiguity as well as with tautological interpretive conventions. What can we do? We can anticipate a variety of suggestions on these issues. Some suggest that we change our scale of investigation and look at the actual distribution of artifacts across a landscape rather than concentrate our efforts on "sites." The ontological question may even be posed, do sites exist? (See Dunnell, this volume.) Others may prefer the suggestion that we investigate through excavation "good sites"—those in which the associations present are unambiguously referable to a single occupational episode. They believe that only in this way can we gain an understanding of "systems" when they are uncomplicated by "time's arrow" (Ascher 1968) and the effects of "distorting" (Schiffer 1976; cf. Binford 1981b) natural and cultural processes, such as recycling and reuse (see Dunnell, this volume). Finally, we can expect to encounter the claim of the statistically minded researcher who believes that if we just used the newest statistical technique we might more clearly see a "true" past.

Are these productive suggestions for guiding the development of a reliable methodology for accurately describing pasts of potentially great variety? I think not. Are these suggestions therefore of little value? I think they are valuable, but we can expect little from them with regard to accomplishing our methodological goals. They are all "let's-look-through-different-glasses" suggestions. When we look at the world with different strategies for seeing, we can generally expect to see things we have not seen before, and we will commonly expand our sense of problem and at the same time complicate our lives with questions about what these new observations might mean. Rarely do these new observations solve our old problems, contrary to what most empiricists might expect. In short, the relationships between our new observations and our old problems are not generally clear, and they do not intrude on us in any self-evident fashion. I might add that if they do appear self-evident, then one should be suspect of these empiricist "intuitions." The history of science strongly suggests that our alleged knowledge at the time of a learning opportunity is commonly inadequate to permit rapid judgments regarding the accuracy and "plausibility" of the novel suggestions that may be forthcoming from such opportunities.

Certainly, novel ways of looking are excellent strategies for creating learning opportunities. Looking through a microscope forces a discussion in terms totally different from those used when observing only with the unaided eye. Judging from the chapters in this volume, we are not apt to hear much about changing the character of our "eyes"; rather, we are likely to hear about changing the scales at which we use our eyes.

By changing our observational scales for looking, do we place ourselves in a strong learning posture? Potentially. For instance, by expanding our scale to landscapes instead of aggregates of artifacts, we clearly gain the opportunity to see patterning among artifacts that are not commonly discarded or lost in human settlements. Similarly we gain the opportunity to relate forms of artifact distributions to geomorphological forms as well as variation in the stability and conditioned dynamics of landforms in more sophisticated ways than might be possible if we had less-complete distributional information or information biased in favor of high-artifact-density areas. We may even be able to demonstrate convincingly that many locations with high densities of artifacts are the by-products of erosional processes or of time-averaged use of relatively stable landscapes. In short, we may find that the archaeological record cannot be directly equated with descriptive statements about discrete episodes of human occupation or even redundancy in such episodes. This is an old message. Nevertheless, it is an important one that needs to be repeated in as many different ways as possible. Working at a landscape scale is an important domain to investigate because the subject matter of archaeology is the archaeological record.

The success we have in making statements about the past, as seen at whatever scale, is directly proportional to our understanding of the consequences of dynamics and how these are manifest in static form, the archaeological record. So far so good. Some positions adopt a very different view, however. I have heard it said that "the interpretative baggage that the site concept, and related concepts such as component, activity area," and so forth are obsolete in view of "a sophisticated understanding of the archaeological record." What's wrong with the "site concept"? As I stated earlier, a site is operationally defined as a spatially clustered concentration of artifacts. Do such high-density concentrations of artifacts exist? Of course they do. What then is wrong with using the site concept to designate such clusters?

What about the other concepts sometimes said to be baggage—the component or the activity area. Do stratigraphically or otherwise spatially separated archaeological associations of artifacts reflect different periods of deposition seen in the archaeological record? Of course. What then is the objection to recognizing these properties of the archaeological record with a term like *component?* Similarly, are there activity areas? The answer is yes. In any system, differentially organized activities are conducted in different places, making use of different things. Should we ignore reality in our discussions of variability in the archaeological record?

In order to have a sophisticated view of the archaeological record we must recognize that it represents an enormous range of variation in structure and patterning. I have criticized the reconstructionists for their desire to see an archaeological record composed of the remains of neat behavioral episodes reflective of the kind of "reality" an ethnographer might observe, which ironically is what Dunnell (this volume) wants to "construct." When we realize that we may not regularly be presented with such neat episodes, should we conclude that the archaeological record is distorted? This is the wrong way to view the archaeological record. It is our task to investigate this record and to understand it in all its variation. It is the variability, after all, that offers us the opportunity to discuss cultural processes at multiple scales of space and time in organizational terms, something that is denied to ethnographers limited by their own life spans and the even shorter episodes of field observation.

Equally misguided is the view that "there are no sites" in the sense of structured consequences of short-term organizations and events of the past. These consequences certainly exist, and this scalar variability, which is differentially accessible in the archaeological record, places the archaeologist in the position of having to recognize the different scales of process, tempos, and durations that stand behind the variably conditioned patterning. Questions of "integrity," "grain," and "processual tempo" must be continually evaluated by the archaeologist working with different expressions of the archaeological record (Binford 1981a).

Many of the authors represented in this volume have taken this challenge to heart and sought to change their scales for "looking" in order to make explicit patterning that may have reference to very long-term processes. Discoveries at this level cannot help but expose new types of patterning and new types of problems for those working at different scales of observation. This is extremely important. We need to know the character of the determinants that condition the structure of the archaeological record in all its scalar variation.

Gaining the insights that almost inevitably derive from changing our scales for looking, and hence our abilities to track dynamics of differing tempos, does not, however, solve the fundamental problem facing archaeologists. This problem was summarized briefly in the beginning of this discussion. How do we explain patterned relationships in terms of the organizing principles that operated in the past to bring into being the relationships we can observe at whatever scale?

Many of the trends in analysis and observation represented in this volume are very provocative. They represent "biting-the-bullet" approaches that seek to make arguments about the integration of structured relationships among different things. Refitting, sequential modification, the study of the consequences of dynamic participation of things (the roles of tools) in ancient systems are most welcome trends in contemporary archaeology. These approaches are moving in productive directions to solve the problem of how to argue reliably for the integration of different things into organized life in the past. Finding a "similarity," in a Kriegerian sense, and using a bad theory, such as that which stands behind "stylistic seriation," to categorize cases as integrated, and then studying the spatially associated residuals is an expedient method that is justified neither by research nor by our increasing understanding of how the world of cultural systems generates static remains. This approach adopts an unthinking, independently reasoned general ontological expectation about the world rather than demanding an understanding of the nature of variable archaeological consequences of differing organizations. It is conventionalism at its worst.

Only a theoretically sophisticated understanding can make explanations of patterning in the archaeological record possible and in turn make the interpretation of the past possible. How do we argue for complementarity or the structured consequences of organized relations among different things, as is common in feature interpretation? Why do we assume that similarities reliably refer to similar organizations? Is it not well known that one characteristic of systems is variation in the way similar things are organized? Is not social organization itself a major "cautionary tale," wherein males and females, young and old, are similar constituents organized differently in different social organizations?

The situation that irritates many of us (including the editors of this volume) is that archaeologists continue to invent false pasts using logically unjustified conventions remaining among us from the days of traditional archaeology. If we hope to investigate process, we cannot assume we know *a priori* how process is manifest. The wedding of the assumptions of stylistic seriation and settlement-pattern studies into a simple convention for interpreting "site" survey data is sure to result in the invention of a false past. Changing our scales of observation may permit us to demonstrate this condition and broaden our appreciation of the long-term processes standing behind segments of the archaeological record, but these approaches do not solve the fundamental need for research aimed at theory building, or at a growth in our understanding of the organized dynamics that produce the patterning we are able to see. We need to know how the dynamics of organized cultural systems condition the patterning remaining for us to see. Only then can we interpret site or landscape, long or short duration, episodal or naturally restructured segments of the archaeological record in accurate ways.

STABILITY AND CHANGE: WHY WE ARGUE ABOUT ORGANIZATION

In the statements I have militantly used the word *organized* for a reason. At least one of the authors in this volume takes a dim view of anyone who speaks of organization. For Dunnell, organization is said to imply "units" given by nature and, as such, warrants his label for such thinkers as "essentialist" (which is a term he uses incorrectly—to assert that there are important organizational properties out there in the external world is not to make the essentialist error that the explanation for those properties rests exclusively in their unique or essential characteristics).

Dunnell's (1986) critique of the Ford–Spaulding debates is one of the more fascinating and, to the naive, convincing essays on this issue. Because Dunnell believes his critique to be accurate and germane, one can understand how he might claim that shifting to a nonsite approach demands a fundamental change in perspective. As I have suggested, it does not demand such a change; it simply involves a change of scale for conducting pattern-recognition studies. For Dunnell, however, it represents a return to the "good old days"; whereas artifact frequencies were previously used to measure time, they can now be used to measure space if you study big enough units.

For Dunnell (this volume), "sites" are bad ideas stemming from an essentialist's ontological bias. All that exists are frequencies continuously varying in time and space (Dunnell 1980:84). (For an update on this position, see Leonard and Jones 1987.) According to Dunnell, we should stop our search for organizational phenomena and stipulate the meaning of our classificatory devices so they (tautologically) reflect our beliefs about the world (see Dunnell 1978a,b and particularly 1986). For Dunnell, "theory" informs us at the level of deciding what to look for in the archaeological record. Although it is unclear from Dunnell's discussions, it would appear that general theory guides the development of "instruments for measurement" (as in the Leonard and Jones example), thus making a direct link between theory and the empirical observational world. Patterning that one might see as a result of using these "instruments for measurement" is then said to be directly understandable in terms of the general theory that guided their stipulation (see Dunnell 1986). This tautological loop can be rightfully criticized with such pet phrases as "all observations are theory-dependent" and "objectivity is impossible; hence science is impossible" (see Binford 1982a for a discussion of this issue; see also Fodor 1984; Rescher 1973; Scheffler 1967).

For me, the design of classifications is one thing and the explanation of patterning is quite another. One cannot anticipate the character of patterning with even a complete theory-based understanding of the "instruments for measurement" used in looking at the world; the derivative patterning must be understandable in *independent* theoretical terms (see Binford 1989b). It is this derivative patterning that is potentially informative regarding organization, and it is theories of organization, such as that given in the example about feature recognition, that render this patterning understandable. But Dunnell does not treat the patterning as anything more than larger-scale expressions of the stipulated meanings justifying his paradigmatic classification. My concern is for the explanation of patterning, no matter how well justified our instruments for measurement might be. *Explanation* is the pivotal goal of archaeological science, *not* classification. Explanation is possible only under "covering law" types of logic. Thus theory must operate on several levels with regard to the logic of learning. Dunnell's demand is for one "right-thinking" view to which all observation is accommodated (see Dunnell 1986).

Dunnell bypasses the challenge of theory development completely, as far as I can see. For him, organizational questions (mere functional concerns) do not matter; it is only continuously varying empirical frequencies that matter, and as Leonard and Jones suggest, these frequencies are measures of "fitness" as manifest by their relative "replicative success." I would argue against this position on several points. For example, Dunnell (1980:88, among others) seems to think that current statements of evolutionary biologists are statements of *theory*. I think they are statements of *mechanism* and that theory development in evolutionary ecology is only occurring where the issue is an understanding of selection and how it differentially impacts breeding populations that may be organized differently.

Darwin made an argument that change occurred, and he suggested how it might have done so. He made an assertion, based on empirical evidence, and he presented arguments to warrant his assertion. In the absence of an accurate understanding of the mechanism of change (which did not occur until the "great synthesis" of the early 1950s), he even attempted to build a theory of change. Since the 1950s, evolutionary biology has focused on the mechanisms that make change possible and has resulted in impressive gains in knowledge. For the most part, however, researchers have not concentrated on the next step: to build a theory that takes into account our new understanding of the mechanism.

In terms of cultural evolution, we know change occurred—that is no longer problematic. We still do not know what the mechanisms of change are with regard to cultural systems, however, and on top of this our challenge is to explain change, not simply to document its reality or the plausibility of it. We cannot look to contemporary biology for either (a) an understanding of extrasomatic mechanisms or (b) a theory that permits us to anticipate grades, characteristics, or scales of change because biology has largely avoided these issues.

As I see the situation at the present time, no evolutionary theory exists for anticipating changes in the organized products of the human experience. (These products are dismissed in most modern "evolutionary biology" discussions.) Nor is there a theory that explains the enormous diversity of organized forms in the biological world, except in a *post hoc* accommodative manner or by making up "adaptationalist" scenarios after the fact. Without a germane theory, one that relates causes and consequences in a predictable fashion, we cannot have explanations. Causes, to my way of thinking, are the relationships between impacted phenomena and impacting forces. This means that one must give consideration in theory building to the character of what is said to be acted upon. A constant set of impacting forces ("selective forces") operating on a population of mice and a population of elephants will have different consequences, depending on the organizational properties (e.g., the "anatomy") of the units said to be acted upon.

Organization *is* important. Evolutionary changes occur with respect to different organizational properties at different tempos and at different rates. Different species are organized differently and hence are subject to selection in different ways; the same is true of different human groups. Archaeologists have long been aware of the advantages of the archaeological record for permitting the investigation of evolutionary processes operative over a long time. In our field of study, organizations are commonly extrasomatically integrated systems, but they are not reducible to simple biological individuals. In biology, isomorphism is assumed between the unit of biological reproduction and the unit through which information is transmitted, thereby affecting phenotypes, which are said to be equivalent to "cultural traits" in Dunnell's classifications. Instead, the transmission of the types of information that strongly affect "cultural" phenotypes may occur independent of biological reproduction, which magnifies enormously the variety of units that might be subject to selection. At the same time, the potential for organizational restructuring within and among units exceeds that of their biological counterparts. This reorganizational "freedom" also permits *stability* in the outward ("phenotypic") appearance of similar "things," although they may be, nevertheless, organized quite differentially.

One might reasonably ask, what does all this about rates and tempos, stability and change, organization and reorganization have to do with archaeological landscapes and sites? What's wrong with the site concept? Why are some of us upset with the common practice of "identifying" hunting camps, transient camps, base camps, and so forth as interpretive conclusions presented after having conducted a major regional survey using a "site" approach? For example, if the focus is on places, particular localizations of systems functions, what can we learn from them? Against a backdrop of my experiences with the Nunamiut I have explored what a system looks like from the perspective of a single place (see Binford 1977, 1978a,b, 1979, 1980, 1981a,b, 1982b, 1983a). In contrast to the way in which many archaeologists have viewed the utility of the study of places (e.g., methodological individualists), I have suggested that the perspective of the individual participant is inappropriate to the task of the archaeologist (Binford 1986, 1987). I have strongly urged that we adopt an etic perspective of an overall system within which humans participated (Binford 1981b).

From a methodological perspective I have urged the adoption of middle-range research strategies, which focus on the explanation of patterning, as the only theoretically independent approach that gives the external world a chance to "talk back" to our ideas about it. Using this tactic we avoid the damning criticism of tautology by virtue of "theory-dependent observation." We need many more middle-range theories, as was exemplified in the discussion of the logic of interpreting features as opposed to sites. Whether one looks at sites or landscapes, the logical tactics are the same, and what is needed is to put in place sufficient knowledge—understanding through theory building—to explain our observations of patterning at either scale. This position is at loggerheads with Dunnell, who decries the past as inference and wants a direct link between phenomena and meaning, which is of course the empiricist's elusive dream (see Dunnell 1980:88).

In another discussion regarding middle-range research, Schiffer (1988) acknowledges the need for links between our thoughts about the world and the observations on the archaeological record, but he somehow believes that descriptions of the world are our ideas about the world. He continually discusses the role of empirical generalizations (he likes to call them "experimental laws") as playing a major role in theory building. I can see no role in theory building for these generalizations; they are the observations in need of explanation, or alternatively the observations that may prompt us to articulate provocative theoretical arguments. They are what we need theories about or are they stimuli to theory building, contrary to the old empiricist's idea that "higher-level generalizations" were theory. Thus, in common with many empiricists, Schiffer wants to argue about the ontological properties of archaeologists' problems and activities, classifying them into little boxes of similarity and difference (Dunnell's label of "essentialist" may be appropriate to Schiffer's work), rather than addressing the processes of learning and the tactical characteristics of logical and investigatory procedures. Unlike Schiffer, Dunnell *is* addressing the latter concerns; I just do not see how this suggestion can work in the best interests of knowledge growth.

From the standpoint of investigatory procedures, we can rarely hope to be able to see the material remains of a complete system. A complete inventory of places used, and a knowledge of the organizational dimensions that might crosscut the dynamics at all of these places, is an unlikely database for us to expect to uncover. Most of the time we have one or a very few sites that must guide our appreciation for the types of systems that once existed. If we are to use site information we must learn to see a past system from a site perspective. I have likened this perspective to that of a "rock with eyes" down in a deep hole (Binford 1983c). What this rock would see are little glimpses or segments of a system that passes over its hole. In addition, our rock's vision would be biased in terms of the matter that happened to fall into its hole as the living system passes overhead. Our job is to learn how to (a) identify the segment or part of the whole that "passed over" each particular site, (b) understand the implications of these identifiable parts for the kinds of organized systems represented, and finally (c) understand what conditions the biases in the systems parts represented from site to site (Binford 1983a:224–225). This is a difficult challenge.

Can we change observational scales and thereby gain some advantage in facing this challenge? The answer is a loud and resounding yes. Unlike Darwin's problem (a focus on change and its plausibility), our contemporary evolutionary problems cannot be addressed without simultaneously considering change *and* stability. (The failure to do this is a major weakness of all contemporary sociobiological approaches using sexual-selection approaches and is the root of the macro-/microevolution debate [see Vrba 1985].) The same theory must permit explanation of tempo differentials. We should be able to anticipate with a viable theory both the forces driving organizational change and those favoring stability.

Documenting landscapes is one way to approach this problem. Science is continually seeking to use tactics that at one level are perceived of as a weakness but when viewed at a different scale are seen as a strength. This potential ability to monitor organizational variables at any scale is the strength of the archaeological endeavor. Painting our observational frameworks "large" is a very important suggestion.

Many will say that landscape archaeology is a waste of energy because one cannot control for time in a surface survey, regardless of the recording accuracy employed. Although this claim may be germane, the answer to this criticism is simply that we are addressing the issue of stability here and are seeking to recognize stabilizing conditions. We want to be able to "see" stability with respect to landforms and what this implies in terms of botanical, faunal, and other natural resources; accumulated changes in the distribution of those resources, including perhaps archaeological sites themselves (which can be used as lithic sources at later time periods); and stabilizing forces related to prior investments in the built environment—such as animal drive lines, dams, fish weirs, and the like. One can expect that stabilizing forces will be demonstrable at very different temporal scales than those characteristic of the forces that promote change.

Looking at sites with the goal of understanding stability and change is difficult because variation cannot be directly equated with evolutionary change (*contra* Dunnell). Some variability may reflect fluctuating system states within organizational parameters that are in fact stable, whereas other changes are of organizational significance. The site "scale" is too narrow to permit an evaluation of what we are seeing. If we can relate what we see at the local scale to what we see in terms of stability at a very large scale, however, we will be in a much better position to understand sites. More important, we can begin the interesting job of theory building, which simultaneously permits us to anticipate the character of stabilizing selective forces as well as those that drive organizational change.

Unlike most of the authors in this volume, Dunnell advocates a change in the character of the problem that archaeologists are said to be facing and finds nonsite approaches consistent with his programmatic suggestions. Dunnell believes that, using theory-based or "paradigmatic" classifications, we can directly infer causation from the material record as accurately as we can infer the presence of fire from the remains of a hearth. I do not deny that this can be done in those few cases where we have viable middle-range theory in place. In general, however, such a program essentially denies that there is anything left to learn. In my opinion, current theories are inadequate; the challenge is an enormous ignorance of the past, which can only be addressed by putting in place viable learning strategies rather than sterile diagnostic procedures that accommodate the archaeological record to what we already allegedly know.

ACKNOWLEDGMENTS

I would like to thank Jackie Rossignol, Eileen Camili, and Jim Ebert, the symposium organizers, and LuAnn Wandsnider, the volume coeditor, for inviting me to participate in this exchange of views. Their comments, as well as those of my fellow participants and other colleagues, have been very helpful (even though

I don't always agree with them). I also appreciate June-el Piper's assistance in translating my original paper into a manuscript suitable for publication.

REFERENCES

Ascher, R., 1968, Time's Arrow and the Archaeology of a Contemporary Community, in: *Settlement Archaeology* (K. C. Chang, ed.), National Press Books, Palo Alto, pp. 43–52.
Binford, Lewis R., 1967, Reply to K. C. Change's "Major Aspects of the Interrelationship of Archaeology and Ethnology," *Current Anthropology* 8:234–234.
Binford, Lewis R., 1968, Review of K. C. Chang's *Rethinking Archaeology, Ethnohistory* 15:422–426.
Binford, Lewis R., 1977, Forty-Seven Trips: A Case Study in the Character of Archaeological Formation Processes, in: *Stone Tools as Cultural Markers* (R. V. S. Wright, ed.), Australian Institute of Aboriginal Studies, Canberra, pp. 24–36.
Binford, Lewis R., 1978a, Dimensional Analysis of Behavior and Site Structure: Learning from an Eskimo Hunting Stand, *American Antiquity* 43:330–361.
Binford, Lewis R., 1978b, *Nunamiut Ethnoarchaeology*, Academic Press, New York.
Binford, Lewis R., 1979, Organization and Formation Processes: Looking at Curated Technologies, *Journal of Anthropological Research* 35:172–197.
Binford, Lewis R., 1980, Willow Smoke and Dogs' Tails: Hunter–Gatherer Settlement Systems and Archaeological Site Formation, *American Antiquity* 45:4–20.
Binford, Lewis R., 1981a, *Bones: Ancient Men and Modern Myths*, Academic Press, New York.
Binford, Lewis R., 1981b, Behavioral Archaeology and the Pompeii Premise, *Journal of Anthropological Research* 37:195–208.
Binford, Lewis R., 1982a, Objectivity-Explanation-Archaeology 1981, in: *Theory and Explanation in Archaeology* (C. Renfrew, M. J. Rowlands, and B. A. Segraves, eds.), Academic Press, New York, pp. 125–138.
Binford, Lewis R., 1982b, The Archaeology of Place, *Journal of Anthropological Archaeology* 1:1–31.
Binford, Lewis R., 1983a, *In Pursuit of the Past: Decoding the Archaeological Record*, Thames and Hudson, London.
Binford, Lewis R., 1983b, Long-Term Land Use Patterns: Some Implications for Archaeology, in: *Lulu Linear Punctated: Essays in Honor of George Irving Quimby* (Robert C. Dunnell and Donald K. Grayson, eds.), Anthropological Papers No. 72, Museum of Anthropology, University of Michigan, Ann Arbor, pp. 27–54.
Binford, Lewis R., 1983c, *Working at Archaeology*, Academic Press, New York.
Binford, Lewis R., 1986, In Pursuit of the Future, in: *American Archaeology Past and Future: Papers Presented at the Special Anniversary Session for the 50th Annual Meeting of the Society for American Archaeology, Denver* (David J. Meltzer *et al.*, eds.), Smithsonian Institution Press, Washington, D.C., pp. 459–479.
Binford, Lewis R., 1987, Data, Relativism, and Archaeological Science, Man n.s. 22:391–404.
Binford, Lewis R., 1989a, Systematic Integration of "Fragmentary Oddments": The Challenge of Settlement Pattern Approaches, prepared for a volume edited by Bradley J. Vierra, submitted for publication to Eastern New Mexico University Press, Portales.
Binford, Lewis R., 1989b, Science to Seance, or Processual to "Post-Processual" Archaeology, in: *Debating Archaeology* (by Lewis R. Binford), Academic Press, New York, pp. 27–40.
Camilli, Eileen L., 1983, *Site Occupational History and Lithic Assemblage Structure: An Example from Cedar Mesa, Southeastern Utah*, Ph.D. dissertation, Department of Anthropology, University of New Mexico, Albuquerque.
Chang, K. C., 1967a, *Rethinking Archaeology*, Random House, New York.

Chang, K. C., 1967b, Major Aspects of the Interrelationship of Archaeology and Ethnology, *Current Anthropology* 8:227–243.

Coe, Joffre, 1964, *The Formative Cultures of the Carolina Piedmont*, Transactions of the American Philosophical Society n.s. 54(Part 5), Philadelphia.

Dunnell, Robert C., 1978a, Archaeological Potential of Anthropological and Scientific Models of Function, in: *Archaeological Essays in Honor of Irving B. Rouse* (Robert C. Dunnell and Edwin S. Hall, eds.), Mouton, The Hague, pp. 41–74.

Dunnell, Robert C., 1978b, Style and Function: A Fundamental Dichotomy, *American Antiquity* 43:192–202.

Dunnell, Robert C., 1980, Evolutionary Theory and Archaeology, in: *Advances in Archaeological Method and Theory*, vol. 3 (Michael B. Schiffer, ed.), Academic Press, New York, pp. 38–100.

Dunnell, Robert C., 1986, Methodological Issues in Americanist Artifact Classification, in: *Advances in Archaeological Method and Theory*, vol. 9 (Michael B. Schiffer, ed.), Academic Press, New York, pp. 149–208.

Dunnell, Robert C., 1989, Aspects of the Application of Evolutionary Theory in Archaeology, in: *Archaeological Thought in America* (C. C. Lamberg-Karlovsky, ed.), Cambridge University Press, Cambridge, pp. 35–49.

Fodor, J., 1984, Observation Reconsidered, *Philosophy of Science* 51:23–43.

Ford, James A., 1954, The Type Concept Revisited, *American Anthropologist* 56:42–54.

Ford, James A., 1962, *A Quantitative Method for Deriving Cultural Chronology*, Technical Manual I, Pan American Union, General Secretariat, Organization of American States, Washington, D.C.

Holland, C. G., 1955, Analysis of Projectile Points and Blades, in: *A Ceramic Study of Virginia Archaeology* (by Clifford Evans). Bureau of American Ethnology Bulletin 160. Washington, D.C.

Leonard, Robert D., and Jones, George T., 1987, Elements of an Inclusive Evolutionary Model for Archaeology, *Journal of Anthropological Archaeology* 6:199–219.

Luchterhand, Kubet, 1970, *Early Archaic Projectile Points and Hunting Patterns in the Lower Illinois Valley*, Illinois Archaeological Survey Monograph 2, Illinois Valley Archaeological Program Research Papers No. 3, Springfield.

MacNeish, R. S., 1958, *Preliminary Archaeological Investigations in the Sierra de Tamaulipas, Mexico*, Transactions of the American Philosophical Society 48(6), Philadelphia.

Rescher, N., 1973, *The Coherence Theory of Truth*, Clarendon Press, Oxford.

Scheffler, I., 1967, *Science and Subjectivity*, Bobbs-Merrill, Indianapolis.

Schiffer, Michael B., 1976, *Behavioral Archaeology*, Academic Press, New York.

Schiffer, Michael B., 1982, Hohokam Chronology: An Essay on History and Method, in: *Hohokam and Patayan: Prehistory of Southwestern Arizona* (Randall H. McGuire and Michael B. Schiffer, eds.), Academic Press, New York, pp. 299–344.

Schiffer, Michael B., 1988, The Structure of Archaeological Theory, *American Antiquity* 53:461–485.

Spaulding, Albert C., 1960, The Dimensions of Archaeology, in: *Essays in the Science of Culture: In Honor of Leslie A. White* (Gertrude E. Dole and Robert L. Carniero, eds.), Thomas Y. Crowell, New York, pp. 437–456.

Vrba, E. S. (ed.), 1985, *Species and Speciation*, Transvaal Museum Monograph No. 4, Pretoria, South Africa.

Willey Gordon, 1953, *Prehistoric Settlement Patterns in the Viru Valley, Peru*, Bureau of American Ethnology Bulletin 155, Washington, D.C.

Part III

The Spatial Dimension of Archaeological Landscapes

The domain of settlement pattern analysis includes the spatial distribution of archaeological sites across regions and the spatial dimension of inferred human activities. The four chapters that make up this section evaluate the use of both site and standard settlement-pattern analysis. Archaeological interpretations of past human activities across the landscape have been hampered by (1) the assumption that loci of well-preserved or high-quantity remains are necessarily the focus of settlement systems, (2) the confusion of settlement system with settlement pattern during analysis and interpretation, and (3) attempts to fit settlement systems into ideal or templated settlement types.

Beyond fundamental problems of definition, epistemology, and ontology discussed for the site concept in the last section, *site* presents conceptual problems in terms of its *role* in settlement pattern analysis. Archaeologists have unconsciously allowed the site concept to dictate arbitrarily the most relevant human system–landscape interface: Places with dense, highly visible collections of artifacts are reckoned, *a priori*, to be the focus of landscape analysis. Off-site and distributional data recovery has confirmed that valuable archaeological material exists in low-density and between-site contexts. When sites are no longer, *a priori*, the focus of analysis, the character of the landscape *per se* as a component of human subsistence systems comes to the fore. In the chapters that follow in this section and the next, off-site (Schlanger; Dewar and McBride)[1] and nonsite distributional approaches (Chang; Camilli and Ebert; Stafford and Hajic;

---

[1] Schlanger's and Dewar and McBride's approach are "off-site" in so far as Foley's off-site approach subsumes sites into a regional approach. Foley notes "the differences between site and off-site material are the results of differences in the frequencies of activities rather than qualitative differences" (Foley 1981a:11). Foley's approach, however, explicitly incorporates regional geomorphology.

Jones and Beck; Zvelebil, Green, and Macklin) avoid site centric bias and redirect attention to a more complete interaction between past human systems and the landscape.

The relationship between settlement system and archaeological settlement pattern is also problematic. Many archaeologists have assumed that the often complex components of archaeological sites can be interpreted by direct analogy with ethnographically derived, and idealized, settlement systems. The relationships between the artifact diversity of components and their inferred functional type, as well as the relationship between archaeological settlement size and inferred settlement type, are in fact poorly understood (Thomas 1986; Dewar and McBride, this volume). This problem is attributable to the failure of many archaeologists to acknowledge that hunter–gatherers and agropastoralists effect strategies of land use through an ever-changing, flexible array of tactics. Agropastoralists, especially, often combine permanent residences with daily mobility and seasonal, long-distance transhumance. Finally, the temporal complexity of sites is often lost in the attempt to associate sites with synchronic models of land use, a problem explored more thoroughly in the "time" section (Dewar and McBride).

The first two chapters of the "space" section explore the distribution of activities over space by directing attention away from the site concept. By incorporating a series of regional "overlays" consisting of environmental and physiographic variables over locations of artifact and feature assemblages, a conceptual tool of potentially great power is generated—the concept of *place*.

The place concept, in opposition to the site concept, is an attempt to reconceptualize the interaction between human subsistence strategies and landscape environment and physiography by focusing on locations on the landscapes where these elements conjoin. Places are locations of varying size and scale consisting of resources or topographic, microclimatic, and anthropogenic features that participate in systems of land use. Although sites can exist on places, places have an existence independent of sites. As such, they are not fundamentally archaeological in nature, although some places incorporate sites over time. The concept of place was introduced by Binford (1982) but has taken on additional dimensions in this volume.

In her ethnoarchaeological study of modern Greek pastoralists, Chang shifts the scale of observation from site to pastoral architectural features, which operate as "superartifacts distributed in space and over time and subject to reuse and remodeling," and investigates the role of places in strategies of land use. By utilizing the superartifact in a distributional approach, she observes variability in the pastoral record previously obscured by rigid adherence to the notion of site and obviates the widely held idea that pastoral systems are invisible in the archaeological record. Chang gains insight into the organization underlying the pastoral system by relating the distribution of facilities to demographic pressure on resources across environmental zones.

In her study of prehistoric agricultural landscape and places in the Southwest, Schlanger uses an off-site approach to integrate multicomponent site data and isolated finds in an investigation of long-term land use. By concentrating on the role of persistent places in focusing reoccupation within the region during periods of residential abandonment, Schlanger is able to demonstrate functional change in these places. She concludes that continued, functionally diverse use of an economic landscape after residential abandonment may have "held" land for eventual residential reoccupation, a pattern with implications for the long-term land use of the region.

In the last two chapters of this section, Camilli and Ebert and Stafford and Hajic explore the complex relationship between formation processes and the organization underlying cultural deposition in their respective interpretations of prehistoric hunter–gatherer subsistence systems. Both chapters avoid simplistic, "templated" settlement types, concentrating on local formation processes and large-scale geomorphological patterns, combining this focus with ethnoarchaeological studies of mobility and foraging strategies.

Using distributionally collected data and indexes of chipped stone core and flake reduction, Camilli and Ebert examine how local formation processes, regional geomorphology, and reuse and recycling of artifacts affect the visibility and structure of nonsite artifactual assemblages. These variables are used in combination to study the affect of variable visibility on prehistoric hunter–gatherer land use strategies in the American Southwest. Camilli and Ebert conclude that the placement of hunter–gatherer camps is conditioned by past visibility of assemblages resulting from postdepositional agents: Elevated surfaces are subject to deflation, exposing buried assemblages, and attracting hunter–gatherers in a reuse and recycling strategy.

Stafford and Hajic emphasize a geomorphic perspective and a distributional approach to data collection in building a method for defining and measuring elements of the paleolandscape. They rely on ethnoarchaeological studies of hunter–gatherer mobility to interpret spatial patterning of artifacts. By examining the changing rates of deposition in response to different functional uses of landscapes (as revealed in different spatial patterns of debris), Stafford and Hajic are able to show that the spatial patterning of artifacts is at least partially a function of the scale of landforms and the arrangement of landscape elements that serve as stopping points (places) on those landforms.

This section demonstrates how a landscape perspective combining off-site or distributional data collection, formation processes, and ethnoarchaeological studies of mobility and foraging strategies provide valuable insight into systems of land use. Integrating landscape parameters with theories of mobility and foraging strategies results in a conceptualization of "place." The place concept allows archaeologists to, in effect, identify and potentially quantify the range of variable temporal and spatial uses of the landscape that are obscured by settlement-pattern templates. The editors of this volume see potential for deriving analytical tools—based on the place concept—that would allow archaeologists not only to conceptualize land use problems in a productive way but also to *measure* the interaction between landscape variables and depositional patterns. This fundamental reorientation to the archaeological record, combined with potentially powerful tools for measurement and analysis, directs the study of land use toward profitable development of theory.

REFERENCES

Binford, L. R., 1982, The Archaeology of Place, *Journal of Anthropological Archaeology* 1(1):5–31.
Foley, R., 1981a, *Off-site Archaeology and Human Adaptation in Eastern Africa: Analysis of Regional Artifact Density in the Amboseli, Southern Kenya*, Cambridge Monographs in African Archaeology 3. British Archaeological Reports, International Series 97.
Thomas, D. H., 1986, Contemporary Hunter–Gatherer Archaeology in America, in: *American Archaeology Past and Future* (D. J. Meltzer, Don D. Fowler, and J. A. Sabloff, eds.), Smithsonian Institution Press, Washington, pp. 237–276.

Chapter 4

Archaeological Landscapes
The Ethnoarchaeology of Pastoral Land Use in the Grevena Province of Greece

CLAUDIA CHANG

INTRODUCTION

This chapter documents an intellectual journey: the process by which I have conceptualized the spatial organization of a contemporary Greek herding system and its relationship to an archaeological landscape. Archaeologists often discuss how spatial patterning and settlement systems can be inferred from archaeological site locations. They also bring to this discussion the assumption that given production systems such as foraging, agriculture, and pastoralism follow a given set of rules dictating where sites will be located and how settlement patterns inform the archaeologist about the mobility, resource use, and environmental settings exploited by past peoples. In this chapter, I start with a different assumption: that the spatial organization of pastoral systems existing on the contemporary landscape provides a basis for investigating how pastoralism may be rendered visible in the archaeological record. My intention is to demonstrate in the ethnographic present how herdsmen organize their use of landscapes through the construction of pastoral facilities and the use of pasture lands and other vital resources. Archaeological questions about how pastoral activities are organized

CLAUDIA CHANG • Department of Anthropology–Sociology, Sweet Briar College, Sweet Briar, Virginia 24595.

Space, Time, and Archaeological Landscapes, edited by Jacqueline Rossignol and LuAnn Wandsnider. Plenum Press, New York, 1992.

on a landscape, or what constitutes a pastoral site or place can then be answered.

I begin with the ethnographic observation that each component of the regional pastoral system in the Grevena Province of southern Macedonia, ranging from upland summer transhumance (pastoralists who move twice yearly between upland summer pastures and lowland winter pastures) to year-round sedentary village pastoralism, is part of an interlocking system of resource exploitation. I then set forth some underlying principles of decision making used by both transhumant herders and village herders for locating their pastoral facilities and use areas in the uplands of the Grevena Province. The tactics and long-term strategies used by herders in organizing activities over the regional landscape are shaped by both ecological/economic aspects of stock raising and a set of cognitive rules regarding the location of herding activities in relation to village habitations, agricultural activities, and physical attributes of the landscape itself.

How may such data be used by archaeologists and what significance do these ethnographic observations have for archaeological surveys? First, I shall argue that our conceptualization about what pastoralism is and what consititutes a pastoral site or "place" must be derived from ethnographic analogy. Second, archaeologists have overlooked the rigorous study of pastoralism because of a failure to understand how the pastoral system operates across landscapes, and even to recognize pastoralism in the archaeological record. The landscape approach to pastoral land use becomes a necessary strategy for discovering whether the spatial distribution of pastoral facilities over a varied terrain could be identifiable in the archaeological record.

My approach to describing and analyzing the spatial distribution of pastoral facilities in Grevena is to develop a new set of terms for describing pastoral loci. Archaeological terms such as *site, catchment area,* and *settlement pattern* are inadequate for accurately describing the pastoral loci used by Grevena herders. These terms have specific connotations in the minds of archaeologists and obscure our ability to observe, describe, and analyze the spatial patterns of human activities found in the archaeological record. Moreover, pastoralism, a mobile economy, does not conform to typological categories of spatial behavior. Throughout this chapter, I will define and introduce the following terms: *place, use area* or *grazing territory,* and *"superartifact."* When these terms are first introduced in the text, they will be defined.

First, I shall depart from using the site concept by adopting the more flexible concept of *place.* Why place and not site? The site concept for many archaeologists has loaded connotations; sites are defined as places where material residues of past behaviors are located and identified. In the ethnographic record, it is often the case that herders use places on the landscape without leaving any traces or material residues. To label such "places" as sites would only confound the links I wish to make between ethnographic observations, pastoral spatial organization, and the archaeological landscape itself.

Place is defined as any location on the landscape that is a part of the herding system. The place concept differs from the site concept in the explicit sense that a place may or may not be visible in the archaeological record. Herders graze their animals over a wide range of environments; their movement patterns are represented by places that are essential to the total spatial and temporal dimensions of pastoral land use. The places used by Greek shepherds and goatherds range from facilities such as corrals, animal folds, enclosures, watering troughs and wells, and storage barns to use areas such as grazing territories, paths, trails, springs, and watering areas along streams and rivers. These places are interspersed among other places of human activities such as seasonal and year-round habitations, field cultivation, woodcutting, and the like. Herders often incorporate features of the natural landscape such as ravines, ridge tops, and stream beds into their own boundary maintenance system separating individual flocks.

In conventional archaeological usage, the site concept is used to label the locations of the pastoral facilities; at best the "grazing territory" or use area might be defined as a site territory (Higgs 1975). If the distinction between use areas and facilities is made clearly, then the archaeologist is more capable of conceptualizing the total regional landscape of a given area as a system, rather than as an array of site locations or settlement patterns. Once archaeologists come to understand pastoralism as a system of spatial organization over a total landscape, they can then establish links between this spatial system and its material correlates. For a pastoralist, it may be that a particularly rich grazing area is a use area situated in the vicinity of a facility location but not directly adjacent to this locus. I describe these use areas as "grazing territories." Although these territories may not have indications of material remains such as artifacts, architecture, and structures, locational attributes of vegetation, slope, aspect, and landform indicate that this is the use area directly associated with the pastoral facility itself. If archaeologists understand the system of pastoral spatial organization, then pastoral use areas will, in fact, be recognizable in the record.

Why has the spatial organization of pastoral systems been largely overlooked by archaeologists? When mobile production systems are studied archaeologically, the focus has been on hunter–gatherer spatial organization. Pastoralism is often seen as a problematic production strategy to recover in the archaeological record because it cannot be seen in isolation or as a pristine system. On the more positive side, because pastoral studies in archaeology are still in gestation, the intellectual baggage that has unduly burdened archaeological conceptualizations of hunter–gatherer settlement-subsistence systems can be avoided. If archaeologists begin first with a conceptualization of pastoral spatial organization and then use this conceptualization to build linkages between the spatial system and the archaeological record, we will in fact discover that pastoral adaptations are far from being either ephemeral or invisible. How will archaeologists come to render pastoralism visible in the material record? The methods best available involve archaeological survey in areas where pastoral locations can be positively identified as the artifacts or residues of the total system. Although in this chapter I only allude to possible strategies in archaeological surveys for the recovery of pastoralism, my ultimate research goal is to fully develop such strategies. In this sense, I view ethnoarchaeology as a "means to an end," a set of research strategies that may ultimately render the archaeological record more intelligible for understanding the past.

How does the specific case of Greek sheep and goat pastoralism in a modern peasant context contribute to an understanding of prehistoric pastoralism on Mediterranean landscapes? By exploring the variability in spatial organization of a regional pastoral system in a contemporary context, archaeologists may begin to develop the appropriate theory and method needed to study pastoralism. What ethnoarchaeology does, in this case, is to set up a base line for developing useful strategies for interpreting Mediterranean landscapes where pastoralism occurred.

THE ETHNOGRAPHIC CASE

Greek pastoralism is based on the husbandry of sheep and goats, herded either in separate or mixed flocks. Although well integrated into a market economy, Greek pastoralists also depend on herd-animal products for subsistence. Management strategies reflect a dual dependency upon meat and milk products as well as fibers, skins, and manure. Contemporary Greek pastoralism usually articulates directly with the agricultural regime of cereal, tree, or vine cultivation, and is rarely divorced completely from agricultural land use. Flocks graze on natural grass, shrubs, woodland vegetation, cultivated green fodder, and agricultural stubble and fallow.

An essential variable of Greek pastoralism is seasonal mobility because both mobility and seasonal use are important factors of land use patterning. The general pattern of seasonal mobility consists of three strategies: (1) summer transhumance at the higher elevations of 1,000 to 1,600 meters, where pastoralists are primarily seasonal long-distance transhumants, using natural grazing lands from late April to early October, and residing in upland summer villages; (2) year-round village herding, from 500 to 1,000 meters (encompassing topographic regimes from the foothills of the Pindos Mountains to the agricultural valleys and plains of the Grevena Basin), where sedentary village pastoralists keep flocks on a year-round basis in agricultural as well as natural grazing areas but move their flocks on a daily and seasonal basis within the local commune (village) area; and (3) in addition to permanent year-round mixed herding and farming systems at 500 m in the agricultural plains, there is some winter settlement of transhumants.

There are a number of variations, however, on this general theme, so that occasionally long-distance summer transhumants occupy open niches in village communal lands at lower elevations during the summer. Most upland summer transhumant pastoralists will travel 150 to 200 km with large flocks (300 head or more) to lowland pasture areas outside of the Grevena Province (the agricultural plains of Thessaly or Elassona) for winter grazing from October to April/May. However, some stay within the Grevena Province but move to lower elevations during the winter months. The diversity of individual herding strategies are often played out in the contexts of ethnicity and complex socioeconomic relationships between herders and villagers (Wace and Thompson 1914; Sivignon 1968).

The ethnographic case study of Grevena pastoralists is particularly complicated by a set of historical conditions by which different pastoral strategies are also associated with specific ethnic groups. The long-distance twice yearly movement of the transhumant herders between upland summer pastures and lowland winter pastures is associated with the Koutsovlach or Vlach, an ethnic group of Aroumani-speaking herders. Two other ethnic groups involved in pastoralism include the Sarakatsani (Campbell 1964), who are Greek-speaking nomadic herdsmen, and the Kupatshar, hellenized Vlach who speak Greek and no longer associate their origins with the Vlach.

Each of these groups has its own settlement and pastoral strategies in Grevena. The Vlach occupy the High Pindos Mountains (defined as Zone 1) during the summer months, where they reside in large, summer villages. Vlach herders may live at their pastoral facilities as well as own a permanent summer home in the village itself. The Kupatshar occupy the Lower Pindos (defined as Zone 2) and other lower elevations (includes Zone 3 and Zone 4). They may engage in long-distance seasonal transhumance, settled village pastoralism, and agriculture. All Kupatshar herders live in villages, either on a seasonal basis or year round. Occasionally they stay in huts near pastoral facilities, but increasingly they opt to travel from their pastoral facilities to the village on a daily basis. Today, Kupatshar is not a widely used term, and most villagers claim their ethnic identity as Greek. Historically, the Sarakatsani were pastoral nomads who had no permanent villages but lived with their flocks of sheep and goats at winter and summer pastures in herder's huts (Campbell 1964). The Sarakatsani define themselves as a separate ethnic group, based upon folkloric customs, rituals, and a commitment to pastoral nomadism. Today, only a few transhumant Sarakatsani occupy the Grevena area.

ARCHAEOLOGICAL LANDSCAPES AND PASTORAL LAND USE

I shall address the central issues of pastoral mobility and resource exploitation by examining the distribution of architectural features over landscapes. This represents a departure from the traditional archaeological convention of describing spatial organization by referring to the concept of settlement type. Pastoralists in Grevena do not conform to models of "ideal" settlement types; many live in permanent or semipermanent village habitations and also keep animal facilities in locations distant from their village habitations. Although the herders may appear to be "peasants" and not nomadic pastoralists, they also move considerable distances—both on a daily basis (10 to 15 km daily) and on a seasonal basis (100 to 150 km between summer and winter pastures). For this reason alone, the actual patterns of pastoral spatial organization in Grevena cannot be explained by the use of site types such as villages, habitations, and special use sites.

Pastoral facilities do not fit our traditional notions of an ideal site type. They can be found in conjunction with or separate from village habitations. The facility itself, although used to enclose and shelter animals, is also an informal marker of grazing territories. I describe these facilities as "superartifacts"—because in a formal sense, they share more properties with artifacts than they do with traditional architectural features. Although architectural features are units of bounded space, they, like artifacts, are distributed in space and over time. They are subject to the similar processes of abandonment, reuse, remodeling, and deposition that occur regularly in the archaeological record. Moreover, because facilities and use areas comprise the major pastoral places used by Grevena herders, their locations also reflect how pastoralists organize herding activities across the landscape. The landscape becomes an important unit of analysis because this approach allows the ethnoarchaeologist to examine a regional spatial system, and not just a single, fragmented piece of the total pastoral system.

This ethnoarchaeological study of pastoral land use in Greece emphasizes a landscape archaeology comprised of two research strategies: (1) the analysis of the distribution of architectural features over space and (2) the analysis of the spatial distribution of pastoral facilities in four environmental zones of an upland region in Northern Greece. These environmental zones constitute the primary analytical unit, and are defined by vegetation, elevation, and physical landforms.

In the first strategy, I consider pastoral facilities such as corrals, barns, milking pens, and animal folds to be "superartifacts," or large-scale artifacts. Their distribution over a landscape differs with regard to scale from a lithic or ceramic scatter but cannot be considered as bounded wholes. Architectural features are distributed over space and through time and have real behavioral meaning, but what is defined archaeologically as discrete architectural units or components are no more bounded wholes of pastoral activities than artifact distributions are bounded wholes of human activities.

In the second strategy, the concept of landscape is used to explain how pastoral facilities are distributed over four distinct environmental zones. Here, the "superartifacts" or pastoral facilities are part of a larger system of pastoral land use, in which different mobility strategies are emphasized at different elevational zones. Each component of the larger regional pastoral system is linked to a specific set of vegetational, topographic, and elevational variables. The summer pastoral facilities of transhumant herders are part of the larger system of agropastoralism that occurs at lower elevations. An understanding of one part of the system cannot be understood without linking it to another part of the system.

Each component in the regional pastoral system articulates with another component. Then, within each environmental zone, predictions are made about the spatial distribution of pastoral places.

To fully appreciate how the regional spatial organization of pastoralism operates in Grevena, I shall reintroduce the *place* concept. As stated earlier, pastoral resource use extends from the pastoral facilities to include use areas. *Use areas* are defined as the loci for herding activities such as grazing, feeding, and watering animals. The use area represents a cognized map of resource use for individual pastoralists; a herder will evaluate on a daily basis the grazing potential of the use area surrounding his pastoral facility. Grazing lands may be frequently parceled into informal territories used by herding households and delimited by the spatial arrangements of pastoral architectural features such as animal folds and enclosures that are bound by topographic features such as ravines, rock outcrops, and other physical features.

The placement of herding facilities across a landscape is directly related to demographic pressure on resources. The facility and its accompanying use area marks the informal grazing territories of individual herdsmen. For archaeological interpretation this is especially important. The distribution of facilities across landscapes reflects how many flock animals and pastoralists can successfully use a particular landscape given its resource base. For archaeologists, this demonstrates that a set of relationships between facility locations, use areas, and resource distribution (vegetation, water) in the archaeological record may directly reflect how pastoral spatial organization operated in the past with regard to environmental conditions and population dynamics.

How will archaeologists render the archaeological record of pastoralists meaningful? My study suggests that archaeologists must first examine the spatial patterning of pastoral places by distinguishing between facilities and use areas. The archaeology of pastoralism must go beyond the quest for the typical pastoral site, to include a fuller understanding of how pastoralists have used landscapes. To do this, archaeologists must recognize the aggregate patterning of pastoral places. Such patterns can be observed, measured, and interpreted by archaeologists. Then the spatial patterning must be linked to key variables of location, resource base, and vegetation. Archaeologists employing such a method will be able to discover how the pastoral system operated in the past.

THE CASE STUDY—THE ETHNOARCHAEOLOGY OF PASTORAL LAND USE IN THE GREVENA PROVINCE OF NORTHERN GREECE

The examination of pastoral land use in the Grevena region of Northern Greece is based on a preliminary ethnoarchaeological survey conducted in the village of Megaron, situated in the foothills of the Pindos Mountains, by Perry A. Tourtellotte and myself during the summer of 1988. These observations are used to explore land use strategies across four environmental zones.

The Grevena Province is situated on the eastern flanks of the Pindos Mountain Range and opens up to the heavily dissected plain of the Grevena Basin. This province makes up the southwest area of Greek Macedonia and is bounded by Epirus to the west and Thessaly to the south (see Figure 1). The Grevena Province, an area 75 km by 45 km, is comprised of eight major environmental zones. In this chapter, four zones are discussed, making up roughly one-third of the total area. The climate of this region is described by Moody and Rackham

Figure 1. Greece showing the location of the Grevena Province.

(1987) as sub-Mediterranean, that is to say, the summers are hot and dry, typical of most regions of Greece, and the winters are inclement with rain, snow, and hard frosts for 3 months out of the year, typical of Central European winters. Natural vegetational regimes include woodland areas found in both the semiarid plains and the high mountains. Although the plains and foothills are dominated by oak woods, the mountains are dominated by pine and beech woods (Moody and Rackham 1987).

Koster (1987) has tentatively characterized the region into eight provisional pastoral land use zones, ranging from zones where long-distance transhumant pastoralism is present to zones of permanent mixed herding and farming villages. For purposes of this discussion, I will concentrate on the first four land use zones—those associated with the dominant landform, the Pindos Mountains: Zone 1—High Pindos; Zone 2—Lower Pindos; Zone 3—Pindos Foothills; and Zone 4—Central Agricultural Plains (see Figure 2). The first three pastoral land use zones are contiguous. For each land use zone, Koster (1987) has described the vegetation regimes used by pastoralists, the nature of their flock composition (sheep, goat, or mixed sheep and goat flocks), the ethnic identity of pastoral groups, stocking rates, and the facilities used by the herders.

The Megaron Survey

The 1988 Megaron survey provides a base line for developing a conceptual framework for examining pastoralism across four environmental zones of the Grevena Province. The small-scale analysis of the distribution of facilities and use area of the village settlement of Megaron can be extrapolated to derive a set of strategies for examining regional pastoral dynamics. This includes an analysis of several different pastoral production systems ranging from transhumant Vlach pastoralism to the mixed agropastoralism of Kupatshar groups (Wace and Thompson 1914). The distribution of pastoral facilities located during the 1988 Megaron Survey is presented in Figure 3. The information from this map will be referred to throughout the next two sections.

I selected Megaron, an area of mixed farming and herding located in Zone 3, because of the range of land use strategies available there for study. Current agricultural practices in this zone consist of cereal/pulse production, fruit and nut orchards, and kitchen gardens. Today, herd animal production has both a market and subsistence focus. Milk, meat, and wool are either sold to cheese and wool merchants and butchers or used by individual households.

Megaron is situated at an elevation of 960 m and has a population of under 1,000 permanent residents. Megaron consists of 24,800 hectares, of which 13,700 ha have been designated as pasture lands. Pastoral strategies are apparent from the community tax records of 1987, where villages reported a total of 2,445 sheep, 2,068 goats, and 839 lambs and kids. The last category, lambs and kids, includes

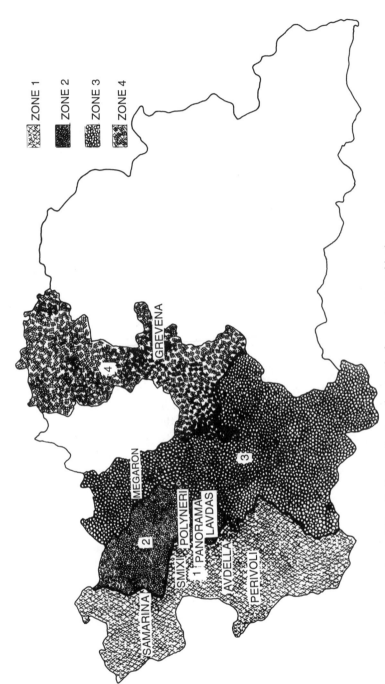

Figure 2. Grevena Province showing the four environmental land use zones.

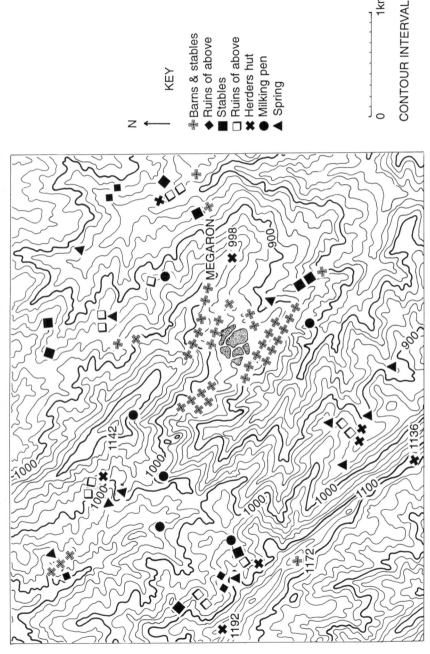

Figure 3. Megaron showing the locations of pastoral facilities.

only those animals registered as taxable livestock, not the total number of young born in the 12-month period. In the mixed flocks, sheep are often found in a greater number than goats. Among the 88 registered owners of livestock, only 1 individual is registered as having a flock comprised only of goats (112 head). During the months of June and July, we observed a predominant pattern of mixed sheep and goat flocks (usually under 100 head, with sheep in slightly higher proportions) grazed on agricultural fallow and stubble and the native oak scrub land vegetation.[1]

The mosaiclike patchiness of the landscape is exploited by both agricultural and pastoral production systems. Although some vertical zonation of vegetation occurs in Megaron, the dissected limestone ridges have been modified more significantly by deforestation, agricultural terracing, and grazing combined with natural factors of erosion and colluviation. Contemporary agricultural land use on this heavily dissected, eroded landscape is restricted to the most fertile valley and slope areas in the immediate proximity of the village settlement. This patchiness extends to distant areas used by pastoralists where field or orchard cultivation occurs as well. Here, pastoralists must keep their flocks out of cereal fields and tend to flocks grazing under orchard trees during summer months. Once harvests are completed, herders are able to graze their animals on agricultural stubble, so long as they establish previous economic arrangements with field owners. In this case, the scheduling of activities is tied to the pastoral exploitation of patchy resources.

Implications of the Megaron Survey for the Landscape Approach

The theoretical context for studying the pastoral spatial organization in Megaron has been derived from an ecological model of pastoral dynamics, in which herd-animal population pressure on natural and cultivated pasture, competition among herders for grazing resources, and the articulation between animal husbandry production and crop cultivation are essential to Mediterranean land use (Koster 1977; Chang 1981). The pastoral facilities and use areas are the material residues of the pastoral spatial organization. The architectural structures at pastoral facilities are the superartifacts distributed over the landscape. The task is then to draw inferences between the patterning of the architectural structures and how the system actually operates in a given area.

Pastoral architecture such as *mandria* (animal folds), corrals, and *strunga* (milking pens) are all bounded features used to enclose animals—and therefore are related to herd population dynamics. Barns are necessary for fodder storage and therefore are indirectly indicative of grazing requirements. Pastoralism as a total system is only partially observable archaeologically. These archaeological

---

[1] Supplemental feeds and oak shreddings are also brought to the animal folds.

observations of the pastoral material record, however, have enormous potential for interpreting relationships between human and herd demography, fodder requirements, and population pressure on available resources. The facilities and their use areas can be observed, measured, and interpreted according to standard archaeological procedures.

The question I ask of the ethnographic data is simple; how do village herders distribute their herd animals over a landscape of finite resources? Village herders may "push" a grazing area to its limits—even overgrazing natural grass or scrub lands, but they will do so knowing that returns in dairy production will suffer as will long-term recovery of their pastures. Herders may also attempt to "invade" agricultural areas by grazing near fields or orchards but will risk the consequences of offending neighbors and creating undue social tensions. More likely, they will attempt to maintain "balances" among flock numbers and grazing resources. When they attempt to drive the system beyond this balance, such actions or tactics are done "on the sly," and as a short-term strategy.

How then do these ethnographic observations translate into archaeological problems? If herders are pushing a use area to its limit, then the spatial distribution of facilities and use areas should in some way reflect the demographic pressure on resources. Archaeologists may then begin to design regional surveys that recover data on the location and nature of pastoral places. When pastoral places are identified in the archaeological record, archaeologists can finally begin to assume that such places are "artifacts" of population dynamics in relation to critical resources.

In Megaron, three distinct facility types exist: (1) the *mandri* (animal fold) associated with storage barn found in or on the periphery of the village habitation area (see Figure 4), (2) the *mandri* (animal fold) found in areas away from the village (usually on protected hillsides), and (3) the *strunga* ⟨milking pen or holding areas) used to enclose flocks at night during the summer months in distant pasture areas (see Figure 5). The spatial distribution of these facility types (see Figure 3) can be analyzed in terms of the seasonal use of the facilities, the differences in topographic setting of these facility types, and the catchment areas associated with the facilities.

The aggregate spatial patterning represents the total distribution of facility locations without attention to seasonal use or distribution of agricultural and pastoral resources. If vegetational factors are considered, the relation between population dynamics, spatial organization, and resource use can be understood more fully. Facility location also directly reflects the combined strategies of field cultivation and sheep and goat herding. By careful evaluation of vegetational regimes and agricultural potential in relationship to actual facility location, archaeologists could determine the relationship between facility loci, resource patchiness, and population (human and herd-animal demography).

The multiresource nature of village agropastoralism, from both spatial and

Figure 4. A Megaron village *mandri* (animal fold).

temporal perspectives, presents a particularly compelling landscape problem. Abandoned agricultural land in upland regions opened up new areas for pastoral land use.[2] Present-day pastoral use probably reflects the in-filling of empty niches or pockets of field cultivation. Villagers suggest that this has been the case. In the archaeological record, the in-filling of pastoral facilities "invading" areas of field cultivation would appear as overlapping sets of architectural features, especially in "optimal zones" where both agriculture and pastoralism are possible. The overlapping architectural features of pastoral facilities, agricultural terraces, field markers, and the like, although confounding interpretation, reflect in fact the dynamic, fluctuating nature of human activities over a single landscape. The ethnoarchaeological survey of these facilities can be used to chart these diachronic changes in pastoral and agricultural strategies over time.

What the Megaron survey demonstrates is that (1) the pastoral facilities are located in relation to grazing resources, (2) the total spatial of organization of the pastoral systems is driven by dynamics of population pressure on critical resourc-

---

[2] Heavy equipment could not be brought into these upland fields, so they were abandoned.

Figure 5. A village *strunga* (milking pen).

es, and (3) the facilities as material correlates of the total system are part of a larger mosaic of agricultural and land use. In the archaeological record, I predict that pastoral places will reflect the numbers of animals placed over a given territory, resource use, and the articulation of pastoral systems with other forms of production like foraging and agriculture.

Research Strategies for the Distribution of Pastoral Facilities in Four Pastoral Land Use Zones in Grevena

The model of spatial distribution of pastoral facilities for four land use zones of the Grevena region introduces further variability into isolating economic and ecological patterns of pastoral mobility. Research strategies for applying a distributional approach to these landscapes are based on Koster's preliminary ethnographic survey of the Grevena region (Koster 1987). The reader may wish to refer to Figure 2, the map showing the location of the four zones of pastoral land use discussed here.

Zone 1

The High Pindos Mountains are characterized as a zone of summer trans-humance, where in villages such as Samarina, Avdella, Smixi, and Perivoli (Wace and Thompson 1914; Sivignon 1968), Vlach pastoralists use these upland grass-lands for grazing large flocks of sheep. Herders own substantial summer homes. They often reside at their summer *stani* (pastoral facilities) in huts. For the last 10 years herders have been able to travel between their village homes and their pastoral facilities by pick-up truck. Usually one herder spends the night at the facility with the flock and guard dogs. Facilities used by Vlach transhumants in this area consist of *korda*, a holding area for the flock constructed of staked wire fencing and brush, the *strunga*, a brush or wire-fenced milking pen, and *kaliva*, a herder's hut and campsite. In addition, the Greek government has built large concrete loading platforms, where herders can unload their large flocks from trucks. Figure 6 depicts a summer transhumant camp.

Pastoral land use in Zone 1 has (1) less overall variability in the kinds of architectural features present than in the Megaron village example because only features related to spring and summer use exist; (2) spatial patterning that conforms to local topography and not to mosaic patchiness of agropastoral settings; and (3) facilities located farther away from the village settlement and more evenly dispersed throughout the region, to accommodate larger flock sizes (200 to 1,000+ sheep).

Vlach pastoralists claim residency in these summer villages. In the fall, they travel to a number of villages in the lowland plains in this region and neighboring regions, where they will enter into contractual arrangements for winter grazing lands. The organizational principles for facility location in this zone, as observed during 1989 include the following strategies: (1) Vlach herders attempt to dis-perse features evenly in good pasture areas so as to reduce potential competition among one another; (2) some herders will cluster their facilities near summer village residences so that they can maintain important social and familial contacts in the village; and (3) shepherds who locate their facilities in forested areas, seek access to open pasture lands, which may be distant from their facility.

Competition among herdsmen is less of a problem than in the other zones, although stocking rates are high. Reduced pressure for grazing lands is related to how herders exploit seasonal flushes of vegetation. They attempt to keep flocks at lower elevations during the early summer months until snow melt has oc-curred and they can move into higher elevations. By carefully monitoring vertical changes in grazing resources, they are able to schedule pasture use over vast areas and not openly compete with other herders.

By and large, grazing lands are well maintained and not overgrazed, except during extremely dry seasons. One strategy always open to long-distance trans-humants is to move to winter pastures, if summer pastures are depleted. During

Figure 6. A summer *stani* (animal enclosure and associated features) used by transhumant herders.

the summer of 1990, we observed the reverse version of this mobility tactic; herders traveled in late April and early May to upland pastures because of the extreme aridity of the winter pastures in the plains. Although Koster (1987) notes a relatively high density of small stock to unit area, between 3.2 to 7.5 head per *stremma* (a *stremma* equals .1 ha) for this area, there is a relatively low density of features per square area. In 1990, we recorded a total of 25 facilities in Perivoli, a village of 137,200 ha (32,000 ha of pasture lands). This is easily contrasted with 30 or more facilities found in Megaron (Zone 3) in a total area of 24,800 ha (13,700 ha of pasture lands). However, the high feature size per unit area in Zone 1 reflects a constant population pressure on the grazing resources.

Such variables as distribution of facilities, density of facilities per unit area, and vegetation cover can help archaeologists predict pastoral strategies from the material record and landscape attributes. More important they also enable archaeologists to also reconstruct population dynamics and resource use of past herding systems through the recovery of the spatial patterning of facilities across the landscape.

Zone 2

The Lower Pindos is an area for Kupatshar transhumant pastoralism and settled village pastoralism. Pastoral facilities consist of similar summer facilities found in Zone 1, the *korda* (holding enclosures), *strunga* (milking pens) and *kaliva* (herder's huts), as well as the *mandri* (animal fold) and storage barns, found in the Megaron example from Zone 3.

The mixed agricultural and pastoral production systems and the intense competition result in the following spatial patterns: (1) there is greater variability in the kinds of pastoral facilities found than in Zone 1, (2) facilities such as the *korda, strunga,* and *kaliva* used primarily during the spring and summer are situated in areas where natural pastures in the form of grasslands are found, (3) facilities used on a year-round basis such as the *mandria* (animal folds) and storage barns are either attached to the peripheries of village settlements or found in clumps or clusters interspersed with agricultural fields or oak woods, and (4) there is a higher density of facilities per unit area than in the previous zone— especially as the transition to year-round pastoralism at lower elevations increases.

In 1989 and 1990, we observed the following pastoral dynamics at work in Zone 2: (1) a tendency to overstock available grassland, resulting in a high number of large area size animal enclosures per unit area, (2) the use of as much abandoned agricultural land as possible by herders, and (3) intense competition among herders and concomitantly extremely tight scheduling of daily herding activities.

Why have the transhumant and village herders of Zone 2 intensified their grazing situation, so as to create overgrazing, and why are their strategies so different from herders' strategies in Zone 1? Two environmentally related explanations come to mind. First, Zone 2 is a transitional region between "pure" summer transhumance and village pastoralism. It is situated at an elevation where agriculture is difficult but not completely impossible. The area surrounding the village of Polyneri has an inviting topographic setting for agriculture and pastoralism.[3] Active deforestation began in the 1920s. The geological setting is ideal; the topography is less rugged and has more open exposures than in Zone 1. Yet the vegetational regime and climatic conditions are similar to those of Zone 1, allowing herders to extend their milking season into mid-July.

I put forth the hypothesis that Zone 2 has always been a transitional land use zone. Historically, the mid-nineteenth century was a difficult time for the Vlach transhumant herding in the High Pindos (Zone 1) (Wace and Thompson 1914: 163). Among the many historical factors involved were wars, uprisings, and the

---

[3] Polyneri has over 6,000 head of animals and is the most overgrazed area in this zone.

disappearance of some large parcels of winter pastures in Thessaly.[4] All this affected what happened in the uplands. Whereas Zone 1 has only been suitable for pastoralism, Zone 2 has always had a greater range of land use alternatives. When large-scale summer transhumant pastoralism in Zone 2 was difficult, people had the choice of expanding their upland cereal, vineyard, or orchard cultivation by clearing land. Abandoned terraces, field systems, and orchards are still visible throughout Zone 2.[5] The alternating dynamics between upland field cultivation and large-scale pastoralism should be visible in the material record, especially in recent periods. I have observed stone agricultural terraces and field markers of abandoned field plots as well as abandoned pastoral facilities (stone enclosures). In 1990, we recorded a total of 20 facilities in Polyneri (Zone 2), which has a total area of 10,300 ha (6,500 hectares of pasture). When contrasted with the number of facilities per village area in either Zone 1 or Zone 3, this is high. Why does such a high density of facilities per unit area exist in Zone 2? Does this overpacking of transhumant flocks explain why the area appears to be overgrazed and subject to erosion? If Zone 2 were interpreted archaeologically, simply in terms of numbers of facilities per unit area, I would predict an extremely high population density of herd animals over finite resources leading to the eventual collapse and failure of the pastoral system.

Zone 3

The Pindos Foothills is the zone where Megaron is situated. The inventory of facilities is comprised of *strunga* (milking pens), *kaliva* (herder's huts), *mandria* (animal folds), and storage barns. The isolated *korda*, or holding area, is uncommon. Mixed herding and farming systems prevail in this area, although Koster (1987) suggests that some transhumance by ethnic groups like the Sarakatsani takes place in this zone. The Sarakatsani herders build *kalivas* and enclosures in these summer pasture areas. The interplay between ethnicity and pastoral strategy is fascinating here; the only long-distance transhumance practiced in Zone 3 is done by an outside ethnic group.

In Zone 3, herders use the following strategies: (1) they reduce overall flock size to cope with the problem of supplying winter fodder for flocks who are confined to stables and folds during the rainy weather or when snow cover prevents open grazing; (2) they locate facilities near available resources, whether

---

[4] Former land-holding units under the jurisdiction of the Ottoman Empire were later distributed to Greek farmers who no longer wished to rent winter pasture to the pastoralists.

[5] Oral testimony confirms that during the 1920s, an era of population explosion and a failing market economy, there was an expansion of the subsistence economy and increased deforestation of Zone 2 (Riki van Boeschoten, personal communication).

pastoral or agricultural; and (3) they schedule the use of pastures, either in oak woodlands, or cultivated areas according to the agricultural harvest cycle.[6]

Extrapolating from the Megaron pattern, I would expect spatial arrangements of pastoral facilities to include (1) the clustering of facilities used during the winter on the periphery of the village, (2) the dispersal of summer facilities in distant pasture areas near oak woods and natural springs, and (3) a tight clustering of facilities found in areas that are left "empty" by agriculturalists or that can be used in conjunction with cereal or arboriculture regimes.[7] Storage for fodder and winter folds are found on the periphery of the village to minimize the distance of the flock from the village residence. During the summer, folds are kept near or in oak woods, both as a means for providing shade for animals and because animals are grazed in oak forests and natural grasslands away from agricultural fields. In the historic past, some village herders would spend the summer in hamlets away from the village, where they would tend their animals and plant and harvest crops. Often clusters of these facilities are in actuality summer settlements for herders and farmers.

Zone 4

Although the ethnoarchaeological survey of pastoral facilities in Grevena during 1989 did not extend to include Zone 4, some ethnographic observations and archaeological inferences can be made about spatial distributions in the agricultural plains.

Zone 4, the central agricultural villages in the Grevena Basin, is where mixed herding and farming systems are fully integrated within individual household economies (Koster 1987). Here, over one-half of the land area is used for agricultural cultivation, a higher proportion than all other zones. Facilities comprise the full range found in Zone 3. Koster (1987) notes that in these villages, the winter fold facility is often attached to the village home itself, in contrast to previous historic periods when the winter fold was situated away from the village. Because his data are based on preliminary observations, it is possible that pastoral facilities in this zone may be found in, on the periphery of, and distant from the village settlement similar to the pattern found in Megaron.

My predictions for spatial patterning in this zone are (1) the clumping of facilities found in those niches, where the pastoral sector can be tolerated or can at least articulate directly with agricultural pursuits; (2) concentrations of facilities on the periphery of, or in oak woodlands, where grazing is communal; and

---

[6] Oak forest is used as communal grazing land. The pastoral facilities in the oak forest areas mark informal grazing territories and are more evenly spaced than facilities found on the periphery of the village settlement.

[7] Sheep and goats feed off agricultural stubble while manuring fields or orchards.

(3) a moderate density of pastoral facilities per unit area, reflecting smaller flock numbers per household. Because agriculture is the dominant strategy of land use in this zone, one might assume that pastoral facilities will be located in places where agriculture is considered unproductive or at least at the edge of cultivation areas. Here the mosaic patchiness of agropastoral land use and the spatial distribution of pastoral facilities must be examined closely.

For archaeologists, Zone 4 represents a situation similar to what may have occurred during the Early Neolithic in areas where agriculture was a predominant strategy and sheep/goat raising a secondary strategy. In mixed farming and herding systems where farming of broad alluvial terraces is the predominant strategy, separate pastoral facilities may not be located far from the village community. The superartifacts found away from village settlements may be combined field houses/animal shelters. Here more careful survey of Neolithic period use areas as well as facilities must be conducted.

LANDSCAPE APPROACHES TO PASTORAL LAND USE

A landscape approach documenting the location of pastoral facilities and use areas in all four pastoral land use zones has considerable potential for developing behavioral models of pastoral production in this region. First, pastoral facilities and their locational variables found in Zone 1, the High Pindos Mountains, should differ considerably from those found in lower elevations of Zones 2, 3, and 4 because this is a summer area for transhumant pastoralists. All other zones are used by either summer transhumants and year-round herders, or year-round herders alone. Although contemporary records provide good indication of density-dependent variables of pastoral production in these four zones, it is also apparent that animal numbers per unit area are not necessarily reflected in number of architectural features found in each zone. This has great importance for a landscape approach in archaeology.

Why should the numbers of herd animals kept in a given environmental zone be related to the amount of available natural pastures, the amount of land put under agricultural cultivation, the amount of available woodlands, seasons of use, and other climatic, elevational, topographic, or vegetational factors? My assumption is that facility size might be a rough indication of stocking rates per individual herding household in a given zone. Thus in Zone 1 there are few facilities per unit area but relatively large facility size over the zone. Moreover, the numbers of architectural features are not really an accurate indication of overall animal population per zone, unless other landscape variables are considered. In Zone 2, the Lower Pindos, and Zone 3, the Pindos Foothills, there may be no material correlates or any set of locational variables that would indicate the mix or combination of mobility strategies. The difference between winter fold facilities attached to permanent residences in Zone 4 and those detached from homes in Zone 3 must be more fully explored. Here, architecture associated with pastoralism must be seen as superartifacts having multiple purposes and differential spatial distributions.

This change in scale size can be investigated more fully, when the distribution of facilities and their relationship to vegetation zones or agricultural fields is examined in four pastoral land use zones. It is likely that the filling in of empty spaces, or the abandonment of former niches by either transhumant or village pastoralists does not focus on the single facility, but rather on clumps or clusters of facilities. Here the distributions are generated from aggregate patterning and not from a single point ont a map and its relation to other points. I suggest that the landscape approach may resolve the analytical problem of resolution between point patterning and cluster patterning inherent in archaeological spatial analysis (Hodder and Orton 1976).

I wish finally to recapitulate how both the distributional and landscape approaches have contributed to a better strategy for interpreting the spatial organization of Grevena pastoralism. First, once the site concept is replaced with the concept of superartifact, it is then possible to adopt a distributional approach to the spatial patterning of pastoral facilities. The architectural features are superartifacts distributed over landscapes. Their spatial dispersal articulates with other landscape features such as village settlements, local topography, and vegetation. This application of the distributional approach grants the investigator freedom from the tyranny of settlement pattern typologies. As I have argued throughout this Chapter, the archaeological search for the "ideal pastoral site" would only obscure the importance of the aggregate spatial patterning of pastoral facilities.

Second, I have adopted a landscape approach because of my own dissatisfaction with the analytical tools available for understanding pastoral spatial organization. Ethnographers rarely discuss exactly how pastoralists organize their resources, grazing territories, and material places over a landscape. Instead they focus on the social, political, or economic structure of pastoral production. Archaeologists do have a conceptual framework for interpreting spatial patterning over landscapes. The artifacts of spatial organization, such as pastoral facilities and use area are observable from the material record. The herders' placement of these superartifacts over four environmental zones demonstrates how the total system functions.

A working knowledge of how pastoral systems operate over space has great significance for both archaeological and ethnographic studies. For archaeologists, this research provides the requisite method and theory needed to identify herding systems in the archaeological record. For ethnographers, this research demonstrates that pastoral economies have a visible, material presence on landscapes. With this database, ethnographers can then measure the degree of environmental impact that herding systems have on the regional landscape.

CONCLUSIONS

What does the ethnoarchaeological study of pastoral strategies in the Grevena region have to offer larger theoretical concerns in Mediterranean archaeology? From the Neolithic period onward, there is archaeological evidence of sheep and goat husbandry throughout the Balkan Peninsula. Archaeologists have only begun to speculate on the nature of pastoralism; most discussions center around the origins of long-distance seasonal transhumance. From my vantage point, I believe that because Mediterranean pastoralism is never divorced from cultivation regimes, the archaeological recognition of pastoral systems in the record must depend upon survey methodologies that emphasize the recovery of facilities and use areas across landscapes. The spatial patterns of pastoral places in the archaeological record will undoubtedly overlap with material remains of agricultural systems such as terraces, field houses, and the like.

The task requires that archaeologists develop a theory of pastoralism that goes beyond the questions concerning its origins and development. Such questions engender normative notions of pastoral settlement, including the notion that pastoralism should be represented by an ideal site type. Archaeologists cannot begin to formulate the diachronic development of pastoralism without a more basic understanding of how pastoralists use landscapes today. For the archaeological study of Mediterranean pastoralism, ethnoarchaeology proves to be an immensely rich source for researching the dynamics of pastoral spatial organization across landscapes, the very same landscapes that have been used for 8,000 years of farming and herding activities.

Mobility strategies employed by pastoralists cannot be easily discovered in the archaeological record. This, I believe, is due to a basic lack of understanding concerning the variability of pastoral dynamics over regional landscapes, either by archaeologists or anthropologists. The limits of pastoral production, when considered from economic, social, or ideological frameworks, are more often discussed in normative ways. Too often the spatial organization by which individual herders place their herds over diverse landscapes is only examined in the most cursory fashion. When the distribution of pastoralists on regional landscapes is addressed in a general way without considering the pastoral facility itself as the nexus from which the spacing of resources, animals, and humans is organized, useful variability in spatial organization is obscured. The locus for herd animal production activities is the facility itself. This is where the strongest case will be made for establishing the relationship between the spatial behavior of pastoralists and its material correlates. The record of diachronic change of pastoral adaptations either in historic or prehistoric contexts is most appropriately documented by this material record of pastoral peoples.

The archaeology of pastoralism may be developed for this region when environmental zones become the unit of observation and the distribution of architectural features becomes the key artifact of pastoral adaptations. Essentialist approaches to the diversity and range of pastoral strategies are readily discarded when a landscape and land use patterning are investigated over environmental zones. The distribution of pastoral architectural features over the landscape is a descriptive tool by which pastoral mobility and resource exploitation strategies can now be examined in relation to critical resources, cultivation regimes, and other interlocking components of a regional pastoral system. The material correlates of pastoral spatial organization can be tested against ethnographically known strategies of herders who compete for grazing territories, place pressure on existing pastures, and must schedule and articulate animal husbandry activities with crop cultivation regimes. I have focused on the dynamics of pastoral ecology, including the balance between humans, herds, and grazing lands, because this is the model that will best show long-term diachronic changes and is present in the archaeological record.

The variation within and between environmental zones in Grevena demonstrates the degree to which Greek pastoralists must devise short-term tactics and long-term strategies to effectively exploit a region of varied landforms, vertical zonation of vegetation, and an ever-changing set of economic conditions. What ethnoarchaeological survey of pastoral land use so dramatically illustrates is the dynamic nature of landscapes—a fact frequently ignored in archaeological spatial models. Here, the dynamic nature of the landscape and the architectural distribution of pastoral facilities over space and through time can be documented as an artifact of both changing human behavioral systems and changing natural conditions.

ACKNOWLEDGMENTS

This work was conducted in conjunction with the Grevena Archaeological Survey, directed by Nancy Wilkie. A Wenner-Gren Foundation grand-in-aid supported this research in 1988 and 1989. Sabbatical leave from Sweet Briar College allowed for a second field season in 1989. A Sweet Briar summer grant provided support in 1990.

The technical responsibilities of survey work were taken on by Perry A. Tourtellotte. Our daughter Laura participated in the Grevena fieldwork from 1988 through 1990. Stan Aschenbrenner, Mari Clark, Harold Koster, Mary Savina, Nancy Wilkie, and Riki van Boeschoten generously shared their knowledge of the Grevena Region. Albert J. Ammerman expanded my limited knowledge of Mediterranean landscapes and taught me how to conceptualize the Grevena landscape. I am intellectually indebted to Jackie Rossignol for her editorial forebearance and honest appraisals of earlier drafts of this chapter. Alix Ingber provided editorial assistance. Karla Faulconer drafted the figures.

Finally, I owe much gratitude to our hospitable informants from the villages of Perivoli, Polyneri, Ziakas, Megaron, and Rodia, and most of all, to Georgios Kaloyeros, who let us in on a few horse trades in true Vlach style.

REFERENCES

Campbell, J. K., 1964, *Honour, Family, and Patronage: A Study of Institutions and Moral Values in a Greek Mountain Village*, Oxford University Press, Oxford.

Chang, C., 1981, The Archaeology of Contemporary Herding Sites in Didyma, Greece, unpublished Ph.D. dissertation, Anthropology Department, State University of New York at Binghamton.

Chang, C., and Koster, H. A., 1986, Beyond Bones: Toward an Archaeology of Pastoralism, in: *Advances in Archaeological Method and Theory*, Volume 9 (M. B. Schiffer, ed.), Academic Press, New York, pp. 97–148.

Higgs, E. S., (ed.), 1975, *Paleoeconomy*, Cambridge University Press, Cambridge.

Hodder, I., and Orton, C., 1976, *Spatial Analysis in Archaeology*, Cambridge University Press, Cambridge.

Koster, H. A., 1977, The Ecology of Pastoralism in Relation to Changing Patterns of Land Use in the Northeast Peloponnese, unpublished Ph.D. dissertation, Department of Anthropology, University of Pennsylvania.

Koster, H. A., 1987, Appendix IV: The Ethnography of Herding in the Grevena Area, in: The Grevena Report (N. C. Wilkie, ed.), unpublished manuscript, Department of Anthropology, Carleton College.

Moody, J. A., and Rackham, O., 1987, Appendix III: Studies in Vegetation and the Environment, in: The Grevena Report (N. C. Wilkie, ed.), unpublished manuscript, Department of Anthropology, Carleton College.

Sivignon, M., 1968, Les Pasteurs du Pinde Septentrional, *Revue de geographie de Lyon* 43: 5–43.

Wace, A. J. B., and Thompson, M. S., 1914, *Nomads of the Balkans*. Reprinted Freeport. Books for Libraries Press, New York (1971).

Chapter 5

Recognizing Persistent Places in Anasazi Settlement Systems

SARAH H. SCHLANGER

INTRODUCTION

As other chapters in this volume illustrate, analytical methods that build an archaeological record from individual artifacts have been most often and most successfully applied in the context of hunter–gatherer archaeology. The study of prehistoric horticulturalists and agriculturalists has more often begun with the notion of the site, with artifact analyses and other work proceeding from there. The reasons for this are partly historical (see Binford, this volume, and Dunnell, this volume), partly based on the very different land and tool use strategies of hunter–gatherers and food producers, and partly practical. Hunter–gatherers maintain relatively small tool inventories, and hunter–gatherer-derived artifact populations tend to be slight, whereas farmers maintain larger tool inventories, and artifact populations generated by farmers tend to be large. Hunter–gatherers tend to move frequently and hunter–gatherer-derived artifact distributions tend to be dispersed; farmers move less frequently, and artifacts discarded by farmers are often clustered around highly visible architectural features. Together, these

SARAH H. SCHLANGER • Museum of New Mexico, Office of Archaeological Studies, P.O. Box 2087, Santa Fe, New Mexico 87504.

Space, Time, and Archaeological Landscapes, edited by Jacqueline Rossignol and LuAnn Wandsnider. Plenum Press, New York, 1992.

factors make it easier to identify some kinds of concentrations of farmer-generated materials in the field, and more difficult to do the same for hunter–gatherer artifacts. Lacking until recently methods for rapid recording of the thousands of artifacts associated with even small agricultural and horticultural settlements (but see Bintliff and Snodgrass 1988; Cherry and Davis 1988), most have opted to record the archaeology of agriculturalists and horticulturalists in terms of artifact concentrations—sites—rather than individual artifacts. A compromise of sorts has been reached to accommodate very small artifact concentrations and individual artifacts: These are often recorded as "isolated finds" and treated separately from "sites" with their richer artifact and architectural inventories. In this chapter, I propose to treat both the isolated finds and the sites together and to employ them as tools for studying the use of a landscape occupied by prehistoric horticulturalists. The concept I use to link sites and isolated finds to landscapes is the concept of the "persistent place," a place that is used repeatedly during the long-term occupation of a region.

For the millennium before the late twelfth century A.D., arable upland mesas, productive lowland basins, and sheltered canyons of the northern American Southwest were repeatedly colonized and abandoned in coordinated patterns that suggest a delicate interplay between simple prehistoric agricultural methods and uncontrollable environmental processes (Gumerman 1988; Kohler and Matthews 1988; Schlanger 1988). Each cycle of renewed occupation brought people into a landscape rich in cultural features, a landscape dotted with abandoned home sites, fields, and camps. In a broad sense, these landscapes are the persistent places of Anasazi settlement systems. Their archaeology is the archaeology of repeated abandonments and reoccupations, of population retreats and population returns. In a much narrower sense, the cultural features on the landscape are also persistent places that structure the use and reuse of the larger landscape. Their archaeology is the archaeology of the particular, of the facility that may serve as a home for a resident population and later as a temporary shelter for those who have moved elsewhere, of the collecting camp that is used intermittently for hundreds of years, and of the field shelter that becomes the homestead for a returning family.

This chapter explores the archaeology of one such landscape and examines the nature of the persistent places established there by the prehistoric Anasazi of southwestern Colorado. As my primary database, I use the most accessible source of information on the use of the landscape—the archaeological materials present on the modern ground surface of the study area. Consequently, this discussion returns at several points to the question of how well surface materials reflect the postresidential occupation and to the larger question of how to use surface materials to study long-term land use. For the sake of both simplicity and convenience, I have restricted my analysis of surface finds to just a subset of the artifact types present in the surface archaeology of the area. I use temporally sensitive ceramic artifacts to establish both a general time frame and to identify multicomponent assemblages that result from the reuse or long-term use of certain places. I use projectile points, a tool type with a relatively unambiguous functional interpretation and a common component of the Anasazi toolkit, as a means of discussing shifts in the function of places, their associated facilities, and their associated artifact assemblages.

THE NATURE OF THE STUDY AREA

The landscape of interest here is a small section of the southward sloping, gently rolling uplands bordering the Dolores River in extreme southwestern Colorado (Figure 1). This area was studied by a multidisciplinary team of archaeologists, geologists, and paleoenvironmental specialists with the Dolores Archaeological Program (DAP), a cultural resources mitigation project concerned with the archaeological record within the pool area and canal lines for a dam, reservoir, and irrigation system (Robinson *et al.* 1986). The study area environment and prehistory are well described elsewhere (Peterson *et al.* 1985; Robinson *et al.* 1986; Peterson and Orcutt 1987; Schlanger 1988; Kohler and Matthews 1988; Orcutt *et al.* 1990), and the following brief description is intended only to alert the reader to the nature of the local environment, the character of the modern ground surface, and the general outline of local prehistory.

Architectural rubble from occupations dating back to A.D. 600 is still visible on the modern ground surface, and the prehistoric ground surface is apparently not deeply buried on the rolling ridges and shallow basins that make up the study area. The sediments in the area are derived from weathered sandstones and from loess deposits that mantle the sandstone bedrock (Leonhardy and Clay 1985a:134; Leonhardy and Clay 1985b:139–153; Holliday and Piety 1985:173–183), and the ground cover is composed of sagebrush at the lower elevations and mixed stands of sage, dense scrub oak, and open pinyon–juniper woodlands at the higher elevations. With the exception of the scrub oak patches, ground visibility is generally very good.

There are three localized features of the landscape that may have influenced the prehistoric occupation and long-term use of the area: permanent water, which is available in the Dolores River; the marsh at the southern margin of the study area, which dried and filled several times during the period of prehistoric occupation in the area (Clay 1985; Petersen 1985); and the breaks in the Dolores River canyon walls that provide good access between the Dolores River and the study area uplands (Figure 2).

These uplands initially were colonized around A.D. 600 by farmers who established dispersed, single-household hamlets. By A.D. 800, continued immigration and local population increase put sufficient stress on local farm lands that the

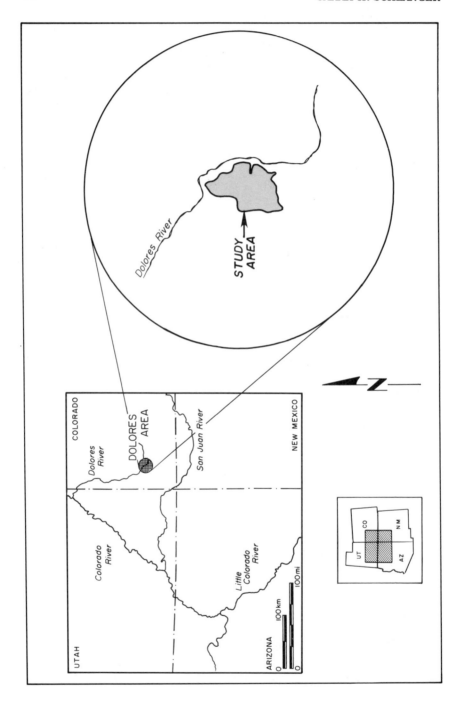

population left their scattered hamlets and aggregated in multihousehold villages, located so as to minimize conflict over farmlands and other local resources (Orcutt *et al.* 1990). The villages were abandoned in turn by A.D. 900, when the combination of high population and poor agricultural conditions led to a general abandonment of the area. Although a very few people returned briefly to the area to live after A.D. 900, reestablishing a small residential population between A.D. 1000 and A.D. 1100 (Schlanger 1988), my interest here is in the post-A.D. 900 use of the area, when it changed from a primarily residential landscape to a place used as an outlying farming and collecting zone for people living elsewhere.

Before I began this research, I had a strong suspicion that the Dolores landscape had not been abandoned until long after the houses, shelters, and field camps had collapsed. Although survey work revealed a substantial use of the area after A.D. 900, marked by the recovery of sherds from vessels manufactured after that time on the modern ground surface, excavations at a sample of residential locations found that the places so marked were abandoned as residences well before the vessels were made. Who was using the landscape after A.D. 900? The demographic trends in my study area are complemented by those immediately to the south and southwest, where population peaks and lows fit the lows and highs found in the study area. Residential populations to the southwest grew as the villages of the study area were abandoned. Elsewhere, I have interpreted this as evidence that the study area was just a small section of a considerably larger region occupied by a population that shifted residential locations in response to climatic and other environmental changes in prehistoric productivity (Schlanger 1988). Although I cannot be certain that the former residents of the study area are the same people who began to build residences a day's walk away in the southern sections of the region, the circumstantial evidence is good. It seems very likely that the former residents (or their descendants) were continuing to make use of the uplands adjacent to the Dolores River, if not as a place for building homes, then as a place for hunting, collecting, and other logistically organized activities.

My primary concern here is to document these suspicions. I begin this process with a discussion of the qualities of persistent places in general. I then turn to expectations for long-term land use patterning among logistically organized systems such as the Anasazi. Next, I discuss the distribution of surface materials in the study area, focusing first on the character of the use of the landscape and then on the problem of identifying particular "persistent places" on

---

Figure 1. Location of the study area. Bottom left, the "Four Corners" states of the American Southwest: Arizona, Utah, Colorado, and New Mexico; top left, the study area and major features of the Four Corners area; top right, the study area and the Dolores River.

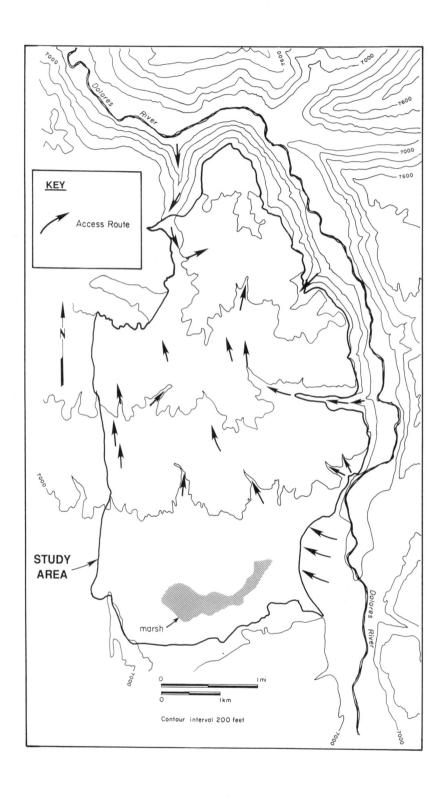

KEY

→ Access Route

N

STUDY
AREA

marsh

Dolores River

7000
7600
7000
7600
7000
7000
7000
7000

0   1 mi

0   1 km

Contour interval 200 feet

that landscape. Finally, I present an analysis of the changing functions of such "persistent places" on my Anasazi landscape.

THE NATURE OF PERSISTENT PLACES

What makes a persistent place? Persistent places are places that were repeatedly used during long-term occupations of regions. They are neither strictly sites (that is, concentrations of cultural materials) nor simply features of a landscape. Instead, they represent the conjunction of particular human behaviors on a particular landscape. Persistent places fall into one or more of the following categories. First, a persistent place may have unique qualities that make it particularly suited for certain activities, practices, or behaviors. Examples of the larger kinds of places that fit this definition include stretches of farmland, open marshlands, riparian bottomlands, stands of good graze for large mammals and cover for smaller mammals, good stands of timber for construction and consumption, and outcrops of workable stone or clay. Smaller, more spatially localized, or more clearly defined features with the potential to become persistent places include springs, streams, topographic breaks that provide access from one area to another, unique topographic situations such as ridge tops, cliff margins, and other vantage points, and preestablished cultural features such as houses, shelters, caches, and campsites. Second, a persistent place may be marked by certain features that serve to focus reoccupations. Whether the place consists of the features or the features serve to mark the place is a subtlety I cannot entirely resolve. At any rate, once built, hearths, shelters, storage features, and other such constructions create their own environment, both attracting reuse and reoccupation and structuring the activities associated with those various occupations. Finally, persistent places may form on landscapes through a long process of occupation and revisitation that is independent of cultural features but is dependent on the presence of cultural materials. In these cases, the artifact assemblages that accumulates at both the larger places, the more spatially localized places, and the "cultural feature" places may serve as a structuring component of the cultural landscape and provide an exploitable resource for people in need of expedient tools or of cached tools.

Figure 2. Landscape features in the study area. Access to the study area uplands is easiest from the southern end, where the valley walls are very low, and through the steep drainages that pierce the valley walls along the west margin of the Dolores River. The river, the marsh, and the access routes appear to have structured long-term land use in the study area.

ANASAZI SETTLEMENT ORGANIZATION AND LONG-TERM LAND USE PATTERNING

The prehistoric Anasazi practiced a mixed subsistence economy based on a variety of domesticates, including corn, beans, and squash, and the exploitation of an equally great variety of wild resources (Lipe 1983; Cordell 1984; Matson 1991). It appears that the cyclical patterns of expanding and contracting regional occupations that characterize the Anasazi occupation developed in the first centuries A.D., after the Anasazi began to use dry farming techniques that allowed them to make use of the northern Southwest's plentiful acreage of poorly watered but fertile uplands (Matson 1991). These farming techniques were but a small part of the technological and behavioral repertoires maintained by the Anasazi for coping with the unpredictable climatic fluctuations that threatened farmers in the prehistoric Southwest.

The Technological Repertoire

In addition to agricultural fields and farming techniques, the Anasazi technological repertoire included domestic structures, storage facilities, agricultural processing facilities, field camps from which wild resources and raw materials were collected, and the tools needed for planting, harvesting, processing, and preparing a wide variety of foods. The Anasazi established at least two types of facilities on the landscape: *habitation loci* and *limited activity loci*. Previous work (Schlanger and Orcutt 1986) suggests that habitation loci were used as residential components and were the site of several features including domestic structures, substantial shelters for inhabitants and for storing goods, and facilities for carrying out personal maintenance activities including food preparation, storage, consumption, tool manufacture, tool repair, and other activities associated with living at a residential base. Limited activity loci served as bases for activities performed at a remove from the residence and contained facilities for short-term, camping occupations. A third kind of activity, a *seasonal locus,* was introduced to the Anasazi repertoire after A.D. 600 and is associated with the development of aggregated populations residing in multihousehold villages (Kohler 1989). This facility serves as a seasonally occupied residential base located near agricultural fields and contains facilities for sheltering farmers and their produce.

The Behavioral Repertoire

The Anasazi also maintained an inventory of organizational strategies and responses to environmental stress. Their organization strategies included independent households occupying spatially segregated hamlets; multihousehold communities of aggregated, often architecturally dependent, densely occupied villages; and regionally coordinated, spatially segregated population aggregates (Cordell 1984). Social responses to local difficulties in agricultural production or to local conditions of environmental degradation were to relocate in a more productive region (Schlanger 1988) or to practice a pattern of seasonal transhumance to and from environmentally distinct bases (Powell 1983; Kohler 1989). Between the organizational responses and the settlement relocation options, the Anasazi created a cultural landscape with numerous temporarily abandoned or more permanently abandoned features that could serve as resources for later occupants and that could eventually become persistent places.

Facilities as Cultural Resources on a Landscape

The kind of use that these various "abandoned" features receive on a longterm basis depends on the scale of residential relocation. As noted by Kohler and Matthews (1988:559–560), the Anasazi moved residences at three different scales: household relocations every generation, or even more frequently (Ahlstrom 1985; Schlanger 1988:783), which may have involved very short moves; community relocations that may have occurred every few generations and that probably involved moves of 3 or more kilometers; and long-distance relocations of regional populations, which seem to have taken place every 200 to 300 years.

As the residential focus of a settlement system moves laterally across the landscape, various places previously used from the former residential locus may change roles in a very systematic way (see Binford 1983 for a discussion of these issues with regard to hunter–gatherer long-term land use patterns). If the distances involved are not prohibitive, former habitation loci may be used as bases for short stays and for logistical forays aimed at collecting materials, hunting, and so on, so that they function as limited activity loci; or they may be maintained as potential bases for agricultural operations, functioning now as seasonal loci. Former limited activity loci may be transformed into seasonal facilities or even into new residential loci as the residential focus shifts across the landscape. Former seasonal loci may be brought into service as habitation loci for the laterally shifted population, may remain in use as alternate seasonal facilities, or they may be used as limited activity loci. Of course, any or all of the former facilities may simply fall out of use as the residential focus shifts elsewhere.

Which of these possibilities is most likely? Binford's observations of modern logistically organized hunter–gatherers (Binford 1982) have led him to suggest some generalizations that may be applicable to the Anasazi situation. Binford notes that logistically used sites, which are the equivalent of the limited activity loci described for the Anasazi, tend to remain in use as logistical camps or special purpose places when the residential focus shifts across the landscape. We can expect that this situation will hold true in general for the Anasazi as well because limited activity loci are developed to take advantage of particular resources or particular landscape features and may not ordinarily be suitable for the variety of activities that must be carried out at long-term occupation loci. Former residential loci, the habitation loci of this study, tend to exhibit functional shifts from residences to special purpose places. For the Anasazi, I expect the greatest degree of functional shifting to take place at habitation loci and seasonal loci. Habitation loci and seasonal loci are close enough in overall function that former habitation loci may sometimes be called into play for seasonal use if the shifted system overlaps the old agricultural range. Former habitation loci and seasonal loci may also be used as limited activity loci as the Anasazi carried out more radical shifts in the residential focus of their settlement systems.

THE CHARACTER OF THE MODERN GROUND SURFACE RECORD

The surface archaeology of the study area was recorded in terms of "isolated finds" and "sites." Isolated finds were those artifacts that occurred in clusters of fewer than 20 items. Surface materials recorded as sites consisted of larger clusters of artifacts, often found in close proximity to architectural rubble, stains, rock alignments, or other indicators of buried features. (The survey methods used in DAP fieldwork are described in a number of DAP reports and interested readers are referred to these reports for further details [Bohnenkamp *et al.* 1982; Goulding and Orcutt 1986:137–139; Schlanger 1986:384–387]). All materials collected were examined by the lab personnel at the field laboratory operated by the Dolores Program (Blinman 1986; Phagan 1986).

The Archaeological Database

DAP survey crews identified 377 prehistoric sites and 62 isolated finds within the 9.46 sq. miles (24.5 km²) of the study area. Of the sites, 202 gave no evidence of structures or architecture on the modern ground surface, thus falling into the limited activity site category, whereas 175 contained building stone, depressions, dark ashy middens, or some combination of these attributes indicating the presence of buried structures, which makes them candidates for habitation loci or seasonal loci. Of the isolated finds recorded within the study area, half consisted of a small number of unmodified flakes and modest flake tools, one-quarter were projectile points, and the remainder were mixed, small assemblages of flakes and plain sherds, mixed assemblages of plain sherds and a projectile point, or small assemblages of plain or corrugated sherds. The plain gray sherds come from vessels that were manufactured throughout the prehistoric Anasazi occupation of the area; the corrugated sherds come from vessels manufactured after A.D. 920

(Dykeman 1986) and thus can be used as a marker for the postresidential, post-A.D. 900 occupation of the area.

The Distribution of "Sites"

Sites occur across the study area (Figure 3) but tend to cluster along a long ridge in the northern section of the study area, around the north and east margins of the area, near access routes from the Dolores River up the entrenched drainages, and just to the north of the marsh. Most are associated with ceramic assemblages indicating a pre-A.D. 900 occupation, with a smaller number of multicomponent sites representing both pre-A.D. 900 and post-A.D. 900 occupations, and an even smaller number featuring a surface ceramic assemblage that dates entirely to the post-A.D. 900 use of the area.

The Distribution of "Isolated Finds"

As a group, isolated artifacts are distributed in much the same pattern as sites (Figure 4). Finds of unmodified flakes are concentrated around the marsh, whereas finds of plain and corrugated sherds are found primarily in the northern section of the area. Mixed finds, consisting of plain gray sherds and flakes, or plain gray sherds and projectile points, are found in the south half of the area, especially in the southeastern section and near the marsh. Projectile point finds are widely distributed across the area, although, like the isolated sherd finds, they occur primarily well north of the marsh.

THE LONG-TERM USE OF THE STUDY AREA

The two kinds of surface manifestations recorded by the DAP—isolated finds and sites—yield different perspectives on the prehistoric use of the study area. The following section exploits the differences between these classes to illuminate the long-term use of the Dolores uplands.

Isolated Finds and the Dolores Landscape as a Persistent Place

Isolated finds give us an indication of the use of the area that was not tied to preexisting cultural features; they point to the use of the landscape itself as a persistent place. Most isolated finds located within the study unit could not be placed into any particular portion of the long occupation of the area and so could not be assigned either to the pre-A.D. 900, primarily residential occupation, or the post-A.D. 900, primarily nonresidential occupation. The ceramic finds are the

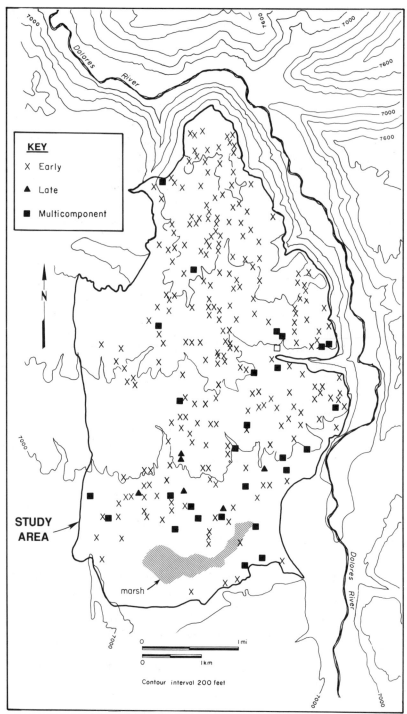

Figure 3. The distribution of sites in the study area.

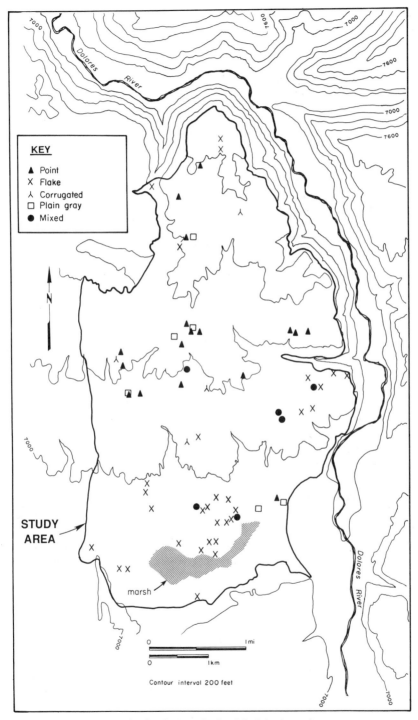

Figure 4. The distribution of isolated finds in the study area.

exception. These artifacts date to no earlier than about A.D. 600, when pottery-using Anasazi colonists first began to occupy the study area. Ordinarily, single sherds or small assemblages of fewer than 20 items such as were recorded as isolated finds cannot be confidently assigned to any particular segment of the Anasazi occupation. There are several reasons for this: The decorative styles used on Anasazi ceramics were popular for varying lengths of time; choices in Anasazi vessel decoration did not always follow a strict chronology; and systemic ceramic inventories may contain vessels produced over considerable time spans (Blinman 1988:532–534). Any single sherd may have been deposited either shortly after production or not until some time after production.

In the study area, however, the utility wares, used for cooking and for storage, show a clear change in decoration style that can be used to identify some vessels produced after A.D. 900 or A.D. 920 (Dykeman 1986; Blinman 1988:514–531). After A.D. 900, the coils forming the bodies of these vessels were pinched to produce a decoration known as corrugation. Such "corrugated" vessels were not used during the occupation of the pre-A.D. 800 hamlets, nor were they used at the villages abandoned by A.D. 900.

Isolated finds of corrugated sherds are found only in the northern two-thirds of the study area, away from the river valley. The presence of these sherds attests to an ongoing use of the uplands, at a distance from abandoned facilities (compare Figure 4 with Figure 3). Evidently, the retreat of the residential population did not bring about a complete abandonment of the study area. Active, nonresidential use of the uplands continued after the initial abandonment of the settlements and may link the periods of residential usage seen in the population reconstructions discussed at the beginning of this paper. Indeed, such continued use of an economic landscape considerably larger than the small portion in active residential use may have established precedents for eventual reoccupation as a residential locus and could allow a group of people to claim a landscape as a persistent place in the absence of an occupying population. Because of the nature of the design variation in ceramic vessels produced in the study area, it is only possible to detect the nonresidential use that follows the village abandonments. There may have been other nonresidential use periods—perhaps between the abandonment of the hamlets and the construction of the villages, or perhaps at some other times before A.D. 900, and again following the A.D. 1000 small reoccupation of the area—but it is not possible to see these shifts in the archaeological record of the Dolores uplands.

Sites and Cultural Facilities as Persistent Places

The site record yields information on the long-term use of specific parts of the study area landscape; this record is more directly tied to the use of cultural features as persistent places, or at the least, as markers of persistent places.

Multicomponent assemblages are the clearest indicators of persistent places that can be identified from the archaeological record preserved on the modern ground surface. In the Dolores study area, there are 31 such sites (Figure 5). (Because I am using surface collection data, with its attendant problems of small sample size and possible lack of congruence with subsurface deposits, these 31 cases must represent only a subset of all the places that experienced repeated occupations during the prehistoric use of the study area.) These multicomponent, persistent places are quite noticeably clustered just north and south of the marsh, along the easy access route to the uplands where the canyon walls are very low, and around the major eastern upland access route. The single multicomponent site in the north-central part of the study area is a large, multihousehold habitation abandoned as a residential facility before A.D. 900.

The Nature of Persistent Places in the Study Area

The distribution of multicomponent sites suggests that two features influenced the development of these persistent places: the marsh, or proximity to the marsh, which would allow permanent occupants and infrequent visitors to the area to exploit both good farmland and the marsh resources, and proximity to an access route to the uplands. Rather than being maintained over the long term because of unique cultural facilities, the sites were kept as part of the technological repertoire because they were located in places convenient to nonresidential users of the study area. This puts these places into the first category of persistent places discussed previously: The marsh and the access route constitute places with unique qualities, and sites nearby become persistent places because of those qualities and not because of the presence of preexisting cultural features and artifact deposits.

In this regard, it is also interesting to consider the types of facilities that are being maintained as part of the long-term occupation of the study area. Both general types of facilities—sites with architectural features and sites lacking such features—appear to have attracted use following the residential occupation of the study area. Although more than half of the 31 multicomponent sites (19 of the 31) exhibit indications of buried structures, which suggests that these were originally habitation loci or seasonal loci, contingency table analyses indicate that there is no statistically significant relationship between sites types and the frequency of multicomponent occupations. Evidently the kinds of cultural facilities originally present at reoccupied sites (at least those with a reoccupation marked by the presence of a small number of corrugated sherds on the site surface) had little bearing on the choice of the site as a persistent place. This pattern fits nicely with our current understanding of the pre-A.D. 900 architecture in the area, which consisted of mud-and-stick wall construction for the free-standing rooms (with low rock foundations), and semisubterranean, earth- and wood-roofed pit struc-

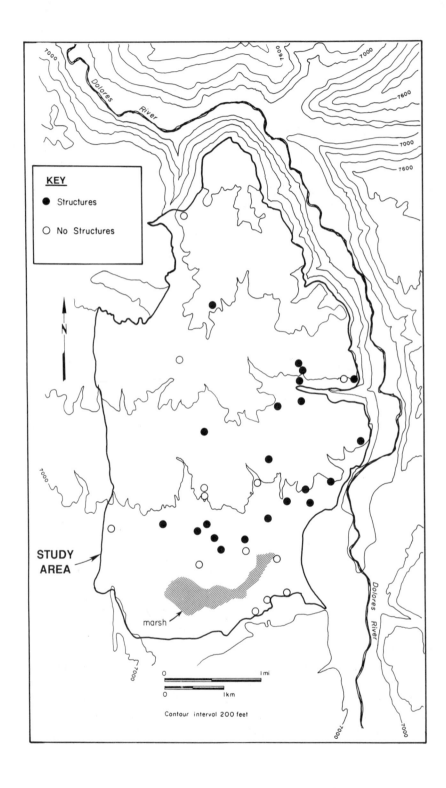

KEY

● Structures

○ No Structures

N

STUDY
AREA

marsh

Dolores River

7000

7600

7000

7600

7000

STUDY
AREA

0   1 mi

0   1 km

Contour interval 200 feet

tures for the primary habitation structures. These facilities would have decayed and collapsed rapidly after only a short abandonment and would offer little in the way of solid shelter for those returning to these sites on an intermittent basis.

THE CHANGING FUNCTION OF PERSISTENT PLACES

Finally, let me turn to the question of how places were used following the residential abandonment of the study area. The model of Anasazi settlement organization presented earlier outlines the most likely possibilities for the development of persistent places. According to this model, when residential populations withdraw from an area, limited activity loci would continue in use as limited activity loci, habitation loci might be used as seasonal loci, and seasonal loci might continue in use as either limited activity loci or seasonal loci. If the settlement shift model is correct, persistent places should be used as camps for hunting, collecting, and possibly some farming in an area at a distance from residential bases. The evidence for such shifts should be preserved in the uppermost fill of persistent places, now exposed as materials on the modern ground surface.

Surface Finds of Projectile Points as an Indicator of Functional Changes

Projectile points were chosen to open this study of long-term functional changes in the use of the study area because they are a specialized tool, used primarily as hunting weapons and as butchering implements. Discarded projectile points occurring in high frequencies at persistent places should be good evidence for hunting during the postresidential use of the landscape.

Projectile points are a common element of the surface archaeology of the study area (Figure 6). Almost one-half of the surface assemblages collected from sites (167 of 377) contained projectile points, with a total of 338 projectile points retrieved in surface collections at archaeological finds recorded as sites. A smaller, but still sizable fraction of the isolated finds, 16 of 62, contained a projectile point in the collection. Most of the modern ground surface assemblages at sites contain a single point, although 3 had close to 20. These last collections were made at sites located close to the marsh; the other collections containing more than one point are distributed more evenly across the study area.

Can I interpret high numbers of projectile points on the surface of some sites

---

Figure 5. The distribution of multicomponent, persistent places in the study area. Note the association of these sites with the landscape features in Figure 2.

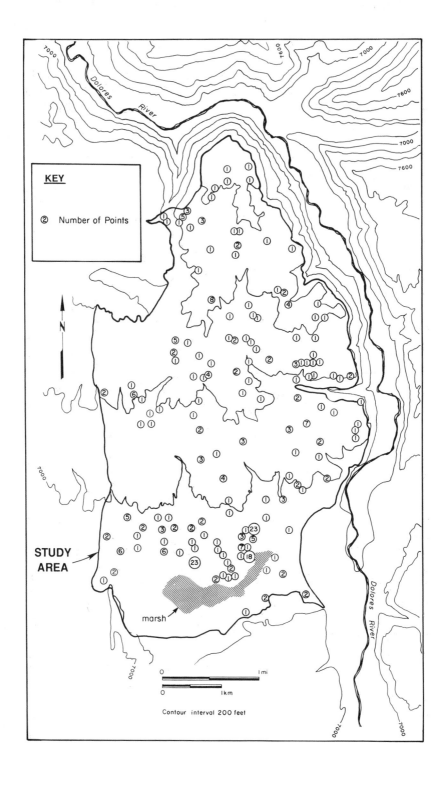

KEY

② Number of Points

N

STUDY
AREA

marsh

Dolores River

Contour interval 200 feet

7000
7600
1 mi
1 km

in the study area as evidence for hunting expeditions conducted from persistent places? That is, can I use the high number of projectile points as evidence that habitation and seasonal loci were used as limited activity loci when they became persistent places on the Dolores landscape? To answer these questions fully, I would have to be able to place individual points accurately in time, so that I could distinguish points deposited during the residential use of the area from those used later during the nonresidential occupation of the Dolores landscape. Unfortunately, this direct approach is not possible at the present time. It is possible, however, to take a more indirect approach and look at the relation between projectile points and persistent places on the Dolores landscape.

Persistent places differ from single-component sites in several significant ways. More projectile points are found in surface assemblages associated with multicomponent occupations than in single-component assemblages ($\chi^2 = 6.9$, df $= 1$, $p < 0.01$). Even more telling, significantly more projectile points are found in surface assemblages from sites in use *only after* A.D. 900 than are found in assemblages from sites occupied prior to A.D. 900 ($\chi^2 = 13.3$, df $= 1$, $p < 0.01$). In addition, places with multicomponent occupations frequently contain two or more projectile points in the surface collection, whereas surface collections made at single-component places generally yield only one or two projectile points.

Although this is not direct evidence—the points themselves are not datable except by association with ceramic assemblages—it seems reasonable to interpret these distributions as evidence of a long-term use of the study area for hunting after the residential abandonment. It is unlikely that the long-term use of the area was restricted to hunting alone, however. Persistent places seem to develop in those spots that afford good access to many parts of the Dolores area, and this suggests that there may have been a number of resources exploited from these bases. The distribution of projectile points does support the model of changes in the function of places outlined. Limited activity loci remained in use as limited activity loci. Habitation and seasonal loci may indicate that these places served as long-term limited activity loci as well.

SUMMARY AND CONCLUSIONS

The concept of the persistent place makes it possible to link the dense artifact and architectural feature concentrations we ordinarily associate with prehistoric horticulturalists and agriculturalists with the more dispersed "isolated find" record that they also generate during the course of a long-term occupation of a

Figure 6. Surface finds of projectile points in the study area. Note that the greatest number of points come from surface collections in the vicinity of the marsh.

landscape. Viewed from the standpoint of the persistent place, both at the scale of the landscape and at the smaller scale of the cultural feature, the surface archaeology of the study area gives a surprisingly detailed picture of long-term, nonresidential use of an area that was occupied by Anasazi horticulturalists for over 600 years. Previous research has focused on the use of this area for residential purposes, documenting repeated occupations and abandonments. My analysis of persistent places and their function suggests this occupation and abandonment scenario oversimplifies the actual long-term land use pattern. The distribution of temporally sensitive ceramics and functionally distinctive tools such as projectile points indicates that certain places played long-term roles in local land use patterns; such "persistent places" were maintained within the cultural repertoire even when residents had moved well out of the study area. I have concentrated here on the later occupation sequence, with its clear ceramic indicators of multicomponent, or long-term, use. The earlier portion of the occupation may also have had a similar long-term land use pattern, made archaeologically invisible by our inability to make positive temporal distinctions with the most abundant ceramics in use at this time.

The persistent places discussed here are neither strictly sites nor are they simply features of the physical landscape. For the archaeologist, they link periods of residential usage with periods of population withdrawal and apparent abandonment, filling in some details of prehistoric use previously unseen. For the prehistoric occupants of the Dolores area, these places may have maintained their claims to land or landscape during periods of population withdrawal, and established both a means and a focus for eventual reoccupation.

ACKNOWLEDGMENTS

This chapter has benefited greatly from comments and suggestions made by Jacqueline Rossignol and LuAnn Wandsnider, who invited me to present the work at their symposium at the 53rd Society for American Archaeology Annual Meeting in Phoenix, Arizona, and who then arranged for its subsequent publication in this volume. Timothy Kohler, Signa Larralde, and R. G. Matson showed extreme patience and kindness in reading through several drafts and provided me with invaluable advice on improving presentation and contents. Advice on figures and expert drafting was provided by Scott Geister, Office of Archaeological Studies, Museum of New Mexico. Victoria Atkins and Shela McFarlin of the Anasazi Heritage Center, Dolores, Colorado, helped me retrieve the Dolores Archaeological Program data used here; this material was originally gathered under Contract No. 8-07-40-S0562, Bureau of Reclamation, U.S. Department of the Interior. Financial and technical support for preparing and presenting the original paper and for preparing this version was provided by the Navajo Nation Archaeology Department, the Department of Anthropology, University of Louisville, the Committee on Research and Publications, Office of Archaeological Studies, Museum of New Mexico, and the Committee on Excellence, Museum of New Mexico.

REFERENCES

Ahlstrom, R. V. N., 1985, The Interpretation of Archaeological Tree-Ring Dates, Unpublished Ph.D. dissertation, University of Arizona, Tucson, Arizona.

Binford, L. R., 1982, The Archaeology of Place, *Journal of Anthropological Archaeology* 1:5–31.

Binford, L. R., 1983, Long-Term Land-use Patterning: Some Implications for Archaeology, in: *Lulu Linear Punctated: Essays in Honor of George Irving Quimby*, University of Michigan Museum of Anthropology *Anthropological Papers* 72 (R. C. Dunnell and D. K. Grayson, eds.), pp. 27–54.

Bintliff, J., and Snodgrass, A., 1988, Off-site Pottery Distributions: A Regional and Interregional Perspective, *Current Anthropology* 29:506–513.

Blinman, E., 1986, Additive Technologies Group Midlevel Research Design, in: *Dolores Archaeological Program Research Designs and Initial Survey Results* (A. E. Kane, W. D. Lipe, T. A. Kohler, and C. K. Robinson, compilers), Bureau of Reclamation, Engineering and Research Center, Denver, pp. 57–75.

Blinman, E., 1988, Justification and Procedures for Ceramic Dating, in: *Dolores Archaeological Program Supporting Studies: Additive and Reductive Technologies* (E. Blinman, C. J. Phagan, and R. Wilshusen, compilers), Bureau of Reclamation, Engineering and Research Center, Denver, pp. 501–544.

Bohnenkamp, W., Goulding, D. A., Goulding, S. L. B., Ives, G. A., Orcutt, J. D., and Walkenhorst, R. N., 1982, The Dolores Archaeological Program Survey Field Manual, *Dolores Archaeological Program Technical Reports* DAP-147. First draft submitted to the Bureau of Reclamation, Upper Colorado Region, Salt Lake City, in compliance with Contract No. 8-07-40-S0562.

Cherry, J. S., and Davis, J. L., 1988, High-Density Distributional Archaeology: A Mediterranean Perspective, presented at the 53rd Annual Meeting of the Society for American Archaeology, Phoenix, Arizona.

Clay, V. L., 1985, The History of the Marsh in Sagehen Flats: The Sedimentary Record, in: *Dolores Archaeological Program Studies in Environmental Archaeology* (K. L. Peterson, V. L. Clay, M. H. Matthews, and S. W. Neusius, compilers), Bureau of Reclamation, Engineering and Research Center, Denver, pp. 217–227.

Cordell, L., 1984, *Prehistory of the Southwest*, Academic Press, New York.

Dykeman, D. D., 1986, Excavations at 5MT8371, an Isolated Pueblo II Pit Structure in Montezuma County, Colorado, *San Juan County Museum Association Studies in Archaeology* 2.

Goulding, D., and Orcutt, J., 1986, Cultural Resources Survey of Dolores Project Central Impact Areas: Borrow Areas A, B, and E, Great Cut Dike and Pumping Plant, McPhee Dam Site, and McPhee Dam Site Access Road Part II, in: *Dolores Archaeological Program Research Designs and Initial Survey Results* (A. E. Kane, W. D. Lipe, T. A. Kohler, and C. K. Robinson, compilers), Bureau of Reclamation Engineering and Research Center, Denver, pp. 127–184.

Gumerman, G., (ed.), 1988, *The Anasazi in a Changing Environment*, Cambridge University Press, Cambridge.

Holliday, V. T., and Piety, L. A., 1985, Surficial Geological Investigations—1980, in: *Dolores Archaeological Program Studies in Environmental Archaeology* (K. L. Petersen, V. L. Clay, M. H. Matthews, and S. W. Neusius, compilers), Bureau of Reclamation, Engineering and Research Center, Denver, pp. 155–183.

Kohler, T. A., 1989, Field Houses and the Tragedy of the Commons in the Anasazi Southwest, presented at the 54th Annual Meeting of the Society for American Archaeology, Atlanta, Georgia.

Kohler, T. A., and Matthews, M. H., 1988, Long-Term Anasazi Land Use and Forest Reduction: A Case Study from Southwest Colorado, *American Antiquity* 53:537–564.

Lipe, W. D., 1983, The Southwest, in: *Ancient Native Americans* (J. D. Jennings, ed.), W. H. Freeman, San Francisco, pp. 421–493.

Leonhardy, F. C., and Clay, V. L., 1985a, Bedrock Geology, Quaternary Stratigraphy, and Geomorphology, in: *Dolores Archaeological Program Studies in Environmental Archaeology* (K. L. Petersen, V. L. Clay, M. H. Matthews, and S. W. Neusius, compilers), Bureau of Reclamation, Engineering and Research Center, Denver, pp. 131–137.

Leonhardy, F. C., and Clay, V. L., 1985b, Soils, in: *Dolores Archaeological Program Studies in Environmental Archaeology* (K. L. Petersen, V. L. Clay, M. H. Matthews, and S. W. Neusius, compilers), Bureau of Reclamation, Engineering and Research Center, Denver, pp. 139–153.

Matson, R. G., 1991, *The Origins of Southwestern Agriculture,* University of Arizona Press, Tucson, Arizona.

Orcutt, J. D., Blinman, E., and Kohler, T. A., 1990, Explanations of Population Aggregation in the Mesa Verde Region Prior to A.D. 900, in: *Perspectives on Southwestern Prehistory* (P. E. Minnis and C. L. Redman, eds.), Westview Press, Boulder, Colorado, pp. 196–212.

Petersen, K. L., 1985, The History of the Marsh in Sagehen Flats: The Pollen Record, in: *Dolores Archaeological Program Studies in Environmental Archaeology* (K. L. Petersen, V. L. Clay, M. H. Matthews, and S. W. Neusius, compilers), Bureau of Reclamation, Engineering and Research Center, Denver, pp. 229–238.

Petersen, K. L., 1988, Climate and the Dolores River Anasazi, *University of Utah Anthropological Papers* 113.

Petersen, K. L., and Orcutt, J. D. (compilers), 1987, *Dolores Archaeological Program Supporting Studies: Settlement and Environment,* Bureau of Reclamation, Engineering and Research Center, Denver.

Petersen, K. L., Clay, V. L., Matthews, M. H., and Neusius, S. W. (compilers), 1985, *Dolores Archaeological Program Studies in Environmental Archaeology,* Bureau of Reclamation, Engineering and Research Center, Denver.

Phagan, C., 1986, Reductive Technologies Group Midlevel Research Design, in: *Dolores Archaeological Program Research Designs and Initial Survey Results* (A. E. Kane, W. D. Lipe, T. A. Kohler, and C. K. Robinson, compilers), Bureau of Reclamation, Engineering and Research Center, Denver, pp. 79–91.

Powell, S., 1983, *Mobility and Adaptation: The Anasazi of Black Mesa,* Southern Illinois University Press, Carbondale.

Robinson, C. K., Gross, G. T., and Breternitz, D. A., 1986, Overview of the Dolores Archaeological Program, in: *Dolores Archaeological Program Final Synthetic Report* (D. A. Breternitz, C. K. Robinson, and G. T. Gross, compilers), Bureau of Reclamation, Engineering and Research Center, Denver, pp. 3–50.

Schlanger, S. H., 1986, 1982 Probabilistic Sampling Survey of Windy Ruin and Yellowjacket Crest Localities, in: *Dolores Archaeological Program Research Designs and Initial Survey Results* (A. E. Kane, W. D. Lipe, T. A. Kohler, and C. K. Robinson, compilers), Bureau of Reclamation, Engineering and Research Center, Denver, pp. 449–466.

Schlanger, S. H., 1988, Patterns of Population Movement and Long-Term Population Growth in Southwestern Colorado, *American Antiquity* 53:773–793.

Schlanger, S. H., and Orcutt, J. D., 1986, Site Surface Characteristics and Functional Inferences, *American Antiquity* 51:296–312.

Chapter 6

Artifact Reuse and Recycling in Continuous Surface Distributions and Implications for Interpreting Land Use Patterns

EILEEN L. CAMILLI AND JAMES I. EBERT

INTRODUCTION

Archaeological surface distributions have, for the past 20 years, been the subject of survey approaches that focus on the artifact as the unit of discovery and observation, and the survey unit itself within which artifacts are discovered, as the unit of analysis. These approaches, often referred to as "off-site" or "nonsite" survey methods, have been variously motivated by the relatively continuous archaeological materials found in arid lands (Thomas 1971, 1975; Irwin-Williams *et al.* 1988), by remains left over extremely long time periods and the multiple disturbance processes these undergo after deposition (Isaac and Harris 1975;

EILEEN L. CAMILLI • Department of Anthropology, University of New Mexico, Albuquerque, New Mexico 87131 and JAMES I. EBERT • Ebert and Associates, 3700 Rio Grande Boulevard NW, Suite 3, Albuquerque, New Mexico 87107.

Space, Time, and Archaeological Landscapes, edited by Jacqueline Rossignol and LuAnn Wandsnider. Plenum Press, New York, 1992.

113

Isaac 1981), by exposures of materials in modern agricultural fields (O'Brien *et al.* 1982; Dunnell 1988), or by the sporadic exposures of archaeological materials found in more heavily vegetated areas, sometimes requiring extensive shovel testing (McManamon 1986).

The archaeological surface record has, in the course of studies like these, been recognized as "an appropriate source of data independent of subsurface remains" (Dunnell and Dancey 1983:70). The argument that postdepositional processes and disturbance renders surface distributions of artifacts of little use for analysis has also been countered with the assertion that almost all assemblages, presently buried or on the surface, have been subjected to these "disarranging" processes because all assemblages are originally surface assemblages (Lewarch and O'Brien 1983). Along this vein, the spatial integrity of sealed deposits has recently been likened to no more than that of surface deposits (Ebert 1992).

If postdepositional processes do considerably influence the placement of items in the archaeological record, then an important area of inquiry is to quantify and control for these influences. Collecting archaeological data at scales of resolution compatible with the highest frequency of spatial displacement is required for recognizing the interactive roles of depositional and postdepositional processes and for determining the scales at which regional landforms interface with cultural deposits.

This study examines areas of low surface artifact density peripheral to the Rio Grande floodplain of southern New Mexico. Conventional attempts at reconstructing settlement systems from continuous low-density surfaces consider small, spatially bounded clusters of artifacts on these surfaces as the sites of temporally specific activity episodes. Debris in most locations within the study region can, however, also be viewed as representing spatially and temporally unbounded accumulations of material. Given this latter perception of the composition of archaeological surfaces, identifying activity-specific assemblages may not be a realistic analytical goal or even an attainable one. Examining the secondary use of artifacts in archaeological deposits here can, in contrast, contribute to better identification of locations with different histories of use over the long term. Further identifying differences in the tempo and degree of overlap in the reoccupation of locations can lead to a basis for distinguishing between past systems of land use.

Natural processes of deposition and erosion, their effects on the archaeological surface, and their interaction with ongoing behavioral systems must be considered in examining secondary use of archaeological deposits. Surface exposure and the visibility and discoverability of the archaeological surface record can be viewed as operating with cultural deposition in a set of interactive depositional and postdepositional processes. Differential exposure affects visibility and, thus, discoverability of archaeological surface materials in the present and has done so in the past to facilitate differential reuse of the natural and cultural landscape. The explanatory importance of these mechanisms lies in linking the surface context of the archaeological record with secondary use of items and reuse of locations that can, in turn, inform on systemic prehistoric land use. Our focus here is on correspondences between archaeological surface visibility and lithic artifact attributes indicative of artifact reuse and recycling.

TOPOGRAPHIC VARIATION IN ARTIFACT DENSITY AS A RECYCLING INDICATOR

Approximately 16,000 acres in the Mesilla Bolson of south-central New Mexico were sampled through surface survey to obtain the data presented here. The geographic province encompassing this region includes internally drained basins, or bolsons, and low mountain ranges. The Mesilla Bolson is one of a number of broad structural basins in this portion of New Mexico (Hawley 1965). West of the Rio Grande, the relict bolson floor forms a level plain, the West Mesa (O'Laughlin 1980), that extends from the international border to about 15 kilometers west of the Rio Grande valley rim scarp. The topography in most places here is dominated by sand dunes alternating with interdunal Pleistocene-floored deflations. Archaeological materials in the wind-scoured flats between dunes are not stratified, but have been deflated, or have remained since their deposition in a single horizontal layer that contains the accumulated archaeological record.

This depositional context does not, however, negate their archaeological potential. In most cultural systems, at least some and often almost all places can be expected to be reused for functionally different purposes during the course of a year (see for example, Ascher 1968; Gould 1968; Yellen 1977:67; Binford 1978a,b: Janes 1983; Newell 1987; Schiffer 1987:104). If this is the case, then the archaeological record contained in a single "stratum" may be of a composite, overlapping nature regardless of relatively constant deposition and sediment layering. Thus the archaeological record in virtually all places—buried or on the surface—may to some degree lack the vertical differentiation necessary to separate episodes of activity or occupation.

Strong associations between geologic units and archaeological surface distributions have been observed on the West Mesa (Camilli *et al.* 1988; Pierce and Durand 1988). Although previous researchers have attributed this pattern to intentional placing of camps in areas with a good view (Pierce and Durand 1988:252), redundancy in this pattern throughout the area implies the work of postdepositional agents to increase visibility of archaeological remains on elevated, exposed surfaces. Elevated surfaces experience deflation, whereas those at lower elevations are encompassed by depressions where sediment is accumulating. Highest artifact densities in the study area (Figure 1) are located on low hills

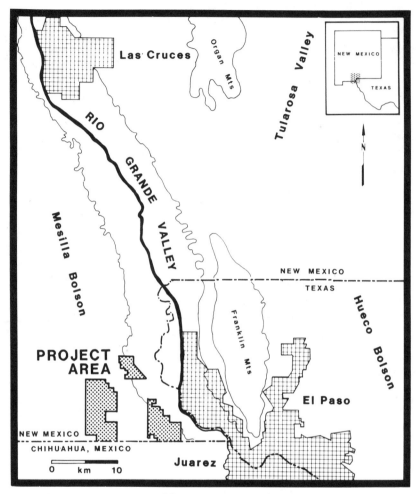

Figure 1. Location of the project area in south-central New Mexico.

and linear rises bordered by low-lying structural basins (Camilli *et al.* 1988). Linear patterns of high artifact frequency follow low scarps in the adjacent Santa Teresa study area (Pierce and Durand 1988), with highest artifact densities on the elevated points between scarps. Broken down by artifact class, groundstone concentrations were found to be restricted to areas of low scarps; chipped stone occurred more ubiquitously but with concentrations on the higher ground between scarps. These observations indicate topographic patterning in artifact density is related to depth of sand cover and, thus, degree of archaeological visibility.

Recent experimental research on the effects of natural aeolian processes on archaeological remains suggests a mechanical interpretation for differential visibility and discovery of artifacts. Wandsnider (1989:42), in the course of experimental studies in sanddunes, has found that small, thin artifacts are those first buried by windblown sand, the percentage of artifacts buried being negatively related to average artifact size. A higher proportion of small artifacts were buried at exposed experimental stations where deposition was occurring. Subsequent deflation at experimental stations resulted in the reexposure of moderate- and small-sized artifacts. These experimental results show that the differential burial of artifacts can introduce a size bias into discovered surface assemblages due to postdepositional geomorphological and mechanical processes (Dunnell 1988; Wandsnider 1988) and that such effects may become more pronounced through time.

Exposure of high frequencies of artifacts in the small to moderate size range and, therefore, high local overall artifact densities can facilitate artifact discovery, as high artifact density or clusteredness has been recognized as a major contributor to generally high artifact discovery rates (Wandsnider 1986; Camilli *et al.* 1988:5–11). Considering this effect, if differential visibility in the prehistoric past conditioned the discoverability, and thus, the availability of material for reuse or recycling, archaeological surface visibility must be considered in modeling the operation of past settlement systems. From a perspective of continuous use of the landscape, surface visibility can be seen as a variable that links the past availability of lithic materials for recycling or reuse and the contemporary discovery of archaeological materials. In the desert basins of south-central New Mexico, the most likely locations of active deflation occur on ridges and exposed scarps bounding structural basins and playas. The correspondence between artifact occurrence and topography in this region should be considered as at least partial evidence that the differential visibility of the archaeological surface in desert basins can play a role in determining what is discovered on that surface in the present, as well as in the past.

On the West Mesa lithic raw materials of all kinds (except the caliche substrate that is quarried for hearth rock) are lacking. In this raw material-poor environment, large cores and pieces of debris, hammerstones and groundstone constitute reusable items and, as such, were good candidates for caching. One attribute of caching locations proposed by Schlanger (1988) is that the locations of cached materials are marked on the landscape with features such as rock cairns. On the generally featureless West Mesa landscape, mounded accumulations of fire-altered rock and ash-stained soil, some incorporating hammerstones and groundstone fragments, may serve this purpose. Very likely, however, recognition of the relationship between topography and artifact density could have served to direct past activities requiring lithic raw materials to areas where suitable materials had been previously deposited.

Exposed surfaces where lithic resources are abundant would have served as targeted locales, that is general areas, for the reuse and/or recycling of suitable discarded lithic material in the course of activities that may also have required groundstone and hearth rock, or vice versa. In this case targeting exposed surfaces for reuse and recycling results in a kind of "feedback" process. Raw material requirements are satisfied through the use of discarded "cached" artifacts for the manufacture of new tools, and the reuse of discarded artifacts directs attention to the obvious known sources of visible discarded artifacts, exposed elevated surfaces. Requirements for chipped stone raw materials accompanied by the need for hearth rock result not only in the reuse of chipped stone cores and tools but also in the recycling of appropriate groundstone materials as chipped stone cores and other groundstone items as hearth rock. This process results in the accumulation of even higher frequencies of all artifact classes in areas where artifacts have been exposed, and therefore, available for reuse since their original discard. Although this process may, upon initial consideration, seem limited to a few unique topographic, geological, and cultural contexts, the ethnographic literature points to secondary use of this kind, commonly referred to as scavenging, as a widespread tactic for raw material provisioning (see, for example, Spier 1933:127, 130; Kelly 1934:138–141, 1964:37; Hill 1938:96–97; Stewart 1941:431, 1942:339; M. E. Opler 1946:84; Downs 1961:371; Goodwin 1971:231; M. K. Opler 1971:77; Riddell 1978:50; Fowler and Matley 1979:84; Janes 1983:26–27; Kelley 1986:204–205).

In contrast to this model, there is no justification for treating the gross amount of debris found at a place as a simple episodic phenomenon, such as optimal camp placement, rather than as a cumulative one, unless the options for raw material acquisition and lithic reduction technique have been determined. In raw-material-poor environments, introduction of carried raw material and tools and reuse of previously discarded items are the two provisioning options. By comparing technological components of a system involving the use of carried, prepared items with use of encountered, "scavenged" sources of lithic raw material in areas where raw materials are not immediately available, the relationship between manufacturing by-products and manufacturing or maintenance events could be expected to be diagnostic. Reduction of curated, carried raw materials in the form of prepared cores and tools used as "blanks" for flakes or other tools could be modeled as an efficient provisioning tactic with each manufacturing event resulting in a minimum of discarded flakes and by-products. On the other hand, if lithic materials were found and used at a place and not transported by the persons doing the immediate reduction, manufacturing events could be expected to be less efficient; more fragments could be expected to result from each manufacturing (reuse) blow.

Independent of provisioning strategy, an exponential relationship can be expected between number of production events and amount of debris given a constant amount of raw material. It must also be considered, however, that different production techniques will produce variable amounts of debris during a single production event. Bipolar smashing of core material, for example, will produce more debris than controlled percussion flaking. In the context of lithic reuse, a few inefficient production events may produce as much debris as numerous production events with controlled techniques.

Optimal camp placement may, therefore, not be indicated by abundant debris because few tools and very little debris might be left at the field locations of groups who are geared-up with curated tools regardless of the number of activities or occupations undertaken. On the other hand, reworking of previously deposited chipped stone material and inefficient production techniques can generate abundant debris. Thus reuse or recycling, in contrast to the use of carried materials, could result in greater numbers of lithic "pieces" per manufacturing event. The generalization could be made that greater raw numbers of items will be found in areas where secondary use of deposits constitutes the major mode of lithic provisioning than in areas where imported tools and debris have simply been discarded, especially in environments that lack primary sources of raw material. Over the long term many, in fact, hundreds of separate activities including reuse and recycling events may serve to reinforce a pattern of more frequent material discard and secondary use on exposed surfaces. In this context, behavioral (cultural) processes disassociate items that were used together in the past and associate other items that were not. On the West Mesa landscape these repetitive activities included the recycling of groundstone into hearth features, observed in most areas except those where the caliche substrate is readily accessible. Another such activity is the discard of potential core material in such a way that, over the long term, the landscape may be furnished with it in most places.

A reuse and recycling strategy for raw material provisioning also introduces interplay between the episodic use of places and previously discarded archaeological materials at these places. Reuse and recycling of core material and hearth rock result in the recurrent, short-distance movement of these items, and can, thus, serve to associate in a very systematic fashion items that were never used together in the past. Natural depositional and postdepositional processes further insure that artifacts are differentially visible, and therefore available, while artifact recycling and reuse is ongoing. Systemic interaction between cultural and natural processes occurs in this way to pose another disjuncture in the continuum between activities and their archaeological equivalents—a continuum that conventional methods of site interpretation seek to reconstruct in a far more simplistic manner.

LITHIC REUSE AND RECYCLING ON THE WEST MESA

Comparison of lithic assemblage characteristics between the West Mesa and adjacent physiographic zones where raw materials are abundant point to the common practice of lithic reuse on the interior West Mesa (Camilli 1988). Because local lithic raw materials on the West Mesa are restricted to obsidian and chert nodules less than 6 cm in diameter, secondary use of archaeological deposits constituted a major form of raw material provisioning. Almost all lithic material here, has, in fact, been imported, with major primary sources located along the Rio Grande floodplain and in the Franklin Mountains to the east. Here we control for the abundance of secondary source materials, in the form of archaeological surface deposits, on the West Mesa itself by differentiating between surfaces with low and high visibility, to examine artifact reuse within this region.

The terms *reuse* and *recycling* are applied here to different mechanisms for the reworking and use of discarded materials. The term *recycling* is used to mean secondary use of items whose original function changes (see Schiffer 1976:38). The reworking of groundstone as hearth rock or as chipped stone cores are two examples of recycling. *Reuse* consists of secondary use whereby the original function of objects is maintained. Secondary use and scavenging, therefore, refer to both reuse and recycling. Discarded materials that have not undergone secondary use have been viewed as entering into an archaeological context removed from ongoing behavioral processes (Schiffer 1972:158–159, 1987:28). Recognizing discarded items as potentially reusable or recyclable adds another dimension to models of artifact life histories because refuse may be "reborn"; and, discarded objects may, through secondary use, function as agents in the interaction between depositional and postdepositional processes.

Differentiating between reuse and recycling is important for modeling secondary use of chipped stone artifacts. Unless evidence for refashioning a previously shaped tool edge is present, chipped stone reuse, in the form of further reduction of "core" material, is not directly observable in the archaeological record. The form, and thus the extent of reduction, of parent core material can be deduced, however, from flake attributes by distinguishing among flakes produced during initial as opposed to final stages of a reduction sequence. If this distinction can be made, attributes indicative of later reduction sequences provide one line of evidence for reuse of core materials.

Chipped stone artifacts may also be produced through recycling of groundstone with hammerstones, manos, and metates recycled as core material to produce flakes and other tools. Attributes indicative of recycling in this context include those related to early stages of a core-reduction sequence because groundstone and hammerstones essentially possess the attributes of lithic raw materials, that is, a cortical rind and little previous reduction by means of percussion flaking.

Flake debris exhibiting the attributes indicative of late-stage reduction may predominate in places that have witnessed extensive reworking of exposed archaeological lithic deposits in the form of reuse. Reuse will occur when scavenged core materials can yield flakes within the size range of those preferred for utilization. Recycling, on the other hand, would lead to the opposite effect with high frequencies of flake debris produced during initial or early stages of core reduction where archaeological deposits are exposed and, thus, accessible for secondary use.

If lack of archaeological visibility limits the availability of potential core material in surface deposits, then more reuse as evidenced by a greater degree of core reduction should occur in areas of low visibility. Factors reducing archaeological visibility on the West Mesa include heavy sand cover that restricts available surface materials to localized deposits. Where surface remains are highly visible, widespread, and thus locally available, on the other hand, less reduction should occur because core materials are more readily accessible. On the West Mesa, areas of high visibility include the elevated surfaces exposed to the prevailing southwesterly winds.

The issue of visibility is also important for considering groundstone recycling. Although recycling groundstone as hearth rock was a common practice prehistorically, the source of the largest volume of rock used in hearths on the West Mesa is calcium carbonate caliche deposits that floor a Pleistocene soil horizon. Caliche outcrops on exposed surfaces scoured of loose sediment. Where it is easily quarried, caliche was more frequently used as hearth rock. Deflated surfaces where archaeological visibility is high contain features incorporating both quarried caliche and groundstone hearth rock. In areas where the caliche substrate is deeply buried, its inaccessibility should cause groundstone recycling to be an attractive option for hearth rock procurement. Because a considerable volume of material is necessary for roasting with heated rock, a common practice in this area, localized and less visible archaeological deposits may not have permitted recycling of an adequate amount discarded groundstone. Less use of facilities that incorporate hearth rock, therefore, may occur in areas of low surface visibility for this reason.

RELATING SECONDARY USE TO POSTDEPOSITIONAL AND BEHAVIORAL PROCESSES

The action of aeolian processes on the coppice dune topography of the West Mesa results in differential visibility, and therefore, discoverability of artifacts. If these processes were acting in the past to facilitate secondary use of surface deposits, as asserted here, the abundance of debris and type of secondary use of lithic materials should vary between locations with contrasting degrees of archaeological visibility. Our purpose will be to demonstrate the prevalence of secondary use of deposits, in the form of groundstone recycling, on surfaces with a high visibility and to contrast degree of lithic artifact reuse between surfaces with low and high visibility.

Assemblages are first partitioned into groups for which contrasting visibility can be argued. Amount of lithic waste is also controlled in examining secondary use of deposits. Waste production can be anticipated as heaviest for locations hosting long-term occupations but may also result from repeated reuse and recycling events. In the latter case, reuse may result in flake attributes indicative of more intensive core reduction even though debris abundance is similar to that of a long-term occupation. Assemblages are classed, based on debris abundance to control variation in amount of core reduction, without distinguishing between occupation types.

Distributional Survey Techniques

Surface data examined here were collected through distributional archaeological survey. A 4.48 km² sample of the study area was investigated with a distributional survey that employed features and artifact attributes as units of mapping and data recording. Survey, discovery, and recording processes were planned and executed in several ways that differ from the procedures employed by traditional surveys. Data recovery was organized around three separate crews, a discovery crew, a data recording crew, and a mapping crew. The discovery crew was responsible for locating artifacts and features and providing summary discovery information with which to guide later analysis and mapping. Survey units were laid out as 400 × 400 meter quadrats and surveyed with a crew spacing of 5 meters. Five surveyors pinflagged the locations of discovered artifact and features with orange-colored pinflags in each of 16 survey sweeps.

Analysis crews subsequently logged numbers assigned to artifacts and artifact grids while performing a detailed infield analysis of lithic and ceramic artifacts. In addition, analysis crews commonly discovered other artifacts that they flagged with red-colored pinflags (Flag color was coded as one of the artifact attributes). All surface features encountered were also described with a consistent format. In instances where dense artifactual materials occurred over limited areas, a 1 × 1 meter grid system was superimposed on the distribution and artifact locations subsequently recorded by grid squares. Mapping crews recorded the locations of numbered artifacts, features, and grids in a consecutive tally with an electronic distance meter. The angle and distance to each artifact or feature marker, or grid corner in the case of gridded surfaces, was recorded from a mapping station established in each unit. Eight 400 × 400 meter and five 800 × 800 meter survey units containing 40,350 artifacts and 155 surface-visible features were recorded in this manner.

Surface Visibility and Debris Production

The cumulative areal extent of surface artifact distributions is used to contrast visibility between surveyed areas with survey quadrats providing the analytical framework for discriminating between surfaces. The surface area of distributions was devised by summing the areas in which artifacts were found to cluster for each of 12 selected 400 × 400 meter survey quadrats. Associations of artifacts were first devised by clustering the x and y locational coordinates of recorded items using a centroid sorting procedure (see Camilli et al. 1988). These clusters of spatially concentrated material lie on portions of interdunal surfaces where aeolian sediment has been deflated to expose the artifact-bearing substrate. Using the clustering procedure, interdunal distributions were divided into relatively compact associations, the center points of which are located no more than 20 meters from one another. Cluster area was calculated using the range of x and y coordinates occurring between the 75th and the 25th percentile that were then included in a formula for the derivation of the area of an oval (see Camilli et al. 1988). The average cluster area is 49.62 square meters, and average artifact density in clusters is less than 1 per square meter.

The topography of this region lends itself to the use of a measure of cluster area as an indicator of the degree of exposed artifact-bearing surface. Photointerpretation of ground surface cover types in this region reveals that two topographic zones dominate the West Mesa (Nials 1988). Mesquite coppice dunes cover an estimated 25 to 60% of the surface in one zone with local relief from 2 to 5 meters. Vegetation includes mesquite (*Prosopis glandulosa*) as the primary anchor for coppice accumulations, although some accumulations also occur with saltbush (*Atriplex canascens*) and yucca (*Yucca elata*). Archaeological manifestations in this zone have been rated by means of photointerpretation as highly visible where not covered by modern dunes. A yucca dunes zone includes dunes with 1 to 3 meters of relief where anchoring vegetation is primarily yucca. Interdunal deflations expose only an estimated 10% or less of the substrate here. Archaeological visibility in this zone has been rated as very low, with the exception of localized areas near some deflations. Both zones also encompass depressions .5 km or larger in maximum dimension interpreted as relict large-scale deflation basins. Depressions are floored by a partially modern sand sheet insuring low archaeological visibility.

The extensive exposure of archaeological materials within portions of the dune zones emphasizes the continuous nature of surface distributions in these areas. Assuming relatively continuous distributions of archaeological surface material partially obscured by accumulations of aeolian sediment in dunes, summed artifact cluster area represents the amount of exposed archaeological surface. The exposed surface in 12 quadrats, measuring 400 meters on a side, is comprised of some 864 artifact clusters (Table 1). The proportion of quadrat area represented by summed cluster area in each quadrat is offered here as a measure of degree of archaeological surface exposure. The proportion of cluster area in quadrats, each of which are approximately .16 km^2 in size, ranges from less than 0.01% to almost 5%. Using the mean 2.22%, quadrats were divided into two groups classed as having relatively low and high degrees of surface exposure.

The frequency of lithic angular debris is used to class assemblages into groups reflecting different amounts of waste production. Angular debris is not the end product of a production sequence like unutilized flakes or tools that may have been manufactured elsewhere and subsequently imported; it may, thus, reflect waste production more directly than other types of lithic items. Assemblages fall into four groups: those (1) lacking debris altogether, (2) with 1 to 2 pieces of debris, (3) with 3 to 9 pieces of debris and (4) with greater than 10 pieces of debris (Table 2). Close to half of all clusters contain no angular debris. These low frequency clusters average 2 flakes and a single piece of groundstone. A third of the clusters have a debris count of between 3 and 9, averaging 8 flakes, 5 pieces of groundstone, and a single utilized item. Five percent of clusters contain more than 10 pieces of debris, chipped and ground stone frequency averaging 50. Weak positive correlations between small cores (those less than 6 cm in maximum dimension) and flakes, debris, utilized tools and hearth rock indicate that some waste buildup accompanies tool manufacture for assemblages in Groups 3 and 4

Table 1.   Surface Exposure as Measured by Cluster Area and Artifact Frequency

Survey area	Number of clusters	Cluster Area/quadrat area[a]	Mean cluster area[b]	Mean cluster artifact frequency	Mean cluster artifact density[b]
45NE	102	0.0363	56.95	13.49	0.23
45NW	81	0.0287	56.75	19.96	0.35
45SE	142	0.0402	45.37	33.76	0.74
48NE	32	0.0065	32.62	6.71	0.20
48NW	58	0.0193	53.48	17.87	0.33
48SE	6	0.00004	2.18	2.00	0.91
48SW	29	0.0052	29.00	20.00	0.68
25	74	0.0222	48.22	22.43	0.46
32	48	0.0107	37.20	14.25	0.38
50	92	0.0277	48.86	22.65	0.46
75	128	0.0494	62.98	15.92	0.35
110	75	0.0209	43.31	16.84	0.38
Total	864				
Means		0.0222	49.65	20.05	0.71

[a] Total quadrat area averges .16 km^2.
[b] m^2.

Table 2. Artifact Clusters by Angular Debris and Exposure Classes

Archaeological visibility	Angular debris count				
	Absent	1–2	3–9	>10	Total
High	226	182	106	31	545
	41.47	33.39	19.45	5.69	63.08
Low	152	102	52	13	319
	47.65	31.91	16.30	4.08	36.92
Total	378	284	158	44	864
	43.75	32.87	18.29	5.09	100.00

(Table 3). These relationships do not hold in Group 1 and 2 assemblages suggesting extremely short-term events or event sequences are represented. In addition, the occurrence of small cores is weakly correlated with that of large ones (over 6 cm maximum dimension) for Groups 1 and 3, implying that as core material is consumed, some new core material is resupplied. Groundstone fragments and groundstone recycled as hearth rock increase together in all groups possibly indicating continuous recycling, whereas utilized and undifferentiated flakes do the same indicating production of flake waste along with discard of flake tools.

Clusters are segregated by degree of surface exposure and debris abundance in Table 2. This classification yields more clusters in the "high" surface exposure class with survey units in the "low" exposure class, evidencing expectably fewer localized exposures of the artifact-bearing substrate. Slightly higher percentages of clusters in the low surface exposure category occur in low-frequency angular debris classes, as well. Distributions of the clusters among angular debris categories are, thus, determined to some extent by surface visibility with fewer high-density artifact clusters discovered in units classed as those with low surface exposure.

Recycled Groundstone, Hearth Use, and Surface Visibility

Impromptu gathering of discarded groundstone artifacts and previously quarried caliche constitute efficient hearth construction methods in this region given the difficulty of mining fresh rock from the caliche substrate. That groundstone artifacts are recycled as hearth rock regardless of their degree of use-wear indicates expedient appropriation of discarded groundstone rather than anticipated recycling of well-worn, stockpiled artifacts.

An activity-specific dichotomy between hearths containing burned caliche and those containing other rock types as proposed by O'Laughlin (1979:69) is not indicated by the contents of West Mesa hearths because rock types are often

Table 3. Lithic Type Correlations[a] among Assemblages
Segregated by Debris Count

Types		Debris count		
r	0	1–2	3–9	>10
Prob(r)	n = 378	n = 284	n = 158	n = 44
Small cores/flakes	0.032	0.084	0.324	0.359
	0.531	0.154	0.0001	0.016
Small cones/large cores	0.147	0.004	0.206	−0.046
	0.004	0.934	0.009	0.764
Small cones/nonlocal	−0.001	−0.062	0.167	0.391
hearth rock	0.976	0.291	0.035	0.008
Small cones/angular debris		0.018	0.281	0.350
	—	0.760	0.0003	0.019
Small cones/utilized items	0.007	0.057	0.265	0.514
	0.884	0.335	0.0007	0.0004
Utilized items/angular		0.110	0.254	0.582
debris	—	0.062	0.001	0.0001

[a] Pearson's Product Moment Correlation Coefficient.

mixed within a single feature. Burned rock features that contain recycled ground-stone also invariably contain burned caliche, which has been locally quarried, but the reverse is not true. Some features containing abundant quarried caliche do not contain other rock types. Nor does variety in hearth rock types necessarily suggest that distance from rock sources dictates rock type used as suggested by Carmichael (1983:201) because caliche arid discarded groundstone can be considered "locally" available materials. The quantity of hearth rock required for processing may be a more likely determinant of hearth rock type because, due to low archaeological densities, only large volumes of caliche can be used.

The burned and angular appearance of groundstone whether or not it was discovered incorporated in hearths and roasting pits is evidence that pieces of groundstone have been recycled. About 30% of sandstone and volcanic ground-stone and about 46% of quartzite groundstone appear to be burned. The size range of quartzite is skewed toward smaller items as it is an extremely friable rock type. Because of this characteristic, quartzite frequencies are not a good representation of rock volume and are not included in this analysis. In addition to groundstone, burned and angular sandstone and crystalline volcanic rocks exhibiting no ground surfaces are also treated here as recycled groundstone, because they are nonlocal rock probably imported in the form of groundstone.

Highest densities of features containing hearth rock are present in areas of highest visibility (Table 4). Feature densities were arrived at using summed cluster area to control for amount of exposed surface. Average feature densities also tend to increase with greater surface visibility, as measured by the percentage of exposed archaeological surface, pointing to more use of hearths on high visibility surfaces. The tendency is also for more groundstone to occur as hearth rock than as unrecycled artifacts on some surfaces with higher visibility, and, expectably, more caliche than recycled groundstone is used in features on surfaces with greater visibility as well. Comparing angular debris classes (Table 5), mean groundstone hearth rock and groundstone artifact frequencies are highest for assemblages with abundant debris in areas of high visibility. Similar-sized assemblages, in terms of chipped stone debris frequency, in low visibility areas have significantly fewer groundstone artifacts. These comparisons point to a tendency for more hearth construction, heaviest use of groundstone implements, and more recycling of groundstone artifacts on surfaces with higher visibility.

Table 4. Features, Groundstone, and Hearth Rock Compared with Archaeological Surface Visibility in Survey Units

Survey unit	Feature density[a]	Groundstone hearth rock: Groundstone artifacts	Caliche: Groundstone hearth rock	Percentage exposed archaeological surface
48SW	0.00	0.84	0.98	0.52
48NE	0.00	1.11	0.43	0.65
32	0.56	0.92	2.25	1.07
48NW	1.28	0.66	0.95	1.93
110	1.23	0.87	3.67	2.09
25	1.12	1.57	0.40	2.22
50	1.11	1.01	0.46	2.77
45NW	1.30	1.06	6.29	2.87
45NE	1.89	1.09	3.64	3.63
45SE	2.17	1.31	1.78	4.02
75	0.62	0.83	0.80	4.94

[a] Number/1000m^2 exposed archaeological surface.

Table 5. Groundstone Artifact and Recycled Groundstone
Frequencies in Assemblages

Angular debris class	Groundstone type	Number of clusters	Artifact			Standard deviation
			Mean	Minimum	Maximum	
		High visibility units				
0	Fire-altered groundstone	109	1.41	0	22.0	2.82
	Groundstone	109	0.91	0	6.0	1.09
1–2	Fire-altered groundstone	108	2.15	0	12.0	2.27
	Groundstone	108	0.98	0	10.0	1.58
3–9	Fire-altered groundstone	86	4.94	0	71.0	9.75
	Groundstone	86	1.90	0	11.0	2.06
>10	Fire-altered groundstone	28	7.39	1.0	17.0	4.82
	Groundstone[a]	28	4.39	0	14.0	2.98
		Low visibility units				
0	Fire-altered groundstone	89	1.49	0	13.0	1.79
	Groundstone	89	0.61	0	4.0	0.08
1–2	Fire-altered groundstone	60	2.10	0	11.0	2.69
	Groundstone	60	0.83	0	4.0	0.95
3–9	Fire-altered groundstone	46	3.34	0	26.0	4.74
	Groundstone	46	2.30	0	12.0	2.92
>10	Fire-altered groundstone	12	4.91	1.0	12.0	3.34
	Groundstone	12	1.41	0	8.0	2.23

[a] Groundstone frequency compared between high visibility and low visibility units.
KS = 0.305; D = 0.666; KSa = 1.93; Prob > KSa = 0.0011.

Lithic Artifact Reuse and Surface Visibility

Assemblages on low and high visibility surfaces were also compared for degree of core reduction to determine the extent of lithic artifact reuse on each.

Building upon previous studies, a measure of flake reduction stage was calculated for those flakes determined to lack distal fracturing. This measure informs on the extent of core reduction and, in turn, on the potential degree of secondary use experienced by surface assemblages. A number of attributes have been used to monitor the position of flakes along a reduction continuum with flake size, number of dorsal scars, platform damage, and amount of dorsal cortex having been shown to be some of the more sensitive indicators of reduction stage (Phagan 1976; Magne and Pokotylo 1980, 1981).

Dorsal scar count density, flake thinness, amount of dorsal cortex, and platform type were incorporated into a measure of flake reduction stage. Dorsal scar count density is a standardized measure of number of dorsal scars divided by flake length. This index ensures that the number of dorsal scars is not automatically tied to flake size. An index of flake thinness was calculated dividing flake length by thickness to distinguish among flake shapes. Platform types include missing, cortical, single-facet and multifaceted platforms. Cortex was recorded in four categories: none, 1–50%, 51–99%, and 100%. Because each of these attributes possesses a different numerical range, each was scaled to range between 0 and 10 and then summed for each complete flake.

A scaled index of flake stage was also set to range from 0 to 10 with 10 indicating late stage reduction. Flake stage was found to be a useful general indicator of degree of core reduction by comparing subjectively classified un-differentiated, biface reduction and pressure flake types. The stage measure proved to be consistent with expectations for measures of reduction stage for these types (Camilli *et al*. 1988), although in retrospect it may better distinguish between production techniques as they reflect reduction stage rather than simply degree of core reduction. This is because increasingly thinner flakes are produced during bifacial reduction. Examining only flakes produced from undifferentiated, as opposed to bifacial, cores, a measure of flake size rather than flake thinness may better inform of reduction stage. Flake length does, however, correlate in a negative and significant fashion with the reduction stage measure for chert and volcanic flakes in the undifferentiated category $(p[r] = .0001)$. As the stage index increases, then, flake size decreases as would be expected for flakes produced from increasingly reduced core material.

Assemblages from survey units differing in their degree of archaeological visibility were compared for flake stage in each of the four debris classes (Table 6). Flake reduction stage does not differ between assemblages in the high and low visibility categories for the three debris classes with little or no debris. Where debris production was abundant in the fourth debris class, a difference in flake stage does exist between high and low visibility surfaces. Surface assemblages in areas of low visibility have a higher measure of flake reduction stage. This difference implies heavier reuse of lithic artifacts where archaeological surfaces are less visible. If, in fact, reuse does determine this pattern, more debris should be accompanied by more reuse in low visibility assemblages. Degree of core reduction as measured by flake stage, should not, however, necessarily increase with amount of debris in high visibility assemblages where secondary material sources may not have been as restricted.

Comparing low visibility assemblages among debris classes, flake stage and debris frequency do increase together in a fairly consistent fashion for chert and

Table 6. Comparison of Chert and Volcanic Flake Reduction
Stage for Visibility and Debris Classes

Debris class	Visibility class	N	Mean	Standard Deviation
Chert				
0	High	136	4.70	1.56
	Low	46	4.98	1.57
1–2	High	251	5.05	1.55
	Low	57	4.77	1.86
3–9	High	393	5.03	1.53
	Low	143	5.02	1.54
>10[a]	High	470	4.94	1.66
	Low	133	5.31	1.47
Volcanic				
0	High	57	4.43	1.66
	Low	33	3.98	1.84
1–2	High	98	4.33	1.60
	Low	44	4.58	1.60
3–9	High	202	4.23	1.64
	Low	71	4.29	1.57
>10[b]	High	163	4.36	1.67
	Low	64	5.15	1.47

[a] 3-9 and >10 debris classes compared for chert low visibility group. KS = 0.066;
D = 0.16; KSa = 1.64; Prob > KSa = 0.009.
[b] 3-9 and >10 debris classes compared for volcanic low visibility group. KS =
0.119; D = 0.266; KSa = 1.805; Prob > KSa = 0.003.

volcanic material types. Flake stage differs in a significant fashion for both material types when compared between the two highest debris classes within the low visibility group (Table 6). Directionality in a measure of flake stage as it relates to debris frequency is not, however, apparent for assemblages in high visibility areas for which measures of flake stage remain relatively constant among debris classes. This dichotomy between high and low visibility assemblages can be offered as evidence that raw material provisioning was satisfied with a reuse option to a greater degree on surfaces with low visibility than it was on those with high visibility. Some lower measures of volcanic flake stage on high visibility surfaces may also be attributed in part to more recycling, the use of groundstone for producing chipped stone tools, which introduces flakes produced during initial stages of core reduction. Widespread recycling here may not have been linked to areas of heaviest lithic tool production, checking directionality in a flake stage measure with respect to debris abundance.

CONCLUSIONS: SECONDARY USE OF ARCHAEOLOGICAL DEPOSITS AND IMPLICATIONS FOR INTERPRETING PAST LAND USE PATTERNS

Where sources of secondary raw material are limited in areas of low visibility, the degree to which core material has been reduced indicates chipped stone reuse as a prevalent provisioning strategy. Where surfaces exhibit high archaeological visibility, and thus contain more widely available deposits of secondary raw material, less core reduction, and by implication less reuse of discarded material, is observed. Recycling of groundstone is more prevalent in areas with highest archaeological visibility. These are places that witness more use of hearth features where both primary and secondary sources of hearth rock are abundant. More frequent manufacturing of chipped stone on high visibility surfaces is also linked to areas where use of groundstone implements was heaviest. Groundstone recycling and chipped tool manufacture do not co-occur to this extent on low visibility surfaces where less use and recycling of groundstone is observed at places containing largest chipped stone assemblages.

Differences implied for the secondary use of chipped stone and groundstone deposits also suggest that the spatial structure of deposits should vary between areas differing in archaeological visibility due to the interplay of depositional and postdepositional processes. A greater degree of core reduction on heavily used, low visibility surfaces indicates small pockets of exposed artifact-bearing substrate in areas of low visibility may experience superimposed events, that is, deposition from recurrent occupations will be horizontally restricted. Where the entire artifact-bearing surface exposed in these areas, small high-density accumulations should punctuate the surface distribution. Where, in contrast, surface visibility is high, less depositional overlap, and thus, greater horizontal spread of cultural deposits, could be expected due to more widespread availability and use of secondary lithic sources. The spatial structure of the surface distribution in areas of high visibility can be seen as formed through a feedback process of deposition, exposure, and repetitive secondary use of deposits due to the ubiquitous potential for recycling.

Circumscribed versus continuous distributions in areas of fluctuating surface visibility can implicate systems of land use for which advantageous positioning of occupations on the landscape differ. Anticipated reuse of locations such as seasonal residences in relatively sedentary system, for example, may be accompanied by superimposition of deposits (Binford 1982:21; Camilli 1983:64; Kelley 1985:202–284). Alternatively, cultural deposits may be overlain to varying degrees when targeted locales (general areas, *sensu* Wandsnider 1989:164), rather than particular locations, are repeatedly occupied. This latter pattern of landscape use, which is in part determined by the presence of cultural deposits from previous occupations, is attributed to mobile systems for which the settlement role of locations varies through time (see Binford 1982, 1983).

With greater group mobility, feedback between depositional and postdepositional processes can be expected. Given a pattern of reoccupation of locales, rather than superimposed reuse of particular locations, selection may have been against repeated use of portions of the landscape for which archaeological visibility is low. If camp placement was instead directed to the general areas of previous occupations where extensive archaeological deposits were exposed, a pattern of multiple overlapped occupation would be reinforced in high visibility areas. A strategy of group movement tied to the actual locations of previous occupations in a sedentary system may not experience the same type of feedback. Where reoccupation is restricted to particular, known locations, archaeological visibility in the past may not have been a determining factor for camp placement.

Interpretations utilizing archaeologically derived "camps" in the southern basins of New Mexico can be questioned in light of the potential for repeated occupation of exposed archaeological surfaces over the long term. In this region, the slopes and hilltops around playas and basins constitute surfaces that are exposed to a greater degree than other places in central desert basins. Most surveys of interior desert basin settings have noted "site" locations near playas, a pattern that may be the result of behavioral processes similar to those interpreted for the West Mesa. Beckes and Dibble (1977:76) observed open occupations located "adjacent to a complex of small playas in the central basin" on the McGregor Range. There is a significant tendency for camp and activity areas (sites less than 1 hectare or lacking one of the three major artifact classes) in the Western Hueco Bolson (Piggot 1978:227) to be located within 300 meters of playa rims. In the Eastern Hueco Bolson, camps of all phases were found to be significantly associated with areas within 300 meters of playa rims; 48% of Mesilla Phase sites occur within 450 meters of playa rims, and a significant number of El Paso Phase sites within 1,200 meters of playa rims (Pigott 1978:227). Carmichael (1983:130) also suggests that shifts in site location with more sites oriented around playas may be indicated for the El Paso Phase in Tularosa Basin.

If these documented locations of archaeological sites in desert basins can be attributed to differential surface visibility in the past as well as in the present, then it can be appreciated that reconstructing settlement patterns with associations of artifacts and features that may have never been used together in the past cannot be reliably accomplished. In this context, sites may not be attributable to specific functions or time periods.

In the case of the desert basins of southern New Mexico, identifying portions of the landscape for which archaeological visibility differed prehistorically could, however, be a first step toward isolating surface distributions attributable to aspects of systems differing in their degree of mobility. Attempting to understand how systems were mapped and remapped onto landscapes first dictates field data collection techniques alternative to those that record spatially limited sites, requiring a continuous surface document for recognizing appropriate scales of observation. From the perspective of a continuous and cumulative archaeological record, inferring mobility patterns from the spatial structure of surface distributions in the context of prevailing patterns of archaeological visibility is a more valuable exercise than reconstructing settlement patterns within cultural–historical sequences by attempting to first isolate spatially and temporally restricted surface associations. Pursuing the former course concedes that archaeological associations result from long-term depositional and postdepositional processes. Rather than causing the problem of "multicomponency" for reconstructing settlement systems from an archaeological surface document, however, the reuse of areas and the secondary use of discarded materials can be extended as basic behavioral processes to most places used in the past.

REFERENCES

Ascher, Robert, 1968, Time's Arrow and the Archaeology of a Contemporary Community, in: *Settlement Archaeology* (K. C. Chang, ed.), National Press, Pal Alto, pp. 43–52.

Beckes, Michael, and Dibble, David S., 1977, The Prehistoric Resource, in: *A Cultural Resource Inventory and Assessment of McGregor Guided Missile Range*, Texas Archaeological Survey Research Report 65(1), The University of Texas at Austin, pp. 1–85.

Binford, Lewis R., 1978a, Dimensional Analysis of Behavior and Site Structure: Learning from an Eskimo Hunting Stand, *American Antiquity* 43:330–361.

Binford, Lewis R., 1978b, *Nunamiut Ethnoarchaeology*, Academic Press, New York.

Binford, Lewis R., 1982, The Archaeology of Place, *Journal of Anthropological Archaeology* 1:5–31.

Binford, Lewis R., 1983, Long-Term Land Use Patterns: Some Implications for Archaeology, in: *Lulu Linear Punctated: Essays in Honor of George Irving Quimby* (Robert C. Dunnell and D. K. Grayson, eds.), Anthropological Papers, Museum of Anthropology, University of Michigan, Number 72, pp. 27–54.

Camilli, Eileen L., 1983, Site Occupational History and Lithic Assemblage Structure: An Example from Southeastern Utah, Unpublished Ph.D. Dissertation, Department of Anthropology, University of New Mexico.

Camilli, Eileen L., 1988, Interpreting Long Term Land Use Patterns from Archaeological Landscapes, in: *Issues in Archaeological Surface Survey: Meshing Method and Theory* (LuAnn Wandsnider and James I. Ebert, eds.), *American Archaeology* 7(1):57–64.

Camilli, Eileen L., Wandsnider, LuAnn, and Ebert, James I., 1988, Distributional Survey and Excavation of Archaeological Landscapes in the Vicinity of El Paso, Texas, New Mexico Bureau of Land Management, U.S. Government Printing Office, Washington, D.C.

Carmichael, David L., 1983, Archaeological Survey in the Southern Tularosa Basin, New Mexico, Ms. on file, Environmental Protection Office, Directorate of Engineering and Housing, Fort Bliss Air Defense Center, Fort Bliss, Texas.

Downs, James F., 1961, *Washo Religion*, University of California Press, Berkeley.

Dunnell, Robert C., 1988, Low-Density Archaeological Records from Plowed Surfaces: Some Preliminary Considerations, in: *Issues in Archaeological Surface Survey: Meshing Method and Theory* (LuAnn Wandsnider and James I. Ebert, eds.), *American Archaeology* 7(1):29–37.

Dunnell, Robert C., and Dancey, William S., 1983, The Siteless Survey: A Regional Scale Data Collection Strategy, in: *Advances in Archaeological Method and Theory*, Vol. 6 (Michael B. Schiffer, ed.), Academic Press, New York, pp. 267–287.

Ebert, James I., 1992, *Distributional Archaeology*, University of New Mexico Press, Albuquerque.

Fowler, Donald D., and Matley, John F., 1979, *Material Culture of the Numa; the John Wesley Powell Collection 1867–1880*, Smithsonian Institution Press, Washington, D.C.

Goodwin, Grenville, 1971, *Western Apache Raiding and Warfare from the Notes of Grenville Goodwin* (Keith H. Basso, ed., with assistance from E. W. Jernigan and W. B. Kessel), University of Arizona Press, Tucson.

Gould, Richard A., 1968, Living Archaeology: The Ngatatjara of the Western Australian Desert, *Southwestern Journal of Anthropology* 24:101–122.

Hawley, John W., 1965, Geomorphic Surfaces along the Rio Grande Valley from El Paso, Texas to Caballo Reservoir, New Mexico, in: *Guidebook of Southwestern New Mexico II* (J. P. Fitzsimmons and C. L. Lochman-Balk, eds.), New Mexico Geological Society, 16th Field Conference.

Hill, Willard Williams, 1938, *The Agricultural and Hunting Methods of the Navajo Indians*, Yale University Press, New Haven.

Irwin-Williams, Cynthia, Pierce, Christopher, Durand, Stephen R., and Hicks, Patricia, 1988, The Density Dependent Method: Measuring the Archaeological Record in the Northern Southwest, in: *Issues in Archaeological Surface Survey: Meshing Method and Theory* (LuAnn Wandsnider and James I. Ebert, eds.), *American Archaeology* 7(1):38–48.

Isaac, Glynn, Ll., 1981, Stone Age Visiting Cards: Approaches to the Study of Early Land Use Patterns, in: *Patterns of the Past: Studies in Honor of David Clarke* (Ian Hodder, G. Isaac, and N. Hammonds, eds.), Cambridge University Press, pp. 131–156.

Isaac, Glynn, Ll., and Harris, J. W. K., 1975, The Scatter between the Patches, paper presented to the Kroeber Anthropological Society, May 1975.

Janes, Robert R., 1983, *Archaeological Ethnography of MacKenzie Basin Dene, Canada*, Arctic Institute of North America Technical Paper 28.

Kelley, Klara B., 1986, *Najavo Land Use*. Academic Press.

Kelly, Isabel T., 1934, Ethnography of the Surprise Valley Paiute, *University of California Publications in American Archaeology and Ethnology* 31(3):67–210, pl. 17–22, Berkeley.

Kelly, Isabel T., 1964, *Southern Paiute Ethnography*, Anthropological Papers of the University of Utah 69, Salt Lake City.

Lewarch, Dennis E., and O'Brien, Michael, 1983, The Expanding Role of Surface Assemblages in Archaeological Research, in: *Advances in Archaeological Method and Theory*, Vol. 4 (Michael B. Schiffer, ed.), Academic Press, New York, pp. 297–342.

Magne, Martin P. R., and Pokotylo, David, 1980, Lithic Reduction Sequences: A Controlled Experiment, The Eagle Lake Project, report on the 1979 season, Laboratory of Archaeology, University of British Columbia, Vancouver.

Magne, Martin P. R., and Pokotylo, David, 1981, A Pilot Study in Bifacial Lithic Reduction Sequences, *Lithic Technology* 10(2-3):34–47.

McManamon, Francis P., 1986, Units of Analysis and Prehistoric Land Use on Outer Cape Code, *Man in the Northeast* 31:151–171.

Nials, Fred, 1988, Geomorphological Stratification, Appendix A, in: *Distributional Survey and Excavation of Archaeological Landscapes in the Vicinity of El Paso, Texas*, New Mexico Bureau of Land Management, U.S. Government Printing Office, Washington, D.C.

Newell, Raymond R., 1987, Reconstruction of the Partitioning and Utilization of Outside Space in a Late Prehistoric/Early Historic Inupiat Village, in: *Method and Theory for Activity Area Research:*

An Ethnoarchaeological Approach (Susan Kent, ed.), Columbia University Press, New York, pp. 107–175.

O'Brien, Michael J., Mason, Roger D., Lewarch, Dennis E., and Neely, James A., 1982, *A Late Formative Irrigation Settlement below Monte Albán: Survey and Excavation on the Xoxocotlán Piedmont, Oaxaca, Mexico*, Institute of Latin American Studies, University of Texas Press, Austin.

O'Laughlin, Thomas C., 1979, Excavation at the Transmountain Campus, El Paso Community College, El Paso, Texas, *El Paso Centennial Museum Publication in Anthropology* 7, The University of Texas at El Paso.

O'Laughlin, Thomas C., 1980, The Keystone Dam Site and Other Archaic and Formative sites in Northwest El Paso, Texas, *El Paso Centennial Museum Publications in Anthropology* 8, The University of Texas at El Paso.

Opler, Marvin Kaufmann, 1971, Plains and Pueblo Influences in Mescalero Apache Culture, in: *Themes in Culture* (Mario D. Zamora, J. Michael Hahar, and Henry Orenstein, eds.), Kayumangg Publishing, Quezon City, Philippines.

Opler, Morris Edward, 1946, *Childhood and Youth in Jicarilla Apache Society*, Southwest Museum, Los Angeles.

Phagan, Carl, 1976, A Method for the Analysis of Flakes in Archaeological Assemblages: A Peruvian Example, Ph.D. dissertation, Ohio State University.

Pierce, Christopher, and Durand, Stephen R., 1988, Prehistoric Land-Use and Spatial Patterning in the Mesilla Bolson, in: *Archaeological Resources of the Santa Teresa Study Area, South-Central New Mexico* (John C. Ravesloot, ed.), Cultural Resource Management Division, Arizona State Museum, University of Arizona and Bureau of Land Management, Contract Number Ya-551-CT4-340012, pp. 235–252.

Pigott, John D., 1978, Reconnaissance Geology: Implications for the Analysis of Human Occupation, in: *Settlement Patterns of the Western Hueco Bolson* (Michael E. Whalen, ed.), El Paso Centennial Museum Publications in Anthropology 6, The University of Texas at El Paso.

Riddell, Francis A., 1978, *Honey Lake Paiute Ethnography* (originally published in 1960), Nevada State Museum Occasional Paper, Number 3 (part 1), Carson City.

Schlanger, Sara, 1988, Hunter-gatherer Tool Caching Behavior and the Archaeological Record, manuscript in possession of the author.

Schiffer, Michael B., 1972, Archaeological Context and Systemic Context, *American Antiquity*, 37(2):156–165.

Schiffer, Michael B., 1976, *Behavioral Archaeology*, Academic Press, New York.

Schiffer, Michael B., 1987, *Formation Processes of the Archaeological Record*, University of New Mexico Press, Albuquerque.

Spier, Leslie, 1933, *Yuman Tribes of the Gila River*, University of Chicago Press, Chicago.

Stewart, Omer Call, 1941, *Northern Paiute*, University of California Press, Berkeley.

Stewart, Omer Call, 1942, *Culture Element Distributions: XVIII. Ute-Southern Paiute*, University of California Press, Berkeley.

Thomas, David H., 1971, *Prehistoric Subsistence-Settlement Patterns of the Reese River Valley, Central Nevada*, Ph.D. Dissertation, University of California, Davis, University Microfilms, Ann Arbor.

Thomas, David H., 1975, Nonsite Sampling in Archaeology: Up the Creek without a Site?, in: *Sampling in Archaeology* (J. W. Mueller, ed.), University of Arizona Press, Tucson, pp. 61–81.

Wandsnider, LuAnn, 1986, The Character of Surface Archaeological Deposits and Its Influence on Survey Accuracy, paper presented at the 4th Annual Mogollon Conference (September 1986), Tucson, Arizona.

Wandsnider, LuAnn, 1988, Experimental Investigation of the Effect of Dune Processes on Archaeolog-

  ical Remains, in: *Issues in Archaeological Surface Survey: Meshing Method and Theory* (LuAnn
    Wandsnider and James I. Ebert, eds.), *American Antiquity* 7(1):18–28.
Wandsnider, LuAnn, 1989, Long Term Land Use, Formation Processes, And the Structure of the
    Archaeological Landscape: A Case Study from Southwestern Wyoming, Ph.D. dissertation, De-
    partment of Anthropology, University of New Mexico.
Yellen, John E., 1977, *Archaeological Approaches to the Present,* Academic Press, New York.

Chapter 7

Landscape Scale
Geoenvironmental Approaches to Prehistoric Settlement Strategies

C. RUSSELL STAFFORD AND EDWIN R. HAJIC

INTRODUCTION

Distributional or nonsite approaches have focused on defining a regional archaeological structure (Thomas 1975; Foley 1981; Camille 1983; Dunnell and Dancey 1983; Ebert 1986). These structures are argued to be a function of the interaction between prehistoric groups and definable paleolandscapes. Foley (1981), for instance, has treated the regional archaeological record as a series of varying artifact gradients and has argued that three factors are involved in its formation: (1) behavior and discard, (2) accumulation, and (3) postdeposition. Although this position is similar to that taken by Schiffer (1976), the problem is formulated at a larger scale or in regional terms, rather than aimed at understanding specific sites. Foley (1981:2–8) makes two fundamental points: (1) that there is an interrelationship between settlement strategies, topographic variation, and cul-

C. RUSSELL STAFFORD • Department of Anthropology, Indiana State University, Terre Haute, Indiana 47809.   EDWIN R. HAJIC • Quaternary Studies Program, Illinois State Museum, Springfield, Illinois 62706.

Space, Time, and Archaeological Landscapes, edited by Jacqueline Rossignol and LuAnn Wandsnider. Plenum Press, New York, 1992.

tural deposition and (2) that there is long-term accumulation of cultural debris on stable or degrading landforms. The archaeological record is viewed as the product of repeated depositional events over sometimes long periods of time where characteristics of the landscape determine in part the spatial distribution of cultural remains.

The purpose of this Chapter is to build on Foley's discussion by examining landscapes from a geomorphic perspective and consider the effect of landscape structure on the movement of hunter–gatherers. A key aspect is variation in the scale of landforms making up a landscape that in turn affect hunter–gatherer movement and ultimately cultural deposition. Our work in a temperate region of the midcontinental United States led us to focus on a three-dimensional geomorphic record, where cultural remains are viewed as inclusions in measurable landform/sediment assemblages. The distribution and concentration of artifacts, taken at any spatial scale, are a function of the rate of cultural deposition and past and ongoing surficial processes. Deciphering the positional status of artifacts requires knowledge of the dominant environments, processes, and particularly, process rates. Our principal focus here is on a geoenvironmental analysis of the scale of landforms making up paleolandscapes and the resulting effect on the structuring of the regional archaeological record. These issues are discussed in the context of spatial data relevant to Middle Archaic hunter–gatherer settlement strategies in west-central Illinois.

LANDSCAPES AND SCALE

Hunter–gatherer mobility and land use strategies can profitably be understood within the context of those aspects of foraging ecology (e.g., Stephens and Krebs 1986) and the emerging field of landscape ecology (Forman and Godron 1986), which relate to the spatial use of the environment by organisms. The environmental factors or variables that affect the evolutionary success of organisms are commonly distributed heterogeneously in space and time. Landscapes are essentially land areas where these ecological factors or character states are unevenly distributed. These ecological variables, however, will have differential effects on organisms at different scales. For example, climate at a macroscale ($2 \times 10^5 - 5 \times 10^7$ m) affects the distribution of biomes, whereas within biomes at the microscale ($10^{-2} \times 10^2$ m), daily temperature patterns are modified by topography (Pianka 1983:43–45; Urban et al. 1987). Moreover, relevant scales are "organism defined"; that is, they are determined by the size, mobility, and habits of a population of organisms (cf. Wiens 1976; Winterhalder 1980). Spatial (or temporal) variation at specific scales differentially affect the adaptive success and in turn the spatial behavior of organisms, resulting in a hierarchy of effects. Therefore, variation in vegetation communities at the microscale may not have the significant effect on spatial behavior that it has at larger scales. Because ecological processes are scale dependent, we may expect that causal relationships between the landscape and an organism's use of it use will change with scale (Haggett 1966:263ff; Senft *et al.* 1987).

Winterhalder (1980:152) suggests that for humans three scales are relevant: (1) foraging range, (2) migratory range, and (3) extended interaction through trade. At the scale of foraging, energy and nutrients accumulate in patches. Foraging for resources is not, however, the exclusive concern of organisms at smaller scales. Species use different parts of the landscape for different functions, one of which is foraging. Sleeping, reproduction, raising young (Forman and Godron 1986:471), and other activities (for humans this would include food preparation, tool manufacture among other things) require other landscape characteristics, many of which may be distributed at other, commonly smaller scales. As minimal spatial units, landscape *elements*[1] (Forman and Godron 1986:12) are the sum of ecological and physical characteristics at all scales. They may encompass a resource patch as well as be defined by other characteristics of the landscape like terrain or relief. Landscape elements must be loosely defined because of the scale component in defining their boundaries and the organism dependency of the concept.

Typically, organisms must move across the landscape to make use of energy or nutrient patches in a heterogeneous landscape. Mobility, as defined by ecologists, varies along a continuum from continuous to saltatory movements. Saltatory movement is defined as movement, stop, and movement again (Pielou 1979; Forman and Godron 1986:359). Certain locations on the landscape serve as stopping points because of their characteristics. Human mobility relative to other organisms tends toward saltatory movement, although hunter–gatherer mobility is clearly variable. Elements as locations on the landscape have differential probabilities of being stopping points, and these likelihoods are determined by (1) the mobility strategy of the organism and (2) the sum of environmental characteristics at all scales. The pattern of movement at the scale of foraging is, among other things, a function of the *structure* or spatial arrangement of landscape elements. That is, how are the probabilities that a location will serve as a stopping point spatially distributed across a landscape? A different pattern of movement, for instance, will result if similar probabilities are contiguously distributed versus ones irregularly dispersed across a landscape.

A number of physical properties can be used to define a landscape. Components of a landscape can include plant and animal communities, temperature,

---

[1] For our purposes, landscape elements are the smallest homogeneous unit in contrast to Forman and Godron's (1986:13) further subdivision of elements into tessera. Also, numerous other terms with the same basic meaning as element have been used in landscape ecology, including cell, geotope, facies, and site (Forman and Godron 1986:12).

rainfall, soils, water resources, or relief. From a geomorphic perspective, landform/sediment assemblages[2] form the matrix in which cultural remains occur as a fundamental part of the sedimentary record. Such units have measurable boundaries that reflect, at least indirectly, other aspects of a paleolandscape, and are especially relevant where present vegetation or climate have limited applicability to the past.

A geomorphic landscape also can be defined at different scales (e.g., Ruhe 1975:4). Physiographic provinces or morphogenetic regions (Butzer 1982:63–64) form large-scale geological units. Medium-scale geomorphic zones are composed of a series of landforms formed by closely related genetic processes. Geomorphic zones would generally be smaller in scale than the foraging range of most hunter–gatherers (e.g., Rodgers 1963; Binford 1983). However, resources available to hunter–gatherers may be found in specific geomorphic zones. Individual landforms within geomorphic zones vary at a smaller scale in terms of relief, aspect, elevation, and geometry. The size, frequency, and spatial distribution of landform/sediment assemblages determine the fundamental structure of paleolandscapes. Under this approach landscape elements are minimal spatial locations on landforms with specific geomorphic and topographic characteristics.

SPATIAL AND TEMPORAL SCALES OF HUNTER–GATHERER MOBILITY

The pattern and rate (per unit of time) of movement of hunter–gatherers across a region as in other species (see Forman and Godron 1986) is at least partially in response to the structure or arrangement of elements that make up a landscape. If we view cultural deposition as a continuous process with changing rates in response to the functional use of the landscape, then the spatial pattern of debris ought to be, among other things, a function of that movement. Cultural deposition may be continuous at varying rates, or nonexistent for lengthy time intervals. However, there is always the potential for cultural deposition across the landscape in any given location (Foley 1981).

Moreover, because landscape structure varies with scale, it is reasonable to expect that the structure of the archaeological record might be different at larger or smaller scales. At large to medium scales, it may be the structure of resource patches (i.e., geomorphic zones) that are most critical, whereas at smaller scales relief or microclimatic factors (i.e., landforms or parts of landforms) may be limiting. For instance, the Chipewyan (Sharp 1977) select settlement locations

---

[2] This is an informal stratigraphic unit referring to a landform and its underlying deposits. These units may conform to criteria for lithostratigraphic units (NACSN 1983).

based first on an area where caribou are present (large scale) and then on the type of terrain and firewood availability (small scale).

Places as defined here are spaces of a size and character appropriate for specified functions under a given settlement or mobility strategy (cf. Binford 1982; Rossignol and Wandsnider, this volume). That is, places represent a subset of landscape elements with higher probabilities of serving as stopping points under a given mobility strategy. The size of the place will depend on space needs of these functions. A landform/sediment assemblage may have many elements, with some or all possessing the appropriate characteristics to serve as places. Variation among landform/sediment assemblages or at a larger scale among geomorphic zones in the number of places and their spatial arrangement will affect the pattern of movement of hunter–gatherers, the likelihood of reuse, and ultimately the structure of the archaeological record. Other factors, however, are also of importance in determining this structure: (1) changes in the rate of movement across a landscape, (2) changes in the rate of cultural deposition in space and time, and (3) changes in the rate of sediment deposition and erosion among landform/sediment assemblages as well as through time. The nature and complexity of the archaeological record will be a function of the interrelationship of these variables.

Particular land use strategies result in different patterns and rates of movement across a landscape. Binford (1980; Kelly 1983; Bettinger 1987) has made the useful distinction between foragers and collectors. These two strategies differ in terms of the organization of foraging groups, the scale at which they exploit the environment, and their strategy of movement. Foragers tend to make use of a series of residential moves to resource patches with food obtained on an encounter basis (fine-grained movement relative to the scale of the environment). Collectors, on the other hand, procure specific resources through specially organized foraging groups (coarse-grain movement). Groups are not simply searching for any resource. Most important, resources are being moved to consumers in contrast to the first strategy. Storage, a method of modifying the temporal availability of resources, is also a common component of a collector strategy (Binford 1980; Bettinger 1987). Even though hunter–gatherers may not exclusively use one strategy or the other over the course of their intraannual movements, change in strategies or strategy mix should be detectable in the distribution of cultural remains within a region. One must, however, consider the result of long-term accumulation of remains on a landscape.

A regional archaeological record is not a direct reflection of intraannual or seasonal movements of hunter–gatherers. The temporal scale of the archaeological record is usually much coarser. Many models of hunter–gatherer settlement strategies, however, are based on known ethnographic accounts of seasonal movements. Winterhalder (1980:137ff) comments on the debilitating reliance in ecological anthropology—a principal source of prehistoric models—on the ethnographic year, which limits the temporal scope of studies focusing on adaptation. Binford's (1983:45–47) account of the seasonal movements of the Nunamiut indicate the complex pattern of reuse even within short time spans relative to the temporal scale of much of the archaeological record. Except where rapid sediment deposition buries surfaces and relatively rapid cultural deposition has taken place, the archaeological record is more typically the result of long-term accumulation of cultural remains. The resolution of the archaeological record is largely not at the scale of intraannual movements of hunter–gatherers. In addition, it is unlikely that the archaeological record is the simple additive result of seasonal movements but is significantly more complex.

Models of hunter–gatherer mobility are needed that are congruent with the temporal and spatial scale of the archaeological record (see Thomas 1986). In this regard, the degree to which a mobility strategy is "tied" to places having specific characteristics on the landscape is important. There are obvious factors that may result in reoccupation in the short term, like the construction of storage facilities or domestic structures. In terms of models that consider long-term accumulation of cultural debris, however, such factors, although undoubtedly important, tend to be limiting relative to the structure of much of the archaeological record. More generally, factors associated with patch distribution or smaller-scale terrain characteristics that affect the probability or increase the rates of cultural deposition are at least as critical. For instance, in a foraging strategy where places with appropriate characteristics are *ubiquitous* on a landscape and rates of movement and cultural deposition uniform, the density of remains are likely to be generally low but variable from place to place (due to essentially random reuse). Although in the short term, previous use of a place could have a negative or positive affect on reuse (Dewar 1986; Brooks and Yellen 1987) of that place; in the long term, cultural deposition at a specific location should become increasingly independent as depositional events are separated by larger intervals of time (i.e., decline of temporal autocorrelation).

Because collectors are attempting to reduce incongruities in resource availability, spatially there tend to be fewer places (i.e., landscape elements with high probabilities of serving as stopping points) on the landscape that will satisfy their positioning requirements. The pattern of movement Binford (1982) has termed point-to-point exemplifies this strategy. Because fewer locations exist in the landscape, there tends to be more reoccupation. Therefore there are higher and more uniform densities of cultural remains at residential places. Because of a more heterogeneous functional use of the landscape, however (i.e., place use by task groups as opposed to residential use as by foragers), collectors are more likely to produce widely varying densities across a landscape (i.e., extreme high and low values).

Thus far the assumption has been that places of different types are nearly equal in frequency. Because environments tend to be heterogeneous this is not likely to be the case. As a result, different settlement strategies may produce convergent cumulative records of cultural deposition. If landform surfaces vary in scale by a substantial magnitude, with fewer appropriate landscape elements, then higher than expected cultural deposition by foragers will be found in the long term (assuming a stable surface) at these locations. In the extreme case, a foraging strategy would approach the point-to-point movements of collectors. The spatial pattern of cultural deposition among collectors may not be as dramatically affected because only a subset of locations are already in use. In short, a heterogeneous environment in conjunction with differences in landform scale and frequency of landscape elements will condition the pattern of cultural deposition across the landscape.

LOWER ILLINOIS VALLEY PALEOLANDSCAPES

Extensive joint geomorphic and archaeological studies have identified in detail landforms, associated sediment sequences, and depositional environments in the Lower Illinois Valley (Hajic 1985, 1987, 1990; Hajic and Leigh 1984; Styles 1985). From these studies, it is evident that the artifact distribution for a given time interval may be only fractionally represented on a modern landscape due to postdepositional burial or erosion (Wiant *et al.* 1983). Landscapes are composed of landforms, and although recognition of the landscape and its landform components is important, it is even more important to recognize that the landscape we see today may represent only a spatial and temporal fraction of the late Pleistocene and Holocene. In areas dynamic geologically over this interval, the current landscape may only accurately represent some spatial and temporal fractions where relict landforms are common. The remainder of time is represented in the stratigraphic record below landform surfaces, so interpretation of the vertical dimension is a key to understanding artifact distributions. It is clear from investigations in the Lower Illinois Valley that the early-to-middle Holocene landscape of interest in this study is differentially represented on the modern land surface.

Geological studies in this region also indicate that the size and frequency of landforms differs substantially across the current landscape. There is at least semisystematic spatial variation within some individual landform types because of either preexisting geological conditions or postlandform events. Further, it is possible to measure the frequency and spatial arrangement of landscape elements that may have served as places for Middle Holocene hunter–gatherers in this region.

Four broad geomorphic zones have been defined (Figure 1) in the Lower Illinois Valley: (1) uplands; (2) tributary valleys; (3) a belt of alluvial and colluvial

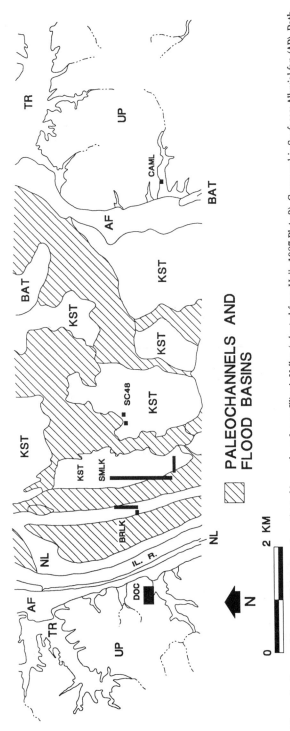

Figure 1. Geomorphic map with locations investigated in northern Lower Illinois Valley (adapted from Hajic 1987:Plate 3). Geomorphic Surfaces: Alluvial fan (AP), Bath Terrace (BAT), Keach School Terrace (KST), Natural levee (NL), Tributary valley (TR), Uplands (UP). Areas Investigated: Campbell Hollow (CAML), Burr Lake (BRLK), DOC, School 48 (SC48), Slim Lake (SMLK).

fans and slopes mantling the valley margin; and (4) the Illinois River, with its terraces, paleochannels, natural levees, flood basins, and related features. The geomorphic stability of landforms and the spatial structure of landscape elements on landforms is described for each geomorphic zone.

The uplands are heavily dissected by east–west-trending tributary valleys within several kilometers of the bedrock valley trench of the Illinois River. This zone has been an erosional geomorphic surface, present throughout the Holocene. There are, in addition, an indefinitely large number of contiguously distributed landscape elements with similar attributes in the uplands.

East–west-trending tributary valleys are asymmetrical with short, steep, gullied north-facing slopes and long, stepped south-facing slopes periodically interrupted by side valleys and lesser but more numerous hillside swales. Unlike the uplands, this geomorphic zone is punctuated by landscape elements of differing small-scale topographic characteristics. Moreover, early to middle Holocene land surfaces may be buried in valley side slopes (Hajic 1985). Tributary valleys probably also acted as conduits or corridors to upland areas.

In this reach of the valley, the eastern valley margin is characterized by broad alluvial fans, whereas those on the western side are small in comparison with generally steeper slopes (Hajic and Leigh 1984; Hajic 1987; Styles 1985). Individual fans clearly vary in size by several orders of magnitude as a result of differences in contributing drainage basin area, ages of underlying surfaces, and erosional activity by the Illinois River. Slope and aspect also varies among fans.

Extensive geomorphic investigations of alluvial and colluvial fans in the region indicate that after limited to moderate early Holocene sedimentation rates, large-scale and rapid sediment influx on fans began about 8500 B.P. Sedimentation rates decreased after about 4000 B.P. with little accumulation after 2500 B.P. Superimposed on this trend of overall decreasing sedimentation rates during the Holocene is a second series of regionally synchronous episodes of waning sedimentation followed by soil formation. Cultural materials younger than 2500 B.P. will generally occur on the surface or by very shallowly buried, whereas older materials will be buried, sometimes to substantial depths (at least 11.3 m). Therefore, the middle Holocene landscape that is of concern here is largely buried in this geomorphic zone.

This belt of generally well-drained alluvial and colluvial fan surfaces occur at the juncture between highly productive aquatic habitats of the Illinois Valley and terrestrial animal and plant resources of the uplands and tributary valleys. There are fewer locations than in the uplands or valley floodplain zones but a larger number than in the tributary valleys. However, these locations vary substantially in their characteristics from relatively small, well-protected locations (especially colluvial fans near tributary valley entrants) to large, exposed alluvial fans at creek-valley mouths.

The final zone is the Illinois River and related features. The most extensive geomorphic surface is the Keach School Terrace, a largely featureless sandy surface except where modified by tributary channel activity. No significant deposition has taken place on the terrace since 9000 B.P. precluding the burial of Archaic or younger remains, except from colluviation on the terrace scarp and upland-derived wash along the valley margin. The Keach School Terrace is well drained and generally has not been subject to flooding since its exposure.

Several major Illinois River paleochannels are evident in this valley reach. They represent various stages in development of the Illinois River floodplain beginning in the very early Holocene. Natural levees present are long, relatively narrow, linear features produced by the Illinois River. Accompanying levee system formation was the establishment of deep, permanent lateral lakes impounded behind the levees. Lateral lakes in-filled between about 6000 and 3000 B.P. with large quantities of sediment delivered largely by tributary streams.

In terms of small-scale terrain variation, many landscape elements on the Keach School Terrace are essentially identical. A subset of these locations, however, were in closer proximity to the paleochannel depressions that supported aquatic resource patches. What relief differences that do exist on the terrace are also correlated with these locations at the terrace edge.

Natural levees vary in size but are generally smaller in area than the Keach School Terrace. Levee surfaces tend to be linear and at times discontinuous. All landscape elements tend to be in close proximity to paleochannel depressions and hence aquatic resource patches. Again, little relief is present along the levees, and many locations have similar characteristics and are contiguously distributed.

The geomorphic surfaces discussed reflect medium-scale landscape variability. Table 1 summarizes the size differences among these geomorphic surfaces in this reach of the Illinois Valley. The dissected uplands and the Keach School Terrace cover by far the largest areas, although the terrace is divided into several

Table 1. Geomorphic Scale Variation in the Northern Lower Illinois Valley[a]

	Area sum[b]	$\bar{x}$	s.d.	c.v.[c]	n^d
Dissected uplands	15.873	7.937	.829	10.44	2
Terraces[e]	7.854	0.978	.724	74.03	7
Alluvial fans	2.064	1.032	.480	46.51	2
Tributary valleys	2.693	0.299	.503	168.23	9
Natural levees	1.324	0.442	.192	43.44	3

[a] Digitized from Hajic (1987:Plate 3).
[b] km²; total area measured equals width of valley plus half that distance away from valley margin on each side; total area = 40.64 km².
[c] Coefficient of variation.
[d] Number of contiguous areas measured.
[e] Keach School and Bath terraces.

discrete areas due to channel activity. The alluvial fan zone is relatively large but is made up of a number of identifiable surfaces that are highly variable in size. As indicated by the coefficient of variation, tributary valleys are the most variable in size. The natural levees of the Illinois River make up a smaller area but are of a relatively uniform size. In addition to these differences in scale, there is further variation in location characteristics between these landform types. In general, there are many more similar locations on the natural levee and Keach School Terrace than there are on alluvial/colluvial fans or tributary valleys in the region.

For instance, the number of landscape elements in the region with south-facing slopes in protected locations (providing a beneficial microclimate) on alluvial/colluvial fans is far smaller than the total number of locations on fans. It is not surprising, therefore, to find extensive evidence that these locations on colluvial fans or valley side slopes repeatedly served as stopping points or places for middle Holocene hunter–gatherers (Brown and Vierra 1983; Wiant *et al.* 1983; Stafford 1985a; B. Stafford and Sant 1985).

The punctuated sedimentation and soil formation on fans has also provided a stratigraphic record of repeated use of these locations throughout the mid-Holocene. Some stratigraphic records on colluvial fans and slopes show relatively continuous use as at Koster (Brown and Vierra 1983), whereas others are more sporadic (e.g., Campbell Hollow [Stafford 1985a] and Smiling Dan [Stafford and Sant 1985]). Because of the punctuated nature of deposition on fans, in conjunction with changes in the functional use of these places, there is substantial variation in the concentration of cultural remains (30 − 2330 gm/m^3). On the larger of these, there is evidence of shifting use of locations on the fan surface (Carlson 1979), whereas use was more restricted on others (Stafford 1985b). The strategic location of places on alluvial/colluvial fans yet the limited number relative to places in other geomorphic zones probably accounts for the frequent reuse of these places during the middle to late Holocene by Archaic hunter–gatherers. In addition, the record of reuse or reoccupation at these locations gives some indication of the potential complexity of spatial patterns on landforms that have remained more stable during the Holocene, such as the Keach School Terrace or some levee locations.

These geomorphic zones mirror the differential spatial distribution of resources important to middle Holocene hunter–gatherer foraging. Distinctive sets of resources are contained in several of the zones. Hickory nuts and deer in the uplands and tributary valleys were likely widely scattered and unpredictable (see Stafford 1991) both temporally and spatially relative to the clumped and linear character of aquatic resources (e.g., fish, shellfish, migratory water fowl) available in Illinois River habitats. As is typical of major river valleys of the midcontinent, the bottomlands of the Illinois River have supported extensive aquatic habitats that form a complex mosaic (based on differences in water depth and flow). The dynamic nature of this fluvial system during the Holocene, however, has resulted in sometimes dramatic changes in patch types, frequency, and distribution.

SPATIAL AND TEMPORAL SCALE OF THE DATABASE

The database used in this analysis reflects at least two temporal and spatial scales. The bulk of the record is from long-term stable geomorphic surfaces that cover large areas of the Illinois River Valley and adjacent uplands. Temporally this record spans a significant portion of the early to middle Holocene, and thus patterning is not at the scale of interannual movements of hunter–gatherers but represents a much coarser temporal scale. One study location does, however, reflect a single place on the landscape of limited temporal duration. It stands in marked contrast to the spatial patterning of debris at other locations that represent long-term use of the landscape on the order of thousands of years.

Archaeological investigations conducted in three of the four geomorphic zones (Table 2) have provided spatial data from five locations: Campbell Hollow, School 48, Slim Lake, Burr Lake, and DOC (Department of Conservation). Although the data used in this analysis were collected under a site-oriented methodology, the extensive nature of the investigations approaches a distributional or nonsite strategy (Thomas 1975; Dunnell and Dancey 1983). At four of these locations, controlled surface collecting was conducted over very large spatial areas (Table 2) and encompassed both low and high debris areas. These investigations focused on the distribution of cultural remains on the landforms rather than arbitrarily defined sites.

Four of the five locations investigated are on Illinois River or related landforms (Figure 1) that were largely stable during the Holocene, and therefore cultural debris is confined for the most part to the surface or plow zone. Slim Lake, Burr Lake, and School 48 are characterized by narrow linear scatters of

Table 2. Sample Characteristics of Locations Studied

Location	Geomorphic zone	Landform	Collection unit size (m^2)	Units collected	Total area collected (m^2)
Campbell Hollow	Tributary valley	Hill Slope	1	150	150
School 48	Illinois River	Terrace	36	297	10,692
Slim Lake	Illinois River	Terrace	36	392	14,112
Burr Lake	Illinois River	Natural levee	36	454	16,344
DOC	Uplands	Upland	144	535	77,040

material of varying density along former channels of the Illinois River, or in the case of School 48, a major tributary meander belt. The Slim Lake and Burr Lake scatters have been traced at least 2.2 and 3.2 km, respectively, along these floodplain landforms. Surface collecting involved either contiguous units with the long axis of the grid distributed roughly parallel to the natural levee (Burr Lake) or terrace (School 48), or as at Slim Lake, linear transects of units oriented both parallel and at right angles to the terrace (Stafford 1989). All materials were collected from each unit.

DOC is an extensive scatter of lithic debris located in the heavily dissected uplands bordering the Illinois Valley (Figure 1). In addition to the intermittent streams that dissect the locality, a sink hole is also present that is a somewhat unique topographic feature in this area. A 7.7 ha cultivated field was entirely collected in contiguous units irrespective of the density of cultural debris (a strictly site-oriented approach would have defined at least three high density areas as individual sites).

The temporal diagnostics recovered from these locations indicate use of these landforms during much of the Holocene. The bulk (50–79%) of the diagnostic artifacts, however, can be assigned to the late Middle Archaic (4000–6000 B.P.).[3] In some locations (e.g., School 48) Early Archaic (8000–10,000 B.P.) artifacts are also common. Later Woodland artifacts are either not present or make up only a small percentage of the total diagnostics recovered (Stafford 1989). These artifact scatters are argued to largely reflect long-term accumulations of perhaps 4 to 5 thousand years during the early to middle Holocene.

In contrast, the Campbell Hollow data represent debris and associated features buried about 2 m below the surface in colluvial/alluvial deposits on a tributary valley side slope (Stafford 1985a). The west gully floor and toe slope containing these remains is a small-scale landform that does not greatly exceed the 150 m^2 encompassed by the excavation block.

This area is small even in comparison to other alluvial/colluvial landforms in the vicinity. Given that the minimum-size requirements of a place are probably not much less than the toe slope leading to the gully floor, this location or place is effectively a point on the landscape. The rise to the west of the gully would have acted as a windbreak to predominately westerly winds, and its southern exposure would have provided large amounts of solar radiation. In effect, a specific microclimate is associated with this location relative to others. Similar locations exist throughout this region along tributary valley side slopes. For the most part, however, these locations are discontinuously distributed in space relative to other types of locations. The landform appears to have been a clear conditioner of debris deposition as well as facility construction on a microscale at Campbell Hollow.

---

[3] Four radiocarbon dates that average about 5300 B.P. were obtained from pits at the Slim Lake site (Stafford 1989).

The linear arrangement of hearths and lithic debitage distribution strongly conform to the paleotopography of the gully (Stafford 1985b).

The locations studied on valley or upland landforms exhibit coarse grain spatial structure. That is, long-term reuse and postdepositional processes (e.g., plowing) have masked individual depositional episodes (cf. Dewer, this volume; Stafford 1985b).[4] In sharp contrast to these other locations is the fine-grain spatial structure and low concentration of remains at Campbell Hollow. Spatial analysis (Stafford 1985b,c, 1987) of the occupation isolated individual depositional events, argued to reflect a brief interval of time and limited reoccupation dating to the early Middle Archaic or about 7600 B.P. (Stafford 1985a).

SPATIAL PATTERNING ACROSS THE LANDSCAPE

Because lithic debitage and chipped stone tools are common remains on these landforms relative to other classes of artifacts, they are the focus of our analysis. Because we have argued that use and movement through the environment by hunter–gatherers is a function of the spatial structure of elements making up the landscape, it is the spatial distribution of these lithic categories across the region that we assert will mimic differential use of the landscape during the middle Holocene.

Given the much higher frequency of debitage on geomorphic surfaces, it is apparent that cultural depositional rates in general are higher for debitage than for tools. This is not unexpected, because debitage is the by-product of tool manufacture and/or repair. Rates of deposition of these classes, however, are not constant; for chipped stone artifacts, expedient tools are likely to have higher rates than curated tools. Moreover, some studies (Binford 1979) indicate that with curated technologies, retooling may be a seasonal task and consequently tool deposition will be episodic, with higher rates during specific intervals (i.e., greater than rates due to incidental loss or breakage). Similarly, debitage rates can vary, with higher rates due to tool manufacture and lower rates resulting from tool resharpening or other repairs.

If the probabilities of deposition for tools and debitage at places are nearly equal, then a spatial correlation will exist in the regional record. If, however, probabilities are differentially distributed among places between these classes of debris because of a heterogeneous functional use of the landscape, then there will

---

[4]As used here, the grain of spatial patterning is derived from Binford's (1980) notion of tool assemblage grain, where fine- or coarse-grain assemblages are a function of the degree to which specific events are represented. In the spatial analog, as the duration of occupation lengthens or as reuse increases, there is less reoslution likely among observed spatial patterns and individual depositional events (see Stafford 1985b,c).

be a lack of covariation. The presence or lack of spatial covariation between tools and debitage should then map these underlying probabilities and hence patterns of land use.

Differences in deposition were investigated by examining the spatial correlation between chipped stone debitage and tools at the locations described previously. Units of analysis at Campbell Hollow were at the scale of 1 m^2, whereas at the upland DOC location one collection unit (144 m^2) essentially encompasses the entire Campbell Hollow occupation. Campbell Hollow is a useful starting place for the analysis because it approaches a minimal place on the landscape and in addition reflects a short segment of time relative to the temporal and spatial scales at the other locations.

Previous analysis (Stafford 1985b,c) of Campbell Hollow data indicated that tools and debitage had a globally moderate correlation ($r = .467$, $P < .001$) that appears to be largely a function of generalized activities carried out around six hearths. There were, however, significant deviations from this global pattern as reflected in the lack of tools in areas of highest debitage density (>80th quantile). These and other analysis results (Stafford 1985b, 1987) indicated that the fineness of the spatial distribution reflected relatively few depositional events, where activities were not uniformally carried out across this landform, even at this microscale.

The locations in the valley and uplands represent long-term accumulations scattered across large-scale landforms. Further, these locations entail vastly larger collection units and areas investigated. As the scale of analysis is increased, there should be an increase in the global trend of tool/debitage covariance, if tool/debitage deposition is tied to relatively discrete places on the landscape, like at Campbell Hollow. Deviations from this pattern should indicate that different patterns of cultural deposition were in operation, reflecting alternative positioning tactics associated with mobility strategies (see Binford 1982).

In order to accommodate different sample characteristics and data distributions, a contingency table analysis was conducted using the debitage and tool data collected from the five locations investigated. By partitioning the table (cf. Simek and Leslie 1983), it is possible to examine both global and local trends among the cells (5 × 3 table; see Table 3), the equivalent of examining residuals in other analyses. The significance of deviations in the observed/expected frequencies in tables and subtables was determined with the log-likelihood chi-square[5] (L^2), which is amenable to partitioning (Reynolds 1984).

Although the log-likelihood chi-square is significant for each location (Table 3), indicating tool and debitage density are not independent, the correlation coefficients (V and Lambda), with the exception of Slim Lake, decline with

---

[5] SYSTAT 2.0; $L^2 = 2\Sigma\, f_{ij}\, Ln(f_{ij}/F_{ij})$, F = expected cell frequencies, f = observed cell frequencies (Knoke and Burke 1980:30).

Table 3. Log Likelihood Contingency Table Analysis[a]

Location	L^2	P	df	V^b	Lambda[c]
CAML[d]	64.56	.000	8	.4647	.2072
SC48	66.11	.000	8	.3405	.1082
SMLK	175.02	.000	8	.4695	.2207
BRLK	87.03	.000	8	.3231	.1239
DOC	36.06	.000	8	.1957	.0732

[a] 5 × 3 table consisting of five debitage density classes based on .2 quantile intervals (00.−.20, .21−.40, .41−.60, .61−.80, .81−1.0) and three tool density classes (0, 1, ≥2).
[b] Cramer's V.
[c] Asymmetric Lambda (row dependent).
[d] Campbell Hollow (CAML), School 48 (SC48), Slim Lake (SMLK), Burr Lake (BRLK).

increasing scale (Table 3). The subtable partition indicates a general pattern of covariation within the tables (Table 4 and 5). In all cases, the subtable that includes only the highest- and lowest-density debitage cells (i.e., first and last row) are significant ($P = .000$), with substantial correlations. However, at intermediate density analyzed in Subtable B (row 2–4), only the Campbell Hollow and Slim Lake log-likelihood chi-squares and associated correlations are significant (i.e., $P < .05$; see Tables 4 and 5). At these latter two locations, deviations from expected frequencies are more evenly distributed across the table, although a major contribution is still being made by the high and low density cells.

Ignoring Slim Lake for a moment, there appears to be a consistent trend of declining association that can be linked to increases in scale of both the analytical units and the landforms from which the remains were recovered. Of particular significance is the pattern observed at DOC, where only a very low correlation is

Table 4. Log Likelihood Subtable Analysis

Location	Subtable A[a]			Subtable B[b]		
	L^2	P	df	L^2	P	df
CAML[c]	31.64	.000	2	13.96	.004	4
SC48	35.85	.000	1	2.19	.334	2[d]
SMLK	133.35	.000	2	21.00	.000	4
BRLK	60.86	.000	2	4.73	.094	2[d]
DOC	29.91	.000	2	1.61	.807	4

[a] Subtable A partition based on rows 1 and 5 of original 5 × 3 table.
[b] Subtable B partition based on rows 2, 3, and 4 of original 5 × 3 table.
[c] Campbell Hollow (CAML), School 48 (SC48), Slim Lake (SMLK), Burr Lake (BRLK).
[d] L^2 based on collapsed 2 × 3 table due to low expected cell frequencies.

Table 5. Subtable Associations

Location	Subtable A		Subtable B	
	V[a]	Lambda[b]	V	Lambda
CAML[c]	.7082	.6786	.3005	.1636
SC48	.4692	.4194	.1130	.0288
SMLK	.8117	.7875	.2160	.1128
BRLK	.5182	.4681	.1012	.0417
DOC	.3526	.3000	.0492	.0230

[a] Cramer's V.
[b] Asymmetric Lambda (row dependent).
[c] Campbell Hollow (CAML), School 48 (SC48), Slim Lake (SMLK), Burr Lake (BRLK).

present and at intermediate densities debitage and tools are uncorrelated. It would appear that differential deposition of tools and debitage are a function of the scale of the landform and the ubiquity of appropriate places. Based on isopleth maps of DOC (Stafford 1991), it appears that high debitage density is correlated with distinctive topographic locations (i.e., the sinkhole and ridge spurs), and that tool deposition, being largely independent, is controlled by other land use factors related to the high frequency of similar places in the uplands. In short, it would appear that the DOC distribution is a function of cultural depositional patterns different from the smallest scale. That is, DOC is not simply the accumulation of multiple Campbell Hollow-like occupations but is more complex (see Stafford 1991).

The Slim Lake results depart quite substantially from the DOC pattern. The association between tools and debitage is equal to that at Campbell Hollow. The nature of this patterning at Slim Lake is further indicated by the examination of spatial autocorrelation of these debris classes. Figure 2 is a plot of debitage density in the north–south surface collection transect. An analysis of both the north–south and east–west transects as spatial series[6] (Hodder and Orton 1976; McCleary and Hay 1980) indicates that there is significant autocorrelation (i.e., adjacent

[6] In parts of the transects, multiple contiguous units were collected. In these cases, the mean value from multiple units was used in the series. SYSTAT 2.0 autocorrelation function (ACF) was employed (see McCleary and Hays 1980:66).

$$ACF(k) = \frac{\sum\limits_{t=1}^{N-k} (X_t - \bar{X})(X_{t+k} - \bar{X})}{\sum\limits_{t=1}^{N} (X_t - \bar{X})^2} \quad [N/N-k]$$

X_t = set of ordered observations

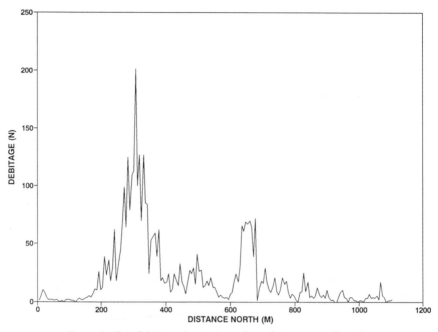

Figure 2. Plot of debitage density in north-south transect at Slim Lake.

collection units have similar density values) in both the spatial distribution of tools and debitage (Table 6). At the first and second spatial lag,[7] the autocorrelations are similar for debitage but substantially less for tools (Table 6). The decay in autocorrelation is markedly different between the two series for both material classes, probably reflecting the different orientations of the transects to the terrace (especially as reflected in the negative values at lag = 6 in the east–west transect; Table 6). The decay in the autocorrelation function also indicates the size of clustering in each series and between material classes. The autocorrelation is greater than two standard errors in the north–south transect up to lag 9 and 8 for tools and debitage, respectively. This indicates a cluster size of about 54 m.

　　Figure 2 suggests that debris is concentrated in a few locations with a moderate scattering of material between these clusters. In fact the highest concentration of material between 200 and 400 m north may be producing the high correlation between tools and debitage in this series. It is in this location that pit features were discovered after removal of the plow zone, as well as a concentration of partially buried trash on the terrace scarp (Stafford 1989).

---

[7] Lag (see Hodder and Orton 1976:179ff) refers to successive autocorrelation functions calculated between X_i and $X_i + 1, X_i + 2 \ldots X_i + n$ collection units (6 m in length).

Table 6.   Slim Lake Spatial Autocorrelation
Function (ACF) Analysis

	Transects			
	North–South		East–West	
Lag	Tool	Debitage	Tool	Debitage
1	.746[a]	.807	.313	.802
2	.676	.835	.471	.666
3	.711	.721	.179	.450
4	.669	.742	.136	.254
5	.636	.649	.136	.065
6	.527	.594	.213	−.005
7	.483	.494	.089	−.213
8	.489	.437	.234	−.268
9	.432	.370	−.011	−.324
10	.375	.333	−.107	−.321
$\bar{x}^b$	.913	20.842	0.670	7.080
s.d.	1.456	30.190	0.846	7.154
n	184	184	44	44

[a] Bold-faced ACF greater than two standard errors.
[b] Debris density statistics for series.

The presence of substantial facilities may have increased the probability that this location was reoccupied or reused in the short term, whereas the remaining scatter of material was the product of longer-term cultural deposition, where probabilities of reuse were quite independent. In order to test this proposition, this area was excluded from the contingency table and autocorrelation analyses. The results, however, indicate that the strength of the correlation between debitage and tools in the north–south transect is not reduced ($V = .4148$, Lambda $= .1803$; $P = .000$, $df = 8$). In addition, there is still significant autocorrelation in the series (Table 7), although the scale of the clustering is somewhat smaller (lag $= 5$), and the tool autocorrelation is reduced. The results suggest that the spatial structure observed at Slim Lake reflects a long-term use pattern where tools and debitage are being deposited under similar conditions (i.e., tools and debitage are associated and clustered); these are conditions much different from those observed at the upland DOC location, or possibly at Burr Lake and School 48.

Table 8 summarizes the differences between DOC and Slim Lake. The ubiquity of similar landscape elements is comparable, although their arrangement with respect to associated resources is different. That is, the structure of landscape elements that served as stopping points (i.e., places) are distinctive: planar (up-

Table 7.　Slim Lake Spatial Autocorrelation
Function (ACF) for North Transect without
Debris Concentration

Lag	Tool	Debitage
1	**.391**[a]	.757
2	.342	.720
3	.403	.608
4	.346	.473
5	.293	.433
6	.151	.289
7	.132	.241
$\bar{x}^b$	.497	12.736
s.d.	.819	16.060
n	159	159

[a] Bold-faced ACF greater than two standard errors.
[b] Debris statistics for series.

lands) and linear (Illinois River). Artifact associations, consistency of association, and density of artifacts also discriminate these two locations (Table 8). We contend that the differences between DOC and Slim Lake reflect long-term differences in the tactics used to forage for distinctive sets of resources associated with upland (e.g., nuts, deer) versus aquatic (e.g., fish, shell fish) habitats.

CONCLUSIONS: MIDDLE ARCHAIC SETTLEMENT STRATEGIES

The differential spatial patterns and by implication patterns of middle Holocene cultural deposition discriminated in the tool-debitage analysis bears on settlement models proposed for the late Middle Archaic in the Lower Illinois River

Table 8.　Comparison of Landscape and Artifact Characteristics
at DOC and Slim Lake

Location	Landscape characteristics				Archaeological record		
			Landscape elements				
	Geomorphic				Artifact	Spatial	Association
	zone	Resources	Ubiquity	Structure	density	association	consistency
DOC	Uplands	Dispersed	Higher	Planar	Low	Low	Variable
Slim Lake	Illinois River	Clumped	High	Linear	High	High	Uniform

valley. Brown and Vierra (1983) contend that after 7000 B.P. there is a shift from high residential mobility associated with a foraging strategy toward more permanent settlement and a logistically organized strategy of resource procurement. In addition to hickory nuts and deer, subsistence appears to be increasingly focused on aquatic resources, especially those in rich backwater habitats in the river valley (Brown and Vierra 1983). The extensive stratigraphic record at the Koster site located in the alluvial/colluvial fan zone (Hajic 1990) reflects this trend (Brown and Vierra 1983). Twenty Archaic components have been identified at Koster dating from 8700 B.P. to 2950 B.P. (Brown and Vierra 1983:175). Prior to about 7000 B.P., occupations are ephemeral (with the exception of Horizon 11), consisting primarily of hearths and associated refuse areas. After 7000 B.P. more substantial occupations are present that are characterized by dense refuse deposits, large pits, burials, and structures (Brown and Vierra 1983). The data recovered from Koster, however, samples only a single location on the landscape. An important indicator of a logistical collector strategy during this period would be the presence of places that served as resource-extractive camps or camps that served other functions associated with a logistical strategy located in other geomorphic zones (i.e., other habitats).

The low-density scatter punctuated by higher-density clusters of cultural remains observed at the DOC location is typical of the upland record in west–central Illinois (Stafford *et al.* 1983; Hassen 1981). Binford (1980) suggests that foragers are more likely to produce such a regional record as a result of low-bulk extraction activities and low redundancy of locations on the landscape (i.e., many places serve as stopping points). However, collector strategies are likely to possess the basic tactics of a foraging pattern plus other tactics specific to a logistical strategy (Binford 1980). The pattern of artifactual debris at the DOC location and presumably in the uplands in general (to the extent it is due to Middle Archaic use) is argued to reflect this type of land use. This low-bulk resource procurement may have been oriented toward dispersed terrestrial animals in the uplands or perhaps opportunistic use of other resources like nuts (see Stafford 1991). Although not a part of this analysis, a high-bulk hickory-nut-processing camp also associated with this late Middle Archaic logistical foraging strategy has also been observed in an upland/tributary valley context (Stafford 1991).

In contrast, the aggregated aquatic resources in the floodplain of the Illinois River probably involved higher-bulk extraction and redundancy of occupation both in the short and long term; hence the different tool/debitage pattern observed at the Slim Lake location. There are other attributes of this record (e.g., large volume pits, shell middens) that also support this contention (Stafford 1991).

The results of this analysis and other data (e.g., Brown and Vierra 1983; Stafford 1985a, 1991) indicate that by 4000–5000 B.P. a settlement strategy had emerged in west–central Illinois that involved the logistical procurement of food resources from riverine and extravalley habitats. Resource extraction was staged from base camps strategically located in the alluvial fan zone but also involved both low- and high-bulk extraction of resources in other geoenvironmental zones that were transported back to base camp locations.

In our view, however, this settlement strategy is not entirely evident unless the regional makeup of the archaeological record is considered in the context of landscape scale. This study strongly suggests that the spatial patterning of artifacts across the landscape is a function of the scale of landforms and the arrangement of landscape elements that served as stopping points (places) on those landforms. The temporal and spatial resolution of the regional record, however, is not uniform. The more stable geomorphic zones contain coarser grain records that require models at congruent scales (see Thomas 1986) and compatible strategies of analysis. A consideration of the scale of landscape variability is a vital component of such modeling and analysis.

ACKNOWLEDGMENTS

Funding for projects summarized in this chapter was provided by the Illinois Department of Transportation. John Walthall's (Chief Archaeologist) support is greatly appreciated. Projects were conducted by the Center for American Archeology, Kampsville, Illinois. We thank Jacqueline Rossignol, LuAnn Wandsnider, Robert Dunnell, and Barbara Stafford for their useful comments on various drafts of this paper. Any errors are of course our own.

REFERENCES

Binford, L. R., 1979, Organization and Formation Processes: Looking at Curated Technologies, *Journal of Anthropological Research* 35:255–273.
Binford, L. R., 1980, Willow Smoke and Dog's Tails: Hunter-Gatherer Settlement Systems and Archaeological Site Formation, *American Antiquity* 45:4–20.
Binford, L. R., 1982, The Archaeology of Place, *Journal of Anthropological Archaeology* 1:5–31.
Binford, L. R., 1983, Long Term Land Use Patterns: Some Implications for Archaeology, in: *Lulu Liner Punctated: Essays in Honor of George Irving Quimby*, Volume 72 (R. Dunnell and D. Grayson, eds.), University of Michigan, Museum of Anthropology, Anthropology Papers, pp. 27–54.
Bettinger, R. L., 1987, Archaeological Approaches to Hunter-Gatherers, *Annual Review of Anthropology* 16:121–142.
Brooks, A., and Yellen J., 1987, The Preservation of Activity Areas in the Archaeological Record: Ethnoarchaeological and Archaeological Work in Northwest Ngamiland, Botswana, in: *Method and Theory for Activity Area Research: An Ethnoarchaeological Approach* (S. Kent, ed.), Columbia University Press, New York, pp. 63–106.
Brown, J. A., and Vierra, R., 1983, What Happened in the Middle Archaic? An Introduction to an Ecological Approach to Koster Site Archaeology, in: *Archaic Hunter-Gatherers in the American*

Midwest: Multidisciplinary Studies of the Archaic Period (J. Phillips and J. Brown, eds.), Academic Press, New York, pp. 165–195.

Butzer, K. W., 1982, *Archaeology as Human Ecology,* Cambridge University Press, Cambridge.

Camilli, E., 1983, Site Occupational History and Lithic Assemblage Structure: An Example From Southeastern Utah, Unpublished Ph.D. dissertation, Department of Anthropology, University of New Mexico.

Carlson, D. L., 1979, Hunter-Gatherer Mobility Strategies: An Example From the Koster Site in the Lower Illinois valley, Ph.D. dissertation, Department of Anthropology, Northwestern University, Evanston, Illinois.

Dewar, R. E., 1986, Discovering Settlement Systems of the Past in New England Site Distributions, *Man in the Northeast* 31:77–88.

Dunnell, R. C., and Dancey,W., 1983, The Siteless Survey: A Regional Scale Data Collection Strategy, in: *Advances in Archaeological Method and Theory* 6:267–287.

Ebert, J. I., 1986, Distributional Archaeology: Nonsite Discovery, Recording and Analytical Methods for Application to Surface Archaeological Records, Unpublished Ph.D. dissertation, Department of Anthropology, University of New Mexico.

Foley, R., 1981, A Model of Regional Archaeological Structure, *Proceedings of the Prehistoric Society* 47:1–18.

Forman, R. T., and Godron, M., 1986, *Landscape Ecology,* John Wiley, New York.

Haggett, P., 1966, *Locational Analysis in Human Geography,* St. Martin's, New York.

Hajic, E. R., 1985, Geomorphic and Stratigraphic Investigations at Campbell Hollow, in: *The Campbell Hollow Archaic Occupations: A Study of Intrasite Spatial Structure in the Lower Illinois Valley,* Volume 4 (C. R. Stafford, ed.), Center for American Archaeology, Kampsville Archeological Center, Research Series, pp. 53–81.

Hajic, E. R., 1987, *Geoenvironmental Context for Archeological Sites in the Lower Illinois River Valley,* Volume 34, U.S. Army Corps of Engineers, St. Louis District Historic Properties Management Report.

Hajic, E. R., 1990, *Koster Site Archeology I: Stratigraphy and Landscape Evolution,* Volume 8, Center for American Archeology, Kampsville Archaeological Center, Research Series.

Hajic, E. R., and Leigh, D. S., 1984, *Shallow Subsurface Geology, Geomorphology and Limited Cultural Resource Investigations of the Meredosia Lake Levee and Drainage District, Scott, Morgan, and Cass Counties, Illinois,* Volume 158, Kampsville Archeological Center, Contract Archeology Program, Reports of Investigations.

Hassen, H., 1981, *Archeological Reconnaissance of a proposed Soyland Power Cooperative Electrical Generating Complex Encompassing 5 Square Kilometers of Dissected Bluffs and Uplands adjacent to the Illinois River, Pike County, Illinois, Volume 111,* Center for American Archeology, Contract Archeology Program, Reports of Investigations.

Hodder, I., and Orton, C., 1976, *Spatial Analysis in Archaeology,* Cambridge University Press, London.

Kelly, R. L., 1983, Hunter-Gatherer Mobility Strategies, *Journal of Anthropological Research,* 39:277–306.

Knoke, D., and Burke, P., 1980, *Log-Linear Models,* Sage Press, Beverly Hills.

McLeary, R., and Hay, Jr., R., 1980, *Applied Time Series Analysis for the Social Sciences,* Sage Press, Beverly Hills.

NACSN (North American Commission on Stratigraphic Nomenclature), 1983, North American Stratigraphic Code, *American Association of Petroleum Geologists Bulletin,* 67:841–875.

Pianka, E. R., 1983, *Evolutionary Ecology,* Harper & Row, New York.

Pielou, E. C., 1979, *Biogeography,* John Wiley, New York.

Reynolds, H. T., 1984, *Analysis of Nominal Data* (2nd ed.), Sage Press, Beverly Hills.

Rodgers, E. S., 1963, *The Hunting Group—Hunting Territory Complex among the Mistassini Indians*, Volume 63, National Museum of Canada, Anthropology Series, Ottawa.

Ruhe, R. V., 1975, Geomorphology: Geomorphic Process and Suficial Geology, Houghton Mifflin, Boston.

Schiffer, M. B., 1976, *Behavioral Archeology*, Academic Press, New York.

Sharp, H. S., 1977, The Caribou-Eater Chipewyan: Bilaterality, Strategies in Caribou Hunting and the Fur Trade, *Artic Anthropology* 14:35–40.

Simek, J., and Leslie, P., 1983, Partitioning Chi-Square for the Analysis of Frequency Table Data: An Archaeological Application, *Journal of Archaeological Science* 10:79–85.

Senft, R. L., Coushenour, M. B., Bailey, D. W., Rittenhouse, L. R., Sala, O. E., and Swift, D. M., 1987, Large Herbivore Foraging and Ecological Hierarchies, *Bioscience* 37:789–799.

Stafford, B. D., 1989, *Central Illinois Expressway Archeology: Floodplain Archaic Occupations of the Illinois Valley Crossing*, Volume 4, Center for American Archeology, Kampsville Archeological Center, Technical Report.

Stafford, B. D., and Sant, M. B. (eds.), 1985, *Smiling Dan: Structure and Function at a Middle Woodland Settlement in the Illinois Valley*, Volume 2, Center for American Archeology, Kampsville Archeological Center, Research Series.

Stafford, C. R. (ed.), 1985a, *The Campbell Hollow Archaic Occupations: A Study of Intrasite Spatial Structure in the Lower Illinois Valley*, Volume 4, Center for American Archeology, Kampsville Archeological Center, Research Series.

Stafford, C. R., 1985b, Spatial Structure of the Middle Archaic Component, in: *The Campbell Hollow Archaic Occupations: A Study of Intrasite Spatial Structure in the Lower Illinois Valley* (C. R. Stafford, ed.), Volume 4, Center for American Archeology, Kampsville Archeological Center, Research Series, pp. 177–235.

Stafford, C. R., 1985c, Hunter-gatherer settlement strategies: A regional perspective on intrasite spatial analysis, Paper presented at the 50th Annual Meeting of the Society for American Archaeology, Denver.

Stafford, C. R., 1987, Settlement Strategies and Lithic Tool Recycling: Analysis of an Early Middle Archaic Occupation in the Lower Illinois Valley, in: *Coasts, Plains and Deserts: Papers in Honor of Reynold Ruppé* (S. Gaines, ed.), Volume 37, Arizona State University, Anthropological Research Paper, pp. 227–238.

Stafford, C. R., 1991, Archaic Period Logistical Foraging Strategies in West-Central Illinois, *Midcontinental Journal of Archaeology*, 16:212–246.

Stafford, C. Russell, Deiss, Ronald, Hajic, Edwin R., and Leigh, Davis S., 1983, Archeological Survey and Limited Soil Coring and Test Excavations of Cultural Resources in the FAP 408 Flint and Blue Creek Alternates of the Illinois Crossing, Pike and Scott Counties, Illinois, Volume 140, Contract Archeology Program, Center for American Archeology, Reports of Investigations.

Stephens, D. W., and Krebs, J. R., 1986, *Foraging Theory*, Princeton University Press, Princeton, New Jersey.

Styles, T. R., 1985, *Holocene and Late Pleistocene Geology of the Napoleon Hollow Site in the Lower Illinois Valley*, Volume 5, Center for American Archeology, Kampsville Archeological Center, Research Series.

Thomas, D. H., 1975, Nonsite Sampling in Archaeology: Up the Creek Without a Site?, in: *Sampling in Archaeology* (J. Mueller, ed.), University of Arizona Press, Tucson, pp. 61–81.

Thomas, D. H., 1986, Contemporary Hunter-Gatherer Archaeology in America, in: *American Archaeology: Past and Future* (D. Meltzer, D. Fowler, and J. Sabloff, eds.), Smithsonian Institution Press, Washington, pp. 237–276.

Urban, D. L., O'Neill, R. V., and Shugart, Jr., H. H., 1987, Landscape Ecology, *Bioscience*, 37:119–127.

Wiant, M. D., Hajic, E. R., and Styles, T. R., 1983, Napoleon Hollow and Koster Site Stratigraphy: Implications for Holocene Landscape Evolution and Studies of Archaic Period Settlement Patterns in the Lower Illinois River Valley, in: *Archaic Hunter-Gatherers in the American Midwest: Multidisciplinary Studies of the Archaic Period* (J. Phillips and J. Brown, eds.), Academic Press, New York, pp. 147–164.

Wiens, J. A., 1976, Pattern and Process in Grassland Bird Communities, *Ecological Monographs* 43:237–270.

Winterhalder, B., 1980, Environmental Analysis in Human Evolution and Adaptation Research, *Human Ecology* 8:135–155.

Part IV

The Temporal Dimension of Archaeological Landscapes

This section focuses attention on a perennial problem in archaeology: determining the scale and resolution of occupations (temporally discrete cultural episodes of deposition) and components (temporally discrete archaeological deposits) and the nature of their interaction. The investigation of organization, and change in organization, underlying the interaction of subsistence strategies and environment is reflected archaeologically as an investigation of the relationship between occupation and component. *Occupation* can have the traditional sense of a temporally discrete activity or set of activities taking place in a highly localized or spatially bounded area. In this discussion, however, and in the chapters that follow, occupation expands spatially to cover entire regions, and stretches temporally over millennia. Likewise, *component* can be perceived as part or all of a traditionally conceived, spatially bounded, temporally specific site. With a landscape perspective, however, a component can cover square meters or hundreds of hectares, with a temporal resolution affixed to a chronologically precise "phase" of decades, or representing units of time resolved no finer than thousands of years.

Investigating the interaction of occupation and component, and by implication the investigation of organization, is partially a problem of space and location on the landscape—as discussed in the previous section. Making sense of the interaction is, however, also complicated by problems of temporal resolution. The inability to determine temporal scale often underlies the difficulty in understanding the occupation–component relationship.

In the first chapter of this section, Jones and Beck review two strategies often used for deriving temporal measures in the archaeological record, association and covariation; point out some (often overlooked) difficulties in applying these chronological approaches to dispersed distributional patterns; and argue for developing multiple classes of time-sensitive artifacts. The authors promote an obsidian hydration dating technique that can potentially reference every obsidian manufacturing event for prehistoric hunter–gatherers in the late Pleistocene–early Holocene record of Nevada, where obsidian makes up a substantial part of the chipped stone assemblage. This method consists of producing a serial order for each separate obsidian source, together providing a cross-checking chronology of production events and their frequency through time. This approach not only refines dating but serves as a potentially powerful analytical method for discerning the relationships between occupation and component and ultimately addresses patterns of land use.

Zvelebil, Green, and Macklin provide an overview of archaeological conventions used to infer cultural and behavioral change through time; explore the concepts of linear, durational, static, and cyclic time; and focus on two temporal relations within linear time: episodal time and processual time. The authors argue that incorporation of taphonomic approaches to the landscape makes it possible to apply simultaneously episodal and processual time to the behavioral–chronological matrix, and in so doing, begin to sort out the relationship between occupation and component.

In their investigation of the indigenous versus derived origin for the Neolithic of southeastern Ireland, the authors examine variability in the size and composition of lithic artifacts, drawing theoretically on actualistic studies of foraging strategy. Preliminary results call into question the "widely held assumption that the technological change marking the shift from the Mesolithic to the Neolithic is paralleled by the rapid replacement of foraging by farming." Instead, the transition seems to have been gradual, with substantial interaction between the two economies.

Dewar and McBride evaluate the relationship between component and occupation and suggest a solution based on behavioral links with formation processes rather than on alternative chronological measures (Jones and Beck) or oscillating temporal scales (Zvelebil, Green, and Macklin). The authors propose "medium-term processes," those processes that affect reuse of an area over years and decades, as a way to explicate the relationship between occupation and component. The authors are able to show how medium-term processes (as opposed to shifts in settlement strategy) might have reshaped the "remnant settlement pattern" of prehistoric hunter–gatherers in the Lower Connecticut River Valley of New England.

In the last chapter of this section, Wandsnider takes Dewar and McBride's middle-term processes as a point of departure. She asks how archaeological landscapes, subject to different frequencies and periods of use—that is, responsive to middle-term processes of varying character—might develop? She uses simulation analysis to explore this question, deriving implications for the spatial structure of archaeological variation. Analysis results suggest fruitful domains for the actualistic study of developing archaeological landscapes.

Time has been conceptualized traditionally in very limited ways. Dating is either absolute within the limitations of radiocarbon, dendrochronological, and other forms of dating or restricted to phases assigned to spatially constricted components of sites. The chapters in this section demonstrate that time can vary considerably from absolute dating in resolution and still be useful for resolving temporal problems of the record. Likewise, the behavioral systems underlying the structure of the record can be conceptualized at different scales, unfolding over years, decades, centuries, and millennia. In other words, behavioral scales range from individual activities to evolutionary shifts in strategy. In turn, investigating shifts in tempos of abandonment and reoccupation revealed in the structure of the archaeological record discloses the character of land use and ultimately the organization of behavioral systems.

Distributional forms of data recovery, the study of site-level formation processes, and the study of the tempo of behavioral systems all contribute to an expanded understanding of the full range of temporal scales and behavioral resolutions represented in the archaeological record. These approaches help augment our notions of archaeological time. Jones and Beck expand the definition of *contemporaneity* beyond its common usage in describing simultaneously created deposits. Zvelebil and colleagues redefine *episode* to refer to a temporal unit corresponding to the total length of time over which an archaeological deposit has accumulated. In defining episode this way, they expand its use beyond the ethnographic framework of the behavioral archaeologists (e.g., Schiffer 1976) into a wider archaeological arena. Dewar and McBride's medium-term processes allow archaeologists to examine time spans intermediate to ethnographic annual round and evolutionary change.

A landscape perspective combining off-site or distributional data collection, formation processes, ethnoarchaeological studies of mobility and foraging strategies, and ethnographic studies of abandonment provide a setting for investigating the entire scope of the temporal resolution problem. Augmenting our concepts of time beyond absolute dating and site-oriented "phases" allows archaeologists to reformulate the occupation–component interaction, providing direction for productive theory building.

REFERENCES

Schiffer, M. B., 1976, *Behavioral Archeology*, Academic Press, New York.

Chapter 8

Chronological Resolution in Distributional Archaeology

GEORGE T. JONES AND CHARLOTTE BECK

INTRODUCTION

The paradigmatic changes in archaeology during the 1960s and 1970s saw re-focusing of research interests from culture–historical problems to issues of human adaptation and attendant shifts in research design, from concentration on single sites to a concern with entire regions. Early in these considerations, some archaeologists concerned with the prehistory of mobile hunter–gatherers recognized that the study of land use, adaptation, and processes leading to stability or change could not be conducted solely in terms of regional site records (e.g., Thomas 1971, 1975; Dancey 1973, 1974). Undoubtedly, those aspects of land use that contributed rather small quantities of material remains to the archaeological record that might be widely dispersed over space was an important analytic domain. They suggested instead that artifacts, all artifacts, rather than sites become the focus of discovery and analysis. We refer to this perspective as distributional archaeology, although other terms like *nonsite approach* (Thomas 1975) and *off-site archaeology* (e.g., Foley 1981a) are presently in use.

GEORGE T. JONES and CHARLOTTE BECK • Department of Anthropology, Hamilton College, Clinton, New York 13323.

Space, Time, and Archaeological Landscapes, edited by Jacqueline Rossignol and LuAnn Wandsnider. Plenum Press, New York, 1992.

With this more inclusive view of the archaeological record of regions came heightened problems in dating, primarily because distributional archaeology (1) almost always is surface archaeology (but see Isaac 1981) and (2) characteristically concerns highly dispersed artifact distributions. On this point, Foley (1981a:197) remarks that the enhanced attention to the spatial dimension accompanying distributional approaches has come at the expense of temporal control. This is not to say that attempts have not been made to date surface assemblages (see Beck 1984; Bettinger 1975; Jones 1984; Thomas 1971); rather, that many of the questions now of concern to archaeologists, such as delimiting the processes leading to the formation of regional artifact records, require fine levels of temporal resolution, often greater than can even be achieved in well-stratified archaeological deposits.

In attempting to build cultural chronologies from the archaeological record of landscapes, particularly those parts that lie beyond the boundaries of dense, tightly clustered phenomena, that is, sites, we are reminded of just how complex chronological inference can be. At least two problems exist. First, most dating methods are appropriately applied only to buried deposits and cannot be used in surface contexts. Even if this were not the case, a second and more substantial problem remains: Chronological associations are exceedingly difficult to demonstrate in those settings in which low-density artifact distributions predominate. How then do we establish chronological controls for the dispersed, surface-artifact records of landscapes?

In this chapter we explore the problems of temporal resolution in surface contexts, particularly for those parts of landscapes comprising low-density artifact records. We then demonstrate the difficulties of formulating such chronologies by developing three examples. Two are from the archaeological literature of the Great Basin, where distributional studies began two decades ago, and the third considers our current efforts to apply obsidian hydration dating to a surface artifact record from eastern Nevada. Throughout, our discussions assume a distributional focus; we will supply no justification for this strategy, leaving that to other authors in this volume. We begin by outlining some of the methodological difficulties posed by dispersed artifact distributions.

CHRONOLOGY AND ASSOCIATION

Almost from the beginning of our formal training in archaeology we learn of the importance of archaeological associations for dating; indeed, Fagan (1978) elevates this concept to a general principle or law. Association refers to two or more artifacts residing in the same stratigraphic unit in close spatial proximity. The clear significance for dating is that, based on associational arguments, we are able to transfer an age determination, however obtained, to all associated items.

In the case of artifact-based dating approaches, the temporal meaning of one artifact is transferred to other associated, but less temporally sensitive, artifacts. In other words, artifacts within a single stratum are considered *contemporaneous*. In this sense, the term *contemporaneity* is relative in that the stratum in question may represent 50, 1,000, or even several thousand years of accumulation. Thus, when two artifacts are said to be contemporaneous, the scale of their association is wholly dependent upon the temporal resolution in that particular situation (see Raymond 1984/1985).

Such arguments of association are so routine in archaeology as to normally require little attention. However, in the surface record where stratigraphy is absent, associational arguments often must be based solely on proximity,[1] with the strength of the argument diminishing with lessening artifact density. Take as an example the artifact cluster shown in Figure 1. Among the 1,600 artifacts on this surface are 11 projectile points that represent four periods spanning some 4,000 years of use (see Beck 1984). Here there is no clear spatial basis by which to identify artifacts associated with projectile points of specific periods. A contrasting situation is shown in Figure 2 in which distinct spatial clustering is evident. Once again, four temporal periods are represented, this time by 13 projectile points. However, in this example points associated with a particular cluster, for the most part, represent the same temporal period.[2] Thus, in the latter case, discontinuities in the spatial dispersion of artifacts are the bases for distinguishing separate clusters, each with a coherent chronological signature. In contrast, because distribution of artifacts is continuous over the entire site, the first case does not yield to further chronological refinement based upon distributional characteristics alone.

Our confidence in the strength of association drops, generally speaking, as distances increase between items. In cases of extreme spatial dispersion, associational arguments based on proximity break down completely. Under the most familiar circumstances, as when radiocarbon dating is applied to stratigraphically discrete artifact assemblages, archaeologists commonly speak of dating occupations or components. Although an *occupation* need not literally mean a single, continuous episode of site use, the term normally implies a brief interval of time, a seasonal occupation perhaps or some similarly conceived ethnographic unit of time. However, when attention is shifted to dating artifacts widely distributed over a landscape, the discreteness of the time interval being assessed is far less certain. As a result, such considerations often turn to the duration of use of the

[1] Associational arguments can be bolstered by, for example, refitting studies. But this evidence, too, can be questioned by recounting the potential of reuse of a locality.

[2] The Elko type is shown separately because its presence is not indicative of any particular period. In the Steens area, for example, it is present for at least 7,000 years and thus is not useful by itself as a temporal indicator. Its presence neither adds to nor subtracts from temporal information.

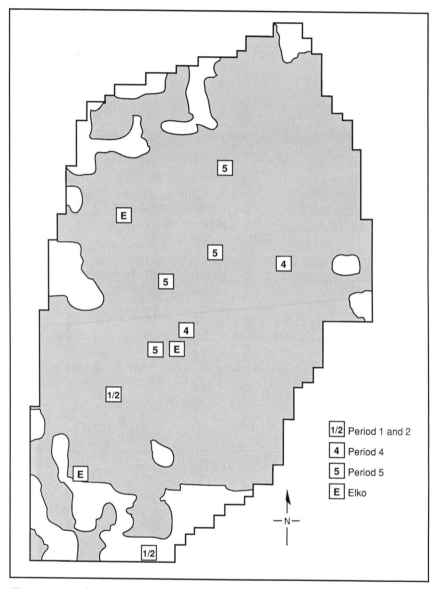

Figure 1. Map of DC1-33/1, a site collected by the Steens Mountain Prehistory Project in southeastern Oregon showing the distribution of artifactual material (stippled area) together with the distribution of period markers (projectile point types) (modified from Beck 1984).

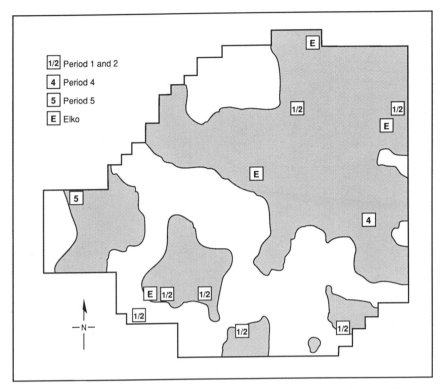

Figure 2. Map of TA-4/1A, a site collected by the Steens Mountain Prehistory Project in southeastern Oregon showing the distribution of artifactual material (stippled areas) together with the distribution of period markers (projectile point types) (modified from Beck 1984).

landscape, with far less emphasis on the actual ages of the events producing the artifacts. Thus we find concern expressed over the length of the interval during which a particular land use pattern persisted, usually considered on the scale of centuries or millennia in the case of hunter–gatherer studies. Under these conditions, the tempo of land use assumes the form of long-term averages.

As part of this different emphasis we also note a shift in the associational argument, from association by virtue of "cluster affiliation" to that of association by virtue of "sample unit" affiliation. Temporal markers are no longer assembled on a site by site basis but instead are tallied usually by more inclusive spatial units, environmental strata (e.g., topographic, vegetational, elevation zones) for instance. This represents a change in the sort of temporal control sought and the kinds of problems addressed, from dating sites and building chronological orders of sites (e.g., occupational events) to assessments of artifact discard rates over time among environmental strata. This emphasis marks another shift in the nature of the chronologic argument; embedded in this kind of associational argument is an assumption regarding a second relational property—covariation.

Whereas patterns of association are founded upon spatial proximity, patterns of covariation (Binford 1972) revolve around correlated frequencies of two or more classes of artifacts (Schiffer 1987). The simplest condition is one in which the frequencies of two classes are related in a positive linear fashion: as the frequency of Class A rises across several collections, the frequency of Class B increases in a proportional manner. Nonlinear and negative patterns are also likely to be expressed archaeologically, as well as instances of no covariation at all. Combinations of these patterns are at the heart of exploratory statistical approaches—pattern search procedures—to uncover spatial patterning and activity areas. It is the simple linear pattern, however, that is adopted for chronological study.

To describe patterns of landscape use as decreasing, increasing, or remaining constant over time, it must be assumed that the discard of all artifacts covaries in a proportional manner to time-sensitive artifacts. In a simple case, for example, we might find that the later of two projectile point types occurs in far greater frequency. Our simple conclusion would be that projectile-point-using events were more common later in time; that is, the intensity of projectile point use increased with time. The assumption of covariation comes into play when we generalize from this pattern that all other kinds of tool categories were deposited over time in the same proportions as the two point styles.

Next we present two extended examples drawn from the Great Basin archaeological literature to show how the assumptions outlined here are used. These examples illustrate two approaches in constructing chronologies for landscapes using time-sensitive classes. Both studies utilize extensive regional artifact samples, in part made up of numerous time-sensitive artifacts, drawn from both clustered (site) and dispersed (off-site) contexts. For these examples, we present in some detail the arguments and assumptions made by each study to show the strengths and liabilities in these approaches. Although the lines of reasoning differ, both approaches ultimately falter around the assumption of covariation.

GREAT BASIN EXAMPLES

Distributional approaches have a long history in the Great Basin of the western United States. Before the late 1960s, a dominant concern over culture–historical issues led archaeologists to emphasize investigations of deeply stratified deposits, usually in rockshelters. However, explicit attempts to evaluate Jennings's Desert Culture model (Jennings and Norbeck 1955) and to assess the temporal depth of the ethnographic pattern described by Steward (1938) led to a rethinking of traditional research designs and brought about not only systematic regional survey but a distributional orientation as well. Key in this shift to a regional approach was the observation that effective prehistoric and historic adaptations emphasized mobility, flexible community patterns, and use of a wide range of resources that could be found distributed over this highly vertical, arid setting.

Throughout this period, Great Basin archaeologists have relied on artifact-based dating approaches—cross-dating—in order to build regional surface chronologies (e.g., Beck 1984; Bettinger 1975; Jones 1984; Thomas 1971, 1981, 1988; Weide 1968). Projectile points receive the greatest attention in these studies, and they figure centrally in the examples provided. We should note, however, that some surface dating studies have made use of geochronological information (e.g., Davis 1975, 1978). Although such investigations hold promise (see Foley 1981a,b for more general consideration), they do not appear suited for use in areas with highly variable depositional histories like those found in the Great Basin.

Example 1: Reese River Survey

Our first example is taken from a familiar case, Thomas's (1971) pioneering research in the Reese River Valley of central Nevada (Figure 3). The Reese River Project was significant along many dimensions, among these problem formulation, sampling, simulation, systematic surface collection, and nonsite orientation. It was grounded in a clear project goal—an archaeological test of Steward's (1938) description of Shoshonean land use practices. Thomas converted Steward's descriptions by means of simulation into expectations for the distribution and density of several classes of artifact assemblages in a large region. The data to evaluate these predictions were generated by nonsite surface survey of 140 randomly drawn quadrats distributed over four environmental zones. The survey of 35 km^2 represented 10% coverage and yielded over 2,500 modified and about 80,000 flake artifacts.

Although Thomas is equally well known for his metrical and typologic studies of Great Basin projectile point styles (e.g., Thomas 1970, 1971, 1978, 1981), his summaries of the Reese River Project (e.g., Thomas 1972, 1973) do not have a temporal focus except in noting that the span of occupation appears to extend from about 2500 B.C. to historic times. In fact, in realizing very high degrees of conformity to model predictions there appears to be little basis for suggesting significant changes in settlement or subsistence patterns throughout this time period. A similar approach was taken by Bettinger (1975) and, although styles of presentation have changed, Thomas's recent Monitor Valley studies (1988) exercise this approach as well.

Several steps are involved in building the Reese River chronology. First, it is demonstrated that projectile point styles are temporally sensitive—they possess limited temporal durations and peaks in popularity. This is done through investigation of distributions of styles in dated, stratigraphic contexts. From this information, phases are constructed. In the Reese River area, Thomas recognizes four phases covering 4,500 years. Identified with each phase is a point style, one that is numerically dominant and that has a temporal span coeval with the phase. The latest of these, the Yankee Blade Phase, for instance, is marked by the presence of Desert Series projectile points (i.e., Desert Side-Notched and Cottonwood Triangular types [Heizer and Hester 1978]) as well as the presence of Shoshonean pottery.

Described thus far is a familiar culture–historical approach, but it begins to differ at the next step. Typically, sites would now be affixed to this phase sequence based upon their projectile point component. Instead, Thomas tabulates the frequencies of phase-marker projectile points by environmental zones (Table 1). This matrix includes projectile points collected from all sample quadrats within a zone, whether they come from dense artifact clusters or areas of low artifact density. Based on the relative proportions of markers by phase, conclusions are drawn concerning patterns of use of each environmental zone throughout the 4,500 years of occupation. Thomas states, for example, "the riverine stratum [A1] demonstrates a continuity throughout the Medithermal period, the relative frequency varying only 4% during the entire period" (1971:181). Although not explicitly discussed, it follows that Thomas assumes phase-diagnostic points covary in a linear fashion with other artifact categories. That is, a change in projectile point frequencies suggests a change in the frequency of stratum use and therefore a change in the frequencies of other functional categories or assemblage types. This assumption, we argue, may be unfounded. We return to this point shortly.

Table 1. Distribution of Phase Markers in Reese River Valley[a]

| | Environmental zone | | | |
Phase	A1	A2	B	C
Yankee Blade	45%	4%	41%	10%
Underdown	46%	12%	35%	8%
Reveille	41%	17%	32%	11%
Devils Gate	44%	12%	18%	26%

[a] After Thomas 1971, Table 5.1.

Example 2: Steens Mountain Prehistory Project

The purpose of studies in the Steens Mountain area of southeastern Oregon (Figure 3) (e.g., Beck 1984; Jones 1984; Jones *et al.* 1989) was to independently establish paleoenvironmental and archaeological records covering the Holocene interval and to investigate cultural change as it might relate to biophysical change. Though not guided by such a detailed settlement–subsistence model as found in the Reese River Project, explicit interest in documenting the nature and duration of land use patterns expressed in this area led to use of a nonsite research design. The Steens Mountain Project involved an artifact-oriented survey of about

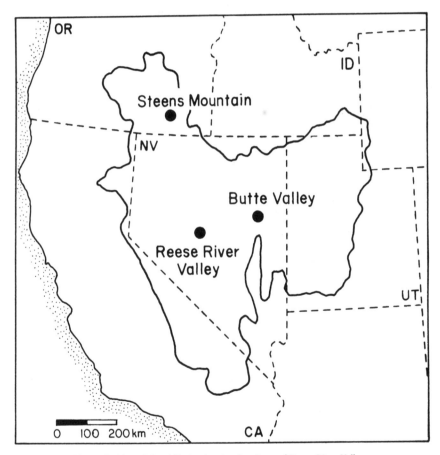

Figure 3. Map of Great Basin showing locations of Reese River Valley, Steens Mountain, and Butte Valley.

78 km² distributed over 85 sample units. These units were drawn randomly from a project area covering nearly 1590 km², which was stratified according to several environmental criteria. Artifacts and provenience information were collected through systematic pedestrian survey by individuals spaced at 15-meter intervals. Areas of high artifact density that precluded accurate provenience recording during survey were flagged and later collected in grids by mapping crews. These areas of high artifact density were called sites. Artifact collections drawn from the remaining low-density areas within sample units were referred to as "offsite" samples. Although no behavioral implications were intended by these different designations, each sample type initially was analyzed separately. A total of 146,028 artifacts were collected (and analyzed)[3] in site contexts while 12,975 artifacts were collected in offsite contexts. Classifiable projectile points represent nearly 3.0% of the off-site component, whereas they represent only 0.6% of the site component.

A somewhat different chronological approach than that used by Thomas was followed in the Steens study (for details see Beck 1984 and Jones 1984), although the results also ultimately rest on an assumption of covariation. Following classification of the projectile points, analyses turned to development of a chronological order of sites using seriation. Using assemblages with sufficiently large numbers of projectile points of clearly limited duration, an initial order of 22 site assemblages was obtained. To place the seriation order in time, relative abundances of projectile point styles at particular positions within the order were compared with those in radiocarbon-dated strata from a number of excavated sites within the region. Using this approach, six periods were defined, each associated with a suite of projectile point styles in more or less fixed proportions (Figure 4). An additional 39 assemblages with smaller samples of projectile points were assigned to one of the six periods, based again on relative proportions of point styles. In all, 61 sites, 75.3% of all clusters collected, were thus ordered chronologically.

Having arrived at a serial order of sites, we were in a position to assess constancy and change in the rate of site formation in this region. We asked next if it might be possible to assess as well chronological patterning in land use that would take into account the off-site record. Unfortunately, samples of projectile points drawn from off-site collections did not meet the conditions of seriation and thus could not be used to generate a chronologic order matching that of the sites. Off-site samples clearly often represent much longer, sometimes interrupted, intervals of use, and are not episodes of comparable duration. Unable to apply seriation to the off-site projectile point samples, we turned to a statistical comparison of site and off-site projectile point frequencies. We reasoned that if site and off-site use varied in a positive, linear fashion through time, the relative abundances of projectile point styles would agree across the two records (i.e., site and

---

[3] Over 300,000 artifacts were actually collected from sites, but some of the larger site assemblages were subsampled for analysis. The figure of 146,028 reflects only those artifacts analyzed.

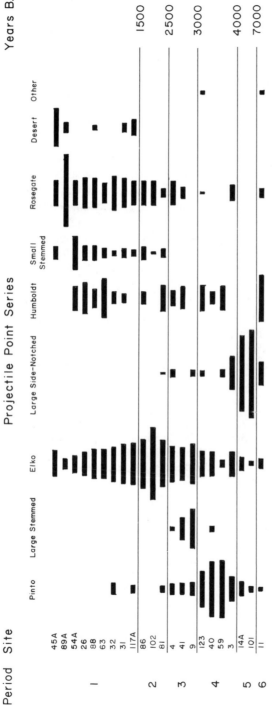

Figure 4. Final seriation order and chronological periods for Steens-area sites (modified from Beck 1984:144).

off-site). Should that be the case, we argued, then rates of change suggested by the site record (i.e., in terms of changes in site number, site size, and functional and technological composition) would apply equally to the off-site record. Discrepancies noted between site and off-site samples would suggest, in contrast, evidence of differences in the intensity of use represented in each context (Jones 1984).

Several statistical comparisons were made, investigating, for example, relationships among environmental strata, between site and off-site samples, among functional assemblage classes composed on the basis of technological and use-wear criteria, and so forth. Table 2 illustrates one such comparison. Here the apportionment of projectile points to various stylistic classes is compared between site and off-site samples from one of the primary environmental strata. For the tabled values a nonsignificant chi-square statistic ($\Sigma^2 = 3.51$; $p > 0.05$) was derived. Adjusted residual statistics (Everitt 1977) were computed to identify those cell frequencies that are significantly above or below their expected size. In this example, no cell frequency exceeds the 0.05 critical value for the statistic, and thus these data indicate nonsignificant associations between point types and sample type.

Based upon sets of comparisons like the one just illustrated, it was argued that site and off-site use, or perhaps put more accurately, those events contributing to dense clusters and dispersed patterns were coeval. Moreover, it appeared that through time, expansion and contraction of site use was mirrored by off-site

**Table 2.   Comparison of Projectile Point Frequencies
between Site and Off-Site Samples from the Catlow Upland
Stratum, Steens Mountain, Oregon (a significant [$p < .05$]
value for the adjusted residual statistic (AR) is ± 1.96)**

	Site		Off-site	
Type	N	AR	N	AR
Early	4	−1.09	3	1.09
Large Side-notch	51	0.45	15	−0.45
Pinto	71	0.72	20	−0.72
Large Stemmed	27	−0.57	11	0.57
Elko	144	−0.86	54	0.86
Humboldt	95	0.47	29	−0.47
Rosegate	79	0.63	23	−0.63
Small Stemmed	34	−0.17	12	0.17
Desert Side-notch	19	−0.56	8	0.56

$\chi^2 = 3.51$; $p \gg .05$

use (Jones 1984), and thus a rate of site formation derived on the basis of typological cross-dating and periodization probably was a close approximation of the rate of artifact discard in areas beyond site boundaries. As a final note we should be clear that such comparisons were based on aggregated data and thus chronological inferences are generalized for the project area as a whole or large segments of it. Attempts to evaluate the tempo of land use at finer geographic scales, as, for example, between sites and off-site records from the same sample unit, were inconclusive because of sample size limitations. Thus, although it is reasonable to suppose that many contiguous site and off-site records were built during the same time interval, and indeed might be both spatially and systemically related with each other, such questions could not be answered with the data at hand.

Evaluation of Examples

In contrasting these two examples, one can readily note that nonsite and site/off-site emphases yield somewhat different approaches to chronology. In Thomas's nonsite study, inferences about temporal variation in settlement pattern proceeded directly from a matrix of projectile point frequencies. Our approach for the Steens material differs to the extent that site and off-site data were compared. In the end, however, both approaches converge with the assumption that the numerical behavior of phase markers holds a proportionate relationship to other artifacts such that temporal trends in the abundances of projectile points indicate proportionate trends among other artifacts. By virtue of a general association, both projectile points and other classes occurring in the same environmental unit, the temporal patterns we determine for one class of artifacts is suggested to be more widely applicable to all artifacts.

The chronological approaches examined thus far, to the extent they are applied to low-density or dispersed distributional patterns, are potentially compromised. The absence of clear associations among artifacts in low-density settings makes extensions of temporal inferences based on time markers to other artifacts suspect. This particular problem is evident when chronologies are sought for small spatial areas with few artifacts among which time markers are likely to be extremely rare. A response to this problem is to broaden the spatial scale at which temporal patterns are sought as we did in the Steens case by aggregating data from several sample units. But this, too, creates difficulties because to do this increases the likelihood that artifacts are not systemically related and thus are not contemporaneous. Most often, probably, aggregation will increase the likelihood that fine temporal patterns are masked.

Both of the approaches described are built on the basic relational assumption that a temporal relationship of positive, linear covariation exists between time markers and other artifacts. In the absence of other chronological information, it is difficult not to make this assumption, but clearly it is also difficult to warrant. Projectile points, for example, carry chronological information, but they also obviously are tied to specific functions and consequently their variation in frequency over time in a particular setting may be quite independent of frequency changes among other functional classes (Bettinger 1980).

When temporal inferences rest on single-artifact categories like projectile points, the assumption of covarying depositional patterns is untested. This condition improves when multiple classes of time-sensitive artifacts are represented, particularly if those classes cross-cut major functional boundaries. Comparisons of the temporal behaviors of these different classes may provide a stronger case for linear covariation or other kinds of covariant relationships. When attention is turned to the Great Basin record, we find that only pottery, and to some extent basketry and beads, fill this need. However, the late appearance of pottery as well as the infrequent occurrence of all three of these artifact classes in surface (and especially in off-site) contexts considerably limit their value in chronological studies.

Unverified association and covariation in the surface artifact record are difficult but not insurmountable problems in the construction of chronologies. Other methods, such as obsidian hydration dating, have the potential for solving these problems. With obsidian artifacts comprising sizable components of regional records throughout the Great Basin and other parts of the Desert West, the prospect of a viable obsidian hydration dating program applied to surface artifacts is very attractive. Indeed, the potential to date *every* artifact should lead us to think very differently about how we organize the archaeological record for analytic purposes (see Dunnell, this volume). Agreement that obsidian hydration can be such a dating tool is far from universal, however; in the minds of many archaeologists there are too many uncontrolled factors that limit or negate the utility of the method in such contexts. To be sure, research on this matter is not definitive. Later we discuss our preliminary investigations of obsidian hydration dating, showing how it might be useful in overcoming the shortcomings of style-based chronologic approaches discussed. We begin with a brief summary of the dating method and recent applications to surface data before moving to an extended example from our current research in eastern Nevada.

OBSIDIAN HYDRATION DATING

The details of obsidian hydration dating (OHD) are provided in several summaries (e.g., Friedman and Smith 1960; Michels 1973; Michels and Tsong 1980) and need not be repeated extensively here. The method is based on the fact that the freshly broken surface of obsidian immediately begins to absorb moisture from its surroundings. This absorption is marked by a hydration rind, the thickness of which is time dependent.

The rate at which the hydration rind expands is a function of both the chemical composition of the obsidian specimen and the temperature of its environment (effective hydration temperature). Neither factor is sufficiently well understood to enable hydration rind values to be converted directly into calendrical dates in the absence of a calibrating scale, such as a radiocarbon sequence (Michels and Tsong 1980). Consequently, as a precise chronometric method, OHD is limited primarily to those circumstances in which obsidian artifacts are recovered from deeply buried, temperature-stable environments. Even then a rate established in one locale will not be applicable to another locale with different temperature characteristics (e.g., Ridings 1991).

At present, the power of OHD lies in its use as a relative dating tool (Jackson 1984; Green 1986; Zeier and Elston 1986). In principle the approach is quite simple, proceeding again from the measured depths of hydration rinds:

> On this basis artifacts can be ordered as a series with relative position determined by successive increments of numerical value: 1.3, 1.9, 2.5 (microns), and so on. Assuming one can hold both chemical composition and EHT [effective hydration temperature] constant for a given population of artifacts, such an ordering permits the various culturally significant attributes of each specimen to be chronologically situated relative to those of every other specimen. (Michels and Tsong 1980:408–409)

Because variation due to chemistry is readily controlled by trace element characterization of sources, the primary obstacle concerns the magnitude of temperature fluctuations at the surface. Trembour and Friedman caution that "even short exposures to abnormally high heat can severely distort the outcome of the dating analysis" (1984:80). Thus, it is not unreasonable to ask if the hydration process is too sensitive to provide interpretable chronological information from obsidian artifacts exposed at the surface. Certainly, we expect that fully contemporaneous artifacts taken from different points along an elevational gradient, for instance, will possess different hydration values. But if collected from the same geographic locale, or from identical topographic circumstances, will a set of artifacts resulting from the same manufacturing event possess the same values? For OHD to be used as a relative dating tool for surface artifacts, this must be the case.

Although few in number, empirical studies in which OHD has been applied to surface data (e.g., Bettinger 1980; Layton 1973; McGonagle 1979; Origer and Wickstrom 1982; Raymond 1984–1985) largely confirm its applicability. For example, in an early study, Layton (1973) showed that among projectile points, the oldest type on stylistic grounds had the widest hydration rinds, whereas younger styles possessed narrower rinds. Layton's data also suggest that artifacts on the surface may hydrate much faster than those in buried contexts (see also Friedman 1976). Raymond's (1984–1985) work demonstrates the usefulness of OHD for establishing associations among surface artifacts within a cluster. He suggests that a set of artifacts of roughly the same age will exhibit a narrow range of hydration values centering on a single mode. In those cases in which more than one geochemical type is present, the more rapidly hydrating types will show less tightly clustered distributions of values, although they still retain symmetry. It follows that these distributional entailments will change if samples comprise noncontemporaneous specimens. In sum, though still at an early point in its development, obsidian hydration dating does appear to have significant potential to provide relative ages of artifacts exposed on the surface.

With obsidian artifacts comprising sizable components of regional records throughout the Desert West, we see many opportunities to develop chronologies that reference every obsidian manufacturing event. In the simplest sense, such a chronology is an arrangement of artifact frequencies by sequential hydration rind widths. In this way a serial order is constructed for each source of obsidian with multiple orders providing a cross-checking chronology of production events and their frequency through time. Further, serial orders of assemblages can be constructed in the same way, based on the mean hydration width for each assemblage, provided individual hydration values within each assemblage exhibit a narrow range and are unimodally distributed. To reduce the confounding effects of temperature, collections are best broken into samples of similar elevation and aspect. We now turn to an example from our recent studies in Butte Valley, Nevada, to consider the implications of such an approach.

BUTTE VALLEY LANDSCAPE CHRONOLOGY

Butte Valley Project

Our present studies in Butte Valley, eastern Nevada (Figure 3), have focused on a regional artifact record largely attributable to the late Pleistocene–early Holocene Western Stemmed Tradition (WST) (Bryan 1980; Willig and Aikens 1988). As is the case elsewhere in the Great Basin, this record, which dates to *ca.* 11,000–8,000 B.P., is most evident on the surfaces of geomorphically stable shorelines and alluvial terraces, suggesting patterns of land use centered on lake and marsh resources. The focus of our research has been the delineation of mobility strategies of these early foraging populations (Beck and Jones 1988, 1990). More specifically, we are attempting to document the territorial scale at which populations operated, primarily through the study of toolstone selection and geologic source attribution (Beck and Jones 1990). At a narrower spatial scale, we are investigating the nature of the relations between landscape and archaeological variables. Beyond the generally accepted observation that WST sites are associated with pluvial landforms, we have asked what kinds of settings witnessed repeated, concentrated use, and which settings, perhaps used differently, have accumulated a more dispersed record. To date, we have observed that the lithic reductions activities as well as reuse of particular localities strongly influence variability expressed in the WST record of Butte Valley (Beck and Jones 1990).

Like its counterparts in many areas of the Great Basin, this early record is preserved largely on the surface, with both clustered and dispersed components. In fact, most of this record probably has never been buried, but if so, not for appreciable periods of time. An artifact-oriented field program has been used to sample this record. Randomly selected 250 × 250-m sample tracts have been surveyed systematically with surveyors spaced at 10-m intervals. Artifacts are located and collected within each 25-m linear interval along a surveyor's traverse. Areas in which artifact density is significantly greater than in surrounding areas have been collected in 2 × 2-m grids. Termed sites or clusters, these areas possess artifact densities ranging between 0.02 and $0.3/m^2$; average artifact density on sample tracts is less than $0.001/m^2$. In order to understand how this record can inform on continuity or change in toolstone procurement, technology, landscape use, or any of a number of other issues, a firm chronology must be created for both clustered and dispersed components.

Traditionally for circumstances like this one, typological cross-dating has assumed the principal role in chronology building. However, for several reasons, not the least of which is the apparent stylistic conservativeness of this tradition, typological efforts have not yielded satisfactory temporal distinctions. As a result, artifacts often are attributed, at best, to periods lasting millennia. In view of the kinds of questions currently being asked about this record, far greater temporal resolution is needed. The inadequacies of the standard typological approach have led us to turn to obsidian hydration dating in an attempt to improve this resolution.

Butte Valley Relative Chronology

For the purpose of constructing serial orders of Butte Valley artifactual material, a pilot project was initiated in which a sample of 115 obsidian objects was selected for source and hydration analyses (see Jones and Beck 1990). The sample consisted of 28 artifacts drawn from 10 quadrats and 87 artifacts from seven site clusters, constituting 48.3% of all obsidian from low-density areas and 12.4% of all obsidian from clusters.

The first step in this analysis was the identification of geological sources represented in the Butte Valley sample through trace element analysis. The results of x-ray fluorescence performed by Richard Hughes suggest that 13 geologic sources are represented. We had, at first, presumed that these obsidians were derived from distant sources, particularly those in west–central Utah; however, source analyses identified only two known sources in the sample, a local Butte Valley pebble source, and the Brown's Bench source, which lies about 200 km north of the project area.

In the next step—hydration analysis—we had several goals. First, relating to the site assemblages, we hoped to determine which represented relatively brief, continuous, episodes of artifact deposition and which might be more appropriately characterized as palimpsests. At least some of the clusters appear to represent the former, containing only projectile points of WST affiliation and none of Archaic affiliation. Moreover, these assemblages appear to represent narrow "behavioral suites" linked to biface production or refurbishment (Beck and Jones 1990), consistent with a relatively brief episode of artifact discard in each case. If this were indeed the case, then, as Raymond (1984–1985) has shown, within a single source the resulting hydration rinds should exhibit a narrow range of values centered around a single mode.

The second goal of the hydration analysis was to create a serial order within each source of the site assemblages, based on the mean hydration values represented in each assemblage. Our third objective was to assess the chronological relationships between artifacts from dense clusters and the low-density survey areas. Because we cannot presume out of hand that the low-density record was deposited by WST populations and not by subsequent occupants of the region, dating by obsidian hydration assumes a critical role if use is to be made of this record.

In an ideal study of this sort, a very large proportion of a regional artifact record would be obsidian and those artifacts would cross-cut a number of dimensions, for example, functional classes, environmental gradients, distributional types. Moreover, every assemblage would share several different chemical types to insure development of independent and cross-checking orders. The Butte Valley sample is less than ideal in these regards. Although the sample of 115 artifacts is a fairly large proportion of all obsidian pieces from our collections, these artifacts are divided among a number of units, making each sample rather small. Also, not all functional classes are well represented in obsidian. The wealth of chemical types, as it turns out, places an additional constraint on the Butte Valley sample. Just four types of obsidian are represented widely among the samples. A number of obsidians are limited in their distributions to single clusters and thus cannot serve in comparisons. Nonetheless, the results of this analysis support our contention that OHD may improve our powers of temporal resolution.

None of the Butte Valley obsidians have been studied in controlled stratigraphic contexts or evaluated experimentally to establish hydration rates. Consequently, hydration measurements were made of every obsidian projectile point to identify an expected range of values for WST artifacts, and by contrast, to establish a range of values for younger specimens. These projectile points (n =

17) consist of three groups. WST examples (n = 11) include Parman (Layton 1970), Silver Lake (Amsden 1937), and Cougar Mountain (Layton 1970) types. Archaic projectile points include single specimens of Humboldt, Pinto, and Elko types. The remaining three examples are stemmed points of uncertain temporal affiliation.

Figure 5 illustrates hydration measurements on these 17 specimens. The sample contains seven distinct geochemical types of which the Brown's Bench glass is the most common and apparently most rapidly hydrating. Multiple examples of types "B" and "G" also occur. Single specimens of four obsidians are present as well, but these are not considered in the subsequent discussion.

Hydration values of the seven Brown's Bench points range between 10.7 microns on a Silver Lake specimen and 13.8 microns on a stem fragment of a

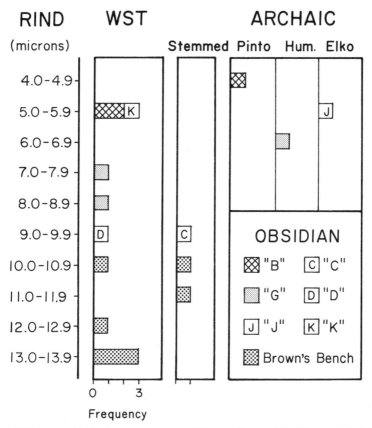

Figure 5. Source and hydration measurements of Western Stemmed Tradition, early Archaic, and several untyped projectile point types from Butte Valley, Nevada (modified from Jones and Beck 1990).

Parman point. Unfortunately, no Archaic representatives are present for comparison. However, two of the stemmed points that could not be associated with an established type possess hydration rinds that fall within the WST range. Obsidians "B" and "G," clearly more slowly hydrating glasses, are represented by both WST and Archaic examples. Two WST specimens of type "G" have close hydration readings (7.7 and 8.4 microns), whereas the single basal section of an Humboldt point, which we regard as an early variant based on its size, has a slightly smaller hydration reading (6.8 microns). Similarly, WST points of "B" have larger hydration values than the single Pinto specimen.

The trends in these data are in the proper direction with WST specimens possessing wider hydration rinds than Archaic projectile points of the same geochemical type. We note, however, that the sample size must be significantly augmented to insure that the hydration values represent largely a temporal signal. We point to the large range of values among Brown's Bench specimens particularly with some concern. In addition to age, these values may reflect as well the confounding effects of temperature histories of each specimen relating to microtopographic differences between localities, subtle variation in aspect, and differences owing to vegetation and sediment at the sites.

If we accept the hydration patterns among projectile points at face value, they provide a basis for assessing the ages of other artifacts from both site and off-site settings. Figure 6 presents a summary of hydration readings from six site

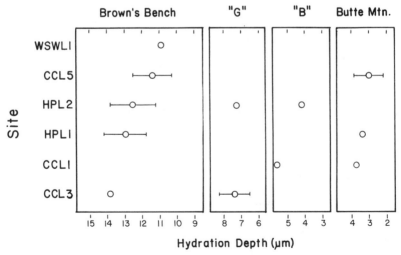

Figure 6. Hydration measurements of four well-represented obsidian types (Brown's Bench, Butte Mountain, "B," and "G") from six Butte Valley site clusters (modified from Jones and Beck 1990).

assemblages. For each of four geochemical types a mean value and standard deviation are shown. The raw data from which this figure is taken reveal in each case a tight distribution of hydration readings. This outcome certainly fits with our interpretations based on technological analyses that at least four of the clusters represent narrow ranges of "behaviors" limited to biface reduction or refurbishment, and consequently perhaps, relatively brief episodes of artifact discard.

In Figure 6, the clusters are arranged along the ordinate such that the hydration mean decreases to the right along the abscissa. Although the Brown's Bench group strongly influences this order, it should be noted that, like a seriation matrix, this arrangement is the single best solution. We suggest the order is chronological. Again, however, we must note that small sample numbers weaken the case. We also acknowledge the significant overlap in the ranges taken by the samples, which might reasonably be ascribed to overlapping occupation/use episodes. The effect, however, of site-specific constraints on fully contemporaneous artifacts cannot be ruled out.

Expanding our observations further on the hydration data, we can consider the conformity of hydration values between specimens from clustered and dispersed assemblages. Figure 7 shows hydration values assembled from sites and off-site quadrat samples in three topographic settings. With the exception of Butte Mountain obsidian artifacts that are made from pebbles occurring in alluvial fan gravels, obsidian artifacts, like artifacts of other toolstones, are rare in off-site settings. Still, it is important to note that the range of hydration values exhibited by these few obsidian artifacts falls within the range of artifacts from sites, and more significantly, they match precisely the values obtained on WST projectile points. Thus, insofar as concerns obsidian artifacts within the Butte Valley collections, most can be inferred to be of the same age. Extending this interpretation beyond the obsidian segment returns us again, however, to issues of association and covariation. We find the case for this extension strengthened if only by the fact that these samples constitute a larger share of the collections than projectile points alone and they cross-cut several artifact categories. Thus quite independent of clustered or dispersed affiliation or environmental association, we can assess changes in frequency of different functional classes through time.

A number of other observations can be made about these data. We point, for example, to artifacts made from the local Butte Mountain source and note that this sample contains no temporal markers. Without temporal markers like projectile points by which to "calibrate" hydration rinds, we are unable to argue with certainty that these are fully contemporaneous with other artifacts. However, this and other observations are most properly fashioned with more thorough attention to spatial patterning and with acquisition of larger samples.

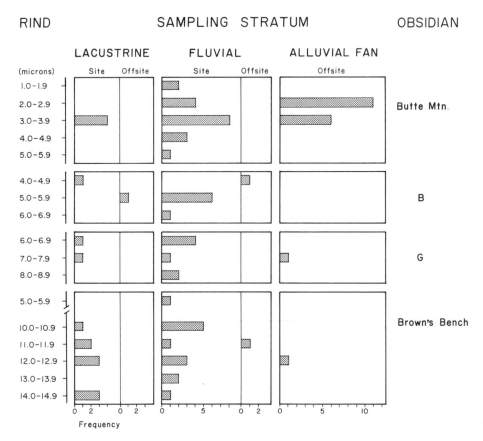

Figure 7. Hydration measurements of obsidian specimens from clustered (site) and dispersed (off-site) settings in four Butte Valley environmental strata. Note that no clusters were found on alluvial fans (modified from Jones and Beck 1991).

CONCLUSIONS

The construction of cultural chronologies will always be fundamental to archaeological research. When this research is undertaken from a distributional perspective, and particularly, as we have illustrated in the previous examples, when the research encounters archaeological expressions across a landscape that are on the surface and highly dispersed in character, chronological determinations are problematic. This is because associations among artifacts, which typically are based on spatial proximity, are difficult to demonstrate in these contexts. As a result, the chronological sensitivity carried by some classes of artifacts is not easily transferred to less sensitive artifacts. This deficiency is often met with another argument, that there is a pattern of linear covariation between temporal markers and other artifacts. That is, it is assumed that chronologically sensitive artifacts bear a proportional relationship to all other artifacts in the general artifact population and the depositional events they represent. Often, perhaps, this assumption is unwarranted.

A general strategy to chronologic resolution in distributional archaeology, one that leads to an evaluation of the linear covariation assumption, is raised by Dunnell (this volume). He calls for methods that permit construction of units of historical association. Distinct from tactics that involve iterative partitioning of the record, often described as "breaking out" spatially, and hence, temporally associated assemblages, these approaches intend to "build upward" from individually dated artifacts. Such approaches give no special priority to dense artifact aggregates for dating purposes, although they will identify those artifacts within spatial aggregates that are contemporaneous and thus may be considered as a group.

One dating method that exhibits some potential in this regard is obsidian hydration. Although questions remain regarding the efficacy of the method for dating artifacts from the surface, a growing number of empirical studies of source and temperature variation are helping to establish the chronological sensitivity of obsidian artifacts. As our pilot study suggests, obsidian artifacts, each bearing an independent temporal signal, may prove especially useful in creating serial orders of artifacts and artifact aggregates, and by extension, may permit one to evaluate assumptions of association and covariation. As a closing note, we suggest that other methods, such as cation dating of desert varnish (e.g., Dorn 1983; Harrington and Whitney 1987; Whitley and Dorn 1987), thermoluminescence (e.g., Fleming 1979; Valladas and Valladas 1987), and analysis of rock weathering (e.g., Colman 1981; Kneupfer 1988) show promise for dating artifacts in low-density settings and/or the surfaces on which they occur. As no single method is applicable to every archaeological situation, further investigation of these approaches seems warranted.

ACKNOWLEDGMENTS

We thank C. M. Aikens, D. K. Grayson, and P. J. Mehringer, Jr., co-directors of the Steens Mountain Prehistory Project, for making available data cited in this Chapter. The Steens Mountain Prehistory Project was funded by National Science Foundation Grants BSN-77-12556 and BNS-80-06277 to C. M. Aikens, D. K. Grayson, and P. J. Mehringer, Jr., and by a grant from Mr. Bingham's Trust for Charity to D. K. Grayson. We gratefully acknowledge the support of these organizations. Obsidian source and hydration analyses for the Butte Valley Project were supported by a faculty research grant from Hamilton College. We thank Sarah Johnston, John Zancanella, and Brian Amme, Bureau of Land Management, Ely District, for continued support of our Butte Valley research. Finally, we thank the editors of this volume for their comments on drafts of this Chapter.

REFERENCES

Amsden, C. A., 1937, The Lake Mohave Artifacts, in: *The Archaeology of Pleistocene Lake Mohave* (E. W. C. Campbell and W. H. Campbell, eds.), Southwest Museum Papers No. 11, pp. 50–97.

Beck, C., 1984, *Steens Mountain Surface Archaeology: The Sites,* Ph.D. dissertation, University of Washington, University Microfilms, Ann Arbor.

Beck, C., and Jones, G. T., 1988, Western Pluvial Lakes Tradition Occupation in Butte Valley, Eastern Nevada, in: *Early Human Occupation in the Arid West: The Clovis-Archaic Interface* (J. Willig, C. M. Aikens, and J. L. Fagan, eds.), Nevada State Museum Anthropological Papers No. 21, pp. 273–301.

Beck, C., and Jones, G. T., 1990, Toolstone Selection and Lithic Technology in Early Great Basin Prehistory, *Journal of Field Archaeology* 17:283–299.

Bettinger, R. L., 1975, *The Surface Archaeology of Owens Valley, Eastern California: Prehistoric Man-Land Relationships in the Great Basin,* Ph.D. dissertation, University of California, Davis, University Microfilms, Ann Arbor.

Bettinger, R. L., 1980, Obsidian Hydration Dates for Owens Valley Settlement Categories, *Journal of California and Great Basin Anthropology* 2:286–292.

Binford, L. R., 1972, Contemporary Model Building: Paradigms and the Current State of Palaeolithic Research, in: *Models in Archaeology* (D. L. Clarke, ed.), Methuen, London, pp. 109–166.

Bryan, A., 1980, The Stemmed Point Tradition: An Early Technological Tradition in Western North America, in: *Anthropological Papers in Memory of Earl H. Swanson, Jr.* (L. B. Harten, C. N. Warren, and D. R. Tuohy, eds.), Special Publication of the Idaho State University Museum of Natural History, pp. 77–107.

Colman, S. M., 1981, Rock-weathering Rates as Functions of Time, *Quaternary Research* 15:250–264.

Dancey, W. S., 1973, *Prehistoric Land Use and Settlement Patterns in the Priest Rapids Area, Washington,* Ph.D. Dissertation, University of Washington, University Microfilms, Ann Arbor.

Dancey, W. S., 1974, The Archaeological Survey: A Reorientation, *Man in the Northeast* 8:98–112.

Davis, E. L., 1975, The "Exposed Archaeology" of China Lake, California, *American Antiquity* 40:39–53.

Davis, E. L. (ed.), 1978, *The Ancient Californians: Rancholabrean Hunters of the Mojave Lakes Country,* Natural History Museum of Los Angeles County, Science Series No. 29.

Dorn, R. I., 1983, Cation-Ratio Dating: A New Rock Varnish Age-Determination Technique, *Quaternary Research* 20:49–73.

Everitt, B. S., 1977, *The Analysis of Contingency Tables,* Halsted Press, New York.

Fagan, B., 1978, *Archaeology: A Brief Introduction,* Little, Brown and Company, Boston.

Fleming, S., 1979, *Thermoluminescence Techniques in Archaeology,* Clarendon Press, Oxford.

Foley, R., 1981a, *Off-site Archaeology and Human Adaptation in Eastern Africa: An Analysis of Regional Artifact Density in the Amboseli, Southern Kenya,* BAR International Series No. 97.

Foley, R., 1981b, Off-site Archaeology: An Alternative Approach for the Short-Sited, in: *Patterns of the Past: Studies in Honour of David Clarke* (I. Hodder, G. Issac, and N. Hammond, eds.), Cambridge University Press, London, pp. 157–183.

Friedman, I., 1976, Calculations of Obsidian Hydration Rates from Temperature Measurements, in: *Advances in Obsidian Glass Studies* (R. E. Taylor, ed.), Noyes Press, Park Ridge, N.J., pp. 173–182.

Friedman, I., and Smith, R. L., 1960, A New Dating Method Using Obsidian: Part I. The Development of the Technique, *American Antiquity* 25:476–522.

Green, J. P., 1986, *Obsidian Hydration Measurement: Are We Getting What We Expect?*, Paper presented at the 20th Biennial Great Basin Anthropological Conference, Las Vegas.

Harrington, C. D., and Whitney, J. W., 1987, Scanning Electron Microscope Method for Rock-Varnish Dating, *Geology* 15:967–970.

Heizer, R. F., and Hester, T. R., 1978, Great Basin, in: *Chronologies in New World Archaeology* (R. E. Taylor and C. W. Meighan, eds.), Academic Press, New York, pp. 147–199.

Isaac, G., 1981, Stone Age Visiting Cards: Approaches to the Study of Early Land Use Patterns, in: *Patterns of the Past: Studies in Honour of David Clarke* (I. Hodder, G. Isaac, and N. Hammond, eds.), Cambridge University Press, London, pp. 131–155.

Jackson, R. J., 1984, Current Problems in Obsidian Hydration Analysis, in: *Obsidian Studies in the Great Basin* (R. E. Hughes, ed.), Contributions of the University of California Archaeological Research Facility No. 45, pp. 103–115.

Jennings, J. D., and Norbeck, E., 1955, Great Basin Prehistory: A Review, *American Antiquity* 21:1–11.

Jones, G. T., 1984, *Prehistoric Land Use in the Steens Mountain Area, Southeastern Oregon*, Ph.D. Dissertation, University of Washington, University Microfilms, Ann Arbor.

Jones, G. T., and Beck, C., 1990, An Obsidian Hydration Chronology of Late Pleistocene-Early Holocene Surface Assemblages from Butte Valley, Nevada, *Journal of California and Great Basin Anthropology* 12:84–100.

Jones, G. T., Beck, C., and Grayson, D. K., 1989, Measures of Diversity and Expedient Lithic Technologies, in: *Quantifying Diversity in Archaeology* (R. D. Leonard and G. T. Jones, eds.), Cambridge University Press, Cambridge, pp. 69–78.

Knuepfer, P. L. K., 1988, Estimating Ages of Late Quaternary Stream Terraces from Analysis of Weathering Rinds and Soils, *Geological Society of American Bulletin* 100:1224–1236.

Layton, T. N., 1970, *High Rock Archaeology: An Interpretation of the Prehistory of the Northwestern Great Basin*, Ph.D. Dissertation, Harvard University, Cambridge.

Layton, T. N., 1973, Temporal Ordering of Surface-Collected Obsidian Artifacts by Hydration Measurement, *Archaeometry* 15:129–132.

McGonagle, R. L., 1979, *Surface Archaeology at High Rock Lake*, Publications in the Social Sciences No. 14, Desert Research Institute, Reno.

Michels, J. W., 1973, *Dating Methods in Archaeology*, Academic Press, New York.

Michels, J. W., and Tsong, I. S. T., 1980, Obsidian Hydration Dating: A Coming of Age, in: *Advances in Archaeological Method and Theory*, vol. 3 (M. B. Schiffer, ed.), Academic Press, New York, pp. 405–444.

Origer, T. M., and Wickstrom, B. P., 1982, The Use of Hydration Measurements to Date Obsidian Materials from Sonoma County, California, *Journal of California and Great Basin Anthropology* 4:123–131.

Raymond, A. W., 1984–1985, Evaluating the Occupational History of Lithic Scatters: Analysis of Obsidian Hydration Measurements, *North American Archaeologist* 6:115–133.

Ridings, R., 1991, Obsidian Hydration Dating: The Effects of Mean Exponential Ground Temperature and Depth of Artifact Recovery, *Journal of Field Archaeology* 18:77–85.

Schiffer, M. B., 1987, *Formation Processes of the Archaeological Record*, University of New Mexico Press, Albuquerque.

Steward, J., 1938, *Basin-Plateau Aboriginal Sociopolitical Groups*, Bureau of American Ethnology Bulletin No. 120.

Thomas, D. H., 1970, Archaeology's Operational Imperative: Great Basin Projectile Points as a Test Case. *University of California Archaeological Survey Report* 12:27–60.

Thomas, D. H., 1971, *Prehistoric Subsistence-Settlement Patterns of the Reese River Valley, Central Nevada,* Ph.D. Dissertation, University of California, Davis, University Microfilms, Ann Arbor.

Thomas, D. H., 1972, A Computer Simulation Model of Great Basin Shoshonean Subsistence and Settlement Patterns, in: *Models in Archaeology* (D. L. Clarke, ed.), Methuen, London, pp. 671–704.

Thomas, D. H., 1973, An Empirical Test for Steward's Model of Great Basin Settlement Patterns, *American Antiquity* 38:155–176.

Thomas, D. H., 1975, Nonsite Sampling in Archaeology: Up the Creek Without a Site?, in: *Sampling in Archaeology* (J. W. Mueller, ed.), University of Arizona Press, Tucson, pp. 61–81.

Thomas, D. H., 1978, Arrowheads and Atlatl Darts: How the Stones Got the Shaft, *American Antiquity* 43:461–472.

Thomas, D. H., 1981, How to Classify the Projectile Points from Monitor Valley, Nevada, *Journal of California and Great Basin Anthropology* 3:7–43.

Thomas, D. H., 1988, *The Archaeology of Monitor Valley: 3. Survey and Additional Excavations,* Anthropological Papers of the American Museum of Natural History, vol. 66, part 2.

Trembour, F., and Friedman, I., 1984, Obsidian Hydration Dating and Field Site Temperature, in: *Obsidian Studies in the Great Basin* (R. E. Hughes, ed.), Contributions of the University of California Archaeological Research Facility No. 45, pp. 79–90.

Valladas, H., and Valladas, G., 1987, Thermoluminescence Dating of Burnt Flint and Quartz: Comparative Results. *Archaeometry* 29:214–220.

Weide, M., 1968, *Cultural Ecology of Lakeside Adaptation in the Western Great Basin,* Ph.D. Dissertation, Department of Anthropology, University of California, Los Angeles.

Willig, J. A., and Aikens, C. M., 1988, The Clovis-Archaic Interface in Far Western North America, in: *Early Human Occupation in Far Western North America: The Clovis-Archaic Interface* (J. A. Willig, C. M. Aikens, and J. L. Fagan, eds.), Nevada State Museum Anthropological, Papers No. 21, pp. 1–40.

Whitley, D. S., and Dorn, R. I., 1987, Rock Art Chronology in Eastern California, *World Archaeology*19:150–164.

Zeier, C. D., and Elston, R. D., 1986, *Effective Hydration Temperature and Quantitative Hydration Rates for Sugarloaf Obsidian Coso Volcanic Field, Inyo County, California,* Paper presented at the 20th Biennial Great Basin Anthropological Conference, Las Vegas.

Chapter 9

Archaeological Landscapes, Lithic Scatters, and Human Behavior

MAREK ZVELEBIL, STANTON W. GREEN,
AND MARK G. MACKLIN

INTRODUCTION

Within the last 20 years or so, the traditional unit of archaeological investigations—the site—has come under increasing criticism. Through the work of Clarke (1972), Schiffer (1972, 1976, 1983), Foley (1981a), Dunnell and Dancey (1983), Binford (1983) and others, it has become clear that structuring of archaeological evidence in terms of such discrete spatiotemporal units is conceptually unsatisfactory, often inapplicable, and highly selective as a record of human behavior.

In this chapter we argue that the concept of a site should be replaced by one of archaeological landscape. This is in keeping with our general view that landscape archaeology must be the most effective way of understanding the past. Nevertheless, the landscape approach faces serious problems of methodology and

MAREK ZVELEBIL • Department of Archaeology and Prehistory, University of Sheffield, Sheffield, England S10 2TN, **STANTON W. GREEN** • Department of Anthropology, University of South Carolina, Columbia, South Carolina 29208, and **MARK G. MACKLIN** • Department of Geography, University of Newcastle-Upon-Tyne, Newcastle-Upon-Tyne, England NE1 7RU.

Space, Time, and Archaeological Landscapes, edited by Jacqueline Rossignol and LuAnn Wandsnider. Plenum Press, New York, 1992.

application to the archaeological record. We consider the approach, the problems involved, and the potential for their resolution in the context of a case study from Co. Waterford, Southeast Ireland.

The many problems which bedevil the site-oriented approach have been noted by many authors in this volume. As Dunnell and Dancey have noted, "using site to structure recovery limits data collection to a small fraction of the total area occupied by any past cultural system and systematically excludes nearly all direct evidence of the actual articulation between people and their environment" (Dunnell and Dancey 1983). This has been particularly noted in the archaeology of hunter–gatherers (Foley 1981b), where we are dealing with complex patterns of mobility and with extensive use of the landscape. Landscape relationships are just as important in farming communities, however, where the relationships between fields, farmsteads, and villages form the basis for the agricultural economy and society (Chisholm 1962). The question arises, then, how to structure our investigations so that we can obtain more complete, representative evidence of past human behavior. The notion of archaeological landscape removes such conceptual, and, in part, methodological problems.

Landscape archaeology looks at the spatial relationships of artifacts and features in order to infer the past use of the landscape (Crumley and Marquardt 1990; Wagstaff 1987). The landscape in this framework then means a set of real-world features, natural or cultural, which give character and diversity to the earth's surface. Archaeological landscapes can then be defined as a past surface within a defined span of time, which is subject to antecedent features and successive modifications. A past landscape surface can be buried, eroded, or modified by successive human activities or geomorphological processes. In landscape archaeology we are dealing, therefore, with both time and spatial dimensions at some hypothetical regional scale. The material residues of the time dimension consist of sedimentary deposits; the spatial dimension is represented by the varied distribution of artifacts and other features over landscape.

Conceptually, such an approach has obvious advantages in that it removes most of the theoretical criticisms leveled at the site-oriented archaeology. First, it reflects more accurately the totality of human activities and provides a more representative basis for the reconstruction of past human behavior. Second, it allows for more accurate definition of artifact clusters that may represent intensive activity areas, traditionally known as *sites*. And third, this approach gives full meaning to the hitherto neglected "off-site" cultural residues and paleoenvironmental data, and, in a more general way, to distributional archaeology by endowing this method with theoretical concepts and explanatory frameworks (Crumley and Marquardt 1990). Such a nonsite or even antisite approach is based on ontological epistemological and theoretical justifications (Dunnell, this volume) that basically can be reduced to the fact that human behavior does not occur in, or indeed generate, spatially or temporally discrete archaeological residues.

Accordingly, in the landscape approach, we regard the archaeological record as one of continuous character within a dynamic geomorphological context. The task for the archaeologist, then, is to interpret the density and character of the more or less continuous distribution or artifacts.

Within this framework, we can draw on a wide range of theoretical and methodological concepts. From the perspective of anthropological and geographical theory, such an approach can draw on significant literature on land use (e.g., Chisholm 1962; Found 1971; von Thünen 1826; Abler *et al.*, 1977). Rather than looking for settlements, huts, camps, or even sites, economic, political, and ideological landscapes can be investigated. For example, the spatial relationship between the farmstead and the fields and the patterning of field use is the basis for economic analysis of agricultural settlement by von Thünen (1826) and Chisholm (1962). The juxtaposition of burial tombs with fields and farmsteads in Northwest Ireland (Caulfield 1983) elucidates the relationship between social and economic landscapes, whereas Bradley's (1984) interpretation of monuments and settlement in Britain serves to recreate a political landscape.

Equally important are the methodological advantages of landscape archaeology. By viewing landscapes as cultural/natural space, we can take advantage of the broad and powerful field of spatial sampling and analysis. Recently, the methodology of Geographic Information systems (GIS) has qualitatively improved our ability to describe and interpret spatially referenced data (Kvamme 1989; Allen, Green, and Zubrow 1990). In simple terms, GISs allow for the mapping of single variables (cultural and natural), so that they can be overlaid and therefore mutually analyzed and investigated. Topography, for example, can be mathematically manipulated to reveal slope, drainage, and accessible routes. These derived variables can then be tied to the distribution of cultural items (artifacts, features, architecture). Landscapes can be literally created through the combination of archaeological and environmental data to view the landscape from the perspective of the researcher's questions.

A combination of landscape archaeology and GIS provides the theory and method to account for the three fundamental elements of the spatial behavior of people: (1) the integration of natural and cultural factors, (2) the continuity of the human use of space; and (3) the importance of "view" as it determines both the use of space and the interpretation of its use by archaeologists (Green 1990).

GISs offer functions that allow for the description and analysis of continuous natural and cultural spatial phenomenon singularly and in combination. Moreover, it allows one to view (that is describe) a landscape from a particular place or point on that landscape. As such, archaeologists can set their analytical view in terms of their position on the landscape (from where they are viewing the archaeological evidence) as well as their analytical view (what types of phenomena they are viewing). Interpretation then involves inferring the view of the past participants (or creators) of the landscape in terms of their view. The view of a prehistoric farmer could be a simple line of sight—or more provocatively a culturally constructed path. A trading pattern via trading partners, middlemen, or perhaps competing groups or raiders might best recreate the social landscape for a farming village (Allen 1990). This combination of landscape archaeology and GIS offers a very powerful problem-oriented approach toward understanding how people perceived, created, and used space.

Our general and methodological framework, the questions we are asking, as well as the nature of the available evidence determine our basic unit of analysis. Although we would not disagree with the distributional notions of artifacts as the basic units of observation (see Dunnell, this volume), we see the *relationships* among these and other features as the more fundamental structural elements within the landscape approach. One reason for this is that artifacts can be only one among several potential units of observation. In this study, we have developed a landscape approach in which spatial samples, in the form of plowed fields, are our basic operational unit of analysis. Various observations are made from these landscape samples, concerning cultural and natural features, their interrelatedness, as well as the relationship between the sample and the world at large. These observations then form the basis for recreating past landscapes in terms of the various cultural and natural questions we may have of them.

On the other side of the coin, landscape archaeology also faces serious methodological problems, some of which are common to any archaeological investigation, whereas others are accentuated by the landscape approach. Some problems, such as those of scale, taphonomy or modern landuse, are more acute in landscape archaeology. This is because of the greater amount of surface that is a part of the investigation, because of the increased importance of scale as an interpretative variable and also because contextual variability and disassociation becomes more common as the scale of investigation increases. Major problems can be summarized as follows:

1. *Lack of chronological resolution.* Surface survey requires commonly discarded artifacts, such as pottery or lithics. Few of these may be chronologically diagnostic, and in the absence of stratigraphic control, many surface scatters cannot be dated accurately. Many surface scatters have to be treated as a single chronologically insensitive assemblage, reflecting the repeated use of an area over a long period of time. As a result, it is the coarse grain of the data that defines the chronological time span. This is often inadequate and at variance with the finer chronological resolution needed to answer questions posed by a problem-oriented approach. The solution may be to redefine the questions—but should the nature of the data really dictate the questions we can ask? We agree with Nash and Petraglia (1987:193) that "research should be directed towards making a satisfactory match between specific research questions and specific properties of the archaeological record."

2. *The palimpsest effect.* Most of the surface residues are palimpsests of

several phases of occupation. The continued exposure of landscape to occupation will result in blurring of spatial patterns and in accumulation and mixing of chronologically unrelated remains.

3. *Definition of a regional scale.* This is defined by the organization of human activities, which take place at different levels of spatial resolution and which change with time. For example, regions can range in extent from periodically used territories comprising a number of settlements to broader units defined by a common geomorphology, a central place, or by shared patterns of human behavior, such as the participation in an exchange system, breeding network, or common ethnic identity. The definition of regional boundaries is bound, therefore, to be difficult, to some extent arbitrary and contingent on the *a priori* models of the anticipated scale of human organization.

4. *Biases introduced through taphonomic processes.* Differential patterns of discard, burial, preservation, and removal to the surface of artifacts all distort the surface distribution patterns. These are further distorted by dislocation on the surface. All these processes are caused by both cultural and natural agencies. As a result, surface material residues of human activities do not reflect directly the behavior that led to their discard. Just as with other forms of archaeological record, surface scatters have to be first understood and interpreted in the light of the processes that led to their formation.

5. *Variation over the landscape.* Taphonomy of surface finds varies over the landscape and is subject to different cultural and natural factors. This further complicates the task of reconstruction of human behavior at a regional scale.

6. *Paleoenvironmental reconstruction.* At the regional scale, two issues are involved. In space, the definition of environmental subareas presents serious problems. In time, we are faced with the problem of accurately dating ecological changes and establishing their controls. The amount of paleoenvironmental work required to understand the evolution of local environment often goes beyond the financial capabilities of archaeological research programs.

7. *Modern land use.* Research design for surface surveys has to balance the requirements for a representative sample against the modern pattern of land use, which often makes large areas of landscape inaccessible for survey or indeed for excavation. As a result, surveys cannot be carried out in some areas, whereas in others, the inferential power of surveys is prejudiced by the differential chances of artifact recovery, which is contingent on modern land use patterns. As a result, regional surveys often fall short of their stated theoretical objectives.

A CASE STUDY: AGRICULTURAL TRANSITION IN SOUTHEAST IRELAND

How do we resolve these problems? Our work on the Bally Lough Archaeological Project illustrates some of the problems involved and suggests some steps toward their resolution. The project was born at the SAA meetings in Minneapolis in 1982 during a meeting between ourselves and Peter Woodman, who was about to become the professor of archaeology at University College, Cork. At that time we were (and still are) interested in the agricultural transition as one of the most important transformations that befell humankind. In the historical context of European prehistory, and subject to our paradigmatic orientation towards cultural ecology and "the original affluent society," the issue has become one of the indigenous versus derived origin of the Neolithic in Europe. The simple models of replacement and assimilation of the indigenous hunter–gatherers by immigrant farmers from the Near East were being challenged. How successful were the indigenous hunter–gatherers in Europe? Was it the immigrants or the indigenous people who adopted farming? If the latter, what compelled them to adopt a more labor-demanding economy? These questions, we felt, could be only answered at a regional scale, integrating settlement–subsistence patterns within a fossil landscape, reconstructed on the basis of a wide range of information.

With this in mind we have initiated, and, since 1983, have been implementing a regional research program designed to systematically recover information about the stone age settlement of the area that incorporates 530 square kilometers around Waterford estuary in Southeast Ireland, of which some 400 sq km has now been sampled (Figure 1). The area includes a range of habitats typical for coastal regions of Ireland: open coasts, estuaries, river valleys, and inland areas. Our research program has been applied as a combination of field walking survey, subsurface test excavation, geophysical, sedimentological, paleoecological, and geomorphological surveys.

The area selected for investigation was virtually devoid of stone age sites other than megalithic tombs. No systematic investigation took place before our arrival. Such a situation was ideally suited for the development of a regional survey design "as the basic recovery technique" (Dunnell and Dancey 1983:28) but offered little in the way of background information.

The main objective of this research was, and still remains, the initial colonization of southern Ireland, the development of hunter–gatherer societies and their subsequent transformation into agricultural societies—a period spanning some 5,000 years from the initial colonization of the island around 7000 B.C. (there is no evidence of Paleolithic settlement at present) to the beginning of the Bronze Age (2000 B.C.). In the process of gathering the basic information about the Stone Age settlement, however, our intermediate goal of modeling the settlement of Ireland and the transition to farming was "put on the back burner"

Figure 1. The location of Bally Lough Archaeological Project, showing the area under investigation and the distribution of diagnostic (Mesolithic and Neolithic) sites.

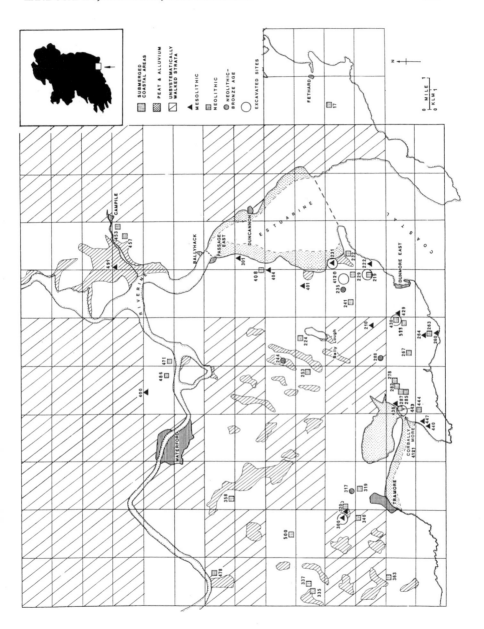

as the complexity of what we were trying to achieve became clear. The methodology and the problems of interpretation of surface lithic scatters and of the reconstruction of ancient landscape became subjects of study in their own right.

We would now like to turn to four particular problems, which encompass both methodology and interpretation: These are survey design, chronological resolution, landscape taphonomy, and behavioral patterns.

Survey Design

The development and application of regional survey designs generated a new set of methodological challenges. These include the problems posed by modern land use, the relative merits of goal-oriented as opposed to general surveys, and the question of cost-effectiveness. As a result, the actual survey procedures adopted in any survey represents, in most cases, a compromise solution to a whole range of considerations. The procedures themselves impose, in turn, further limits on the statistical and behavioral inferences that can be ultimately drawn from the survey work.

Our field survey design is illustrated in Table 1. In order to capture a representative sample of the project area, we opted for a systematic, stratified survey, based on 35 aligned rectangular grids of 15.6 sq km each, adopted from the National Ordnance System (Figure 1). Within each grid, plowed fields composed our cluster sample units. The survey aimed at minimum coverage of 5% of each sampled stratum. Lithic scatters were the principal material collected. Every other grid was sampled to form a checkerboard pattern in order to increase the total coverage with the added benefit of leaving one-half of the project area for further research.

Table 1.   Sampling Methodology

Objective	To collect a stratified sample of archaeological sites within the project area, giving each sampled stratum a minimum coverage of 5%, and an overall coverage of 2.5%.
Strata	Uniform rectangular grids (2 by 3 miles; 15.6 square kilometers)
Cluster sample unit	Ploughed fields, variable size. Each field is walked completely (systematically) at five metre intervals
Sampling strategy interunit intraunit	Alternate strata (chequerboard pattern) Pseudouniform distribution of cluster sample units (i.e., ploughed fields)
Sample size	Regional: 2.5% (minimum); intrastrata: 5% (minimum)

A variety of practical and methodological concerns guide our sampling design. Foremost is the layout of the contemporary Irish landscape. Relatively small fields form a mosaic of arable and pastureland with frequent changes in land use. Plowed fields provide, therefore, the most practical cluster sample. We have managed to use this reality to our advantage by systematically walking fields within each strata to reach our sampling size of 2.5%. Although selection of fields cannot be set out prior to survey, available fields are located on a daily and weekly basis, so that a systematic pattern of fields is walked within each strata. This yields a large set of 20 to 30 samples for each strata, an aspect that is essential for generating a representative sample (Cowgill 1975). This type of cluster sampling is typical in research where independent spatial clusters such as rural counties, parishes, and the like form the most effective sampling unit. As a rule, fields were walked at a regular pace at 5-m intervals. Although artifacts were not point provenienced, artifact clusters were noted on a sketch map of each field.

Chronological Resolution

Lithic scatters collected in our survey reflect both hunter–gatherer and agricultural settlement. From about 400 sampling units, about 50 yielded chronological indicators. This means that our sample of identified Mesolithic (i.e., "hunter–gatherer," *ca.* 6000–3500 B.C.) and Neolithic (i.e., "farming" *ca.* 3500–2000 B.C.) use of the landscape is very small, and most of the surface scatters can only reflect the general patterns of land use in the Stone Age, irrespective of the shift in subsistence practices. On the other hand, those lithic scatters with Mesolithic and/or Neolithic artifacts can be treated as time-sensitive subsets within the large set of Stone Age land use data.

Lack of chronological resolution is a common problem in landscape archaeology. How do we deal with this problem? Time is a continuous phenomenon, packaged into different conceptual frameworks for the benefit of self-orientation, communication, and comprehension. Bloch (1977) draws our attention to different perceptions of time in its social and cultural context. At the very least, a distinction can be made between linear, durational time, and static, cyclic time. The former is associated with "the systems by which we know the world," the latter, ritual and mythological, with "systems by which we hide it" (1977:290). Our own, Western society operates mostly within the framework of linear, measurable time; it is this time perspective that we use to comprehend and communicate our understanding of the past. Pertinent to archaeology is the fact that linear time can be subdivided into smaller units, whether for measurement (i.e., calendar time), to reflect the duration of discrete events (i.e., "episodal time"), or of continuous processes such as genetic interaction with the environment or taphonomic transformation of archaeological record (i.e., "processual time"; Binford 1981; Schiffer 1983; Wandsnider 1987). These relationships are illustrated in Figure 2.

Such perceptions and definitions of time do not, on the whole, correspond to temporal divisions afforded on the basis of archaeological data. Conventionally, archaeological data are divided into periods on the basis of geological strata or the occurrence of type fossils in cultural materials. In making a connection between human behavior and the conventional chronological and stratigraphic schemes, archaeologists assume, often implicitly, such schemes are signatures of cultural and/or behavioral change. Thus the geologically defined boundary between the Pleistocene and the Postglacial is often held to indicate cultural change (Evans 1975; Simmons and Tooley 1981): the boundary between the late Mesolithic and Neolithic, culturally defined by the occurrence of long-bladed lithic technology, pottery, and polished stone is held to indicate a change in human, social, and economic behavior (Ammerman and Cavalli-Sforza 1984; Thomas 1988). These conventional chronostratigraphic frameworks are imposed on us by the limits of archaeological data: they bear no clear relation to significant changes in human behavior. Although we will continue using such frameworks (for the lack of finer chronology), the links between changes in human behavior and chronological frameworks have to be demonstrated, not assumed.

The argument between Binford (1981) and Schiffer (1983) about the episodic as opposed to processual approach to the archaeological record highlights the complex nature of the links between human behavior and the archaeological evidence and points toward a solution. Within the episodic perspective, the archaeological record consists of differentially preserved episodes of human and natural behavior, "ethnographic instants" through time. In the processual perspective, the archaeological record is regarded as forming through the continuous interaction of natural and cultural behavior, where the preservation of "ethnographic instants" is exceedingly rare. The two approaches represent to us a mutually supportive form of inquiry. It is only through the understanding of taphonomic processes and of the filters they impose on the archaeological remains that we can arrive at full understanding of our data, including discrete episodes of human behavior.

In the landscape perspective, we have a dual aim: first, to understand the processes that form and transform archaeological residues and the surrounding landscape, and second, to interpret contemporaneous patterns of behavior and the way they change in time. The first aim is served by taphonomic, processual approach. The second is framed by episodal perception of archaeological record, which in our view can be composed of a complex sequence of events of varied duration. The first aim covers the creation of archaeological residues and their passage through time up to the present. The second aim is constrained by the chronological resolution of specific episodes: in our case by the late Mesolithic, Neolithic and more broadly, Stone Age time frames that are currently the only

CALENDAR TIME

PAST

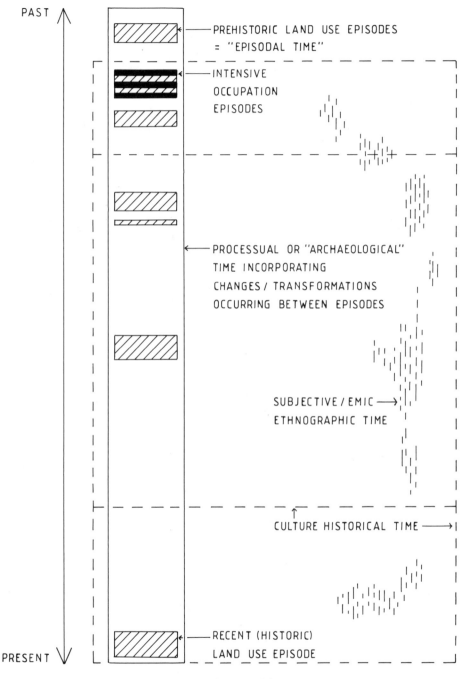

PREHISTORIC LAND USE EPISODES
= "EPISODAL TIME"

INTENSIVE
OCCUPATION
EPISODES

PROCESSUAL OR "ARCHAEOLOGICAL"
TIME INCORPORATING
CHANGES / TRANSFORMATIONS
OCCURRING BETWEEN EPISODES

SUBJECTIVE / EMIC →
ETHNOGRAPHIC TIME

CULTURE HISTORICAL TIME →|

RECENT (HISTORIC)
LAND USE EPISODE

PRESENT

Figure 2. Concepts of time.

ones available. In other words, we cannot, at present, identify more discrete episodes of human behavior than those framed by the conventional typological definitions of lithic assemblages.

Landscape Taphonomy

The aim of landscape taphonomy is to understand the formation of prehistoric landscapes and or archaeological residues that form a part of such landscapes. We are dealing with the time scale that spans the period between the initial cultural event that created the residue and the present. More specifically, in Southeast Ireland, we are dealing, at least initially, with two types of questions: (1) What postdepositional factors lead to the horizontal distribution of surface scatters and (2) what is the vertical relationship between the surface scatters and buried features and assemblages? To answer these questions in the project area, we began geomorphological and sedimentological research and subsurface testing programs.

Preliminary results of the geomorphological survey show that at a local scale, not all surface scatters can be treated as *in situ*. Although Pleistocene river terraces on valley floors, periglacial solifluction terraces near the coast, and inland upland plateau locations can, on the basis of geomorphological evidence, be considered as sites of minimal natural disturbance, single and multifaceted valley slopes show dislocation features that indicate that artifacts recovered at such locations are unlikely to be at the original point of their discard. This means that on 45% of all sampling units in the study area, stratigraphic integrity is in doubt.

Regional landscape transformations caused by climate and sea-level changes during the Postglacial, as well as by anthropogenic activity, have been equally important in affecting the horizontal distribution of finds. In our area, such changes include river and coastal alluviation, peat development, and shoreline displacement, all of which have acted to make parts of the archaeological landscape inaccessible to surface collection. Our own as well as earlier investigations indicate that local shoreline displacement, alluviation, and coastal erosion may have altered beyond recognition prehistoric surfaces in the riverine zone and in the Tramore Bay area (Figure 1).

A close examination of one particular area, a basin of a small stream entering the sea at Fornaught Strand, illustrates how geomorphological studies can contribute to prehistoric landscape reconstruction and surface scatter interpretation (Figure 4). The basin contains a high density of surface scatters (Figures 3 and 4), three of which have been test-excavated (BL 219, 231 and 4120). There are scatters located on the high ground within the basin (BL 4120, 233, 215, 219, etc.), on valley slopes (232, 229) or river terraces (241), or in the lower part of the basin, adjacent to Fornaught Strand, on solifluction terraces (417, 231). All these locations have differing erosional and depositional regimes. In general, headwater

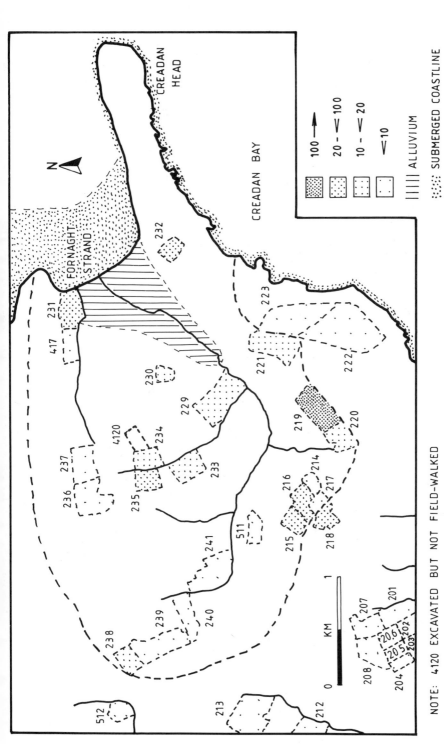

Figure 3. Density of lithic scatters per HA in Fornaught Strand Basin.

NOTE: 4120 EXCAVATED BUT NOT FIELD-WALKED

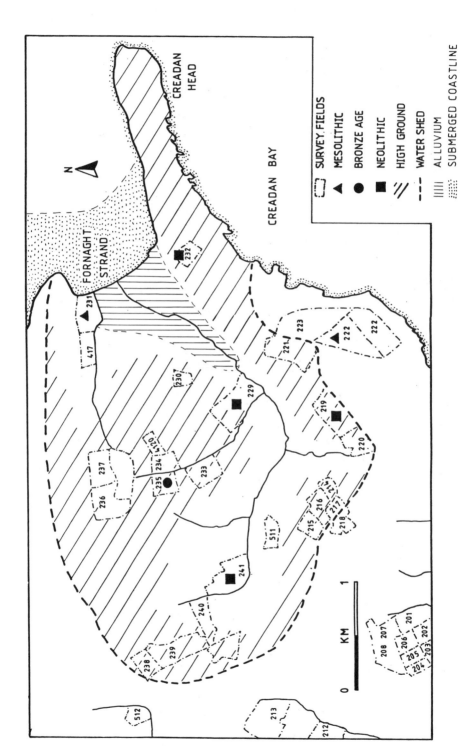

Figure 4. Survey in Fornaught Strand Basin.

and upland plateau area sites have been marked by high locational stability (little erosion or deposition); sites on the upper part of valley slopes have been dominated by erosion with colluviation occurring in Pleistocene river and solifluction terraces closer to the valley bottom. In contrast, sites on the valley floor have been subject to burial by alluvium and peat. This means that upland and some terrace sites would have the best chance of preservation *and* recovering *in situ*.

Geomorphological studies also indicate that *ca.* 8000 B.P.—the time of the earliest known occupation of the area by late Mesolithic groups—the sea level was about 6 meters below the present. Since this time, the lower part of the Fornaught Strand Basin (northeast of site 229) has been infilled by marine, paludal, and freshwater deposits that are locally more than 7 meters thick. Up until *ca.* 3300 B.C., Fornaught Strand was a tidal inlet of much larger dimensions than at present with a shoreline abutting as far inland as high ground adjacent to site 230. After 3320 B.C., a period transitional between the Mesolithic and the Neolithic, a slowing rate of sea-level rise significantly reduced the influx of marine sediment into the basin but continued to maintain high water-table levels on the valley floor. This resulted in peat formation (over 4.5 meters), which continued until late Iron Age times. With deforestation following in the wake of agriculture and with the development of open landscape after about A.D. 300, erosion increased and resulted in the deposition of river alluvium that presently covers most of the valley bottom.

This reconstruction would indicate that three major episodes of valley floor development and sedimentation have occurred during the Postglacial that are of particular importance in the interpretation of the archaeological record: (1) before *ca.* 3500 B.C., marine reworking and deposition of estuarine sediments; (2) 3300 B.C.–A.D. 300 paludification and peat development; (3) post *ca.* A.D. 300 deposition of river alluvium associated with anthropogenically induced erosion.

The low-lying parts of the ancient landscape, particularly the Mesolithic surface has been either covered by peat or alluvial deposits, submerged by the rise in the sea level, or, on the higher ground, truncated by coastal erosion. This is particularly important bearing in mind the coastal orientation of Mesolithic settlements.

It has been noted above that due to geomorphological considerations, the stratigraphic integrity of surface to subsurface finds cannot be taken for granted (see also Haselgrove *et al.*, 1985, etc.). We have now test-excavated five field-walked sites, and our experience confirms the complex nature of the surface to subsurface relationship. We report briefly on our findings next.

Surface–Subsurface Relationships

Excavations at BL 219 represent one of our most intensive efforts to relate the surface distribution of artifacts to the original subsurface occupation. The field is located on an exposed ridgetop overlooking the Fornaught Strand (see Figure 5). Presumably it was not as exposed during the Neolithic when more forested landscapes prevailed (soil samples containing pollen have been taken from the site but not yet analyzed; however, pollen samples taken from cores on the valley floor indicate that the Fornaught Strand Basin was almost certainly tree covered), but at present it is exposed to wind and water erosion. Fieldwalking recovered 2,576 artifacts from the field, of which all diagnostic tools were classified as Neolithic.

The south-eastern part of the field is relatively high and flat (Figure 5) with a gradual slope leading to low, flat area in the western third of the site. Surface collection, carried out in bands about 15 m. wide across the field (Figure 5) revealed high surface densities of artifacts on the high flat area just below the crest, and on the lower part of the shoulder of the slope.

Our excavations set out to investigate intensively the high flat area and to test systematically the rest of the field for cultural materials and to assess the role of geomorphological processes in artifact distribution. The taphonomy of the field, in the end, proved all important. When we compare surface densities, excavated finds and field geomorphology (Figures 5–7, Table 2), three situations, all subject to different processes, emerge. The crest location in the north-west corner of the field consisted of undulating Old Red Sandstone bedrock, covered with thin soil, 30–55 cm. deep, most of it a plow zone. Pockets of soil not reached by the plow were only found filling the hollows in the bedrock. The surface density of finds was highest in this part of the field, just below the crest (Figure 5, Table 2), leading to our decision to excavate extensively in this part of the field. Density of finds was also relatively high in the plow zone but declined markedly in the layers below the plow zone. Although we did find the remains of occupation in this high flat area (remains of features, stone tools, carbonized barley), it became clear that most of this area had been plowed out. The high density of surface scatters did indicate the approximate location of prehistoric activity, but the *in situ* position of finds and features has been lost due to agricultural activity.

On the shoulder of the slope in the central portion of the field, soil depths were greater, ranging from 35 to 60 cm. A thicker sediment cover here appears to have been the result of soil erosion from the top of the field with colluvium being stored on the slope, rather than being washed down to the flat part of the field. Slope wash, in fact, seems to have created a higher density of surface finds at the break of the slope with more level ground as well as creating a relatively high density of finds in the plow zone, which moreover, decreased with depth (Figures 6–7, Table 2). A study by Telfer (1988) of the shape and weight distribution of the surface assemblage revealed the tendency of heavier artifacts to concentrate in the lower part of the field, particularly in the midsection at the break of slope. The overall weight distribution pattern is consistent with the tendency for heavier pieces to be transported further downslope, aided by the selective effect of agricultural tilling machinery.

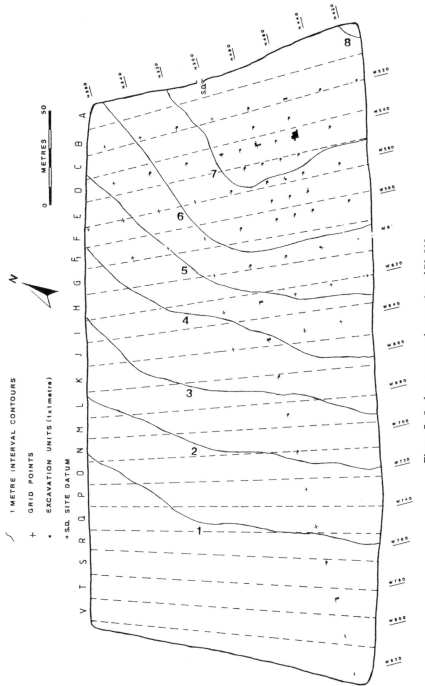

Figure 5. Surface survey and excavation of BL 219.

1 METRE INTERVAL CONTOURS

+ GRID POINTS

• EXCAVATION UNITS (1×1 metre)

○ S.D. SITE DATUM

N

0 METRES 50

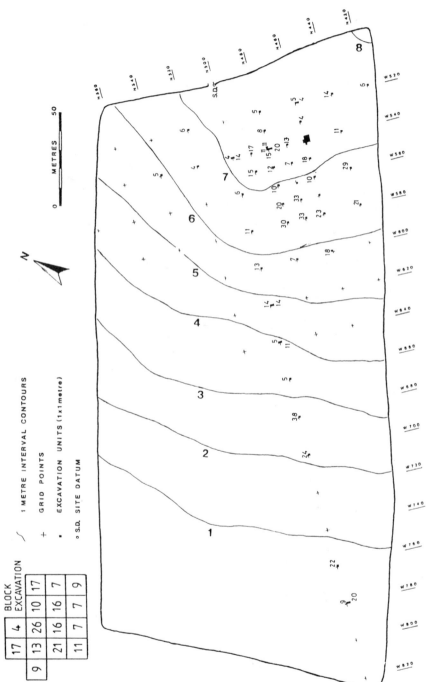

Figure 6. Density of finds from BL 219 excavations.

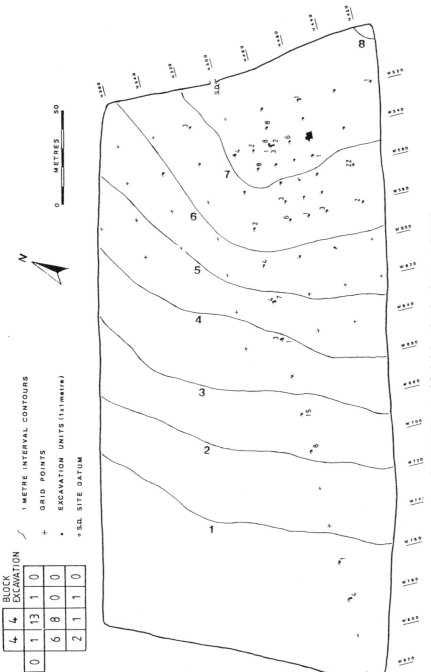

Figure 7. Density of finds below the plough zone at BL 219.

Table 2. Density of Finds from Surface and Subsurface
Investigations at BL 219

Surface finds per transect walked		Surface density per square meter	Excavated total per square meter per tst	Subplough zone total
A	76	0.03	—	—
B	64	0.03	6.66	0.83
C	54	0.02	6.00	4.00
D	46	0.02	12.11	2.57
E	90	0.04	11.88	3.40
F	116	0.05	11.66	1.00
F1	119	0.05	23.60	2.80
G	54	0.02	—	—
H	65	0.03	—	—
I	86	0.04	14.00	5.50
J	123	0.05	8.00	2.00
K	71	0.03	—	—
L	72	0.03	5.00	0.00
M	41	0.02	38.00	15.00
N	68	0.03	24.00	8.00
O	60	0.03	—	—
P	30	0.01	—	—
Q	27	0.01	—	—
R	35	0.02	—	—
S	26	0.01	22.00	1.00
T	46	0.02	15.00	2.00
V	29	0.01	—	—

In the bottom, western section of the field, the soil reaches greater depths of 45 to 75 cm. Unlike in the top eastern section, in the western section glacial deposits appear to overlie the bedrock. The surface density of finds is relatively low; whereas the density of finds excavated from the plow zone *and from the deposits below* is high, indicating that this part of the distribution may have been the least disturbed by plowing and translocation and that some of the finds in this part of the field may have remained *in situ*.

Ultimately, the excavations are consistent with surface collection in terms of chronology and distributional patterns. However, the relationship between the surface and subsurface part of the assemblage is different in each part of the field:

Position	Disturbance	Surface/subsurface dislocation
Ridgetop	Erosion, translocation of finds by plowing to bedrock	Extensive, finds partly *in situ* but destroyed by plowing cultural deposits
Shoulder	Erosion and deposition, translocation of finds by plowing to bedrock	Extensive finds not *in situ*
Bottom	Limited deposition not plowing to bedrock	Limited finds *in situ*

Only the surface scatters in the bottom part of the field are likely to accurately indicate the subsurface distribution patterns. Yet the surface scatter density in this part of the field was low (Table 2) showing that surface scatters on their own are not necessarily a good guide to areas of undisturbed activity below.

At other sites, subsurface testing also confirmed that correspondence between surface scatters and subsurface deposits cannot be taken for granted. At BL 4120, another upland plateau site within the Fornaught Strand Basin, test pit excavations revealed a low-density scatter (51 finds in 61 pits) in a geomorphologically stable matrix, which could be taken as typical of the incidental use of the landscape—a "background scatter."

At BL 231, a coastal site located on a solifluction terrace sloping from the foot of Knockavelish Head toward Fornaught Strand and its alluvial sediments, the high density of surface finds was matched in the northwestern part of the field by excavated finds. The complex geomorphological history of the site was controlled by the downslope movement of material, ranging from soliflucted till in periglacial environment, to more recent erosion processes. Erosion of up to 1 metre below the wall boundary at the top of the field suggest that recent plowing has accelerated this process. The western edge of the field, containing the remains of a shell midden, was lost to the sea within the last 60 years. Finally, the lower part of the terrace was covered by alluvium and peat after *ca.* 3300 B.C.

The consequences are that the surface scatter again does not represent the subsurface pattern of finds *in situ:* It is more likely that the finds, both surface and subsurface, were redeposited by erosion and plow on an earlier solifluction surface. This is supported by the mixed nature of finds, which includes both Mesolithic and Neolithic diagnostics. The high density of lithics, the presence of a hearth and possibly of structural remains indicates, however, that the center of activity was not far away, possibly above the excavated area in the northwestern corner of the field.

At BL 300, a rhyolite quarry, yielding thousands of artifacts in surface collection and subsurface testing, the overall stratigraphy of the site is conditioned by its location on the northeastern slope of the rhyolite ridge and by the agricultural activities that have taken place. The site forms a continuous distributional surface with the neighboring field BL 320, which has yielded the highest density of finds from all the fields walked. In both locations, the slope has an undulating surface, with outcrop locations separated by concave areas of greater soil depth. Despite the potential for soil erosion and slippage, the examination of soil profiles leads to the conclusion that most of the soil formation took place *in situ*. It is more likely that greater disturbance took place by the repeated plowing of the locality and by the dumping of material in and around the outcrop area. In view of these observations, the high density of finds in the plow zone, their relative paucity below the plow zone, and the absence of cultural features all point toward the *in situ* destruction of the fossil occupational surface by farming activities.

Another site, BL 430, located, significantly, on a multifaceted valley slope, contained very few artifacts subsurface, despite very high densities in the plow zone. In this case, a high-density artifact scatter occurred either as a result of downslope movement and accumulation or because the entire site was located in the plow zone and was brought to the surface by repeated plowing.

The lesson learned from these investigations is that it is futile to attempt behavioral interpretation without understanding the geomorphology and the formation of archaeological landscapes first. This requires often detailed testing of the landscape by geomorphologists, palynologists, and other specialists on which paleonenvironmental reconstruction, both on local and regional scales can be based. Despite the cost of such investigations, such cost appears to us justified, if geomorphological studies form an integral part of archaeological research project and are carried out prior as well as in conjunction with excavations. Only in this way, the taphonomic processes of "longue durée" can help to unravel the behavioral patterns, both local and regional, which act as signatures of human behavior in the past.

Behavioral Patterns

The principal value of landscape archaeology rests in its potential for the better understanding of human behavioral patterns. One of the first steps in this direction consists of understanding the structure and the variation of material residues over landscape. In our case, we have used the variation in the density, size, and composition of lithic scatters as the point of departure for making basic observations about the nature of our data.

As noted earlier, our data can be organized chronologically into three time frames: Stone Age, late Mesolithic, and Neolithic. These periods are defined by technological changes that can be observed in artifact collections; on their own, they do not indicate changes other than in technological behavior; although, associated paleoeconomic and other evidence suggests that the Mesolithic–Neolithic transition is associated with the shift from hunting and gathering to farming economy in most, but not all, archaeological contexts.

One obvious feature of most surveys, including ours, is the variation in the size and density of surface scatters. Such variation can reveal the basic organization of land use. These patterns will be subject to both predicted patterns of human behavior and taphonomic processes. Because we are dealing with a period of transition from hunter–gatherer to farming societies, we can advance two settlement–subsistence models. Hunter–gatherer remains can be expected to have a hierarchial structure with base camps/residential sites located along coastlines and in riverine locations (Woodman 1976; Mitchell 1986). Satellite camps, with a restricted range of activities, such as hunting, gathering, tool curation, and raw material procurement would occur in territories surrounding the base camps and result archaeologically in a low-density or background scatter as a basic pattern. The repeated use of some locations will result in artifact accumulations of greater density whose reduced variation in artifact types should distinguish them from residential sites (but see Binford 1983 for general discussion and Zvelebil *et al.* 1987 for a discussion specific to Southeast Ireland regarding the interpretation of artifact patterns). The overall effect should be one of settlement hierarchy and continuous but uneven density distribution of artifacts over landscape (Figure 8).

Bearing in mind the current view regarding the nature of Neolithic farming communities in Ireland (Herity and Eogan 1977; Aalen 1978; Reeves-Smyth and Hammond 1983; O'Kelly 1989; Mitchell 1986), the basic settlement pattern should be created by the remains of hamlets or isolated farmsteads scattered across the landscape. Reduced mobility, a simplified range of activities (chiefly agropastoral farming), and reduced size of territories should produce a "point resource" pattern, with small, dense clusters of artifacts peaking above the background scatter. Preferential settlement of lowland, water-edge areas should be abandoned in favor of lighter, drier soils of upland areas (Figure 8) (Aalen 1978; Peterson 1990). This pattern would have been blurred somewhat if the greater shift towards animal husbandry in later Neolithic resulted in more mobile, pastoral economies. Ceremonial and burial sites (granges, megalithic tombs) would have provided a focus for aggregation, mate exchange, and social reproduction; however, in terms of artifact distribution, such sites are often marked by a paucity, rather than a high density of artifacts.

This is, of course, a simplified picture. When the processual perspective is added, artifact scatters come to represent more than discrete residues of social and economic behaviors. The palimpsest effect, for instance, may result in a pattern that does not distinguish between the repeated use of a locality for different purposes and a residential site, as may be in the case with BL 231. Some activities, such as the procurement of lithic raw material, will produce a high density of nonbiodegradable material, whereas other activities, such as fishing, or

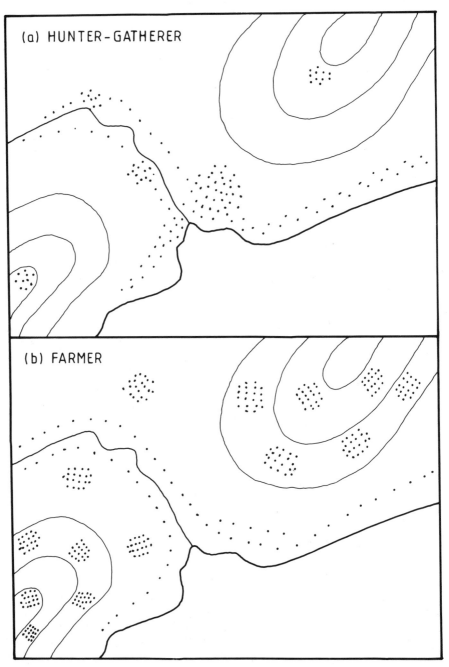

Figure 8. A model of artifact distribution as a residue of hunter–gatherer and farmer settlement.

ritual associated with megalithic tombs, will not. The enormous quantities of rhyolite artifacts from BL 300 are not strictly comparable, then, to shellmidden sites in Corbally More, which lack stone tools. As we have seen in the previous section, a whole host of taphonomic processes can alter the density and distribution of artifacts, and for this reason it is crucial to take these into account. For instance, the status of BL 231 as a residential site is reduced by its possible role as a sediment trap accumulating finds of several periods of occupation to produce a high-density palimpsest. The role of BL 219 as a major focus of Neolithic land use/occupation is confirmed because, despite erosion, a high density of artifacts was recovered.

But the most widespread constraint affecting our analysis is the coarse chronological grain of the "episodes" we are dealing with: Most scatters can be identified as Stone Age only. Nevertheless, at this level of resolution we can profit from the large number of scatters at hand, observe the variation in land use during the Stone Age as such, and attempt to understand the repeated use of certain locations as opposed to others. Let us begin by examining lithic density variation at this broadest level of chronological resolution.

The Lithic Landscape

To distinguish the differences in land use and to express the variation in size and density more accurately, lithic scatters were ranked in a rank/size diagram (Figure 9). Although the size of the scatters does not behave according to a rank/size rule, five distinct groups can be distinguished, ranging from large scatters of 300 to 400 finds/hectare to collections of less than 1 find/hectare. The elbow of the graph marks the beginning of the fourth group, where scatters begin to cluster around the same value of less than 20 finds/hectare:

Group 1: Over 290 finds/hectare (BL 300, 219, and 320)
Group 2: 50 to 80 finds/hectare (BL 232, 235, 132, 3218, 216)
Group 3: 21 to 50 finds/hectare (BL 1231, 135, 133, 231, 215)
Group 4: 10 to 20 finds/hectare (25 cases: groups clustered around the elbows of the graph)
Group 5: less than 10 finds/hectare (243 cases)

In geography, rank-size analysis has been used to infer the existence of settlement hierarchies. In the case of prehistoric settlement, discrete groupings may denote qualitatively different types of land use locations, reflecting the structure of settlement in the region. In the present case, settlement hierarchy was defined as hierarchy of find locations that is defined by the density of artifacts per unit area (cf. Paynter 1983). In fact, a closer look at the finds within different groups (Figure 9) suggests that Group 5, with density of less than 10 finds per hectare (i.e., the tail end to right of the elbow on the graph) probably represent

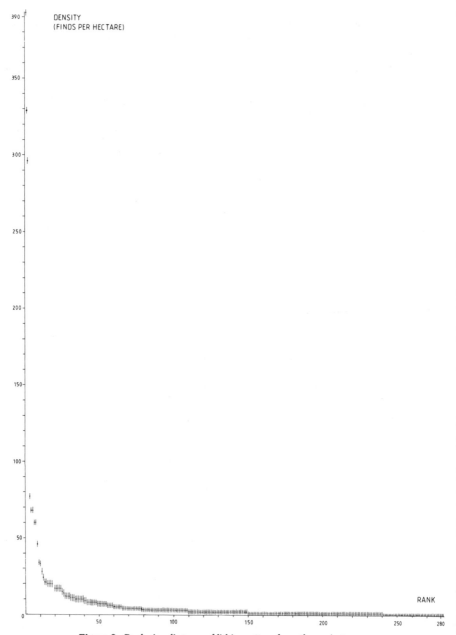

Figure 9. Rank-size diagram of lithic scatters from the project area.

incidental, "off-site" activities, or background scatter. A restricted range of activities was carried out in these locations, showing mainly the remains of tool finishing and tool discard.

In reference to hunter–gatherers, Foley (1981b:19) noted that the ratio of focal points for activities to home bases within a home range should be 5 to 1. In our case, the ratio of Group 5 to large scatters is 7.4 to 1, suggesting that we may be dealing with a broadly similar type of land use structure. All sites surveyed were included in this calculation, even those where only a small area was field-walked and that have yielded only one or two finds. This may have inflated the number of small sites. The "catch 22" problem in this instance is to define a minimum size of an area representative for a field survey, since in order to do that, we have to know the spatial and the hierarchial structure of the settlement pattern.

Larger lithic scatters, comprising Groups 1, 2, 3 and 4 can be best explained as representing manufacturing locations or residential sites, depending on the nature of the debris. Some of these contain tool types such as scrapers, notches, knives, and fabricators, suggesting processing activities. The presence of manufacturing debris from every stage of the reduction sequence suggests that artifacts were manufactured, used, and discarded on location. Excavation on three such locations revealed lithic reduction sequences (BL 300), lenses of shell (BL 231), ash, charcoal, plowed-out features (BL 219 and 231), and a possible habitation feature (BL 231). Figure 10 represents an attempt at a functional interpretation of the lithic scatters in the region, bearing in mind that the depositional integrity of some scatters, such as at BL 231 may be questioned and that parts of the ancient landscape were covered or eroded by subsequent taphonomic processes.

Turning to the variation in the density of lithic scatters over the landscape shown in Figure 11, we can see that the highest densities occur in coastal and estuarine areas. The density of finds is noticeably smaller inland, consisting mainly of scatters that would be viewed here as incidental use of the landscape. The riverine zone has so far yielded only low-density scatters. Many riverine areas supporting Mesolithic settlements, however, may have been subsequently covered by alluvial deposits.

Taking a closer look at the distribution of artifact scatters in the Fornaught Strand Basin (Figure 3), we can see that we are in fact dealing with a continuous distribution pattern, in that all but one field examined yielded stone artifacts. Some locations have been used consistently more often than others. Microenvironmental conditions of these locations are yet to be analyzed, but even at this stage it is clear that lowland coastal locations and upland locations with a good view were used preferentially to valley slopes. Such a pattern could have been produced by the superimposition of the hunter–gatherer and early farming settlement patterns, described earlier. At the same time, the regional density pattern

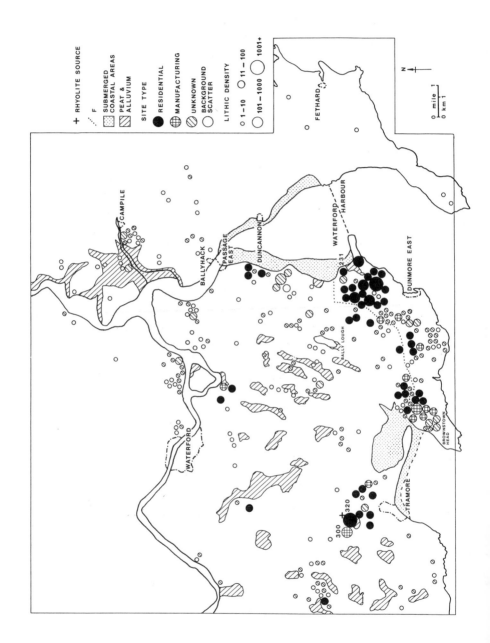

and the hierarchial structure of the settlement pattern (more hunter–gatherer than farming) point to a greater continuity in settlement and land use than is usually acknowledged (Green and Zvelebil 1990; Peterson 1990).

Let us now consider the distribution of lithic scatters with Neolithic and Mesolithic diagnostics (Figure 1). Neolithic scatters appear to be preferentially located on interfluves and on valley terraces close to the valley floor. Artifacts at these locations tend to be less dislocated than is the case with other landforms. The major Mesolithic scatters are located on or near the coast, on landforms prone to surface disturbance and burial. These observations do not take account of the palimpsest effect and have been challenged (Petersen 1990). As it stands, however, the regional distribution of diagnostic locations lends further support to the distribution pattern observed in Fornaught Strand.

Behavioral interpretation of these patterns is complicated by the nonbehavioral variables outlined before. A preliminary interpretation, however, is possible. Low-density scatters occur throughout the project area, demonstrating the continuous use of the landscape during the Stone Age. Most of these scatters consist of what we regard as incidental discard.

Higher-density scatters occur mainly in former and present coastal and estuarine areas. This must be due to two factors: the presence of raw material—either poor quality flint pebbles or rhyolite (Figure 10)—and proximity to the coast. Here we can recognize two types of locations: manufacturing sites or quarries and processing or habitation sites. The overall organization of land use both in the Mesolithic and Neolithic appears to have been similar: Major sites were located within easy reach of the coast with the land use catchments extending inland. At a microscale, Neolithic settlement extended further inland than that of the hunter–gatherers.

If this picture is borne out by further investigations, then it would support the following propositions regarding the Stone Age in Ireland.

1. Land use patterns of foragers and farmers were not remarkably different, suggesting perhaps greater continuity in population, resource use, and social organization during the transition to farming than generally assumed.
2. With the development of farming, settlement, and land use extended from the coastal areas inland, reflecting the gradual intensification of farming or a shift to a more pastoral economy.
3. The gradual nature of this process calls into the question the widely held assumption that the technological change marking the shift from the

Figure 10. A functional interpretation of lithic scatters in the project area.

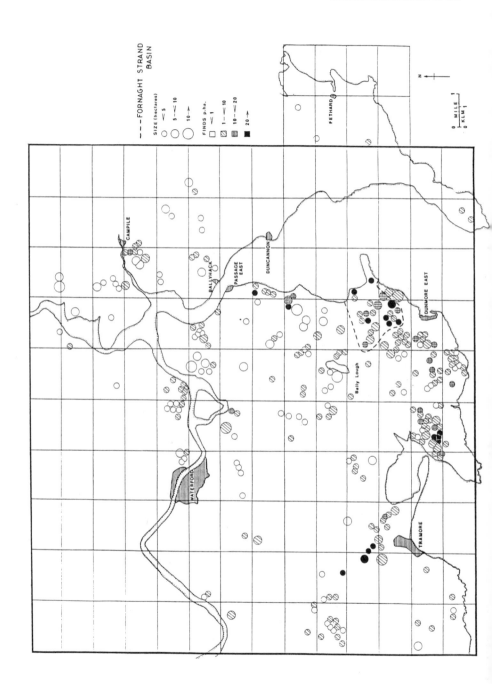

Mesolithic to Neolithic is paralleled by the rapid replacement of foraging by farming (see also Green and Zvelebil 1990); Petersen 1990; Dennell 1983; Zvelebil 1986).

CONCLUSIONS

Until now, our research in Southeast Ireland has been aimed at understanding the basic structure of our data. This research has illustrated both the advantages and difficulties associated with landscape-oriented archaeology. Without such an approach, however, we could not even begin to understand the organization of human societies in the Stone Age.

Bearing in mind the body of data available in Southeast Ireland, the site-oriented approach would have been of little use. Within the site approach, surface scatters are perceived in terms of concept, method, and practice, as indicators of subsurface settlement remains. Our examination of surface scatters has shown quite clearly that this is not the case. Surface scatters may indicate plowed-out subsurface remains of a specialized activity repeated over a long period of time (as at BL 300), plowed-out and dislocated site remains within the same sampling area (as at BL 219), remains of activity deposited from outside the sampling area (as at BL 430), a background scatter (as at BL 4120), or a palimpsest of cultural activity brought together by repeated downslope movement of material (as was probably the case at BL 231). It is clear, then, that surface scatters form a poor search strategy for locating preserved sites under the surface. Viewed as a means to this end, surface scatter expose, if anything, the unbearable lightness of the archaeological record.

Viewed as a distributional surface over landscape invested with a meaning of its own, surface scatters provide the basis for the reconstruction and transformation of ancient landscapes and for elucidating past human behavior embedded within them. As we have shown, there are problems as well: the peaks in the distribution density of finds may be signatures of reoccupation, intensive use, or geological superimposition of strata; the gaps may indicate genuine avoidance by prehistoric communities or burial by later deposits. This does not detract from the potential of the landscape approach for understanding the past. When we moved into the Waterford Harbor area of Southeast Ireland, the pre-Neolithic cultural landscape was a matter of conjecture, and, the Neolithic one barely existed in the form of isolated megaliths. We now have a record of intensive land use in the Stone Age, with differential, yet continuous and overlapping patterns of land use

Figure 11. Density of lithic finds per HA in the project area.

by the late Mesolithic and Neolithic communities. This is just a beginning; more specific information has to be extracted of course—the point is that within the landscape approach, it is extractable.

Two avenues are crucial, in our view, in advancing our research toward more specific conclusions: geomorphological studies and the use of geographic information systems (GIS).

As human behavior and natural processes transform the landscape in time, the record of human behavior is embedded in the physical matrix of which the landscape is composed. Although human behavior is complex and often unpredictable, the natural forces active in the landscape are more patterned, regular, and ultimately subject to the basic laws of physics. The physical matrix of archaeological residues, through the natural component of which it is mostly composed, provides, therefore, an unequivocal and intelligible framework against which human behavior can be interpreted.

The next step must be the development and testing of models of organization and land use of foraging and farming communities. This can only be done, however, with detailed knowledge of processes responsible for the formation of surface residues and with the development of middle-range theory that would make such models operational within the constraints imposed by our data.

ACKNOWLEDGMENTS

We wish to thank all the members of the Bally Lough Archaeological Project team: Chris Judge, Eddie Moth, Jane Peterson, and Christina Rushe, and all the Irish, British, and American students, as well as all the Earthwatch volunteers, who have walked the fields with us to lay the basis for interpreting the landscape of Southeast Ireland. We thank the British Academy, the Center for Field Research, the National Geographic Society, and our respective universities for their financial support. We should also like to thank Willie Lodge, Edward Flynn, Richard Jennings, Richard Power, and Patric Crotty for allowing us to excavate in their fields. Stan thanks Claudia, Harrison, Devin, and especially little Sophie who waited for his return before making her debut.

REFERENCES

Aalen, F. H. A. 1978. *Man and Landscape in Ireland,* Academic Press, New York.
Abler, R., Adams, J. S., and Gould, P., 1977, *Spatial Organisation,* Prentice Hall, London.
Allen, K., 1990, Modelling Early Historic Trade in the Eastern Great Lakes using Geographic Information Systems, in: *Interpreting Space: GIS in Archaeology* (K. Allen, S. Green, and E. Zubrow, eds.), Taylor and Francis, London.

Allen, K., Green, S. W., and Zubrow, E. B. W. (eds.), 1990, *Interpreting Space: GIS in Archaeology*, Taylor and Francis, London.

Ammerman, A. J. and L. L. Cavalli-Sforza, 1984, *The Neolithic Transition and the Genetics of Populations in Europe*. Princeton University Press, Princeton.

Binford, L., 1981, Behavior Archaeology and the "Pompeii Premise," *Journal of Anthropological Research* 37:195–208.

Binford, L., 1983, *Working at Archaeology*, Academic Press, New York.

Bloch, M., 1977, The Past and the Present in the Present, *Man* 12:278–292.

Bradley, R., 1978, *The Past and the Prehistoric Settlement of Britain*, Routledge Kegan Paul, Boston.

Bradley, R., 1984, *The Social Foundations of Prehistoric Britain*. Longman, London.

Caufield, S., 1983, The Neolithic Settlement of North Connaught, in: *Landscape Archaeology in Ireland*. (T. Reeves-Smythe and F. Hammond, eds.), BAR British Series 116, pp. 195–215. Oxford.

Chisholm, M., 1962, *Rural Settlement and Land-Use: An Essay on Location*, Hutchinson, London.

Clarke, D., 1973, Archaeology: Loss of Innocence, *Antiquity* 47:7–18.

Cowgill, G., 1975, A Selection of Samples. In: *Sampling in Archaeology* (J. Muller, ed.), University of Arizona Press, Tucson, pp. 258–276.

Crumley, C., and Marquardt, W., 1990, Landscape: A Unifying Concept in Regional Analysis, in: *Interpreting Space: GIS in Archaeology* (K. Allen, S. W. Green, and E. B. W. Zubrow, eds.). Taylor and Francis, London, pp. 73²80.

Dennell, R., 1983, *European Economic Prehistory*, Academic Press, New York.

Dunnell, R. C., and Dancey, W. S., 1983, THe Siteless Survey: A Regional Scale Surface Collection Strategy, in: *Advances in Archaeological Method and Theory* (M. Schiffer, ed.), vol. 267–87.

Evans, J. G. 1975. *The Environment of Early Man in the British Isles*, Paul Elek, London.

Foley, R., 1981a, Off-Site Archaeology: An Alternative Approach for the Short-sighted, in: (I. Hodder, G. Isaac, and N. Hammond, eds.), *Pattern of the Past. Studies in Honour of David Clarke*, pp. 157–183. Cambridge University Press.

Foley, R., 1981b, A Model of Regional Archaeological Structure, *Proceedings of the Prehistoric Society* 47:1–17.

Found, W. C., 1971, *A Theoretical Approach to Rural Land Use Patterns*, Arnold, London.

Green, S., 1990, Sorting Out Settlement in Southeastern Ireland, in: *Interpreting Space: GIS and Archaeology* (K. Allen, S. Green, and E. Zubrow, eds.), Taylor and Francis, London, pp. 356–364.

Green, S., and Zvelebil, M., 1990, The Mesolithic Colonisation to Agricultural Transition of Southeast Ireland, *Proceedings of the Prehistoric Society*, 56:57–88.

Hassan, F., 1987, Reforming Archaeology: A Foreword to Natural Formation Processes and the Archaeological Record, in: (D. T. Nash and M. D. Petralgia, eds.), *Natural Formation Processes and the Archaeological Record*, pp. 1–9. B.A.R. Int. Ser. 352.

Hazelgrove, C., Millet, M., and Smith, I. (eds.), 1985, *Archaeology from the Ploughzone*, University of Sheffield, Sheffield.

Herity, M., and Eogan, G., 1977, *Ireland in Prehistory*, Routledge Kegan Paul, London.

Hodder, I., and Orton, C., 1976, *Spatial Analysis in Archaeology*, Cambridge University Press.

Kvamme, K., 1989, Geographic Information Systems in Regional Archaeological Research and Data Management, in: *Archaeological Method and Theory* (M. Schiffer, ed.), 1:139–204.

Madry, S., and Crumley, C., 1990, Remote Sensing and GIS in Burgundy, in: *Interpreting Space: GIS in Archaeology*, pp. 364–381 (K. Allen, S. W. Green, and E. B. W. Zubrow, eds.), Taylor and Francis, London.

Mitchell, G. F., 1986, *Reading the Irish Landscape*, Amach Faoin Aer Teo, Dublin.

Nash, D. T., and Petraglia, M. D. (eds.), 1987, Natural Formation Processes and the Archaeological Record: Present Problems and Future Requisites, in: *Natural Formation Processes and the Archaeological Record*, B.A.R. I.S., 352:186–204.

O'Kelly, M., 1989, *Early Ireland*, Cambridge University Press.
Paynter, R. W., 1983, Expanding the Scope of Settlement Analysis, in: *Archaeological Hammers and Theories* (J. Moore and A. Keene, eds.), Academic Press, Orlando, pp. 234–277.
Peterson, J. D. 1990, From Foraging to Food Production in Southeast Ireland: Some Lithic Evidence, *Proceedings of the Prehistoric Society* 56:89–103.
Reeves-Smith, T., and Hammond, F. (eds.), 1983, *Landscape Archaeology in Ireland*, B.A.R. Brit Ser. 116.
Schiffer, M., 1972, Archaeological Context and Systematic Context, *American Antiquity* 37:156–165.
Schiffer, M., 1976, *Behavioral Archaeology*, Academic Press, New York.
Schiffer, M., 1983, Towards the Identification of Formation Processes, *American Antiquity* 48:675–706.
Simmons, I., and Tooley, M. J., 1981, The Environment in British Prehistory, Duckworth, London.
Thomas, J., 1988, Neolithic Explanations Revisited: The Mesolithic–Neolithic Transition in Britain and South Scandinavia. *Proceedings of the Prehistoric Society* 54:59–66.
Thünen, von, J. H., 1826, *Der Isolierte Staat in Beziehung auf Landwirtschaft und Nationalokonomic*, Rostock.
Telfer, A., 1988, Going Downhill in Southeast Ireland: Flint Scatters and Site Formation Processes, Unpublished dissertation, Department of Archaeology, University of Sheffield.
Wagstaff, J., 1987, *Landscape and Culture*, Blackwell, London.
Wandsnider, L., 1987, Natural Formation Process Experimentation and Archaeological Analysis, in: *Natural Formation Processes and the Archaeological Record* (D. T. Nash and M. D. Petraglia, eds.), B.A.R. Int. Ser. 352:150–185.
Woodman, P., 1976, The Irish Mesolithic-Neolithic Transition, in: *Acculturation and Continuity in Atlantic Europe* (J. S. DeLaet, ed.), De Tempel, Brugge, Belgium.
Zvelebil, M., Moore, J., Green, S., and Henson, D., 1987, Regional Survey and the Analysis of Lithic Scatters: A Case Study from Southeast Ireland, in: *Mesolithic Northwest Europe: Recent Trends* (P. Rowley-Conwy, M. Zvelebil, and H. P. Blankholm, eds.), Department of Archaeology, University of Sheffield, Sheffield, pp. 9–32.
Zvelebil, M. (ed.), 1986, *Hunters in Transition*, Cambridge University Press.
Zubrow, E. B. W., 1990, Modeling and Prediction with Geographic Information Systems: A Demographic Example from Prehistoric and Historic New York, in: *Interpreting Space: GIS in Archaeology* (K. Allen, S. W. Green, and E. B. W. Zubrow, eds.), Taylor and Francis, London.

Chapter **10**

Remnant Settlement Patterns

ROBERT E. DEWAR AND KEVIN A. MCBRIDE

INTRODUCTION

There are real methodological and theoretical difficulties inherent in classical settlement pattern analysis, especially when it is defined as the analysis of "the distribution of sites across a landscape." All of the contributors to this volume, in one fashion or another, are seeking more satisfactory and productive ways of understanding and interpreting spatial distributions of archaeological materials. There are many ways to refine methods of spatial analysis, and the approach we outline here is but one. Our approach, which we call "remnant settlement pattern analysis" focuses on the spatial and temporal dynamics of past people's use of places and the way those dynamics changed through time. We are seeking a set of concepts and approaches (e.g., Dewar 1986, 1992) that avoid many of the difficulties that are created by a focus on "sites" (cf. Dunnell, this volume and 1988; Binford, this volume; Camilli 1988). Nonetheless, our effort is in some ways an elaboration and reform of the traditional approach to settlement patterns, where archaeologists attempt to interpret the distribution of the places where they find concentrations of artifacts—so-called "sites"—across a landscape to reconstruct the dynamics of ancient cultural systems, estimate population density, and monitor changes in these over time.

Although some archaeologists have shown that it is productive to relate distributions of artifacts and features directly to the landscape, without recourse

ROBERT E. DEWAR and KEVIN A. McBRIDE • Department of Anthropology, University of Connecticut, Storrs, Connecticut 06269.

Space, Time, and Archaeological Landscapes, edited by Jacqueline Rossignol and LuAnn Wandsnider. Plenum Press, New York, 1992.

to "sites" at all (Thomas 1975; Foley 1981; Dunnell and Dancy 1983; Ebert 1988; Camilli 1988), we are not yet prepared to abandon entirely the study of "sites," or in the editors' phrase *dense, highly visible assemblages* (personal communication, 1991). One reason is that in the areas in which we work, surface survey is typically impeded by vegetation, and most artifacts are discovered through subsurface test pitting. Test pitting is both expensive and a guarantee that only relatively dense concentrations of artifacts will usually be discovered in the field. We are forced, then, at least when we are examining a reasonably large area, to examine the distribution of this skewed sample of the total potential record of past human activity. A second reason, related to the first, for attempting to refine a "site-based" approach is that most of the existing archaeological database is presented in this way. Refinement of the theory and the development of appropriate methods to analyze "clumps" of artifacts will allow reinterpretation of previously reported settlement patterns. We are sure that our methods will be more useful in areas where the contemporary archaeological record has a "clumpy" quality and may be less attractive in places where "nonsite" distributions are common and visible. We will discuss first the distinctive features of "remnant settlement pattern analysis" in comparison with more traditional methods and then illustrate our points with data from an archaeological survey of Glastonbury, Connecticut.

SETTLEMENT PATTERNS AND REMNANT SETTLEMENT PATTERNS

The cycle of economic activity over the four seasons of a year is usually treated as the primary determinant of settlement patterns in most discussions (Beardsley *et al.* 1956; Chang 1962, 1967, 1972; Flannery 1968; Struever 1968; Trigger 1968; Parsons 1972; Jochim 1976; Binford 1980). The study of settlement patterns has been cited as a point of articulation between archaeologists and ethnographers (Parsons 1972; Chang 1967, 1972), and many ethnographic and ethnoarchaeological studies have provided detailed and valuable descriptions of the articulation of resource distributions and human residences and exploitation tactics. Understanding subsistence/settlement systems, as these are sometimes called, is clearly necessary to understanding settlement patterns. However, the analysis of prehistoric settlement patterns requires more than simply matching an observed distribution of sites and artifacts with a synchronic model of annual subsistence round drawn through ethnographic analogy. Attempts to compare site distributions to models of an annual subsistence round are quite simply attempts to compare radically different phenomena.

Interpretations of prehistory are distorted in two ways by standard settlement pattern analyses. First, archaeologists have often assumed that the physical qualities of archaeological sites and the associated assemblages can be interpreted by direct analogy to the camps, stations, and locations that are the components of ethnographically described subsistence/settlement systems. Ethnographic descriptions are employed to characterize the spatial size and the diversity of activities of different types of occupations, and these signatures of different occupation types are compared to the archaeological sites and assemblages. Thomas has pointed out the ubiquity of such assessments:

> Smaller, less diverse assemblages have commonly been interpreted as areas of diurnal extraction ("locations"). Larger, more diverse assemblages are often equated with residential utilization ("base camps"). Assemblages of intermediate size and diversity are conventionally viewed as logistic settlements ("field camps"). Although rarely spelled out, the tacit equation of absolute assemblage diversity with discrete settlement types underlies many so-called behavioral interpretations in contemporary hunter-gatherer studies [references deleted]. (Thomas 1986:241–242)

Although Thomas is concerned with the difficulty of linking assemblage diversity with settlement types, we would add that there is a similar tacit equation of settlement size with settlement type. In so doing, analysts ignore the fact that the sites are commonly the product of *many* occupations, not one.

The second problem emerges when archaeologists have sought ethnographic or ethnohistoric analogues of landscape use as templates to which their spatial distributions of archaeological sites can be fitted, disregarding the fact that the inferred articulation of sites is not usually testable with the data they possess. For example, archaeologists in New England have often tried to match archaeological site distributions with Beardsley et al.'s (1956) "community patterns," and thus to distinguish between "restricted wandering" and "central-based-wandering" hunter–gatherer settlement systems (cf. Snow 1980:14–15). This cannot be done, unless it is possible to identify the specific sites that were articulated in a single annual round. Ignoring the difficulties, other archaeologists have moved from the identification of "central-based wandering" to premature and poorly supported discussions of territoriality, seasonal migration distances, ethnic boundaries, and the like (cf. Mulholland 1988). In short, synchronic models of settlement systems, derived from ethnographic analogues, have been imposed upon asynchronic data.

Rouse (1972) distinguished between archaeological and ethnographic analyses of settlement patterns. Ethnographers and geographers study full settlement patterns according to Rouse; archaeologists study *remnant settlement patterns*. Like Rouse, we want to call attention to the fact that the distribution of archaeological sites across a landscape is controlled by many processes that are not salient in an ethnographic description of a "typical year."

A remnant settlement pattern is the product of at least three kinds of processes: (1) those that control site formation and preservation, reflecting both on-site human activity and the burial and preservation of debris (Ascher 1968; Schiffer 1976); (2) those that determine the locational and seasonal features of the sites used during an annual subsistence round and are responsible for some kinds of intersite and interassemblage variability—the result of these latter *short-term* processes is the "dynamic of yearly round" (Binford 1980:19, 1982) (3) those processes that are responsible for year-to-year *variability* in the geographical positioning and content of assemblages of villages, bases, camps, special-purpose sites, and locations. We call these *medium-term processes,* to distinguish them both from the processes that determine annual subsistence/settlement systems and from processes only observable over evolutionary time spans. Short-term processes are described by models of months and seasons, whereas evolution, whether cultural or biological, has impact over generations, but medium-term processes are recognizable only over periods of years and decades.

The size and composition of residential and foraging groups, the timing of the moves, and the resolution of scheduling conflicts are accounted for by subsistence/settlement models that, in addition, often describe the nature and location of the places that will be used during a typical year. In these models of short-term processes, all years are assumed to be much like any other; locations are good or poor for summer or fall or winter occupations. But slower, nonannual medium-term processes can have impact on settlement patterns inexplicable by models of short-term processes alone.

Medium-term processes, for example, include human responses to year-to-year cycles of resource availability, of both natural and human cause. Decreases in shellfish size through time in middens are sometimes interpreted as a result of shifts in the age distribution of the species under the impact of collection. "Strand-looping" (Groube 1971) is a hypothetical pattern of residential mobility designed to deal with declining yields under exploitation: Easily collected seaside resources are vacuumed up without regard for long-term yield, and beds abandoned as they are depleted. Strand-looping settlement shifts are not determined solely by short-term seasonal qualities because an important process underlying the attractiveness of potential new sites is when they were last exploited. In agricultural economies, decreases in soil fertility or depletion of wild resources lead to settlement shifts in a precisely analogous pattern. Potential settlement locations have differential value both because of their permanent features and because of their recent history of use.

The distribution of archaeological materials across a landscape is almost always a product of many years and even generations of use. It reflects not an articulation of "a typical seasonal round" with permanent landscape features but rather many years of the establishment and abandonment of residential occupations on a landscape some of whose features altered over time in response to previous use. One major set of problems with many settlement pattern analysis is due to a failure to employ analytic concepts that clarify rather than conceal the effects of medium-term dynamics on archaeological site distributions.

At this point, we wish to clarify our use of some terms (see Dewar 1986 for a more extended exposition) because we employ them in somewhat more limited fashion than is common. On the other hand, our usages are themselves largely borrowed from the work of others. *Sites* are simply places on the modern landscape where archaeologists find concentrations of human debris. Site distributions are the joint product of past human activity, research efforts of archaeologists and factors of landscape qualities, and dynamics that effect site burial, preservation, and discovery. Sites can be analytically subdivided into *components*, which are the spatial distribution of assemblages of materials that can be temporally distinguished from other assemblages but cannot be temporally subdivided themselves (Chang 1972). Most settlement pattern analyses start with the spatial distribution of components of roughly coeval age. However, components, like sites, cannot be directly interpreted in behavioral terms, for each is the product of one to many occupations. An *occupation* is the archaeological manifestation of a single continuous episode of the residential use of a place. Although the analytic distinction between an occupation and a component is very important, the archaeological discrimination of single occupations is often extremely difficult.

Remnant settlement pattern analysis starts with the premise that components are best regarded as *sequences of occupations*. Each occupation has its own spatial and temporal qualities, and each occupation leaves its own evidence of the nature of activities at this place in the form of artifacts, debris, and features. The archaeological record of an occupation is perhaps interpretable in behavioral terms, and many ethnoarchaeological projects have sought to explore these relations (cf. Yellen 1977). However, because it is often the superposition of several or many occupations that produces a component, the regional distribution of components depends not only upon activity patterns but also the medium term patterns of how often and for how long occupations occurred in the same places, and how exactly subsequent occupations were usually centered upon previous ones. These patterns are reflected in the spatial and temporal qualities of the sequences of occupations that produced our components. These qualities of occupation sequences must be diagnosed, to the best of our skills, before attempting any further analysis of the distribution of components, let alone sites, across a landscape.

TEMPORAL CONTINUITY AND SPATIAL CONGRUENCE

A significant factor affecting sequences of occupations is the duration of use of places, as has long been recognized. Thus, Chang (1962, 1972) draws a major

distinction between temporary and permanent settlements. Relatively little attention has been paid to the impact of changes in patterns of the frequency or average
number of reoccupations on the remnant settlement patterns of hunter–
gatherers or to the relevance of these changes for the interpretation of the
archaeological record. We believe that this is true because (1) year-to-year permanence is not a relevant feature of synchronic models of 12-month subsistence
rounds and (2) the impact of those processes that are important in determining
permanence may not be apparent over ethnographic observation periods of a year
or two.

In order to interpret site distributions by comparison to models of an annual
seasonal round, much settlement pattern theory tacitly assumes that seasonally
occupied bases and most camps of hunter–gatherers are permanent, that is,
perennially reoccupied. Decisions about the location of settlements are envisioned
as optimal solutions to problems created by stable features of the landscape (e.g.,
Jochim 1976; Wood 1978). Typically, settlement locations are discussed with
reference to such variables as distance from water or resource patches, slope,
exposure, elevation, aspect, drainage, and defensibility. Assuming an unchanged
economic system and constant settlement size, it is possible to construct models
predicting a stable measure of attractiveness for any possible site location. If,
however, occupation of a site alters its attractiveness as a future settlement
location, the predictive power of models that only consider landscape features is
likely to be low. What is missed in such models are the medium-term processes
that affect occupation positioning over longer periods.

Occupation may alter a place's attractiveness in subsequent years both
positively and negatively. The construction of expensive, reusable features such
as storage or processing facilities (Flannery 1972) or the caching of difficult to
transport site furniture (Binford 1979) would surely increase its attractiveness.
Past disturbance of nearby plant communities might also increase the density of
some game species (Linares 1976). Whenever occupation increases a place's
attractiveness for future years, then the predictions of a model relying solely upon
permanent landscape features will not be contradicted; the location first selected
will continue to be selected for later occupations, all other things being equal. In
such circumstances, there will be a strong tendency for year-to-year redundancy
in the choice of occupation positioning, and the resulting component will be the
product of a long sequence of occupations.

When occupation reduces a site's future attractiveness as must often hap-
pen, such long sequences of occupation will be the exception rather than the rule.
To take well-known cases, the energetic costs of life in an Amazonian village have
been shown to increase directly with length of occupation; firewood supplies are
depleted, and game becomes scarce in the neighborhood (Johnson 1974, 1982).
Amazonian village relocation has also been attributed to declines in fertility of
arable soils (Gross 1983) and the buildup of village pests (Hames 1983). During

the dry season, !Kung San campsites are always near the same waterholes but the buildup of debris and infestations of parasites often lead to the establishment of camps on less recently occupied places in the vicinity (Yellen 1976, 1977). In New England, seventeenth-century Narragansett abandoned their villages after a period of permanent residence because of exhausted firewood supplies (Williams 1936 cited in Salwen 1978). Simmons reports that the Narragansett shifted residence in midsummer to avoid fleas (1978:191); Mahican villages were shifted every 8 to 12 years "due to the exhaustion of nearby garden plots, a shortage of firewood, and the increasing filthiness in and around the village" (Brasser 1978:198–199). Binford has recently reported a pattern of shift of annual range every 6 to 10 years for Nunamiut "bands" because, in the words of one of his informants,

> as time goes on, things get used up and the place gets full of flies, then people start to fight. When that happens it's time to move to a place where nobody has lived for a long time. (1983:38)

Perennial residence in the same place seemingly always entails added costs, and there is probably usually a tension between repeated use of the *most favorable* place in terms of relatively permanent landscape features, and the attractiveness of uncontaminated, unexploited locations. Local resources that renew only slowly, like firewood, soil fertility, or large game, will always become locally scarcer over the span of occupation of a place and therefore more expensive. In addition, the longer occupation continues, the more likely sanitation measures will become necessary.

Most archaeologists have little difficulty viewing "temporary" and "permanent" as the poles of a temporal continuum: Sites may be occupied for 1, 2, 10, 1,000 seasons. We call this the *continuum of temporal continuity*. More formally, temporal continuity is measured as the number of consecutive years a given place is reoccupied by a seasonally mobile group, or the number of years that a year-round occupation will be maintained in the same place (see Dewar 1986). Recognizing a continuum between "temporary" and "permanent" is important not only in the analysis of seasonally mobile groups but also in the analysis of sedentary, agricultural populations. Dewar (1992) discusses a way to distinguish differences in the average span of use of sedentary villages, and shows how substantially such differences affect the archaeological records of different periods.

Different site types in the same settlement system will probably not have occupation sequences of identical temporal continuity. Binford (1978:488–495), for example, argues that in logistically organized hunter–gatherers there will be a tendency for long-term reuse of special-purpose sites. Certainly, small groups occupying places for short periods will have less environmental impact than the larger, longer occupations associated with base camps. And it follows that previous occupations will be less likely to decrease significantly a place's attractiveness.

Sequences of occupation have variable spatial qualities as well as temporal ones: Reoccupation implies that *the same place* is returned to. But, particularly in the absence of permanent dwellings, each occupation in a sequence may not be located precisely on top of the previous occupation. This raises the question: How close together in space do subsequent occupations have to be for us to regard them as reoccupations of the same place? There is no simple answer to this question, but variation in *spatial congruence* of sequences of occupations is a fundamental cause of variability in remnant settlement patterns. Spatial congruence is measured by the inverse of the average distance separating the centers of sequential occupations of the same place. An example can illustrate the radical effects that changes in spatial congruence have on remnant settlement patterns.

Figure 1 shows schematically three different occupation sequences on a river floodplain. Figures 1d, 1h and 1l show the maximal (i.e., with perfect preservation and 100% effective survey) remnant settlement patterns that would result from the three sequences. In the first sequence, all nine occupations (Figure 1a–1c) occur within 50 m of one another. Without changes in material culture, the archaeological manifestation will be a thick, single component surrounded by several square kilometers of unoccupied space. In the second sequence, each successive occupation is about 300 m from the previous one but always within about 300 m of the center of the distribution. Archaeologically, this produces a cluster of thinner components spread discontinuously over an area of about 9 hectares but once again isolated on the floodplain from contemporary settlements. In the third sequence, subsequent occupations are at least a kilometer from the immediately preceding occupation but always within a kilometer of the center of the cluster. This remnant settlement pattern is spread over 150 hectares. The amount of "empty space" diminishes sharply and so does the apparent integrity of the group of sites as a whole.

These sequences were constructed to illustrate three ideal cases: (1) a *concentrated* sequence of occupations, where previous use has no demonstrable negative impact upon subsequent occupation; (2) a *localized* sequence of moderate congruence where occupations "spoil" the immediate vicinity, for example, by infestation or garbage buildup; (3) a *dispersed* sequence of low congruence where previous occupation transforms a much larger area, for example, by the depletion of firewood.

Several points emerge from this illustration. First, these three different remnant settlement patterns differ *only* in the spatial congruence of the sequence of occupation. This place in the broadest sense was never abandoned, and there was no shift in annual range; there is a high temporal continuity. The remnant settlement patterns are different solely because of differences in spatial continuity controlled by medium-term processes; they are not distinctive for reasons of differences in subsistence patterns or the "dynamic of yearly round." Second, the center of each distribution is identical, and a gravity model such as Jochim's

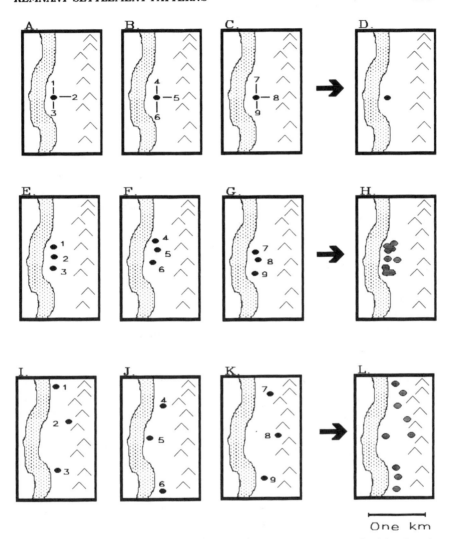

Figure 1. Schematic illustration of three different occupation sequences on a river floodplain. In each sequence, nine separate and sequential occupations are illustrated in the three leftmost maps. The maps on the far right show the maximal (i.e., with perfect preservation and 100% effective survey) remnant settlement patterns that would result from the occupation sequence.

(1976:47–63) might be used to explain the choice of locale with reference to landscape features. However, such a model cannot predict the precise locations of the occupations in the localized or dispersed sequences, nor can it predict whether the sequence should be concentrated, localized, or dispersed. Third, the archaeological visibility of each sequence will be very dissimilar. The site produced by the concentrated sequence is the most visible; it is compact, with detectable boundaries and high densities of artifacts and features. The dispersed sequence would be the least visible. If any or all of the occupations were discovered, they would likely be treated as "separate sites." These deposits would be thin, with lower artifact densities than the single site of the concentrated sequence. For the intermediate case, the localized sequence, it is likely that discovery of any one of the occupations would tend to lead to discovery of others, particularly if there is an attempt to establish site boundaries by intensive survey. The density of artifacts would be similar to the dispersed case. However, it is the methods and skill of the archaeologist (Dincauze 1981) that will determine whether one or five or nine sites will be reported. Fourth, in some interpretations, all may reflect equally permanent occupation sequences, if year-to-year residence in the same "neighborhood" is included within the concept of permanent settlement. Struever reports, for example, such a pattern of site localization on the floodplain of the Illinois River during the Early Woodland period with "repeated occupation . . . of the same *locality* . . . but not . . . of a *specific site locus* (1968:292, emphasis in original). Similar considerations have led to a dichotomy of Yąnomämo village relocations between "micromoves" and "macromoves" (Chagnon 1973; Hames 1983).

Many familiar methods employed in the interpretation of site distributions are frankly inadequate to deal with differences in spatial congruence of occupation sequences. Inferences about population size based upon numbers of sites created per century (Funk and Rippeteau 1977) are widely recognized to require assumptions about temporal continuity because it is evident that "stay-at-home" groups will create fewer sites than more mobile ones. It should be clear, however, that such inferences will also be extremely sensitive to changes in the spatial congruence of occupation sequences. In the example presented in Figure 1, the estimate derived for the dispersed pattern would be almost an order of magnitude greater than for the concentrated sequence. Estimates of population size from site area are similarly compromised. Only when sites are the products of single occupations will their areas directly reflect the space used by a co-resident group, and this is likely to be common only in dispersed occupation sequences. In concentrated sequences, the components are palimpsests of occupations whose centers may or may not be identical. Similarly, the aggregate of site area created per century or phase will obviously reflect in part the extent to which the remains of sequential occupations overlap. The interpretation of site clustering or dispersion also depends upon whether such clusters are regarded as the product of an occupation sequence with spatial congruence or a set of simultaneous occupations.

Let us review the argument to this point. We have identified a substantial difference between settlement patterns viewed from the perspective of an annual round and the remnant settlement patterns that are recovered by archaeologists. These differ principally because (1) taphonomic processes intervene and result in a less than complete record of the use of places prehistorically and (2) differences in medium-term processes affect the temporal continuity and spatial congruence of occupation sequences. These differences in continuity and congruence can have dramatic effects on the number and distribution of archaeological components. When archaeologists examine changing distributions of components over time in a region, they are seeing the products of changes not only in population and in the patterns of exploitation of the landscape but also of changes in the way medium-term processes affect occupation sequences. Analyses of spatial distributions of components that ignore possible differences in continuity and congruence are frankly insufficient and probably often very misleading.

Although changes in temporal continuity and spatial congruence of occupation sequences will have important effects in most regions, they may be particularly important in understanding the archaeology of the floodplain of the Lower Connecticut River. This area has been used for so many thousand years in so many ways that it is tempting to regard it as one big multicomponent site from the Narrows at Middletown to well into Massachusetts. Resource zones and geomorphology parallel the river's banks and terraces so regularly that many places must have been nearly equally attractive in terms of distance to permanent landscape features. In other words, it is precisely the kind of place where problems of local resource depletion, sanitation, and parasites can be expected to affect occupation sequences.

GLASTONBURY

The town of Glastonbury, Connecticut, is located on the eastern bank of the Connecticut River, about midway from Massachusetts to Long Island Sound. The Connecticut River is 200 to 300 meters wide here, and the broad floodplain, 4 to 5 m above normal river height, extends 100 to 1,500 m to the east. Further east are a series of riverine and old lacustrine terraces and an interior, hilly upland, well dissected by small streams and brooks.

The survey of Glastonbury was a 1979 field project of the Public Archaeology Survey Team, Inc., and the coincidence of the survey boundaries and modern political boundaries a purely practical choice. Ninety-three prehistoric components (64% of the total) were discovered through a probabilistic field survey of this area of some 140 km², and the numeric data discussed here all derive from this sample. An additional 52 components were discovered through informants or existing site files, and they are located on later figures.

For sampling, the town was stratified into four zones: (1) the Connecticut River floodplain zone (610 ha); (2) the terrace zone (arbitrarily areas between 15 and 50 m above sealevel, comprising 3,400 ha); (3) the uplands zone (areas above 50 meters above sealevel, comprising 8,500 ha); and (4) the floodplain of the Roaring Brook, a major tributary of the Connecticut that nearly bisects the town, where it crossed the uplands, comprising 1,500 ha. East–west transects within each strata were selected randomly. Because no sites were found in the Roaring Brook stratum, it was combined with the upland stratum in analysis. The floodplain zone and terrace zone strata are parallel bands, approximately north–south (Figure 2).

Field teams of three walked 5 meters apart and excavated 40 cm by 40 cm test pits to a depth of 1 meter every 20 m along linear transects. The total coverage of each of the three strata was uneven. In the floodplain zone, historic records allow the exclusion of 420 ha as having been recently deposited by the shifting river channel; 9.7% of the remaining 190 ha was covered by walking transect crews; 2.1% of the terrace zone stratum was similarly covered, as was only 1.3% of the upland zone stratum. Thus sampling intensity is in a ratio of about 7:1.5:1. The total area covered by the survey crews was 18.4 ha of floodplain, 71.6 ha of the terraces, and 130 ha of uplands. In addition, surface visibility was variable. The entire floodplain was in use as agricultural fields; the terrace and uplands zones were largely covered with forest.

When a prehistoric artifact of any sort was located, the location was designated as a site, given a site number, located on a map and the crew commenced collection at the location. The collections were aimed at finding more artifacts, especially temporally diagnostic forms of lithics and ceramics. All sites, however, were retained in the analysis, no matter the size of the resulting assemblage. Thus a few of the sites are represented by no more than a single artifact.

Collections were made in one of two ways. Sites identified from materials on the surface were almost always in agricultural fields; they were surface-collected in a systematic fashion. In subsurface sites, a variation of transect interval sampling (Chartkoff 1978) was used. We dug the same 40-cm test pits in lines radiating along the major compass axes, from the point of discovery, oriented like checkerboard squares. The lines of pits terminated when sterile test pits were encountered, unless soil disturbance was apparent. In many sites, additional test pits were chosen in an ad hoc fashion. This is particularly true where the collections suggested that there was more than a single component present. Estimates of component area were made using gridded plastic overlays on the polygon with vertices at the most distant nonsterile test pits. We will report here areas for a majority of the components that we could assign to culture–historic periods. Areas were not calculated when time constraints prevented sufficient testing, when neighboring landowners were uncooperative, when components could not be reasonably separated, or when soil disturbance was substantial. Rockshelters

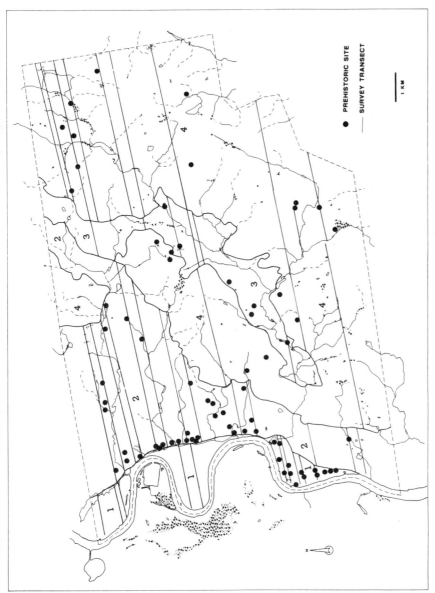

Figure 2. A map of Glastonbury, showing the ecoregions and the location of the survey transects.

were more intensively tested: Usually between 10% and 40% of surface area within and adjacent to the overhang was excavated. As a result there are some biases in our data: 64% of uplands zone and 69% of the floodplain zone components that we could assign to culture–historic periods have area estimates, but only one-half of the terrace zone components have such size estimates. To a large extent, this is because the terraces are the zone of the most intensive modern development.

RESULTS

Table 1 presents a working chronology drawn from work throughout the Lower Connecticut Valley (McBride 1984). The dates assigned to the periods are estimates derived, as much as possible, from local radiocarbon dates. We will add that the chronology of the phases of the Late and Terminal Archaic is a complex and as yet unresolved issue (see later discussion and Pagoulatos 1986). The Late Archaic is divided into two phases, Golet and Tinkham. The Golet Phase is characterized by lithic assemblages that include projectile points similar to the Brewerton series of New York State and a wide variety of raw material types; the Tinkham Phase has assemblages characterized by a very heavy reliance upon quartz and the manufacture of Squibnocket-like points.[1] In Glastonbury, and throughout the lower valley, Golet Phase materials are never seen stratigraphically

Table 1. Lower Connecticut River Valley Prehistoric Chronology[a]

Phase	Approximate time span	Regional "period"
—	12,000–10,000 B.P.	Paleoindian[b]
—	10,000–8,000 B.P.	Early Archaic[b]
—	8000–6000 B.P.	Middle Archaic[b]
Golet	5000–4200 B.P.	Late Archaic, "Laurentian"
Tinkham	4200–3500 B.P.	Late Archaic, "Narrow-stemmed"
Salmon Cove	3600–2700 B.P.	Terminal Archaic
Broeder Point	2700–2000 B.P.	Early Woodland
Roaring Brook	2000–1200 B.P.	Early Middle Woodland
Selden Creek	1200–450 B.P.	Late Middle/Late Woodland
Niantic	450–300 B.P.	Final Woodland

[a] The dates given here reflect radiocarbon dates from the river valley itself. The chronological patterns would be different if the study area were broadened to include more distant parts of Connecticut. The most vexing case is the overlap of some dates for Tinkham and Salmon Cove Phases.
[b] For none of these periods is there sufficient information to define local phases.

[1] In some previous work (e.g., McBride 1984), a third phase, Vibert, intermediate to Golet and Tinkham, was defined. We now include these components in the Tinkham Phase.

above Tinkham Phase components. The Salmon Cove Phase assemblages include much nonlocal lithic material (Calogero 1991) and projectile points of the Susquehanna and Orient series. Sites are assigned to Woodland phases on the basis of ceramic and projectile point typology and radiocarbon dates.

In Table 2, we display the components recovered through the probability survey by phase (where known) and ecozone. Those assigned to "Woodland Unknown" have nondiagnostic lithic and ceramic assemblages; "Archaic Unknown" indicates nondiagnostic assemblages that are stratigraphically pre-Woodland; "Unknown" components have nondiagnostic lithic assemblages. These three categories account for 28 of the 93 components (30%). Compared with the total distribution of components across ecozones, a disproportionate number of these are either on the floodplain (often deeply buried) or in the uplands.

Table 3 presents data on the 37 components for which we have estimates of component area. In this table, no attempt is made to distinguish between areas derived from dispersed, localized, or concentrated occupation sequences. We discuss this later. Note that only 6 of 14 Salmon Cove Phase components have area estimates. However, the aggregated area data for the phase broadly reflects the distribution of occupations across ecozones: 99% of Salmon Cove Phase component area is in the terrace zone, and 5 of the 8 components without size estimates are there as well.

Both the floodplain and the terrace ecozones are variable in east–west breadth, so it is wrong to assume that all floodplain sites are closer to the river than all terrace zone sites. Table 4 regroups data presented in Table 3, combining into a single "riverine zone" floodplain sites and terrace zone sites less than 200 m from the floodplain–terrace zone boundary.

DISCUSSION

These data are the remnant settlement patterns of prehistoric Glastonbury; they are a part of the contemporary archaeological record. In order to use them to understand past settlement systems, we must (1) deal with problems of differential discovery, site destruction, and taphonomy; and (2) attempt to diagnose patterns of site occupation sequences. Only then can we try, with the data we have from studies of site function and seasonality, to interpret these distributions in terms of short-term processes like the "dynamic of yearly round," or in terms of intensity of use. Three questions will guide this discussion. First, what dynamics are responsible for the remnant settlement patterns of the successive periods of local prehistory? Such inferences require the identification of relevant medium-term processes, and the diagnosis of their impact upon the patterns of site distribution, as well as appreciation of differential site preservation. Second, are changes in settlement pattern over time best attributed to changes in the

Table 2. Distribution of Components across Ecozones

	Early Archaic	Golet	Tinkham	Salmon River	Broeder Point	Roaring Brook	Selden Creek/Niantic	Archaic unknown	Woodland unknown	Unknown	Total
Floodplain											
Total	1	1	4	3	1	1	2	3	5	2	23
Terraces											
Total	1	6	12	10	3	3	3	2	2	2	44
Uplands											
Open	0	0	3	0	2	0	1	0	3	7	16
Rockshelters	0	1	3	1	1	1	1	0	2	0	10
Total	0	1	6	1	3	1	2	0	5	7	26
Totals	2	8	22	14	7	5	7	5	12	11	93
Percentage of components by ecozone											
Flood plain	50	12	18	21	14	20	29	60	42	18	26
Terrace	50	75	55	71	43	60	43	40	17	18	46
Upland	0	12	27	7	43	20	29	0	42	64	28

Table 3.   Aggregate of Component Area by Ecozone

	Floodplain		Terraces		Uplands		Total	
	m²	N	m²	N	m²	N	m²	N
Golet	0	0	50	1	100	1	150	2
Tinkham	35,250	3	33,900	7	325	5	69,475	15
Salmon Cove	125	2	20,000	4	—	—	20,125	6
Broeder Point	10,000	1	16,250	2	4,050	2	30,300	5
Roaring Brook	2,000	1	23,750	3	—	—	25,750	4
Selden Creek/Niantic	12,050	2	22,000	2	50	1	34,100	5
Totals	59,425	9	115,950	19	4,525	9	179,900	37

**Table 4.   Aggregate of Component Area by Riverine/Nonriverine
Terrace/Uplands**

	Riverine	Nonriverine terraces	Uplands
Golet	0	50	100
Tinkham	62,100	7,050	325
Salmon Cove	20,125	0	0
Broeder Point	26,250	0	4,050
Roaring Brook	18,250	7,500	0
Selden Creek/Niantic	24,050	10,000	50
Total	150,775	24,600	4,525
Sample size (with area estimate/all sites)			
Golet	0/5	1/2	1/1
Tinkham	8/13	2/3	5/6
Salmon Cove	6/12	0/1	0/1
Broeder Point	3/4	0/0	2/3
Roaring Brook	3/3	1/1	0/1
Selden Creek/Niantic	3/4	1/1	1/2
Total	23/44	5/8	9/14

"dynamic of yearly round" or to changes in the effects of medium-term processes on site permanence? Third, do our data confirm previous descriptions of trends in southern New England cultural evolution?

We will discuss here only the remnant settlement patterns of the Tinkham through the Broeder Point phases. Archaeological material from earlier periods was rarely discovered or yielded unsatisfactory samples. The floodplain is a zone of rapid deposition, and archaeological materials of earlier periods are often very deeply buried; although soil augers were employed to extend the depth of testpits, we are sure we have missed some early components. In addition, the deeper the deposits, the smaller were our assemblages, and thus three of five components known to be stratigraphically pre-Woodland, but otherwise undatable, are from the floodplain (Table 2). We will not discuss the later Woodland periods because it would require consideration of issues extraneous to the point of this chapter.

Throughout the roughly 2,000 years of prehistory discussed here, the prehistoric populations were hunter–gatherers. There is no credible evidence for any form of agriculture in southern New England until roughly 1000 B.P. (Bendremer and Dewar, 1992). In addition, there is no evidence that over these 2,000 years that there was any major change in the list of floral and faunal species that were exploited (McBride 1984), although it is very likely (see later discussions) that patterns of resource exploitation did vary.

Tinkham Phase

"Narrow-stemmed Late Archaic" components dominate many collections from southern New England. In Glastonbury, as elsewhere in the Connecticut River Valley, the striking feature of the Tinkham remnant settlement pattern is the presence of very large sites on the floodplain. These are located on narrow low rises in the floodplain, oriented parallel to the riverbank. Soils on the "knolls" are better drained than the rest of the floodplain. During this phase, all of Glastonbury is occupied (Figure 3). There are three large sites (>15,000 m² in area); two are on the floodplain, and the other on the edge of the first terrace. In addition, there are many medium (1,500 to 7,000 m²) and small (<250 m²) sites on the terraces and in the uplands. In fact, 43% of all identified sites in the uplands are from the Tinkham Phase. Both for number of sites and aggregate site area, the phase dominates the sample. We note that components of this phase have a relatively high visibility, at least in comparison to some periods, as a result of the predominant reliance upon the manufacture of expedient quartz tools. These components yield large numbers of quartz flakes and cores; such artifacts are easy to spot, both on the surface and in test pits.

The remnant settlement pattern of this phase is illuminated by previous work on Tinkham Phase sites in the valley. Just to the north of Glastonbury, a "knoll" site has been extensively excavated: Woodchuck Knoll (McBride 1978;

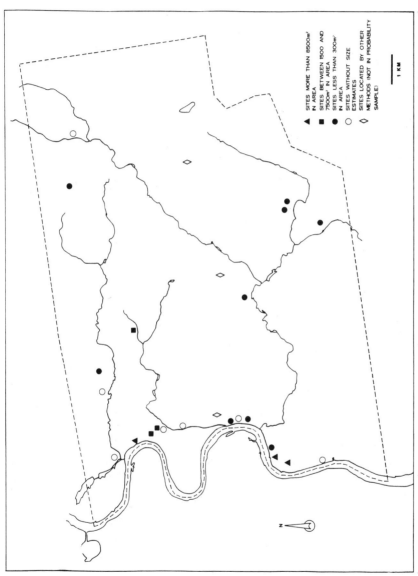

Figure 3. Tinkham Phase components.

McBride *et al.* 1980; D. F. Jordan personal communication). The Tinkham Phase component at Woodchuck Knoll is clearly the product of a long, localized sequence of occupation: high temporal continuity, with moderate spatial congruence. The factor forcing localization is almost certainly the microtopography of the floodplain. Both large Glastonbury floodplain sites are located on similar "knolls." All three of these sites are less than 10 m wide and hundreds of meters long; the occupations are always limited to the knolls. The Tinkham Phase component at Woodchuck Knoll was a thick midden, with many hearths, possible storage pits, and very poor definition of living surfaces. The site is a palimpsest of hundreds of years of seasonal occupation. It is unlikely that any single occupation ever completely covered the knoll. The season of occupation is well established; macrobotanical remains of wild grains, nuts, and lotus seeds strongly suggest occupation during the summer and fall. Although winter occupation cannot be ruled out, the annual flooding of the Connecticut makes the floodplain uninhabitable during early spring. Firewood came from trees characteristic of both the floodplain and the terrace edge. Finally, the carbonized exoskeletons of a granary beetle (*Sitophilus* sp.), an obligate pest of stored grain, in association with carbonized seeds of *Chenopodium* sp., allow the inference of wild grain storage (McBride 1978).

It is possible that the three large Tinkham Phase sites are contemporaneous (see Figure 3), but we cannot rule out a sequence of alternation of occupations among them. Indeed, given the frequent movements of the river's channel, there may well have been other floodplain knolls that were used during Tinkham times but that have now been eroded away. Small- and medium-size sites of the terraces may include occupations during other seasons. In fact, none of the terrace sites can be confidently assigned a season of occupation, for three reasons: First, none has been extensively excavated; second, the acidic soils in our region mitigate against good preservation of bone; and third, there are no botanical indicators of activity from November through May. All of the terrace components seem to be quite thin deposits, suggesting much lower spatial congruence than on the floodplain. There is no way of knowing just how many such sites would have been simultaneously occupied. Finally, there are the many small upland sites. On the basis of size alone, these must have been occupied by small groups. At present we guess that some may have been seasonal camps, and others may have been locations or logistical field camps (*sensu* Binford 1982; see McBride 1984 for data from another nearby region). We do not know the annual range (Binford 1982) of the occupants of the knoll sites, and some winter–spring occupation may have been outside of our survey region.

Salmon Cove Phase

Between the Tinkham and the Salmon Cove phases there is a remarkable change in remnant settlement patterns (compare Figures 3 and 4). The large

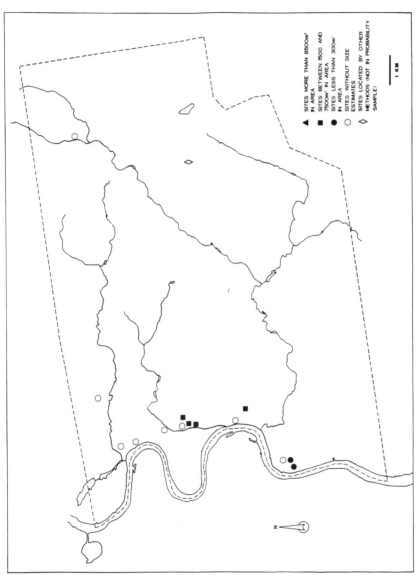

Figure 4. Salmon Cove Phase components.

"knoll" sites of the Tinkham have no analogues. During the Salmon Cove Phase, archaeological materials were deposited on the floodplain only sporadically, and these components are very small (<100 m²); the uplands, too, were occupied much less frequently than before, and settlements are now predominantly on the western edge of the terraces. None of the terrace zone sites has concentrated occupation sequences, and in fact the pattern was apparently a dispersed occupation sequence. One site has been excavated on a large scale: the Timothy Stevens site (Pagoulatos 1990), and at this site it was possible to identify the distribution of activity areas across the site. Such an analysis would be impossible on the Tinkham "knoll" site. Although the relative scarcity of floodplain "knolls" explains the Tinkham localized occupation sequences, there are many more alternative occupation sites on the terraces, which may have permitted more frequent site relocations. Because there are no obvious candidates for seasonal camps either on the floodplain or in the uplands, we infer that the Salmon Cove Phase components were occupied year-round, or else that the annual subsistence range included areas beyond our study region.

Salmon Cove lithic assemblages include much less quartz and more high-quality, nonlocal lithics (Calogero 1991). The use of fine-grained material is rare in Connecticut. In a preceramic context, it usually signals either a very early component or the Salmon Cove Phase. This affects archaeological visibility in two somewhat opposing ways: The absence of abundant quartz debris makes such components less visible to a survey crew, but the presence of fine-grained lithics often led to intensive testing to identify the components present. More important, there is surely a major impact of medium-term processes on these aggregated data: The localized, concentrated, and highly visible components of the Tinkham Phase are surely more completely represented than the dispersed, low continuity and less visible Salmon Cove Phase components. Even with compensations for sampling intensity and differential phase length, using data like these to monitor population density changes or to estimate the size of co-resident groups is unwarranted—though many archaeologists do so (cf. Mulholland 1988).

The Salmon Cove Phase is the local manifestation of the Terminal Archaic, with projectile points like those of the Susquehanna and Orient series of Pennsylvania and New York. The beginning of the Terminal Archaic in southern New England has sometimes been attributed to a migration (see, e.g., Bourque 1975; Cook 1976; Dincauze 1972, 1975; Pagoulatos 1986; Sanger 1975; Snow 1980; Turnbaugh 1975 for a range of views), and the distribution of Terminal Archaic sites has been described as strongly riverine, in regional perspective (Turnbaugh 1975). Recent work by Calogero (1991) has shown that there was a significant increase in the amount of lithics from distant sources deposited in Lower Connecticut River valleys occupations of this phase, and Parry (1989) suggests that northeastern Terminal Archaic tool assemblages have general characteristics that suggest a high degree of residential mobility. We note a curious feature of Salmon

Cove Phase settlement patterns: If the inference of "riverine" orientation were based upon the average distance of base camps to the river, then the Salmon Cove Phase would be judged less riverine than the Tinkham Phase.

We do not believe, however, that the Salmon Cove Phase base camps were moved to the terraces to be closer to terrace zone resources. Instead, the shift may have occurred because the economy of the Salmon Cove Phase was *more* dependent upon the river than that of the Tinkham Phase, at least to the extent that occupation near the river was desirable for a longer period of time. The floodplain and its knolls cannot be occupied for the later winter and much of the spring, because of the annual flooding. Modern shad runs begin about the time of the spring floods, and probably salmon ran at about the same time.[2] If Turnbaugh is right in arguing that Terminal Archaic economies relied upon fishing in deep rivers as opposed to along brooks and at falls, then the terraces would have been the closest habitable area during the runs themselves, and the shift from the floodplain to the terraces not explained with reference to the resources of the terrace zone at all!

Once the primary residential sites moved to the terraces, medium-term processes reshape completely the remnant settlement patterns. On the terraces, there are no microtopographic features that would have led to the spatial congruence characteristic of the knoll sites. As a consequence, Salmon Cove occupation sequences at any particular place were short, and the components relatively thin. In addition, the surface area of Salmon Cove components must more nearly match the surface area of residential use of a single occupation more closely than the area of the Tinkham knoll palimpsests does.

Broeder Point Phase

The Broeder Point remnant settlement pattern (Figure 4) is strikingly different from that of the Salmon Cove Phase—the floodplain and the uplands are once again important areas of occupation, and once again there are large sites on the floodplain and western terrace edge. At the Long Knoll Site, a very large Tinkham Phase component underlay a shallow and very much smaller Salmon Cove Phase component, which itself underlay a Broeder Point occupation of more than 10,000 m[2]. The Broeder Point component has an assemblage of early Woodland ceramics and quartz-cobble lithics that are very difficult to discriminate from Tinkham Phase lithics. We believe the Broeder Point component was the result of a localized occupation sequence very similar to the Tinkham Phase occupation sequence at Long Knoll. There are many ways in which Broeder Point

---

[2] Carlson argues (1988) that salmon were less numerous in the Connecticut than some archaeologists have supposed. We are not wholly convinced by her argument, but there is no doubt that the shad runs remain economically important today and could have been equally important in the past.

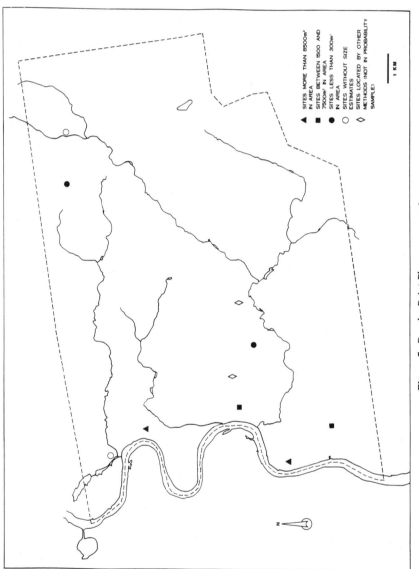

Figure 5. Broeder Point Phase components.

components and assemblages resemble the Tinkham Phase, and this might be the result of direct historical continuity; the Salmon Cove Phase in Glastonbury may be something of an interregnum. This sequence is similar to that reported for Martha's Vineyard (Ritchie 1969).

In terms of archaeological visibility, the Broeder Point Phase is probably similar to the Tinkham Phase. The lithic assemblages are once again largely the product of the expedient manufacture of quartz implements. There are as yet no known differences in the subsistence patterns of these two phases, at least in the Connecticut Valley. The overall similarity of the Broeder Point and Tinkham Phase remnant settlement patterns suggest that they were alike both in terms of patterns of occupation sequences and probably also in annual round. In only one respect do the remnant settlement patterns of these two phases differ, and that is that there are larger Broeder Point upland components than any known in the Tinkham sample. There are two potential explanations of this difference. It may be that there was a change in the size of co-resident groups exploiting the uplands. Alternatively, there may have been a change in the spatial congruence of the upland occupation sequences. At present, we cannot distinguish between these alternatives.

Comparing the Phases

If we are correct in arguing that the Tinkham and Broeder Point phases had similar seasonal rounds, and, at least near the river, similar occupation sequences, then one might argue that one can directly compare the remnant settlement patterns of these two phases. There is no obvious reason to believe that taphonomy, archaeological visibility, or preservation are different in these two cases. Thus, given the similar span of time attributed to each phase, the observed differences in the number and area of Tinkham and Broeder Point components may well be ascribed to differences in population levels. Looking at the floodplain and terrace zones, one might conclude that population levels during the Tinkham Phase were two to three times the size of those during the Broeder Point Phase; such a pattern has been proposed elsewhere in the New England for this period (Dincauze 1974). However, even such a crude guess is subject to the caveat that there were differences in the use of the uplands in these two periods, with unknown effects on the occupation sequences in the floodplain and terrace zones. How one might compare population densities during either the Tinkham or Broeder Point phases to those of the Salmon Cove Phase is another matter altogether.

At present, there is no known difference in the subsistence base of these three phases. All were hunter–gatherers relying upon the same list of known resources. Yet their archaeological records are very different. The distribution of

Tinkham Phase components *looks* like a "central-based wandering" settlement pattern; the Salmon Cove Phase does not. Yet the differences in the component distributions of these phases may be more due to medium-term processes than to differences in annual round. Botanic and faunal analyses have shown that the Tinkham floodplain knoll sites were occupied for the same span as the Salmon Cove terrace sites. There is no known difference in co-resident group size. What is different is the sequence of occupation, with the knolls returned to year after year, and with a dispersed sequence in the Salmon Cove Phase.

CONCLUSIONS

We feel it is clear that the analysis of prehistoric settlement patterns can no longer be construed as merely the analysis of "dots on a map" by direct analogy to ethnographic descriptions of the "dynamic of yearly round." The archaeological record is the product of processes that have their impact over time spans greater than a single year, and this fact can no longer be ignored. We have tried to show that comparisons of remnant settlement patterns of differing ages can be greatly complicated by differences in the medium-term processes that conditioned their respective patterns of occupation sequences.

Examining the remnant settlement patterns of three phases in Glastonbury has shown how differences in annual round, patterns of occupation sequences, and differential site preservation in contrasting environmental zones all combine to produce the remnant settlement patterns that resulted from the archaeological survey. Of these three factors, only differences in annual round, and, to a lesser extent, differences in site formation and preservation, have played a role in most analyses of settlement patterns. We have tried to show, however, that the great contrasts in the distribution of components in these phases is probably not due to these two factors. Rather we drew attention to the changes in the nature of the spatial and temporal qualities of occupation sequences. Differences in occupation sequence are determined by medium-term processes. They directly affect the present-day distribution of archaeological sites of differing ages. Even when subsistence regimes are very similar, differences in sequences of occupation have yielded radically different patterns of site distributions. Remnant settlement pattern analysis offers a start toward the development of more productive approaches to the analysis of the "distribution of sites across a landscape."

ACKNOWLEDGMENTS

The data discussed here were collected as a result of a survey of Glastonbury by the Public Archaeology Survey Team, Inc., with the assistance of a Survey and Planning Grant administered by the Connecticut Historical Commission. We would like to thank D. F. Jordan, R. Potts, A. F. Richard, M. Soulsby, R. Whallon, and J. Rossignol for constructive criticism of earlier drafts. The data for this chapter could not have been collected without the assistance of Bill Wadleigh, and we would like to dedicate this work to the memory of him.

REFERENCES

Ascher, R. A., 1968, Time's Arrow and the Archaeology of a Contemporary Community, in: *Settlement Archaeology* (K. C. Chang, ed.), National Press, Palo Alto, pp. 43–52.

Beardsley, R. K., Holder, P., Krieger, A. D., Meggers, B. J., Rinaldo, J. B., and Kutsche, P., 1956, Functional and Evolutionary Implications of Community Patterning, in: *Seminars in Archaeology: 1955* (R. Wauchope, ed.), Memoir of the Society for American Archaeology, No. 11, pp. 129–155.

Bendremer, J. A., and Dewar, R. E., 1992, The Advent of Prehistoric Maize in New England, in: *Corn and Culture in the Prehistoric New World* (S. Johannessen and C. Hastorf, eds.), Westview Press, Boulder.

Binford, L. R., 1978, *Nunamiut Ethnoarchaeology*, Academic Press, New York.

Binford, L. R., 1979, Organization and Formation Processes: Looking at Curated Technologies, *Journal of Anthropological Research* 35:255–273.

Binford, L. R., 1980, Willow Smoke and Dog's Tails: Hunter-Gatherer Settlement Systems and Archaeological Site Formation, *American Antiquity* 45:1–17.

Binford, L. R., 1982, The Archaeology of Place, *Journal of Anthropological Archaeology* 1:1–31.

Binford, L. R., 1983, Long Term Land Use Patterns: Some Implications for Archaeology, in: *Lulu Linear Punctated: Essays in Honor of George Irving Quimby* (R. C. Dunnell and D. K. Grayson, eds.), Anthropological Papers of the Museum of Anthropology, University of Michigan, no. 72, pp. 27–53.

Bourque, B. J., 1975, Comments on the Late Archaic Populations of Central Maine: The View from the Turner Farm, *Arctic Anthropology* 12(2):35–45.

Brasser, T. J., 1978, Mahican, in: *Handbook of North American Indians, Volume 15, Northeast* (B. G. Trigger, ed.), Smithsonian Institution, Washington, pp. 198–212.

Calogero, B. C., 1991, *Macroscopic and Petrographic Identification of the Rock Types Used for Stone Tools in Central Connecticut*, Ph.D. dissertation, University of Connecticut, Storrs.

Camilli, E., 1988, Interpreting Long-term Land-use Patterns from Archaeological Landscapes, *American Archaeology* 7:57–66.

Carlson, C. C., 1988, "Where's the Salmon?": Reevaluation of the Role of Anadromous Fisheries in Aboriginal New England, in: *Holocene Human Ecology in Northeastern North America* (G. P. Nicholas, ed.), Plenum Press, New York, pp. 47–76.

Chagnon, N. A., 1973, The Culture-ecology of Shifting (Pioneering) Cultivation Among the Yanomamö Indians, in: *Peoples and Cultures of Native South America* (D. R. Gross, ed.), Doubleday and Natural History Press, New York, pp. 126–144.

Chang, K. C., 1962, A Typology of Settlement and Community Patterns in some Circumpolar Societies, *Arctic Anthropology* 1(1):28–40.

Chang, K. C., 1967, Major Aspects of the Interrelationship of Archaeology and Ethnology, *Current Anthropology* 8:227–243.

Chang, K. C., 1972, *Settlement Patterns in Archaeology*, Addison-Wesley Module in Anthropology, 24, Addison-Wesley, Reading, Massachusetts.

Chartkoff, J. L., 1978, Transect Interval Sampling in Forests, *American Antiquity* 43:46–52.

Cook, T. G., 1976, Broadpoint: Culture, Phase, Horizon, Tradition or Knife?, *Journal of Anthropological Research* 32:337–357.

Dewar, R. E., 1986, Discovering Settlement Systems of the Past in New England, *Man in the Northeast* 31:77–88.

Dewar, R. E., 1992, Incorporating Variation in Occupation Span in Settlement-Pattern Analysis, *American Antiquity* 56(4):604–620.

Dincauze, D., 1972, The Atlantic Phase: A Late Archaic Phase in Massachusetts, *Man in the Northeast* 4:40–61.

Dincauze, D., 1974, An Introduction to the Archaeology of the Greater Boston Area, *Archaeology of Eastern North America* 1(1):39–66.

Dincauze, D., 1975, The Late Archaic Period in Southern New England, *Arctic Anthropology* 12(2):23–34.

Dincauze, D., 1981, Paleoenvironmental Reconstruction in the Northeast: The Art of Multidisciplinary Study, in: *Foundations of Northeastern Prehistory* (D. Snow, ed.), Academic Press, New York, pp. 51–96.

Dunnell, R. C., 1988, Low-density Archaeological Records from Plowed Surfaces: Some Preliminary Considerations, *American Archaeology* 7(1):29–38.

Dunnell, R. C., and Dancy, W. S., 1983, The Siteless Survey: A Regional Scale Data Collection Strategy, in: *Advances in Archaeological Method and Theory*, Volume 6 (M. B. Schiffer, ed.), Academic Press, New York, pp. 267–288.

Ebert, J. I., 1988, Modeling Human Systems and "Predicting" the Archaeological Record: The Unavoidable Relationship of Method and Theory, *American Archaeology* 7:3–8.

Flannery, Kent V., 1968, Archaeological Systems Theory and Early Mesoamerica, in: *Anthropological Approaches in the Americas* (B. J. Meggers, ed.), Anthropological Society of Washington, Washington, DC, pp. 67–81.

Flannery, Kent V., 1972, The Origins of the Village as a Settlement Type in Mesoamerica and the Near East, in: *Man, Settlement and Urbanism* (P. J. Ucko, R. Tringham, and G. W. Dimblelby, eds.), Duckworth, London, pp. 25–53.

Foley, R. A., 1981, A Model of Regional Archaeological Structures, *Proceedings of the Prehistoric Society* 47:1–17.

Funk, R., and Rippeteau, B. E., 1977, *Adaptation, Continuity and Change in Upper Susquehanna Prehistory*, Man in the Northeast Occasional Papers in Northeastern Anthropology.

Gross, D. R., 1983, Village Movement in Relation to Resources in Amazonia, in: *Adaptive Responses of Native Amazonians* (R. B. Hames and W. T. Vickers, eds.), Academic Press, New York, pp. 432–449.

Groube, L. M., 1971, Tonga, Lapita Pottery, and Polynesian Origins, *Journal of the Polynesian Society* 80:278–316.

Hames, R. B., 1983, The Settlement Pattern of a Yąnomamö Population Bloc: A Behavioral Ecological Interpretation, in: *Adaptive Responses of Native Amazonians* (R. B. Hames and W. T. Vickers, eds.), Academic Press, New York, pp. 393–427.

Jochim, M. A., 1976, *Hunter-gatherer Subsistence and Settlement: A Predictive Model.* Academic Press, New York.

Johnson, A. W., 1974, "Carrying Capacity" in Machiguenga Ecology: Theory and Practice, Paper presented at the annual meetings of the American Anthropological Association, Mexico City.

Johnson, A. W., 1982, Reductionism in Cultural Ecology: The Amazon Case, *Current Anthropology* 23:413–428.

Linares, O. F., 1976, Garden Hunting in the American Tropics, *Human Ecology* 4:331–350.

McBride, K. A., 1978, Archaic Subsistence in the Lower Connecticut River Valley: An Example from Woodchuck Knoll, *Man in the Northeast* 15-16:124–132.

McBride, K. A., 1984, The Prehistory of the Lower Connecticut River Valley, Ph.D. dissertation, University of Connecticut.

McBride, K. A., and Dewar, R. E., 1987, Agriculture and Cultural Evolution: Causes and Effects in the

Lower Connecticut River Valley, in: *Emergent Horticultural Economies of the Eastern Woodlands* (W. A. Keegan, ed.), Center for Archaeological Investigations, Occasional Papers No. 7, Carbondale, pp. 305–328.

McBride, K. A., Wadleigh, W. M., Dewar, R. E., and Soulsby, M. G., 1980, *Prehistoric Settlements in Eastern Connecticut: The North-Central Lowlands and Northeastern Highlands Surveys: 1979*, Archaeological Research Monograph No. 15, Public Archaeology Survey Team, Storrs.

Mulholland, M. T., 1988, Territoriality and Horticulture: A Perspective for Prehistoric New England, in: *Holocene Human Ecology in Northeastern North America* (G. P. Nicholas, ed.), Plenum Press, New York, pp. 137–164.

Pagoulatos, P., 1986, *Terminal Archaic Settlement and Subsistence in the Connecticut River Valley*, Ph.D. dissertation, University of Connecticut.

Pagoulatos, P., 1990, Terminal Archaic "Living Areas" in the Connecticut River Valley, *Bulletin of the Archaeological Society of Connecticut* No. 53, pp. 59–72.

Parry, W. J., 1989, The Relationship between Lithic Technology and Changing Mobility Strategies in the Middle Atlantic Region, in: *New Approaches to Other Pasts* (W. F. Kinsey and R. W. Moeller, eds.), Archaeological Services, Bethlehem, CT, pp. 29–34.

Parsons, J. R., 1972, Archaeological Settlement Patterns, *Annual Reviews of Anthropology* 1:127–150.

Ritchie, W. A., 1969, *The Archaeology of Martha's Vineyard*, Natural History Press, Garden City.

Rouse, I., 1972, Settlement Patterns in Archaeology, in: *Man, Settlement and Urbanism* (P. J. Ucko, R. Tringham, and G. W. Dimblelby, eds.), Duckworth, London, pp. 95–107.

Salwen, B., 1978, Indians of Southern New England and Long Island: Early Period, in: *Handbook of North American Indians, Volume 15, Northeast* (B. G. Trigger, ed.), Smithsonian, Washington DC, pp. 160–176.

Sanger, D., 1975, Culture Change as an Adaptive Process in the Maine-Maritimes Region, *Arctic Anthropology* 12(2):60–78.

Schiffer, M. B., 1976, *Behavioral Archaeology*, Academic Press, New York.

Simmons, W. S., 1978, Narragansett, in: *Handbook of North American Indians, Volume 15, Northeast* (B. G. Trigger, ed.), Smithsonian, Washington, DC, pp. 190–197.

Snow, D. R., 1980, *The Archaeology of New England*, Academic Press, New York.

Struever. S., 1968, Woodland Subsistence-Settlement Systems in the Lower Illinois Valley, in: *New Perspectives in Archaeology* (L. R. Binford and S. R. Binford, eds.), Aldine, Chicago, pp. 285–312.

Thomas, D. H., 1975, Nonsite Sampling in Archaeology: Up the Creek Without a Site?, in: *Sampling in Archaeology* (J. W. Mueller, ed.), University of Arizona Press, Tucson, pp. 61–81.

Thomas, D. H., 1986, Contemporary Hunter-Gatherer Archaeology in America, in *American Archaeology: Past and Future* (D. J. Meltzer, D. D. Fowler, and J. A. Sabloff, eds.), Smithsonian Institution Press, Washington, pp. 237–276.

Trigger, B. G., 1968, The Determinants of Settlement Patterns, in: *Settlement Archaeology*, (K. C. Chang, ed.), National Press, Palo Alto, pp. 53–78.

Turnbaugh, W. A., 1975, Toward an Explanation of Broadpoint Dispersal in Eastern North American Prehistory, *Journal of Anthropological Research* 31:51–68.

Williams, R., 1936, *A Key into the Language of America* [1636], 5th ed., The Rhode Island and Providence Plantations Tercentenary Commission, Providence.

Wood, J. J., 1978, Optimal Location in Settlement Space: A Model for Describing Location Strategies, *American Antiquity* 43:258–270.

Yellen, J. R., 1976, Settlement Patterns of the !Kung: An Archaeological Perspective, in: *Kalahari Hunter-gatherers* (R. B. Lee and I. DeVore, eds.), Harvard University Press, Cambridge, pp. 47–72.

Yellen, J. R., 1977, *Archaeological Approaches to the Past*, Academic Press, New York.

Chapter 11

The Spatial Dimension of Time

LuAnn Wandsnider

[T]he [jacal habitation] framework is fairly permanent, usually surviving a number of occupancies extending over months or years, and outlasting an equal number of outer coveries; so that all habitable Seriland is dotted sparsely with jacal skeletons, sometimes retaining fragments of walls or roof, but oftener entirely denuded. (McGee 1898:222)

INTRODUCTION

Archaeological research commonly focuses on various temporal aspects of archaeological deposits, such as their age and the sequencing or the relative temporal order of one deposit to another. Another aspect is the concern for temporal scale and resolution, or the degree of contemporaneity shared by deposits, treated elsewhere in this volume by Jones and Beck and also by Zvelebil and colleagues.

Archaeology is also concerned with ethnographic time, that domain in which formation events occur. Here, ethnographic temporal aspects refer to the temporal characteristics of activities with respect to the piece of land on which those activities occur. Thus activities can be distinguished according to duration (Chatters 1987; O'Connell 1987; Yellen 1977), degree of planning (Kent 1991), and

LuANN WANDSNIDER • Department of Anthropology, University of Nebraska–Lincoln, Lincoln, Nebraska 68588-0368.

Space, Time, and Archaeological Landscapes, edited by Jacqueline Rossignol and LuAnn Wandsnider. Plenum Press, New York, 1992.

frequency and syncopation of occurrence, all with respect to a specific location. The last, frequency and syncopation in activities, are part of the larger notion of activity tempo. Binford (1980), Ferring (1986), and others have called attention to the tempo of deposit formation, as contributed by both natural and cultural events, as well as the relationship between deposition tempo and deposit grain.

This chapter focuses on a more general aspect of ethnographic time, the *tempo of locale use,* or the frequency and syncopation with which a specific area (i.e., locale) is occupied. It attempts to relate the differential development of archaeological landscapes to locale use tempo. It suggests that it may be possible to "read" land use tempo through inspection of the spatial distribution and state of contemporaneous archaeological elements within a region. This proposed spatial dimension of time is explored using computer simulation of a general model describing the development of an archaeological landscape. By way of introducing this model, the necessity of archaeologically "reading" tempo is touched upon briefly first.

ECONOMY AND TEMPO OF LOCALE USE

Economy can be described as a configuration of technology and people on the land surface and through time. Thus it is useful to distinguish between a hunting economy based on the spear versus one employing the bow and arrow or the rifle. It is equally useful to distinguish between bow-and-arrow hunters that hunt only one location during one season versus those in which a single location is hunted year round. Finally, distinguishing between economies in which a single location is hunted sporadically throughout the year versus one in which a single location is repeatedly hunted throughout the year is also useful. When one component of the economy changes, there is, of course, a reorganization in the role played by all the other components. For example, Pelto and Müller-Wille (1987) document the reorganization of social, leisure, and production activities in various arctic groups upon the introduction of the snowmobile.

Locale use tempo, then, informs on the role of that locale, and cultural or natural features there, in the settlement–subsistence system. By amassing data points on tactical locale use for multiple locations in disparate contexts, w approach a fuller understanding of land use strategies. In conjunction with independent, particular data, such as how plants or animals were processed at specific locations and times within the locale, determinations of tempo and tactical land use decisions contribute to the emerging picture of the overall organization of the settlement–subsistence system. In turn, it is this system upon which ecological–evolutionary selection acts (Binford 1981; see also Rossignol this volume). To identify and gauge the effects of selective forces, it is necessary to understand the system that modulates such forces. Understanding land use tempo over the medium and long term, then, takes us one step further in the analytic process of reconstructing past systems (Binford 1982, 1983).

Thus it is critical that we attempt to assess the tempo of land use. High-resolution chronometric determinations, for example, dendrochronology, offers one means for reading land use tempo. Indeed, Wills and Windes (1989) employ a sequence of tree-ring dates to partially support their reinterpretation of Shabik'eschee Village as representing periodic rather than two distinct occupations of a Chaco Canyon rim location. It is likely, however, that even dendrochronology, the dating method that affords the highest potential resolution, may be too coarse to monitor land use tempos of interest. Also, tree-ring series that would enable the chronometric determination of locale use tempo have not been developed for all regions of the world.

Gilman's (1987) cross-cultural study of pit structure construction and use suggests that more indirect methods for reading tempo may be developed. She observes that pit structures were a common mode of habitation in circumstances with biseasonal mobility. Biseasonal mobility tethered to pit structures indicates one kind of land use tempo, with repeated, planned use of at least one location on a seasonal basis. Can we also detect repeated but unplanned use of an area or use that is sporadic but planned? Can we understand the tempo of use and in so doing be better able to distinguish one economic organization from another?

Redding (1988:85) suggests that determinations of exactly this sort are necessary in order to archaeologically track subsistence change. He proposes that tactical changes in subsistence activities, that is, changes in the spatial and temporal dimensions of those activities, may herald a subsistence shift. Unfortunately, it is exactly this sort of change for which there are few archaeological indicators.

In the following, I propose to monitor land use tempo though a consideration of the spatial structure of archaeological deposits that show facility refurbishment, deliberate destruction, and apparent decay. Importantly, this proposition offers further insight into the variability in archaeological landscapes documented in this volume and elsewhere.

SYSTEMIC LOCALE USE TEMPO AND ARCHAEOLOGICAL SPATIAL STRUCTURE

In a 1986 article, Robert Dewar introduced the concepts of spatial congruency and temporal continuity to describe the settlement history of a location (see also Brooks and Yellen 1987 and Camilli 1983:74–132). *Spatial congruency* refers to the spatial displacement observed between occupation events with high spatial congruency equivalent to reoccupation with direct superimposition. *Temporal continuity* refers to the degree to which the same location is used through time and incorporates notions of occupation frequency and duration; high temporal continuity means that a location is occupied frequently with each occupation event a lengthy one.

Here, I wish to recast these concepts in terms of tempo of locale use and spatial structure of material remains resulting from occupation events. More critically, I propose to couple them and aim to demonstrate that certain tempos of place use and reoccupation will necessarily result in distinctive spatial distributions. When archaeologically documented, this spatial structure, in turn, may inform on the tempo with which an area has been occupied in the past.

Although the literature on this subject is not overly developed, it is important to be clear about several terms. Brooks and Yellen (1987:69) distinguish between *reuse*, redundant place use that is spatially congruent with previously established facilities, and *reoccupation*, repeated place use without spatial congruency. Camilli (1983:71–134) terms the same phenomena *reoccupation* and *multiple occupation*, respectively. Here, the terms *reuse* and *reoccupation* are used interchangeably to refer to repeated use of a locale; individual events may or may not be spatially congruent with previous occupations.

Model of Locale Reoccupation

The claimed relationship between land use tempo, on the one hand, and spatial structure, on the other, can be described in terms of ethnographic "rules" for reoccupation. Vierra (1985) has distinguished between reoccupation for residential and special purposes. I propose a more functionally general model of reoccupation here but contrast those occupation histories accumulating in constrained (e.g., caves) versus unconstrained (most other places) spaces (see also Wills and Windes 1989:355).

Six different measures of time are important to this discussion of locale occupation history. The first two, reoccupation interval (RI) and reoccupation interval variation (RIV), describe the tempo of land use occupation and reoccupation. Their utility is illustrated in the computer simulation that we discuss later.

The remaining four, facility use-life, site use-life, site regeneration time, and facility decay interval, relate to characteristics of the location being occupied. Facility use-life (FUL) refers to the amount of time a facility or structure endures and is useful in the capacity for which it is designed. Actual FUL is a function of many things such as functional design criteria (Hunter-Anderson 1977), perceived maintenance versus construction costs (McGuire and Schiffer 1983), and expected total use-life (Kent 1991; Hitchcock 1987), encompassing all anticipated future uses. In some cases, meeting the functional needs of any one occupation event will result in a facility that endures beyond the total anticipated use-life of the facility.

Site use-life (SUL) refers to length of time a location may be used before becoming polluted or vermin-ridden, or, before the immediate environment becomes depleted of critical bulky resources. Expected site use-life, of course, determines hygienic practices (cf. Silberbauer 1972:303). Similarly, the nature of the economic organization, dictating and being reflected by the role of individual locations over the short and long term, stipulates site use-life.

Site regeneration interval (SRI) is the time it takes for the pollution problem to abate or for critical bulky resources to rebound. In Brooks Range in Alaska, for example, Binford's (1978:425) informants reported that willow stands, used as fuel by the Nunamiut and exhausted after 2 years of wintertime residency, required 45 years to regenerate.

Finally, the facility decay interval (FDI) is the amount of time after which no trace of the facility remains visible. For wooden structures in biotically active environments, this interval may be very small; masonry structures in an arid environment may have a decay time measured in centuries. The FDI may also be accelerated by humans scavenging materials for other uses (e.g., Lange and Rydberg 1972; see Wandsnider 1989:123–130). Also, facilities may be deliberately destroyed and the site abandoned upon the death of site occupant as related by numerous ethnographic accounts of hunter–gatherers.

Table 1 presents values for these measures for two groups, the western Kalahari !Kung and Amboseli Maasai pastoralists. The !Kung have been intensively studied over the past several decades with the consequence that there exists good information on many of these values. For example, the 1960s wet season camps documented by Yellen (1977) were usually occupied for very brief time periods (i.e., days) and one-quarter of the 16 locations mapped by Yellen were reoccupied. The reoccupation events occurred within the 1-year (Yellen 1977:67) use-life of the huts, and at least some of these huts were reused; others (built by individuals not part of the reoccupying group) were disassembled and used to build huts for new occupants. The tempo of the use of specific wet season

Table 1. Values for Facility and Site Time Measures

Camp	FUL	FDI	SUL	SRI
!Kung (1960s)[a]	Year	Year	Days/weeks	Seasonal recovery
Wet				
Dry	Year	Year	6 months	3–5 years
Maasai pastoralists (1970s)[b]				
"Swamp-far"	Unknown	Unknown	3.7 years	20–25 years
"Near-swamp"	Unknown	Unknown	10 years	20–25 years

[a] Sources: Brooks and Yellen 1987; Patricia Draper, personal communication 1990; Yellen 1977, 1986.
[b] Source: Western and Dunne 1979.

campsites over the very short term (i.e., months) is deliberate. Over the medium and long terms, however, it is seasonal, brief, and generally fortuitous (Brooks and Yellen 1987:87).

The dry season camp at Dobe also is occupied and reoccupied with deliberation, at least over the short term (Brooks and Yellen 1987:87). Occupation durations of between 1 and 22 months (9.89 ± 7.37 months) are reported by Yellen (1986:738), with occupants coming and going throughout the span of the site life. A dry season camp is abandoned "only if a death occurs there or it becomes extremely rank and bug ridden" (Yellen 1977:78). Given that Dobe is a reliable source of water even during the dry season and has been so for many centuries, reuse of a previously camp site is likely over the long term. In the medium term, that is, within the life span of occupants, it seems to have been very rare, as discussed later.

Western and Dunne offer little information on facility use-life or decay interval, noting only that huts and fences attained a poor state of repair after a long (length unspecified) time without occupants (1979:95). Such locations would be forsaken for others to avoid the 4-week labor cost necessary to making the corrals and huts serviceable. They provide relatively more information on site use-life. They note that after a period of 7 to 8 years, a settlement location would become saturated with the urine of the Maasai cattle, at which point drainage at the site was impaired, and the location became undesirable. In the short term, locations were left when the vegetation was depleted or when disease losses mounted (1979:95). Western and Dunne also note that the Maasai they studied would move six to eight times per year among settlements, with settlements in "swamp-far" areas with unpredictable resources being visited a minimum of six times over an average of 3.7 years. Settlements in "near-swamp" areas with forage that is highly predictable but of low quality were being used two to three times per year for up to a decade.

Taken together, these measures reflect the tempo of use received by a location, which in turn informs on the organization of the settlement–subsistence system in that particular environment. In the same environment, a different settlement–subsistence configuration would result in places playing different roles and hence, different values for these temporal measures would be evident. If we had such values for every part of the used landscape, then we would have a very effective currency with which to compare and contrast the configurations of land use systems through time. Indeed, efforts to characterize the archaeological landscape in terms of number of residential-camp versus special-purpose sites (e.g., Upham 1984) are attempting exactly this.

This effort does not attempt to identify archaeological indicators that inform on each of the four individual temporal measures. I also will not address the probability that the archaeological record does not always instruct on which cultural system is making use of a locale, although it perhaps can tell us "one only" or "more than one" system. Instead, I will consider the archaeological consequences of place use tempo with respect to these different measures.

Rules for reoccupation are derived from the ethnographic accounts and are presented in here terms of computer language-like if–then statements. For place use in a situation where space is not constrained, they are:

1. *If the facilities are in good repair and the site is not polluted and resources are not depleted, then reuse both the facilities and the site.* Reoccupation in this case acknowledges the serviceable state of the facilities and site by reusing or refurbishing previously constructed facilities. Examples of this type include the reoccupation of !Kung Camp 1 one month after its abandonment (Yellen 1977); the huts and hearths previously constructed were employed upon reoccupation. Yellen also recorded several other camps (3, 4, and 7) that were reoccupied in which some facilities were reused and others were dissembled and used in building new huts to accommodate newcomers.

2a. *If facilities are in good repair, but site-life has been exceeded, then avoid the site, possibly moving the facilities to a new site location.* Reoccupation acknowledges the previous occupation by avoiding the site or reusing it for very brief visits. Binford's (1978:170) description of reuse of a Nunamiut residential camp, where firewood has been depleted through intensive wintertime occupation, by a small hunting party for a very short span is an example of the second case. Examples of the first case are rare, although accounts of locations being abandoned because site use-life has been approached are common. For example, Denham (1972) describes an Alyawara community shifting between boreholes about every 2 years, as firewood becomes more costly to transport.

2b. *If facilities are in poor repair, but the site is habitable, then conditionally scavenge materials from decaying facilities and move to new position on site.* Reoccupation acknowledges the previous occupation by avoiding specific facility locations at a site. For example, Gould (1980:10) describes Ngatatjara aboriginals, upon arriving at a previously visited water source, scavenging firewood from a decaying sunshade located 30 m from the water source and about 190 m from the new facility location. This same situation may also apply to the continuous use of a site by a group, in which the site use-life is not exceeded but facility life is exhausted. O'Connell (1987:87–88) reports 21 Alyawara households building 105 shelters at 104 locations over an 11-month span, with structures being repositioned because of death, accommodation of visitors, shelter deterioration, domestic strife, and other factors.

2c. *If facilities are in poor repair and site-life has been exceeded, then avoid the location, possibly scavenging material for use elsewhere.* Reoccupation acknowledges previous occupational remains by avoiding both facility and site, and, conditionally scavenging from facilities. Again, few accounts of this aspect of reoccupation have been explicitly documented because ethnographers typically document where a group resides, rather than where it chooses not to reside.

3. *If facilities have decayed and the site is in good repair, then the previous site of a facility or encampment is available for occupation.* Reoccupation does not acknowledge invisible (e.g., subsurface) remains from previous occupations either by avoidance or by deliberate selection. The cultural landscape, however, is populated with locations to which cultural memories are attached, and this knowledge may attract or repel subsequent occupation. For example, Patricia Draper (personal communication 1990) reports that the locations at which !Kung individuals had been buried may be avoided for several months after the death, but this avoidance does not persist beyond that time. The 4-km² area around the Dobe waterhole in the western Kalahari Desert has been a preferred dry camp location for centuries. Within this area, Brooks and Yellen (1987:88) note the reuse of only two locations during the 40-year observation period. In one case, 15 years had transpired between occupation events, during which time the bush had recovered and all obtrusive evidence of the previous occupation had disappeared.

These reoccupation generalizations assume a different form in the situation of socially or physically constrained space. At locations that are preferred but have constrained space, facility maintenance and refurbishing is frequently reported. For example, Solecki (1979:327) describes the repair and reconstruction of huts and corrals by the 1950s Kurdish occupants of Shanidar Cave. A Nunamiut sheep-observation stand reported by Binford (1978:408) is an example of a very specialized, open-air, location that has been used and maintained for generations. The scars of repeated place use by Maasai, whose cattle have settlement requirements met by only a few locations on the landscape (Western and Dunne 1979:95), is evidence of this kind of repeated use history.

When decayed and decaying remains are found at these constrained spaces, the facilities may be destroyed and removed or disassembled and reused. For example, upon reoccupying a cave that has seen previous use, the Alyawara have been observed to burn the extant rubbish, spreading the ash on the surface to create a "clean" surface (Binford, personal communication, cited in Vierra 1985:70). For a Mackenzie Basin Dene group residentially confined to a small spit, houses of frequently disassembled and reassembled nearby, and the residential trash amassed and burned (Janes 1983:29–34).

Although these reoccupation generalizations have been phrased in terms of rules, the basis for why they hold is both axiomatic and theoretically based. To date, humans and their devices are confined to the three dimensions of space and the fourth dimension of time. It is impossible for two solids to exist in the exact same place during the exact same time. Therefore, to occupy a location at which a facility is found entails that either the existing facility be occupied as is, be refurbished, or be destroyed and rebuilt. A final alternative is to avoid the location and build a facility elsewhere. The tactical decision about which of these options to implement seems to be based on cost–benefit determinations. The first option appears to be taken when the facilities are still in "good" repair (no cost); the second, when only minor repair is required (small cost); the third when the location (e.g., a cave) offers special characteristics (absorption of large costs warranted by other benefits); and, the fourth when refurbishment is deemed too costly (see Yellen 1976:58–59). Support for these statements comes from interviews with anthropologists (Patricia Draper, personal communication 1990; Henry Harpending, personal communication 1990) and ethnoarchaeologists (Lewis Binford, personal communication 1990; Robert Hitchcock, personal communication 1990; John Yellen, personal communication 1990) on the abandonment and reoccupation of facilities and sites by groups whom they have studied for other purposes. In fact, little directed research on this topic has occurred and would greatly benefit the understanding of why these generalizations appear to hold.

Recurrent locale use over the short term results in a cultural landscape that is variably rich in abandoned and decaying facilities. McGee's (1898) description of the Seri Indian cultural landscape, with which this chapter opens, nicely illustrates this aspect of the prehistoric landscape. John Wesley Powell's oft-cited report of a Ute camp (see Fowler and Fowler 1971:53), with an extensive distribution of abandoned structures giving an impression of a camp a magnitude larger than it actually was, is another provocative example (see also Woodburn 1972:194). Conversely, Cipriani writes for the Onges on Little Andaman island that "since the same small, well-chosen site may be used for thousands of years, the hut ends up perching on top of a small mound of refuse dating back to ancient times" (1966:54).

The archaeological consequences of these reoccupation rules holding over the long term, developed in the following section, are several and impact both number and distribution of facilities as well as the degree to which they have been refurbished or maintained.

LOCALE REOCCUPATION SIMULATION AND RESULTS

The long-term effects of locale occupation and reoccupation in unconstrained space according to the preceding model are illustrated here through computer simulation.[1] In this exercise, the focus is on facility use-life (FUL) and facility decay interval (FDI), and the interplay of these two with the reoccupation

---

[1] The simulation was written in Borland Turbo Pascal version 5.0 and is available upon request from the author.

interval (RI) and reoccupation interval variation (RIV). Occupation of a near-water locale over a series of 100 occupation events was simulated, with the settlement pattern described by Tindale (1972:244) for the Pitjandjara in the vicinity of ephemeral water serving as a model. The near-water locale, measuring 1,000m × 1,000m, was considered a plain, homogenous in all regards except that of previous or extant occupation debris. With every occupation of the near-water locale, a decision about which of the countless locations to occupy was made based on the state and locations of previously used facilities, but, occupation was elastically constrained to occur within 200 m of the water source.

If reoccupation occurred within the life span of an extant facility, it was reoccupied. If the use-life of a facility had been exceeded, but the facility persisted in a deteriorating state, occupation was constrained to any area 75 m to 200 m away that still fell within the vicinity of the water source. This 75 to 200-m "shifting" distance is commonly mentioned in hunter–gatherer ethnographic accounts (e.g., Woodburn [1972:194] for the Hazda; Yellen [1977:78] for the !Kung); Western and Dunne (1979:95) note for the Maasai pastoralists they studied a shifting distance of several hundred meters. This shifting distance seems to be a compromise between remaining near the desired location, such as a water source, but "far enough" from the abandoned facilities. It is unclear if matters of hygiene or relative abundance of other critical resources such as firewood are responsible for how far is "far enough." If preexisting facilities had decayed to a point where their presence was no longer detectable, then occupation location was randomly determined. Reoccupation occurred according to a specified time interval that was allowed to stochastically vary within predefined limits.

In this simulation, time is measured in relative units. As will be shown later, it is not so much the absolute value of the time units that impacts the character of the distribution of occupation remains, but the values of the facility use-life, decay interval, and reoccupation intervals relative to each other. I nevertheless found it helpful to think of these time intervals in terms of months.

With every occupation, it was assumed that obtrusive, but perishable materials were deposited as well as unobtrusive, but relatively eternal materials. That is, with every occupation event, perishable structures would be constructed at the same time that artifacts were deposited and hearths excavated and used. Upon abandonment, hearth features and durable artifacts would persist even after facilities like sun and wind shelters had decayed or been scavenged. The archaeological landscape of the American West, for example, is resplendent with such enduring features and artifacts, reflecting occupations of varying durations and tempo.

On completion of the simulated occupation history, what does the distribution of these persistent (but unobtrusive) materials look like? Figure 1 through 4 present examples of the completed simulations for four different situations. In the first (Figure 1), reoccupation always occurs at an interval inside that of the use-life

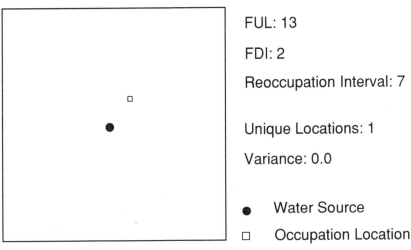

FUL: 13

FDI: 2

Reoccupation Interval: 7

Unique Locations: 1

Variance: 0.0

● Water Source

□ Occupation Location

Figure 1. Simulated locale reoccupation with deliberate superimposition.

of the facility, which is continuously refurbished. Only one unique location was occupied (and presumably well maintained) and is "archaeologically" recognized.

In the second situation (Figure 2), reoccupation usually occurs after the use-life of the facility is exhausted and the facility has decayed. Of the 100 occupation events, 100 randomly determined (albeit constrained by the magnetic water source) locations were occupied. The variance of their distribution, determined with respect to the mean values for northing and easting, is 5,360.6.[2]

The third situation (Figures 3 and 4) considers reoccupation that occurs at an interval greater than the use-life of the facilities but less than the facility decay interval. In the case of Figure 3, the decay interval is almost twice that of the reoccupation interval. According to the reoccupation model, persistent deteriorating facilities preclude some locations from occupation, resulting in a more regular distribution of occupation locations. Again, 100 locations were occupied, and these are spatially distributed such that they have a variance of 12,717.4. Of note is that this variance is larger than that for the randomly determined occupation history depicted in Figure 2.

An even larger disparity between the reoccupation ($RI = 5$) and decay

---

[2]Variance was calculated as

$$var = \frac{\sum ((x - \bar{x})^2 + (y - \bar{y})^2)}{2N}$$

with x and y being the easting and northing coordinates and N the number of unique occupation locations.

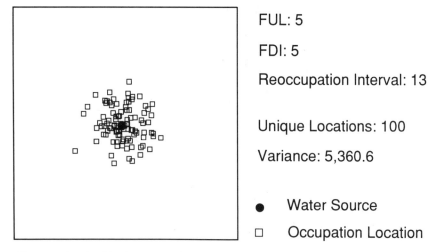

FUL: 5

FDI: 5

Reoccupation Interval: 13

Unique Locations: 100

Variance: 5,360.6

● Water Source

☐ Occupation Location

Figure 2. Simulated locale reoccupation with no deliberate superimposition and no avoidance.

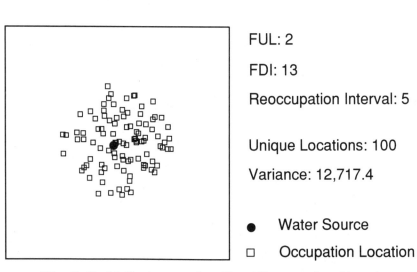

FUL: 2

FDI: 13

Reoccupation Interval: 5

Unique Locations: 100

Variance: 12,717.4

● Water Source

☐ Occupation Location

Figure 3. Simulated locale reoccupation with no deliberate superimposition and some avoidance (FDI is almost three times greater than RI).

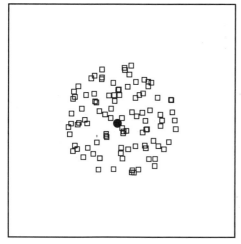

FUL: 2

FDI: 100

Reoccupation Interval: 5

Unique Locations: 100

Variance: 16,096.5

● Water Source

☐ Occupation Location

Figure 4. Simulated locale reoccupation with no deliberate superimposition and with avoidance (FDI is 20 times greater than RI).

(*FDI* = 100) intervals was also simulated, the results of which are presented in Figure 4. Here, the number of unique locations is again 100; their spatial distribution is even more regular, as reflected by the still larger variance (16,096.5).

This preliminary analysis suggests, then, that number of occupation locations and their distribution, whether random or regular, reflects occupation tempo, at least with respect to *FUL* and *FDI*. This relationship is further explored through more extensive simulation. A simulation was run for all combinations of the values of 1, 3, 7, 13, and 27 for each of the parameters of *FUL, FDI,* and *RI*. *RI* was allowed to stochastically vary as well through incorporation of a normal random variate that assumed the same (1, 3, 7, etc.) values. For each of the 625 different configurations of parameter values, 25 trials were run. Mean, minimum, and maximum variances and mean number of occupation locations were recorded for each set of 25 trials.

Figure 5 presents the results of these multiple trials as described by mean number of unique occupation locations and the mean variance of their spatial distribution for only those trials in with a minimal amount (*RIV* = 1) of stochastic variation in reoccupation. Minimum and maximum variance is not treated here because it mirrors the results reported for the mean variance in spatial distribution. In this graph, six clusters of remnant settlement patterns, corresponding to six relationships between *FUL, FDI,* and *RI,* are found.

1. *FUL > RI > FDI:* In the case where reoccupation primarily occurs within the life span of the facility, one or at most two well-maintained occupation locations results. With this total superimposition of occupation events, a variance

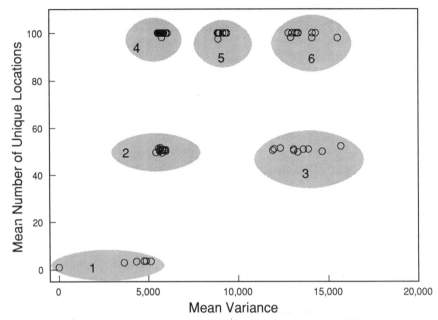

Figure 5. Summary of 125 sets of simulated locale reoccupation (RIV = 1;
see text for interpretation of numbered clusters).

of zero is seen. The five settlement patterns with occupation location variance of
around 5,000 are those in which stochastic variation resulted in reoccupation
outside the use-life of the facility. In these few cases, an additional facility was
constructed at another locale location. The small facility decay interval means that
few facilities persist through time to determine subsequent occupations in the
area. Thus the magnetic quality of the water source is the sole determinant of
occupation. In this simulation, variance values of between 5,000 and 6,000 are
expected with randomly determined locale reoccupation, that is, local reoccupation without superimposition and without avoidance.

  2. *(FUL = RI) > FDI:* In this case, the reoccupation interval is equal to the
facility use-life and, as the actual variation in reoccupation is randomly distributed, half of the time results in reoccupation within the *FUL* and the other half
of the time results in reoccupation just outside the use-life of the facility. For this
reason, half of the occupations result in reuse of extant facilities, and the other
half entail new facilities being built at nearby locations. Thus an average of about
50 occupation locations (out of 100 occupation events) is seen. For this cluster,
facility decay interval is small so that previously occupied locations exert little
influence over which locations are occupied. That is, like the first situation,

reoccupation is a randomly determined, and variance is therefore between 5,000 and 6,000.

3. *FDI > (FUL = RI):* This situation is similar to situation 2 in that reoccupation occurs sometimes within facility use-life and other times outside of it. It differs in that abandoned facilities persist through time and thus influence which locations are available for reoccupation. For this reason, the variance recorded for the easting and northing coordinates of the occupied locations increases to above 12,000. As mentioned for Figures 3 and 4, the degree of regularity (as measured by variance) increases as facilities persist for longer time periods, relative to the reoccupation interval.

4. *RI > FDI > FUL:* In this situation, reoccupation occurs after reparable facility use-life is exhausted. Therefore, reoccupation mostly results in the construction of new facilities, and we see a unique occupation location for almost every of the 100 occupation events. These locations are essentially randomly determined, however, because facilities do not persist to influence subsequent occupations.

5. *(FDI = RI) > FUL:* This situation is similar to situation 4 except that specified reoccupation interval is equal to the facility decay interval. As actual reoccupation interval is modulated by stochastic variation that is normally distributed, half the time this results in reoccupation with standing facilities preventing reoccupation of certain locations and half the time, no facilities persist to deflect reoccupation of a specific location. Thus an intermediate variance of about 8,000 is seen.

6. *FDI > RI > FUL:* Finally, this last situation is likewise similar to situations 4 and 5 in that facility use-life is very small compared with reoccupation interval. Because the facility decay interval is relatively large, however, facilities persist to deflect any potential reoccupation of the same location. Thus a more regular (variance > 12,000) distribution of occupied locations is seen.

In sum, the number of occupied locations reflects the relationship between facility use-life and reoccupation interval. When reoccupation occurs within the use-life of extant facilities, then a single location may continue to be occupied. When reoccupation occurs at an interval greater than the facility use-life (no matter the length of the facility use-life), then new locations will be selected, resulting in higher numbers of locations bearing evidence of occupation.

Concomitantly, high variance in the distribution of occupied locations is seen when facility decay interval, the time it takes for a facility to decay, is also high. The longer the decay interval *relative to the interval at which a locale is revisited,* the greater the observed variance. Variances of about 5,000 reflect randomly determined occupation locations. Intermediate values reflect reoccupation that is sometimes determined by persisting facilities and other times is not.

In that reoccupation in the real world is often tied to other events (e.g.,

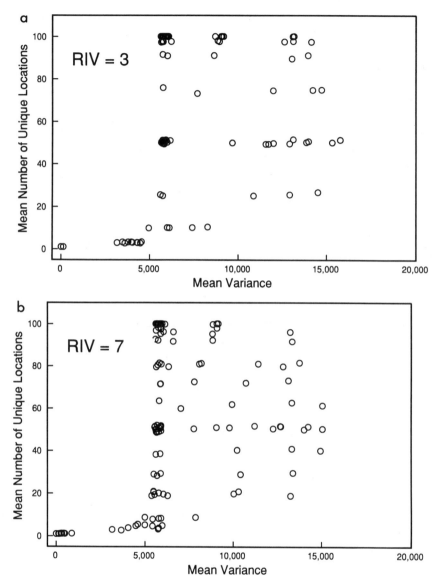

Figure 6. Summary of 125 sets of simulated locale reoccupation:
(a) RIV = 3; (b) RIV = 7; (c) RIV = 13; and (d) RIV = 27.

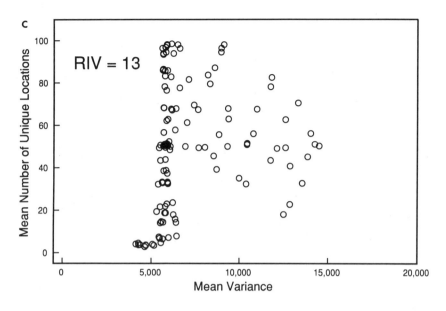

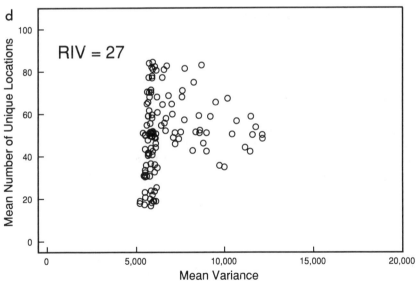

rainfall, hunting success, and so forth) best modeled in terms of stochastic variation, it is useful to consider the effects of variation in reoccupation of the simulated water source locale. The different graphs in Figure 6 correspond to an increasing value for permitted stochastic variation in reoccupation interval. The settlement patterns summarized in Figure 5 reflect a specified reoccupation interval plus a value randomly drawn from a normal distribution with a mean of 0 and a standard deviation of 1, resulting in actual reoccupation intervals that vary little from the specified value. In Figures 6a–d, the mean of the normally distributed random variate added to the specified reoccupation interval is also 0; the standard deviation, however is 3, 7, 13, and 27, respectively. Thus Figure 6a represents a locale that is reoccupied in an almost regular fashion, whereas Figure 6d shows the results of reoccupation for which the interval varies dramatically. The relationship between *FUL, FDI,* and *RI* discussed for Figure 5 and the effects of these with respect to number of unique occupation locations and variance hold here as well with the addition of one other cluster (see Figure 6a). This is the situation in which facility decay interval exceeds facility use-life, which also exceeds reoccupation interval (i.e., *FDI > FUL > RI*). In this case, facilities are created at few unique locations because for the most part, facilities are in good repair and can be reused. When facilities are found to be in poor repair, then a new location is selected. Because the facility decay interval is relatively high, however, certain locations are not available for reoccupation, and a more regular (higher variance) is seen.

Considering all of Figures 6a–d, one trend can be noted. That is, as the occupation interval increasingly varies, the range in the number of unique occupation locations changes from 0–100 to 15–85; where the distribution was previously trimodel, with modes at 0, 50, and 100, it becomes unimodel, with a single mode at 50. Simultaneously, the range in variance values shifts from 0–16,000 to 5,500–12,000. Thus, with locale reoccupation that varies dramatically, we see both reuse of locations as well as construction of new facilities. As reoccupation sometimes occurs in the presence of persistent but decaying facilities and sometimes does not, intermediate amounts of variance in the distribution of occupied locations is observed. Figure 5 (and 6a) reflects reoccupation that may occur in a very stable or predictable environment; Figure 6d presents the long-term results of a highly variable reoccupation interval, as might hold in arid areas that experience spatially and temporally stochastic rainfall.

Figure 7 reiterates the information presented in Figures 5 and 6, summarizing the relationships among and between *RI, FUL,* and *FDI.*

DISCUSSION

This analysis suggests, minimally, that the *relationship* between facility use-life and decay intervals and reoccupation intervals may be inferred through

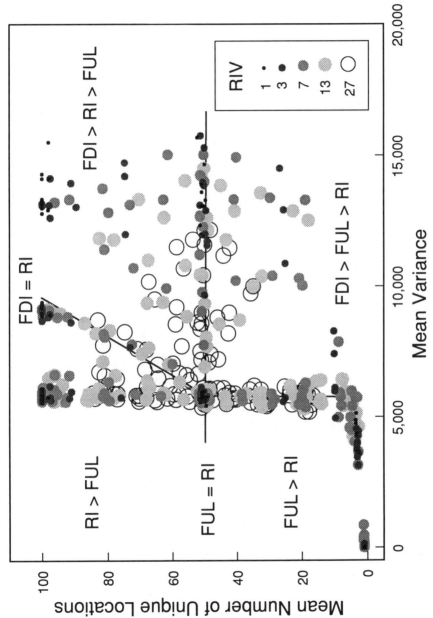

Figure 7. Summary of all simulations of locale reoccupation.

inspection of the number and spatial distribution of occupations found in an area. With knowledge obtained from ethnoarchaeological and ethnographic research on values for the *FUL* and the *FDI*, the reoccupation interval itself might be determined. Such conclusions depend on several critical assumptions, however.

One such assumption is that occupants always behave as described by these empirical generalizations, that is, "rules" for reoccupation. It is likely, however, that such rules apply situationally rather than universally. Therefore, the question becomes under which circumstances do occupants reoccupy still useful facilities if they exist? If the facilities are judged too costly to repair (and what is "too costly"?), but occupation of the locale is desired, how variable is the role that extant but deteriorating facilities have in determining which location to occupy? These are questions that can be addressed through targeted ethnoarchaeological research.

These questions have guided the research I recently initiated on the development of archaeological landscapes over the medium term. The research focuses on the use, abandonment, and reuse of locations by nomadic pastoralists in south–central India. Some preliminary observations emanating from this continuing research are pertinent (Wandsnider 1991).

First, when reoccupation was observed, and, because of an abbreviated observation period only three such reoccupations were observed, it occurred at locations that had previously seen minimal (occupation length of days or weeks within a 6-month period) rather than intensive use (occupation length of months within a 6-month period). At the reoccupied locations, facilities, in the form of boulder platforms on which bulk food is stored and over which tents are erected, were present. In all but one case, the facilities were ignored or avoided, with new facilities constructed amid the persisting facilities. I speculate that the reason why the persistent facilities of boulders were not reused relates to two factors. The first is that sheep herd size varies between occupations received by specific locales and the tent configuration (and hence boulder platform configuration), designed to enclose and protect the sheep during the night, must be constructed to accommodate the current sheep herd size. Persisting, serviceable boulder platforms may not fit the required current tent configuration.

The one case in which a previous facility was acknowledged by the new occupants informs on the second potential factor determining facility reuse—hygiene. Upon reoccupation, one boulder platform was disassembled, moved 1 meter and reassembled. The immediate area of the platform, which had been strewn with debris from the previous occupants, was also cleaned up. Thus hygienic concerns may be of some importance in determining facility reuse. Schebesta's (1973:56) observation that the Malay forest pygmies he documented in the early 1900s preferred new shelters to apparently serviceable structures may be interpreted in this light. It may also reflect, however, a decision on the part of the pygmies that refurbishing was more costly than building anew.

The reason this one boulder facility received the attention it did is, I conjecture, because of its preferred location. It is located at the intersection of two boulder walls, which are also used to contain the sheep. In fact, in all the encampments inspected, "corner" locations always contain a boulder facility, suggesting that they are preferred locations. To make use of this apparently preferred corner location, thus, the shepherds could have just employed the existing platform, but, instead, elected to rebuild it, perhaps for hygienic reasons as indicated. Stafford and Hajic (this volume) introduce the concept of landscape element, which allows us to talk about a landscape in terms of criteria that make some portions "preferred" and, with respect to other criteria, recognize still other preferred locations.

Through actualistic research, it is possible to evaluate the assumptions of the proposed reoccupation model and to learn about the circumstances where it does and, more important, does not track reality. It is likely that we will reach, if and when such research is completed, a conclusion similar to that emerging from research conducted on bone transportation and butchery practices (see Hudson 1992). That is, that decisions about facility reuse or relocation are indeed logical, but, that the content of those decisions is highly contingent on other features of the social and physical environment and on future plans, which are not directly accessible to the archaeologist. This anticipated conclusion does not mean that such research would be conducted in vain. Rather, it signifies to me that research on the medium-term consequences of reoccupation will help us define the parameters of what we do not know about how archaeological landscapes develop (see Chang, this volume, for similar sentiments).

Another critical assumption that must be made if one is to infer locale use tempo from the number and variance in occupation locations is that we can archaeologically detect and identify unique occupation locations. There are two parts to this question. The first is that an accurate and reliable portrait of regional occupation is required. Current archeological field practices cannot guarantee this, and further effort in this area is absolutely necessary (e.g., Cowgill 1990; Wandsnider and Camilli 1992).

Second, even if we had such a high-fidelity archaeological representation, can unique occupation locations be archaeologically recognized? The answer seems to be, contextually, yes. In situations that have not seen reoccupation with overlap or superimposition, we may expect discrete (Chatters 1987:346–347; but see Brooks and Yellen 1987) distributions of features and artifacts and artifact distributions that manifest spatially distinctive size sorting (O'Connell 1987; Simms 1988, 1989; Thomas 1986; Wandsnider 1989:173–216). At a location with a more complex occupation history, the character of the palimpsest will be informative in telling us "more than one occupation event occurred here." Work by Camilli (1983, 1988), among others, focuses on this issue, and the chapters by Stafford and Hajic and by Dewar and McBride (this volume) speak to recognizing and analyzing deposits of this kind.

In addition, the analysis presented here directs attention to the degree and kind of facility refurbishment or destruction, both at individual locations and throughout a locale. Enduring and maintained facilities are expected in the situation with relatively few other occupied locations. In the case of the more random distribution of facilities, little maintenance is to be expected. When occupation location variance is high, as in the case of decaying features that persist on the landscape, little maintenance is likewise to be anticipated.

Other analytic challenges must be solved before tempo can be inferred from spatial structure of archaeological remains. For example, the simulation here focuses on the case in which a point resource attracts occupation, with the probability of a particular location being occupied falling off as distance to the point water source increases. As described by Tindale (1972), such occupations by the Pitjandjara are very brief and tied to unpredictable rainfall events. The role played by other point resources in the landscape economy may be very different. Brooks and Yellen (1987), for example, have characterized occupation in the vicinity of Dobe such that a doughnut of occupation debris has accumulated around the waterhole, with the immediate vicinity of the hole being relatively free of debris. This pattern has resulted from the practice of not camping for long periods of time at the waterhole itself, which would discourage its use by animals in the area. Thus the uses to which all point water sources are put are not equal and should be reflected by the spatial structure of locale archaeological remains.

Additionally, the patch size and shape of resources that attract occupation will influence how the structure of archaeological remains develop there. That is, the archaeological spatial structure in the vicinity of a point resource that is being visited as frequently as a linear (e.g., rivers, trails) resource or an areal (e.g., stands of grasses or mesquite trees) resource will likely be very different by virtue of the geometry of the resource. Thus the variance measure used here to describe randomness or regularity of occupation remains has low general utility. Ebert's (1992) technique for describing frequencies and associations among artifacts at multiple scales, while yielding less than intuitive results, is likely much more useful.

Even if all of these assumptions could be warranted and analytic questions of how best to describe archaeological spatial structure were resolved, it is still unlikely that we would be able to simply read land use tempo from a graph of unique locations versus spatial variance, such as Figure 8. Such attempted de-terminations, however, could provoke other productive research. For example, if a random distribution of highly visible monuments are found in close proximity to each other, a situation not documented ethnographically in repeated use of an area, we may suspect that the features come from a strictly contemporaneous occupation and proceed with analysis to reject or support such a finding.

CONCLUSIONS

As archaeologists confronted with a wind-swept, seemingly vacant expanse, it is sometimes difficult to remember that the landscape visited and used by prehistoric occupants was not a barren land. It was rich with cultural (as well as natural) features that constrained and influenced to varying degrees the subsequent use of entire locales as well as specific locations.

This chapter has attempted to explore the ramifications of differentially enduring features of cultural geography in the medium- and long-term development of archaeological landscapes. I have proposed a simple model that relates tempo of locale use, relative to the persistence of cultural features, to distinctive distributions of remains from reoccupation events. The relationship between past locale use tempo and present archaeological spatial structure, however, is likely to be much more complex than entertained here. Thus this paper has also identified several domains where actualistic and analytic research is necessary to develop our understanding of these complexities.

The spatial dimension of time informs on the tactics of land use for individual locales. In amassing such information for locales from throughout a region, we may construct a composite picture of land use strategy and economic organization. The resulting more detailed picture of the settlement–subsistence system should permit a fuller understanding of the ecological environment within which past selective forces operated.

ACKNOWLEDGMENTS

This chapter is a result of discussions with numerous individuals, including Eileen Camilli, Zarine Cooper, James Ebert, Richa Jhaldiyal, Signa Larralde, K. Paddayya, Sheena Panja, Jackie Rossignol, Sarah Schlanger, Sarah Tarlow, and Patrice Teltser. I also consulted with Lewis Binford, Patricia Draper, Henry Harpending, Bob Hitchcock, Jean Hudson, and John Yellen. Amy Spiess provided technical assistance. I thank these individuals for their insights and remain responsible for errors in reasoning and presentation.

The work reported upon here was supported by the Visiting Scholar program at the Center for Archaeological Investigations at Southern Illinois University–Carbondale, the Fulbright Fellowship program of the Institute for International

Education, Deccan College Post-graduate and Research Institute (Pune, India), and the University of Nebraska–Lincoln.

REFERENCES

Binford, Lewis R., 1978, *Nunamiut Ethnoarchaeology,* Academic Press, New York.

Binford, Lewis R., 1980, Willow Smoke and Dog's Tails: Hunter-Gatherer Settlement Systems and Archaeological Site Formation, *American Antiquity* 45(1):4–20.

Binford, Lewis R., 1981, Behavioral Archaeology and the "Pompeii Premise," *Journal of Anthropological Research* 37(3):195–208.

Binford, Lewis R., 1982, The Archaeology of Place, *Journal of Anthropological Archaeology* 1(1):5–31.

Binford, Lewis R., 1983, Long Term Land Use Patterns: Some Implications for Archaeology, in: *Lulu Linear Punctuated: Essays in Honor George Irving Quimby* (Robert C. Dunnell and Donald K. Grayson, eds.), Museum of Anthropology, University of Michigan Anthropological Papers No. 72, pp. 27–54.

Brooks, Alison, and Yellen, John, 1987, The Preservation of Activity Areas in the Archaeological Record: Ethnoarchaeological and Archaeological Work in Northwest Ngamiland, Botswana, in: *Method and Theory for Activity Areas Research: An Ethnoarchaeological Approach* (Susan Kent, ed.), Columbia University Press, New York, pp. 63–106.

Camilli, Eileen, L., 1983, *Site Occupation History and Lithic Assemblage Structure: An Example from Southeastern Utah,* Ph.D. dissertation, University of New Mexico, University Microfilms, Ann Arbor.

Camilli, Eileen L., 1988, Interpreting Long-Term Land-Use Patterns from Archaeological Landscapes, in: *Issues in Archaeological Surface Survey: Meshing Method and Theory* (LuAnn Wandsnider and James I. Ebert, eds.), *American Archaeology* 7(1):57–66.

Chatters, James C., 1987, Hunter-Gatherer Adaptations and Assemblage Structure, *Journal of Anthropological Archaeology* 6:336–375.

Cipriani, Lidio, 1966, *The Andaman Islanders,* Frederick A. Praeger, New York.

Cowgill, George, 1990, Towards Refining Concepts of Full-Coverage Survey, in: *The Archaeology of Regions* (Suzanne K. Fish and Stephen A. Kowalewski, eds.), Smithsonian Institution Press, Washington, DC, pp. 249–260.

Denham, Woodrow W., 1972, *The Detection of Patterns in Alyawara Nonverbal Behavior,* Ph.D. dissertation, University of Washington, University Microfilms, Ann Arbor.

Dewar, Robert E., 1986, Discovering Settlement Systems of the Past in New England Site Distributions, *Man in the Northeast* 31:77–88.

Ebert, James I., 1992, *Distributional Archaeology,* University of New Mexico Press, Albuquerque.

Ferring, C. Reid, 1986, Rates of Fluvial Sedimentation: Implications for Archaeological Variability, *Geoarchaeology: An International Journal* 1(3):259–274.

Fowler, D. D., and Fowler, C. S., 1971, Anthropology of the Numa: John Wesley Powell's Manuscripts on the Numic Peoples of Western North America, 1868–1880, *Smithsonian Contributions to Anthropology* 14.

Gilman, Patricia A., 1987, Architecture as Artifact: Pit Structures and Pueblos in the American Southwest, *American Antiquity* 52:538–564.

Gould, Richard A., 1980, *Living Archaeology,* Cambridge University Press.

Hitchcock, Robert K., 1987, Sedentism and Site Structure: Organization Changes in Kalahari Baswara Residential Locations, in: *Method and Theory for Activity Areas Research: An Ethnoarchaeological Approach* (Susan Kent, ed.), Columbia University Press, New York, pp. 374–423.

Hudson, Jean (ed.), 1992, *From Bones to Behavior,* Center for Archaeological Investigations, Occasional Paper No. 21, Southern Illinois University–Carbondale, Carbondale.

Hunter-Anderson, Rosalind L., 1977, A Theoretical Approach to the Study of House Form, in: *For Theory-Building in Archaeology* (Lewis R. Binford, ed.), Academic Press, New York, pp. 287–316.

Janes, Robert R., 1983, Archaeology Ethnography among the MacKenzie Basin Dene, Canada, *The Arctic Institute of North America Technical Paper* No. 28.

Kent, Susan, 1991, The Relationship between Mobility Strategies and Site Structure, in: *Interpretation of Archaeological Spatial Patterning* (Ellen Kroll and T. Douglas Price, eds.), Plenum Press, New York, pp. 33–69.

Lange, Frederick W., and Rydberg, Charles R., 1972, Abandonment and Post-abandonment Behavior at a Rural Central American House-site, *American Antiquity* 37:419–432.

McGee, W. J., 1898, The Seri Indians, *Seventeenth Annual Report of the Bureau of American Ethnology,* Part 1 (1895/1896):1–344.

McGuire, Randall H., and Schiffer, Michael B., 1983, A Theory of Architectural Design, *Journal of Anthropological Archaeology* 2(3):277–303.

O'Connell, James F., 1987, Alyawara Site Structure and Its Archaeological Implications, *American Antiquity* 52:74–108.

Pelto, Pertti J., and Müller-Wille, Ludger, 1987, Snowmobiles: Technological Revolution in the Arctic, in: *Technology and Social Change,* 2nd ed. (H. Russell Bernard and Pertti Pelto, eds.), Waveland Press, Prospect Heights, Illinois, pp. 207–242.

Redding, Richard W., 1988, A General Explanation of Subsistence Change: From Hunting and Gathering to Food Production, *Journal of Anthropological Archaeology* 7:56–97.

Schebesta, Paul, 1973 (originally published in 1928), *Among the Forest Dwarfs of Malaya,* Oxford University Press, Singapore.

Silberbauer, George B., 1972, The G/wi Bushman, in: *Hunter-Gatherers Today,* reissued 1988 (M. G. Bicchieri, ed.), Waveland Press, Prospect Heights, Illinois, pp. 271–326.

Simms, Steven R., 1988, The Archaeological Structure of a Bedouin Camp, *Journal of Archaeological Science* 15:197–211.

Simms, Steven R., 1989, The Structure of the Bustos Wickiup Site, Eastern Nevada, *Journal of California and Great Basin Anthropology* 11(1):2–34.

Solecki, Ralph S., 1979, Contemporary Kurdish Winter-time Inhabitants of Shanidar Cave, Iraq, *World Archaeology* 10:318–330.

Thomas, Peter A., 1986, Discerning some Spatial Characteristics of Small, Short-Term, Single Occupation Sites: Implications for New England Archaeology, *Man in the Northeast* 31:99–121.

Tindale, Norman B., 1972, The Pitjandjara, in: *Hunter-Gatherers Today,* reissued 1988 (M. G. Bicchieri, ed.), Waveland Press, Prospect Heights, Illinois, pp. 217–268.

Upham, Steadman, 1984, Adaptive Diversity and Southwestern Abandonment, *Journal of Anthropological Research* 40:235–256.

Vierra, Bradley J., 1985, Hunter-Gatherer Settlement Systems: To Reoccupy or Not To Reoccupy, That is the Question, Unpublished master's thesis, Department of Anthropology, University of New Mexico, Albuquerque.

Wandsnider, LuAnn, 1989, *Long-term Land Use, Formation Processes, and the Structure of the Archaeological Landscape: A Case Study from Southwestern Wyoming,* Ph.D. dissertation, University of New Mexico, University Microfilms, Ann Arbor.

Wandsnider, LuAnn, 1991, Archaeological Landscapes, Nomadism, and Tungabhadra Ethnoarchaeology, Deccan College 1991 Seminar Proceedings (in preparation), Pune.

Wandsnider, LuAnn, and Camilli, Eileen, 1992, The Character of Surface Archaeological Deposits and Its Influence on Survey Accuracy, *Journal of Field Archaeology,* 19(2):169–188.

Western, David and Dunne, Thomas, 1979, Environmental Aspects of Settlement Site Decisions among Pastoral Maasai, *Human Ecology* 7(1):75–98.

Wills, W. H., and Windes, Thomas C., 1989, Evidence for Populations Aggregation and Dispersal During the Basketmaker III Period in Chaco Canyon, New Mexico, *American Antiquity* 54:347–369.

Woodburn, J. C., 1972, Ecology, Nomadic Movement and the Composition of the Local Group among Hunters and Gatherers: An East African Example and Its Implications, in: *Man, Settlement and Urbanism* (Peter J. Ucko, Ruth Tringham, and G. W. Dimbleby, eds.), Schenkman Publishing, Cambridge, Massachusetts, pp. 193–206.

Yellen, John E., 1976, Settlement Pattern of the !Kung Bushmen: An Archaeological Perspective, in: *Kalahari Hunter-Gatherers* (R. B. Lee and I. DeVore, eds.), Harvard University Press, Cambridge, pp. 47–72.

Yellen, John E., 1977, *Archaeological Approaches to the Present: Models for Reconstructing the Past,* Academic Press, New York.

Yellen, John E., 1986, Optimization and Risk in Human Foraging Strategies, *Journal of Human Evolution* 15:733–750.

Part **V**

Postscript and Prospectus

Chapter *12*

Archaeological Landscape Studies

LuAnn Wandsnider

INTRODUCTION

The goal of most processual archaeological studies is to move from a description of regional archaeological variation to an understanding of some aspect of the organization of and change in past human systems, especially the subsistence component. Usually, the subsistence system is rendered in terms of the regional and annual arrangement of technology, consumers, and producers. As discussed in the introductory chapter, settlement pattern studies of the remains of both hunter–gatherer and more complex economies have accomplished this interpretative task through reconstruction of the settlement system. Over the past 20 years, however, formation process research and research on hunter–gatherer systems has made insupportable some of the critical assumptions of settlement system reconstruction. Thus, over this 20-year span, strategies have appeared that approach past subsistence by other avenues. The studies presented here illustrate one such strategy, which we have labeled the *landscape approach*.

By way of assessing what this volume has accomplished, it is worth comparing and contrasting some of the salient features of the settlement pattern and

LuANN WANDSNIDER • Department of Anthropology, University of Nebraska–Lincoln, Lincoln, Nebraska 68588-0368.

Space, Time, and Archaeological Landscapes, edited by Jacqueline Rossignol and LuAnn Wandsnider. Plenum Press, New York, 1992.

285

landscape approaches to regional archaeological variation. Settlement pattern studies usually proceed by considering only those locations at which archaeological materials are recovered, that is, sites. From site architecture (presence and type), artifacts, and local environment, inferences are made about how the location functioned in the settlement system throughout a certain time period. Once these settlement components have been identified, the entire settlement pattern is reconstructed. Referencing implicit or explicit precepts of geographical analysis of settlement patterns, systemic processes responsible for the settlement configuration can then be argued.

Several assumptions are implicit to settlement pattern studies, including that locations served one settlement function for the duration of the period under consideration. For complex economic systems, such an assumption may be warranted, but, for most hunter–gatherer systems, actualistic research has shown that this assumption is likely false. That is, locations may serve several settlement functions, and, further, over both the short and long terms, locations shift in and out of use as a consequence of the natural functioning of the subsistence system. Thus to assign sites one settlement function, as in residential camp or special-purpose site, is to obscure information about other capacities in which the location served. And, to then inventory settlement components in terms of numbers and locations of residential camps, limited-activity camps, and so forth, does not render a satisfactory picture of the settlement system because all were likely not in service for equal amounts of time. The chapters by Binford, Chang, Schlanger, and Dewar and McBride target exactly these issues. Further, they suggest that knowledge of the settlement function of a location may be only one facet of what we would like to know about how the location participated in the subsistence system.

Landscape approaches to regional archaeological variation in pursuit of past system states reflect a strategy different from that pursued by settlement pattern studies. First, rather than beginning with only those loci manifesting archaeological remains, they begin with the entire landscape. Portions of the landscape have differentially attracted human use and, because of surface processes, today differentially manifest evidence of that use. Middle-range research on hunter–gatherer and horticultural use of the landscape as well as on the impacts of surface processes to archaeological deposits means that we can identify landscape dimensions that are sensitive to its processual analysis. Studies of the archaeological landscape take advantage of this secure anchor of knowledge about the landscape.

Second, rather than reconstructing only the settlement system, reconstruction of the formational history of deposits across the landscape is the intermediate goal. In many cases, this reconstruction is facilitated by collecting information on atomic elements (i.e., artifacts and features) of the archaeological record, which in composite inform on formation history (Stein 1987). Thus, through regional analysis of these histories for locations in different landscape contexts, an understanding of organizational aspects of the subsistence system is approached.

TECHNOLOGICAL DEVELOPMENTS

The landscape approach *per se* is not new elements of this strategy have emerged following our increasing understanding of the formation of the archaeological record over the past 20 years. For example, the landscape dimension played a major role in structuring the siteless analyses of Bettinger (1977), Dancey (1973), Foley (1981), and Thomas (1973, 1975). The present studies consider dimensions of the landscape that reflect our increased knowledge of systemic sources—natural and cultural, and interactive—that introduce archaeological variation. Chapters by Camilli and Ebert and by Stafford and Hajic are especially important in this regard.

Atomic, that is, feature and artifact attributes, archaeological data assume a critical role in producing a picture of the formation histories of deposits. It is only recently, however, that technological innovations have allowed the expeditious collection of such data. With the advent of, for example, the electronic distance measuring (EDM) theodolite, siteless data collection similar to that of Dancey (1973) and Davis (1975) can be now completed in a fraction of the time these projects required (e.g., Ebert 1992). Furthermore, Global Positioning System (GPS) technology, which references satellites to absolutely locate features to the nearest meter, will greatly facilitate work like that described by Chang (this volume).

One further technology-related development concerns the storage and manipulation of archaeological data. Precomputer analyses required that archaeological analysis proceed using tools like artifact and site types. The correspondence between the available analytic hardware and the goal of reconstructing the settlement system reinforced this practice. Even with early computer technology, the cost of storing and manipulating archaeological data in units other than artifact or site types was very high. With the advent of low-cost storage and computing power, archaeological analysis according to artifact or deposit attributes or dimensions is possible. Most of the substantive chapters in this volume (see also Dunnell, this volume and examples in other venues abound) illustrate the power of this analytic shift in producing diagnoses of formation history. The potential for Geographic Information System (GIS) technology to expedite archaeological landscape studies of the kind presented here, noted by Zvelebil, Green, and Macklin, is a continuation of this trend.

CONCEPTUAL DEVELOPMENTS

The landscape approach involves, however, more than arguments about how to collect and analyze archaeological data. That is, it is not encompassed by simple statements about site-based data being bad and siteless data good. Rather, it concerns how to analytically proceed from regional archaeological variation to interpretations about past system states given what we currently know about the formation of the archaeological record. Methodological issues are important here, but conceptual matters are equally critical. For this reason, in our section introductions we have emphasized the conceptual additions to the archaeological repertoire that the landscape approach invites, and these bear repeating here.

In this volume, the site as an operational concept receives special attention. In that several volume authors, notably Dewar and McBride, Stafford and Hajic, and Schlanger, make use of site-based data to good effect in discussing formational histories, it is clear that site-based archaeological data and the landscape approach are not incompatible. This observation supports Binford's point that the archaeological site as an explicitly defined unit of analysis is perfectly serviceable. Dunnell's contention about the diminished utility of the site concept as usually made operational in modern site surveys, however, remains viable. How often could analyses of the sort presented here be undertaken with most reported survey data? On the siteless side of the coin, other volume contributors, for example, Camilli and Ebert, and Jones and Beck, demonstrate the ease with which units of analysis can be constructed to meet the analytic challenge at hand.

The concept of the place, useful in discussing the differential development of deposits on the landscape, is further developed in these chapters. Schlanger's notion of persistent places, that is, locations that receive continued use as the subsistence system spatially shifts, and Chang's observation that diagnosable place use need not result in archaeological deposits are especially useful.

Introduced analytic concepts are formational in character and speak directly to the nature of archaeological deposits. Stafford and Hajic's concept of landscape element provides a currency with which to discuss attributes of the environment that condition place use. Shifting more explicitly to the temporal domain, Dewar and McBride's concept of medium-term processes to describe the development of remnant settlement patterns as a matter of the functioning of a subsistence system is an important contribution. The expansion of the ethnographic concepts of episode, by Zvelebil and colleagues, and contemporaneity, by Jones and Beck, again accommodates our evolving knowledge about the formation of archaeological deposits and the information we consequently can extract from them.

An implication of these studies is that concepts attending settlement pattern studies are, within the landscape approach, of reduced utility. For example, identifying residential camps and limited-activity sites seems a self-limiting exercise. Demography, function, and occupation length, three characteristics of occupational events that are confounded by the terms residential camp and limited-activity site, may be considered as isolated dimensions along with occupation frequency, continuity, and spatial contiguity. Archaeological indicators of these dimension states are proposed in studies presented here.

INTERPRETATIVE CHALLENGES

In this volume we have presented a number of case studies that use a landscape treatment of regional archaeological variation to approach some aspect of past system states. Clearly, these studies do not provide the definitive word on archaeological landscape studies. Many challenges remain.

As Dewar and McBride discuss, medium-term processes contribute greatly to the form the archaeological record assumes across the landscape. Yet, about these processes we know very little. Therefore, as identified by Wandsnider, this domain deserves to be a major focus of study over the next decade.

How to research this problem through actualistic study requires some ingenuity because these processes operate at a temporal scale greater than that of most ethnoarchaeological field seasons. Two possibilities exist. First, during the 1970s and 1980s many ethnoarcheological studies were initiated to document some relationship between behavior and archaeological consequences. A 1990s follow-up examination of the same behaviors and materials, to document how they have fared over the medium term, may be appropriate. In addition, attention to how to extend short-term ethnoarchaeological observations to the medium and long terms so as to facilitate archaeological interpretation is required (Stiner 1992). Second, Rothschild and colleagues (1990) are conducting archaeological investigation of locations on the Zuni reservation for which knowledge of the use and abandonment history is known. Studies of this sort should help to refine our abilities to recognize the archaeological consequences of middle-term processes.

Binford's objection that the landscape approach provides us with more archaeological data that require explanation, rather than better explanation, is well taken. He calls attention to the continuing need for middle-range research to understand the necessary links between contemporary archaeological record and past system condition. This volume identifies several areas where such research is best focused, including the investigation of medium-term processes, mentioned before. Certainly, the archaeological indicators that Stafford and Hajic and also Dewar and McBride employ to recognize medium-term processes, although based on current formational knowledge, could stand to be strengthened.

Another potential domain of research is that of landscape dimensions, with attention to their sensitivity to different formational histories and their independent measurement. The case studies here considered specific landscape characteristics, for example, proximity to the sea (Zvelebil and colleagues), differential exposure (Camilli and Ebert), proximity to restricted access routes (Schlanger), and the like, as well as systemic features that appear to track these landscape characteristics. A more general treatment of the landscape, perhaps extending work by Ebert and Kohler (1988) and Stafford and Hajic (this volume), is necessary.

The studies here also suggest that continued emphasis on archaeogeomorphology is critical. Standard geomorphological studies consider phenomenon at a time scale much larger than that usually of interest to archaeologists. When such studies are tailored to archaeological problems, however, critical information on formation history and hence on system condition emerges. The chapters by Zvelebil and colleagues and by Stafford and Hajic reflect an evolving tradition of collaboration between quaternary scientists, that is, archaeologists and geomorphologists, that we see intensifying to mutual benefit of all in the future.

Finally, the landscape approach to the regional archaeological variation generated by hunter–gatherer and horticultural systems has been very productive during the last 20 years. Over the same span, we see settlement pattern studies of more complex systems continue the tradition of Gordon Willey's Viru Valley study (1953). Although there is a developing school of landscape archaeology expressly concerned with complex landscapes (see Wagstaff 1987; Crumley and Marquardt 1990), we see this variety of landscape archaeology as a refinement of the settlement pattern strategy for understanding past systemic organization. In such studies, the landscape plays a prominent role in structuring analysis, but the term *landscape archaeology* seems to refer more to the scope of archaeological phenomenon under consideration; all and sundry archaeological manifestations found across the landscape, rather than major sites only, are the subject of analysis. The strategy of describing system organization in terms of the settlement system remains unchanged. Thus consideration of archaeological landscapes resulting from the operation of more complex economies via the formation histories of these archaeological materials is suggested. Continuing formation process and middle-range research, facilitated by ethnohistorical sources (e.g., Parsons 1990), on the relationship between the condition of archaeological materials and system condition may be productive here.

In addition to methodological growth, it is clear that our conceptual inventory must likewise continue to develop. Both analytic concepts, to describe aspects of system states over the medium and long terms, and operational concepts, to facilitate translation between the archaeological landscape and its interpretation, are critical.

CONCLUDING REMARKS

The study of the formational history of archaeological landscapes offers one avenue to understanding of past subsistence systems. The analytic synergy that results from simultaneously considering systemic and natural formation processes within a landscape framework, we feel, compels consideration of this approach. The potential for this approach to exploit more of the extant regional archaeological variation and to produce rich and well-grounded interpretations of past system states that accommodates the expanding body of formation knowledge we find particularly exciting. We look to a stimulating future for such studies propelled by continued methodological and conceptual development.

REFERENCES

Bettinger, R., 1977, Aboriginal Human Ecology in Owens Valley: Prehistoric Change in the Great Basin, *American Antiquity* 42(1):3–17.

Crumley, C. L., and Marquardt, W. H., 1990, Landscape: A Unifying Concept in Regional Analysis, in: *Interpreting Space: GIS and Archaeology* (K. M. S. Allen, S. W. Green, and E. B. W. Zubrow, eds.), Taylor and Francis, London, pp. 73–79.

Dancey, W. S., 1973, *Prehistoric Land Use and Settlement Patterns in the Priest Rapids Area, Washington*, Ph.D. dissertation, Department of Anthropology, University of Washington, University Microfilms, Ann Arbor.

Davis, E. L., 1975, The "Exposed Archaeology" of China Lake, *American Antiquity* 40(1):29–53.

Ebert, J. I., 1992, *Distributional Archaeology*, University of New Mexico Press, Albuquerque.

Ebert, J. I., and Kohler, T. A., 1988, The Theoretical Basis of Archaeological Predictive Modeling and a Consideration of Appropriate Data-Collection Methods, in: *Quantifying the Present and Predicting the Past—Theory, Method, and Application of Archaeological Predictive Modeling* (W. J. Judge and L. Sebastian, eds.), U.S. Department of Interior, Bureau of Land Management, Denver, pp. 97–171.

Foley, R., 1981, *Off-site Archaeology and Human Adaptation in Eastern Africa: Analysis of Regional Artifact Density in the Amboseli, Southern Kenya*, Cambridge Monographs in African Archaeology 3, British Archaeological Research International Series 97.

Parsons, J. R., 1990, Critical Reflections on a Decade of Full-Coverage Regional Survey in the Valley of Mexico, in: *The Archaeology of Regions: A Case for Full-Coverage Survey* (S. Fish and S. Kowalewski, eds.), Smithsonian Institution Press, Washington, DC, pp. 7–32.

Rothschild, N., Mills, B., Ferguson, T. J., and Dublin, S., 1990, Abandonment at Zuni Farming Villages, paper presented at the Society for American Archaeology Meetings, Las Vegas.

Stein, J., 1987, Deposits for Archaeologists, in: *Advances in Archaeological Method and Theory* 11 (M. B. Schiffer, ed.), Academic Press, Orlando, Florida, pp. 337–392.

Stiner, M., 1992, The Place of Homonids among Predators: Interspecific Comparisons of Food Procurement and Transport, in: *From Bones to Behavior* (Jean Hudson, ed.), Center for Archaeological Investigations Occasional Paper No. 21, Southern Illinois University–Carbondale, Carbondale, in preparation.

Thomas, D. H., 1973, An Empirical Test for Stewards's Model of Great Basin Settlement Patterns, *American Antiquity* 38:155–176.

Thomas, D. H., 1975, Nonsite Sampling in Archaeology: Up the Creek without a Site? in: *Sampling in Archaeology* (J. W. Mueller, ed.), University of Arizona Press, Tucson, pp. 61–81.

Wagstaff, J. M. (ed.), 1987, *Landscape and Culture—Geographical and Archaeological Perspectives,* Basil Blackwell, London.

Willey, G. R., 1953, *Prehistoric Settlement Patterns in the Viru Valley, Peru,* Bureau of American Ethnology, Bulletin 155, Washington, DC.

Willey, G. R., and Sabloff, J. A., 1980, *A History of American Archaeology,* 2nd edition, W. H. Freeman and Company, San Francisco.

Index